ISBN 978-1-333-18121-5
PIBN 10490306

English
Français
Deutsche
Italiano
Español
Português

www.forgottenbooks.com

Mythology Photography **Fiction**
Fishing Christianity **Art** Cooking
Essays Buddhism Freemasonry
Medicine **Biology** Music **Ancient
Egypt** Evolution Carpentry Physics
Dance Geology **Mathematics** Fitness
Shakespeare **Folklore** Yoga Marketing
Confidence Immortality Biographies
Poetry **Psychology** Witchcraft
Electronics Chemistry History **Law**
Accounting **Philosophy** Anthropology
Alchemy Drama Quantum Mechanics
Atheism Sexual Health **Ancient History**
Entrepreneurship Languages Sport
Paleontology Needlework Islam
Metaphysics Investment Archaeology
Parenting Statistics Criminology
Motivational

INDEX OF NAMES

Hughes: PP. 7-76 Includes:

Atkinson, Austin;

Bainbridge, Banner, Barnes, Bell, Beard, Black, Blackwell, Bostick, Bowles, Branson, Bright, Briggs, Buchanan, Bradley;

Caldwell, Camber, Cannon, Campbell, Carr, Carter, Chaetam, Cheeke, Christain, Clark, Clotworthy, Cox, Craig;

Dabney, Dalton, Dandridge, Davis, De Novelle, Dillard, Dickson, Dobson, Doss;

Ewing, Elliott;

Fleming, Fontaine, Fowlks, Frame, Frelinghusan, Fulkerson;

Gaines, Galespie, Gentry, Gifford, Gardner, Graham, Green;

Hailey, Hairston, Hanby, Hardeman, Harrison, Henry, Hicks, Hodgson, Horton, Hendricks, Henderson, Hobson, Howard;

Jones, Johnston;

Lee, Le Vert, Lewis;

Maney, Martin, Matthews, McCabe, McEwen, McFerrin, McGavock, McKenney, Metcalf, Morton, Mooreman, Mosby, Murphy, Merriwether, Moore, Moss;

Neill, Nowlan;

O'Fallon, Oglevie, Oliver;

Penn, Pettus, Perkins, Petway, Poindexter, Powell, Preston, Puryear; Randolph, Ransom, Redd, Roberts,

Scales, Scruggs, Sharp, Sheath, Shelton, Smoot, Smithson, Spencer, Staples, Steel, Stovall, Smith;

Tavenor, Taylor, Todhunter, Tulloss;

Vance, Van Dyke, Van Hook, Vest;

Walton, Walker, Wallace, Warren, Watkins, Webb. Whitfield, Wilson, Winder, Williams, Willhoit, Woodson, Wood, Work, Winston, Wilkin-.son;

Yeatman, Yeamans;

Dalton: PP. 77-122 Includes:

Affleck, Almond, Austin;

Banner, Bellenfont, Berisford, Bird, Bright, Brittain, Bullock;

Martin: PP. 123-199 Includes:

Hickson, Horton, Hopkins, Hodge, Hughes, Hunter;

Ingles;

Jameison, James, Jennings, Johnson;

Keith, King, Kincannon;

Lea, Lewis, Lillard, Lummes, Lyon;

Manlove, Marshall, Mason, McLendon, McCabe, Mestand, Meadows, Minor, Moon, Marks, Mooreman, Moseley, Mosby, Moore;

Overton, Owens;

Page, Pannell, Peeler, Penn, Perkins, Perry, Pringle; Ready, Reynolds, Reid, Ridley, Riddell, Robertson, Rogers, Russwurm, Rucker;

Sartin, Saunders, Sikes, Sheffield, Shipp, Smiley, Smith, Staples, Starling, Stokes, Stockton, Sumner, Steadman, Stonestreet;

Tate, Terry, Tillman, Tippins, Thomas, Thompson, Toulman;

Waller, Warren, Walace, Weatherby, Wellborn, Webb, Whitaker, Williams;

Young;

Henderson: PP. 200-289 Includes:

Alexander, Austruther;

Baker, Baskett, Baxter, Bean, Beckham, Birch, Bradford, Bruce, Brodnax, Boynton, Brewer, Bullock, Butler, Bynum;

Cabell, Carter, Calloway, Chalmers, Clark, Clemens, Compton, Crawford;

Dalton, Darby, Davies, Dow, Duke, Dyer;

Edwards, Estill;

Fenner, Ferrand, Freeman, Fernandee;

Gaines, Galespie. Glenn, Gillespie, Green;

Hamilton, Halle, Hart, Harrison, Hayes, Hawkins, Hill, Horton, Hillard, Hyde, Haile, Hughes;

Jackson, Jowett;

Kavanough, Kendrick, King, Kirkland, Kelynge, Knox;

Lacey, Lewis, Learcey;

Maddox, Martin, McCorry, McDaniel, McKay, Mercer, Meeks,

TO OUR
EARLIEST
AMERICAN
ANCESTORS

LUCY HENDERSON HORTON

Franklin, Tennessee
October
Nineteen Hundred Twenty-two

FOREWORD

Hearing the call of posterity demanding of us a right to know something of their origin, and convinced, too, that in duty to those who have gone before, we should bind together the golden links of the past, I have gathered what I could of family history. This means much labor; but if this backward glance should inspire one person to noble endeavor, I am amply repaid.

An effort has been made to give authority for every assertion. If error is found, I trust someone with broader and clearer vision than mine will rectify the wrong.

I have a great many old family papers, business papers and letters, which came to me through my grandfather, Captain John Hughes (1776-1860). Captain John Hughes administered on the estate of his father, Colonel Archelaus Hughes of the Revolution. Some of these papers date back to colonial times. They throw light on many things. Then history often corroborates what was written many years ago by members of the family. I began to gather data for this work in 1897, when making research to establish my eligibility to membership in National Society of Daughters of the American Revolution. When becoming a member of Colonial Dames of America, in 1904, I went deeper into the study.

We regret exceedingly that the genealogy is incomplete. We wish to acknowledge our indebtedness, for aid given, to Mrs. Ryland Todhunter, of Lexington, Missouri; to Mrs. Susan Letitia Rice Clotworthy, of Hillman, Georgia; to Miss Mary Louise Dalton, for paper written by her grandfather, Dr. Robert Hunter Dalton, who was born in Rockingham County, North Carolina, and died in Tacoma, Washington; to Miss Josephine Robertson, Statesville, North Carolina; and to the Honorable John Wesley Gaines of Tennessee, etc.

In lifting the veil from the past we see that our Hughes branch is of Welsh origin; the Martin branch of Irish descent; the Henderson immigrant ancestors came from Scotland; all of these are descendants of the ancient Britons (see page 15, Abbotsford by Washington Irving). The Daltons came from Yorkshire, England; while in the veins of the writer flows the blood of one ancestor of Dutch descent.

It may seem to some that I have made a vainglory effort to trace our origin back to European nobility, but "I do not think that lords are small things anywhere. Lords are made by kings for great deeds or great virtues." "Then they are lords of their own making. Kings only seal the patent nature has bestowed."

"In looking back through records of noble houses we shall find a sum of deeds and qualities suited to and honored by succeeding ages, which, tried by the standard of the times of men, show that hereditary nobility is not merely an honor won by a worthy father for unworthy children, but a bond to great endeavors, signed by a noble ancestor on behalf of all his descendants."

LUCY HENDERSON HORTON.

HUGHES

Argent (silver), an eagle displayant, with two heads sable (black). Crest, an eagle's head erased sable (black) holding in the beak a staff raguly gules (red) enflamed proper.

Motto: "Fynno Duw Deifydd."

This old Welsh motto signifies in English: "Let what God wills, be."

Orlando, Leander and William Hughes came from Wales to Virginia about 1700. The public records of Powhatan and Goochland counties, Virginia, which we quote later on, bear us out in this assertion.

Mrs. Harriett D. Pitman, who did much research work among the archives of Great Britain, has written a book entitled "Americans of Gentle Birth and Their Ancestors." On page 81, Vol. II, of this work she says that the Hughes family of Virginia descend from Roderic the Great. Bulwer, in "Harold", the last of the Saxon kings, carries us somewhat into a knowledge of the ancient Britons, who, after the Saxon invasion, settled largely in Wales. Many valuable footnotes given from English chronicles are found in "Harold." Roderic the Great, perhaps the most famous of the ancient Britains of whom we have knowledge, governed all Wales. Possibly twenty sub-kings knelt at his throne (see pages 352, 355.) Roderic the Great "came of a race of heroes, whose line transcended by ages all the other royalties of the North." (Bulwer).

The Welsh are among the proudest people on earth. Even the humblest Welshman loves to trace his lineage. It has become a proverb, "His genealogy is as long as that of a Welshman."

Mrs. Pitman says, "About 1700 there appeared in Virginia three brothers, Orlando, Leander and William Hughes, from Wales. Orlando and Leander had land grants in Powhatan and Goochland counties, near Richmond. She speaks of Colonel Archelaus Hughes of the Revolution "who married Mary Dalton of the old Virginia family (see Dalton)," and says that his father's name was Leander.

The county records show that Orlando Hughes, the immigrant, died in 1768, and that his wife's name was Elizabeth. His sons were Anthony, Josiah and Leander. This son, Leander, died in 1775. His sons were Powell, Stephen, John and Archelaus. So that these county records show that Col. Archelaus Hughes, of Revolutionary fame, was of the third generation in America. The Hughes family are long-lived people. Many of them have lived to be more than ninety years old.

Thus, it is not surprising that a man who came to Virginia about 1700 should have died in 1768.

The name Hughes has sometimes been spelled "Hewes." In some of my old family papers I find this the case, but the family themselves always spelled the name "Hughes." The mother of Mary Ball, grandmother of George Washington, was Mrs. Mary Hewes. In the will of Mrs. Mary Hewes, which was probated July 29, 1721, she makes provision for "My daughter, Mary Ball" (see page 302 of the American Monthly Magazine for May, 1917.) Joseph Hewes was one of the signers of the Declaration of Independence from North Carolina.

Burke's Peerage and Burke's Landed Gentry give us much information in regard to Hughes lineage. In Burke's Peerage, page 802, it is said: "This family of Hughes (as testified by theirr emblazoned pedigree, drawn up in 1622 by Jacob Chaloner of London) shows itself to be of royal Welsh origin." In Burke's Peerage and Barontage, page 803, a branch of the Hughes family is shown to have descended from Gwaith Vald Mawr, king of Gwent, a prince of Cardigan, and from Blethyn ap Cynyn, Prince of Powis Arms—Az., A lion, rampant; or Crest—A lion couchant, or Motto: "Dopo il Cimento sequi pace."

Their descent from princes of Wales is many times reiterated by genealogists, both living and past. Frances Cowles says in the Nashville Banner of May 13, 1911, "If you are a Hughes you are almost sure to have Welsh blood in your veins, and Welsh blood to be proud of, too, for the first of the name were princes of the royal line of Wales." Frances Cowles asserts a well known fact—that the Huguenot Hughes family of Hughes Creek plantation above Richmond "intermarried extensively with the Hughes family of Welsh blood." This is also proved on pages 77-78 American Ancestry, Vol. 4, 1889, Muncells Sons, publishers, Albany, New York. The writer, Lucy Henderson Horton, is the offspring of intermarriage between these two branches.

Orlando, Leander and William Hughes came to Virginia from Glamorganshire or Carnarvonshire, Wales. The family had holdings in both of these counties. We are told in Burke's Landed Gentry that Hughes descent in the county of Carnarvon occupies twenty-four pages of the Golden Grove MSS., now in the Record office. We note the fact that Sir Thomas Hughes was knighted at Whitehall, Nov. 4, 1619. He was sixteenth in descent from Gwaith Vald Mawr, King of Gwent, and prince of Cardigan (see page 803, Burke's Peerage and Barontage); and that Sir Richard Hughes had the honor to entertain George III at one time. Both the Huguenot and the Welsh Hughes immigrants had grants of land in Powhatan and Goochland counties, Virginia. The Hughes Creek plantation, which was entailed through four generations, is not far from Richmond. Since one is always interested in knowing something of the social atmosphere in which people live, we will quote from an old chronicle by Paulding, describing the inhabitants in this vicinity in early colonial days.

The first settlement on the sight of Richmond was made by Col.

Wm. Byrd in 1677. Some years later a little village flourished here. Paulding describes the inhabitants as "a race of most ancient and respectable planters, having estates in the country, who chose it for their residence for the sake of social enjoyment. They formed a society now seldom to be met with in any of our cities. A society of people not exclusively monopolized by money-making pursuits, but of liberal education, liberal habits of thinking and acting, and possessing both leisure and inclination to cultivate those feelings and pursue those objects which exalt our nature rather than increase our fortune."

That Archelaus Hughes, son of Leander, son of Orlando, the immigrant, was Colonel of a regiment during the Revolutionary war, see Vol. IX, page 415, Virginia Magazine of History and Biography.

Col. Archelaus Hughes married Mary Dalton, a daughter of Samuel Dalton (1699-1802) of Rockingham county, North Carolina, Sept. 25, 1769. Archelaus was born in Goochland county, Virginia, and died in Patrick county, Virginia. The writer prizes as a treasure an autograph note written by Samuel Dalton to his son-in-law, Col. Archelaus Hughes, in 1796. Samuel Dalton was at this time nearly one hundred years old. This paper is worn, but the penmanship is fine. We will write of the Daltons later.

In the Virginia Magazine of History and Biography, Vol. V, page 208, is given some record of the Hughes family of Powhatan county, Va. It is said that Jesse Hughes, whose wife was a French Huguenot, settled in Powhatan county, Virginia, on a grant of land from Charles the Second of England. His grant was on Hughes Creek, above Richmond, and is known as the Hughes Creek plantation. This was entailed according to the English law, and continued in the family for four generations.

Jesse Hughes' son, Robert, married and left sons and daughters. There are no records of births, marriages and deaths of himself and family now extant.

Robert Hughes, Jr., son of Robert Hughes, Sr., married Ann Hartwell, of New Kent. They had three sons, Jesse, Robert and David; also two daughters, Fanny and Temperance. Temperance married Henry Watkins, of Bush River, Prince Edward county, Va. They had five sons and two daughters.

Jesse Hughes, son of Robert, Jr., was a pioneer and explorer of the mountains of West Virginia. He died on one of these expeditions, and was unmarried. So his brother, Robert, inherited Hughes Creek plantation. At the time of his death he was with his relatives, of the Orlando Hughes branch, in Southwestern Virginia.

Robert Hughes III. served in the Revolutionary war as Captain of a volunteer company. Previous to the war he had married Mary Mosby, daughter of Litterberry Mosby. We will say, in passing, that the name Litterberry, an unusual one, occurs in family connection as late as the middle of the nineteenth century. Robert Hughes III. died soon after the close of the Revolutionary war. He left three daughters, no sons. Martha Hartwell Hughes married Francis Goode, of Withby, October 28, 1795. She died in 1825.

David Hughes, son of Robert Hughes II., and his wife, Ann Hartwell, married Judith Daniel, of North Carolina. They had two sons, Jesse and Robert. Jesse Hughes, born 1788, married Elizabeth Woodson Morton, born 1793. Judge Robert W. Hughes, their son, died unmarried. They had one other son and three daughters.

Fanny, daughter of Robert Hughes and his wife, Ann Hartwell, married Rev. John Williams, of North Carolina. They left a large family of sons and daughters in that State (see Vol. V., Virginia Magazine of History and Biography).

Leander Hughes, son of Orlando, and father of Col. Archelaus Hughes, moved from his father's home in Powhatan county, Va., at the time of his marriage, to their estate in Goochland county, Va. Here all his children were born.

· The Jesse Hughes branch and the Orlando, Leander and William Hughes branch, through many intermarriages, have become the same, if they were not originally identical. Jesse Hughes came to Virginia in 1675. Orlando, Leander and William Hughes came to the same county (Powhatan) about 1700 (see American Ancestry, Vol. IV., 1889, pages 77-78, together with Mrs. Harriet D. Pitman's "Americans of Gentle Birth and Their Ancestors."

One of Jesse Hughes' sons married Sallie Tarlton. Their daughter, Martha Hughes, married George Walton, the uncle and educator of the Walton who signed the Declaration of Independence. The mother of George Walton, signer of the Declaration of Independence, was Sally Hughes (see page 154, North Carolina Register, Vols. 1-2, 1900-1901).

Stephen Hughes, of the Orlando branch of the family, who was born in Wales in 1690, married Elizabeth Tarlton, who was born in 1696 and died in 1775 (see American Ancestry, Vol. IV., 1889, pages 77-78).

The writer has in her possession a deed of gift of land signed by George Walton. The signature is identical with that of George Walton on the Declaration of Independence. This deed of gift is to a kinsman, Daniel Frame, who the writer thinks has descendants in Kentucky by the name Metcalfe. Some of his children settled in Wilkes county, Georgia. This was also the home, later in life, of George Walton, uncle of the signer of the Declaration of Independence. The writer has old letters written by members of this family of Wilkes county, Georgia. We will quote from an article by Frances Cowles in the Nashville Banner of May 13, 1911:

"The Hughes Family

"If you are a Hughes you are almost sure to have Welsh blood in your veins, and Welsh blood to be proud of, too, for the first of the names were princes of the royal line of Wales. One of this family was Sir Richard Hughes, made a baronet by the English king in 1773, when he was commissioner of the dockyard of Plymouth, England. A well known man of the name is Justice Charles E. Hughes, whose father was a Welsh Baptist, and mother a Scotch Presbyterian. The best known English Hughes is, without doubt, Thomas Hughes, who wrote 'Tom Brown's School Days.' He was born in Newbury, in the county of Berkshire, England, less than one hundred miles from the Welsh border. In spite of the Welsh blood of this family, the first man of the name in the Southern part of the United States was of Huguenot origin, and is said to have escaped from France to England at the age of fourteen. With his wife he came to Virginia between 1670 and 1700. This family intermarried extensively with the Hughes family of Welsh blood.

"One of the descendants of this double Hughes connection was Major John Hughes, who married Ann (or Nancy) Merriwether. Another was Major David Hughes, born in Virginia in 1756, who served in the Revolution. His son was Andrew S., born in Kentucky in 1792, who married Dora Metcalfe and had a son, Gen. Bela Metcalfe Hughes, of Denver, Colorado, born in Kentucky in 1817. He married, first, Catherine Neal, and second, Laura Allen.

"Jesse, the Huguenot, settled on Hughes Creek, on the James river, and here his family lived and died. This farm continued in the family for four generations. A granddaughter of Jesse Hughes, the Huguenot, named Martha, married George Walton, an uncle of the Walton who signed the Declaration of Independence."

We have proved elsewhere that the mother of George Walton who signed the Declaration of Independence, was Sally Hughes.

Jesse's son, David, or perhaps Adam, was the father of Robert Hughes of Hughes Creek, and his son was Robert, who married Ann Hartwell. Their son, David Hughes, of Muddy Creek plantation, Va., was a Captain in the Revolutionary war. He married Judith Daniel, and their son was Jesse, born in 1788, who married Elizabeth Morton. They had two sons, Robt. William and John Morton. The elder lived in Norfolk, Virginia. He was born in 1812, and at the age of 29 married Eliza Johnson. They had two sons, Robert M. and Floyd, lawyers of Norfolk. John Morton Hughes established his family at Mobile, Alabama.

In Burke's Landed Gentry is given a Hughes coat-of-arms in which is blended Welsh emblems and the French fleur-de-lis.

In County Carnarvan there is Hughes of Coedhelm. In 1569 the family residence was rebuilt, which, from the color of the stone, acquired the name of Plas Coch (Red Hall). The family seat is Coedhelm, Carnarvan.

We are told by several authorities that the Hughes family of Virginia and the Daltons have a common origin in Roderic the Great.

It was to appease the pride of the Welsh people that the title "Prince of Wales" was, in 1343, given to the heir apparent to the throne of England.

We will next copy from the Genealogical Column of the Times-

Dispatch, published at Richmond, Virginia, Sunday, April 24, 1910. This column is edited by Sallie Nelson Robins:

Hughes Family of Goochland County, Virginia.

First will of the Hughes family in Goochland county is that of Sarah, a widow. Will proved in that county May 19, 1730, mentions children, Robert (2), Stephen (2), Ashford (2), Sarah Atkinson (2), Elizabeth Liles (2), Mary Hughes (2), and Isaac Hughes (2).

Robert Hughes (2) in will dated July 13, 1750, mentions his wife, Martha; daughter, Sarah, who married Tucker Woodson; Mary, wife of George Walton; Temperance, wife of Henry Watkins; Martha Walton; sons, Abram and Robert.

Stephen Hughes' will, made in 1749, mentions wife, Elizabeth; and daughter, Elizabeth, who married Sandbourn Woodson; Judith Cox; sons, John and Joseph.

William Hughes (2) married a Miss Bowles and had a son, John; a daughter, Ann, who married a Mr. Perkins. He married a second wife, Martha Bronson, and had Merriette, Sarah and Charles Wesley. Merriette was a Confederate soldier, killed in battle. Sarah also married a Mr. Perkins, brother to her half-sister's husband. Charles Wesley married Mary Davis and had Martha Jane, Sarah Virginia and William Meritte. Martha Jane married George Miles Bainbridge and had Charles Edmond, Nettie B., Halla, Eva and Gilbert Merriette. Nettie B. graduated in medicine and married a class-mate, Albert E. Powell. They have two children, Emily and Edmond. Sarah Virginia married Samuel M. Graham and had Jesse Hughes and Donald Inkerman. Meritte married Jane Younty and had Charles Wesley, Virginia and Maud.

William married (the third time) Nancy Grayson Blackwell. Col. Joseph Blackwell was an officer in the Revolutionary war. They had Susan, who married Vest; Martha Ann, Mary, Virginia, Elizabeth, Stephen Hughes and George Parnell Hughes. Stephen, named for his great-grandfather, married Miss Hodgson, no children. George Parnell Hughes married Miss George Gardner, and had Mrs. Howard, of Lynchburg, Va., and Mrs. Baxter Wilson, of Richmond. The descendants of William Hughes by his third wife have Revolutionary ancestry through Joseph Blackwell.

We will copy some old family records—county records as furnished us by Mr. William G. Stanard, of Richmond, Va.:

Powhatan and Goochland County Records.

(1) Inventory of personal estate of Ashford Hughes, deceased; recorded March 6, 1750.

(2) Will of Stephen Hughes, dated July 6, 1749, proved June 25, 1753. Legatees: daughter, Judith Cox; sons, John and Joseph; wife, Elizabeth, and daughter, Elizabeth Woodson.

(3) Will of Robert Hughes, dated July 13, 1750, proved Sept. 22, 1755. Legatees: daughter, Sarah Woodson; daughter, Mary Walton; daughter, Martha Woodson; daughter, Susan Hughes; daughter, Tem-

perance Hughes; and wife, Martha. Sons were Abraham and Robert.

(4) Will of Joseph Hughes, dated Nov. 1, 1751, proved June 28, 1756. Legatees: Henry Hobson; brother, John Hughes (confirming gift of the "land given him by my father"); wife, Jane; mother, Elizabeth, etc. Refers to his father's will.

(5) Will of Isaac Hughes, dated Jan. 22, 1758, and proved April 24, 1758. Legatees: wife, Martha; Patty Mosby and said Patty's brother, George Walton.

(6) Will of Robert Hughes, dated Feb. 21, 1760, and proved Oct. 23, 1760. Legatees: oldest son, Jesse; sons, Robert and David; wife, Ann; daughters, Frances and Martha Hughes. Refers to estate which will fall to him at his mother's death.

(7) Will of Abraham Hughes, dated Jan. 10, 1756, proved Feb. 23, 1761. Legatees: mother, Martha Hughes; brother, Robert; cousin, John Walton. Refers to deceased father, Robert Hughes; sister, Mary Winfree.

(8) Will of Orlando Hughes, dated July 25, 1768, proved Sept. 26, 1768. Legatees: wife, Elizabeth; sons, Anthony and Josiah; son-in-law, John Maney and son Leander Hughes, executors.

(The writer throws in parenthesis to say that Orlando Hughes was her ancestor. The line runs thus: Orlando Hughes, son Leander Hughes, son Col. Archelaus Hughes, of the Revolutionary war, son Capt. John Hughes (1776-1860), daughter Rachel Jane Hughes, married Dr. Samuel Henderson (1804-1884), daughter, Lucy Henderson Horton.)

(9) Will of Martha Hughes, dated Sept. 8, 1769, proved March 6, 1770. Legatees: daughter, Martha Walton; three children, George Cox, Nully Cox, and Martha Walton.

(10) Will of John Hughes, dated April 16, 1774, proved Feb. 27, 1775. Legatees: wife and son, John.

(11) Will of Leander Hughes, dated March 4, 1775, proved June 26, 1775. Legatees: the following sons: Powell, Stephen, John and Archelaus (this last is Col. Archelaus Hughes).

(12) Deed, Sept. 10, 1746, from Leander Hughes, of Southran parish, Goochland, to Henry Terry, conveying 390 acres in said parish.

(13) Deed, May 16, 1750, from Stephen Hughes to his daughter, Elizabeth, wife of John Woodson.

Woodson.

Since there have been so many Hughes-Woodson intermarriages, we refer those interested in these things to a beautiful little Revolutionary story entitled "Cornwallis' Kiss," written by Mrs. Williamson, the mother of Mrs. Howard Hodgkins, regent of the District of Columbia Daughters of the American Revolution. Mrs. Hodgkins has filled other offices of distinction in this order.

Lord Cornwallis, on his way to Yorktown, while stopping in Goochland county, made "Dover," the home of the Woodsons, his headquarters. To quiet the mother's fear, Cornwallis kissed her baby, Mary Woodson, in the cradle. This incident forms the theme of Mrs. Williamson's fascinating story.

"Dover" was one of the most imposing homes of colonial Virginia. One of its most attractive features was the lovely stairway. This house was the home of Col. John Woodson, his wife, whose maiden name was Dorothea Randolf, and of his son, Major Josiah Woodson. Here Mary Woodson was born, the baby whom Lord Cornwallis kissed. Her portrait is in the possession of some of the family. In this portrait she wears a colonial cap. Mary Woodson became the wife of Dr. James W. Moss. Her daughter, Keturah Taylor, was the grandmother of James O'Fallon.

The Hughes, Woodsons, and Winstons have intermarried in every generation since colonial times. Some living representatives of the Hughes-Woodson connection (1914) are Judge Archelaus Woodson, of the Supreme Bench of Missouri, and Dr. Randolph W. Woodson, of Missouri, an expert on insanity cases, and their sisters and brothers. They are children of Margaret Hughes Woodson, and all the brothers are distinguished lawyers. There are two sisters, Margaret and Jane. Here, as in every branch of our family, we find family names handed down. Judge Archelaus Woodson was named for Col. Archelaus Hughes. Randolph is a family name on the Woodson side, and Mary and Jane were named for Mary (Dalton) Hughes and for Jeaney (Hughes) Fulkerson. They are children of Margaret Hughes Woodson.

The Redd family of this section, who were descendants of Sir Wm. Lionel Rufus de Redd, married into the Woodson, Hughes, and Dalton families, notably Ann (or Nancy) Redd, who in 1740, married Samuel Dalton (1699-1802). Jesse Redd and Mary Woodson were married in Goochland county, Virginia, Nov. 21, 1785 (see page 160, Virginia County Records, 1909).

W. H. Woodson, of Liberty, Clay county, Missouri, descends from Sarah Hughes, a sister of Col. Archelaus Hughes, and John Woodson, of another generation from the John Woodson spoken of above. They had a son, Samuel Hughes Woodson, and he had a son, W. H. Woodson, now living (1914). This John Woodson of whom we speak married, first, Sarah Hughes. His second wife was Rebecca Redd and his third wife, Alice Cheeke. This Woodson branch descends in direct line from "Dr. John Woodson, who came to America in 1619 on the ship George. He was accompanied by his brother-in-law, Anthony Winston, and by his own wife, Sarah Winston." One of his sons was the father of Governor Silas Woodson, of Missouri, and of Benjamin Jordan Woodson. Benjamin Jordan Woodson was the father of Judge Archelaus Woodson, of the Supreme Bench of Missouri. Benjamin Jordan Woodson married Margaret Fulkerson, of Lee county, Virginia. She was a sister of Mary Dalton Fulkerson, who, by the way, was the grandmother of Mrs. Ryland Todhunter, of Lexington, Missouri. Their father, John Fulkerson, who married Jeancy Hughes, a daughter of Colonel Archelaus Hughes, of Patrick county, Virginia, served at one time in the Virginia senate, while two of his brothers were representatives. John Fulkerson's father was a major in the Revolutionary war from Washington county, Virginia. He was also an early Justice of the Peace and public benefactor. His wife, mother of John Fulkerson, was of a noted family of Long Island Patrons, as was he (see records of old Lennett church, New Jersey). Monmouth Chapter D. A. R., in 1911, were restoring the church yard where some of them are buried.

The granddaughter of Judge Van Hook married James Fulkerson in Virginia in 1747. From this branch of the Fulkersons, that is from the parents of James Fulkerson, are descended the noted families of which General Frelenghusen and Henry Van Dyke are representatives.

The writer has in her possession old family papers, bearing the signatures of Jeancy (Hughes) Fulkerson and her husband, John Fulkerson, of Lee county, Virginia. Jeancy (Hughes) Fulkerson was a sister of the writer's grandfather, Capt. John Hughes (1776-1860).

We failed to state the fact that John Woodson left Virginia and settled in Knox county, Kentucky, after his first marriage.

We will first copy extracts from a book written by Mrs. Elizabeth Winston Campbell Hendricks, of Washington, D. C. These references, showing Hughes-Winston connection, were furnished me by U. S. Senator E. W. Pettus, of Alabama, in 1906:

1. Isaac Winston, the Saxon immigrant, married about 1740 in Virginia, Mary Ann Fontaine. Their son, Peter Winston, married Elizabeth Powell. Their son, John Winston, married Miss Austin. Their daughter, Mary Ann Winston, married Peter Denoville. Their daughter Elizabeth, married William Bright. Their daughter, Susan Bright, married a Mr. Hughes.

2. Sarah Winston, a granddaughter of Isaac Winston, the immigrant, and mother of Patrick Henry, had a daughter named Lucy Henry, who married Valentine Wood. Their daughter married Judge Peter Johnston. Their son, Charles Johnston, married Emily Preston. And their daughter, Elizabeth, married Judge Robert Hughes.

3. William Winston, one of the immigrants, about 1730, married Sarah Dabney (who was the mother of Judge Edmund Winston and Sarah Winston, the mother of Patrick Henry).

4. William Winston and his wife, Sarah Dabney, had another daughter named Mary Ann, who married Dr. John Walker. Their son, also named Dr. John Walker, married Susan Christian. Their daughter, Maria Walker, married Dr. M. Spencer. Their daughter, Ann Spencer, married B. Nowlan, and their daughter, Virginia Nowlan, married John Hughes.

We will quote from the letter of U. S. Senator E. W. Pettus: "So far as I am informed my first known ancestor, on the Winston side, was Isaac Winston, of York, England. Three of his grandsons, Isaac, William and Anthony, settled in Hanover county, Virginia. Isaac Winston, the Saxon, was my first American ancestor, and lived in Hanover county, Virginia, before 1700. His son, Anthony, married Alice

Taylor, Sept. 29, 1723. He lived in Hanover and had a son, named Anthony, born Nov. 27, 1752, and this last named Anthony was my grandfather. He moved to Buckingham county, Virginia, and married Kizia Jones, in 1776. My mother was Alice Taylor Winston and my father was John Pettus, of Fluvana county, Virginia. My grandfather, Anthony Winston, moved to Davidson county, Tennessee, with his family, near the Hermitage, and, later in life, he followed his children to Alabama. Edmund Winston, of Franklin, Tennessee, who died last year, was a son of my uncle, Edmund Winston, of Lagrange, Tennessee."

Then he adds, by way of P. S.: "General Wade Hampton's mother was a Preston and she was of the Winston stock."

Edmund Winston, of Franklin, referred to in this letter, married Josephine Cocke, of Chattanooga, Tenn., who comes of a well-known Virginia family. They had no children. Edmund Winston, of Lagrange, Tenn., was a fine type of the ante-bellum Southern gentleman.

Edmund W. Pettus

Edmund W. Pettus served Alabama in United States senate. He was a man of ability, and his character was such that he held the friendship of Senator Pugh, over whom he was elected to the U. S. senate. Indeed, the friendship of Pugh, Morgan and Pettus, and the combined efforts of these three for public good, caused them to be spoken of as "Alabama's great triumvirate."

Pettus was a man who was quoted by Washington newspaper men a great deal. He was held in great veneration by them, "But his quaint, old-fashioned simplicity, his unfailing good nature, his constant droll humor, terse and frank speech, combined to make him a frequent source of interest, especially to those whose mission it was to supply-anecdotes of public men."

Sometimes these anecdotes were a bit trying on him, but, with his unfailing philosophy, he would say, "Well, I suppose I am legitimate prey."

He by no means escaped life's sorrows. His son, Frank Pettus, who was an honored leader among strong men in Alabama, died in the prime of life. His beloved wife, the companion of his youth and old age, passed over the river before him. Only a few months before her death he had spoken of her as "the handsomest 88-year-old girl in the land."

Senator Pettus was a man trusted in his larger sphere just as he had at home been honored, trusted, and beloved; a man to inspire fresh faith in human nature.

John A. Winston, governor of Alabama 1853-57, was closely related to Senator Pettus. Winston county, Alabama, was named for the Governor.

Preston

The assertion is sometimes made that all old Virginia families are

related. We will quote from the history of Southwestern Virginia, by
Lewis Preston Summers, of Abingdon, Virginia, to show some Hughes
connection with the Preston family. Page 794: "Judge Robert William
Hughes, born in Powhatan county, Virginia, June 16, 1821, was reared
by Mrs. General Carrington, a daughter of General Francis Preston,
of Abingdon. He was educated at Caldwell Institute, Greensboro, N.
C.; tutor in Bingham, N. C., High School 1840-43.; lawyer in Richmond,
Virginia, 1843-53; editor Richmond Examiner 1850-57; commissioned
Judge Eastern District of Virginia by Grant, served until 1898 and resigned. June 4, 1850, at Governor's mansion, Richmond, Virginia, he
married Miss Eliza M. Johnston, daughter of Hon. Charles C. Johnston and Eliza May Preston, niece of General Joseph E. Johnston. He
was author of valuable "Reports," and others, "Lee and His Lieutenants," etc. In 1866 Judge Hughes fought a duel with Cameron, afterward governor of Virginia, and broke his rib at first fire. Judge Hughes
died Dec. 10, 1901, at Sinking Spring. For many years he occupied
a summer home on his fine estate three miles east of Abingdon.

A Preston connection comes through Col. Peter H. Dillard. Col.
Dillard was an uncle of Lucinda Redd, who married Hon. William Ballard Preston, Secretary of Navy in Taylor's cabinet 1849-1850. He
represented Virginia in U. S. congress as a Whig 1847-49. He was a
Confederate Senator in 1862. Preston was born in 1805, and died in
1862 (see Dictionary of U. S. History by Jameson). We have never
been able to trace the relationship of Lucinda Redd's father to the Ann
(or Nancy) Redd, wife of Samuel Dalton (1699-1802). They were
different families; and yet through the Dillard-Hughes line there is
descent from Nancy (Redd) Dalton.

Three members of this family of Redd, of which Lucinda (Redd)
Preston was a member, married grandchildren of Gov. Patrick Henry
by the name of Fontaine.

Frances Cowles says in "A Corner in Ancestors," published in
Nashville Banner, March 28, 1914: "There were many distinguished
men, governors, senators, and soldiers in the Preston family. In fact
there was hardly a son of the family who did not distinguish himself in
some way, and it was proudly said by the Prestons that the members
of this family alone have done quite as much for the service of the
country as all Mayflower descendants put together. This sounds like a
gross exaggeration, but anyone who has studied the annals of the
family during the first one hundred years of their residence in this
country can understand that the proud Preston who made this statement has some ground for his assertion." Frances Cowles further says:
"William Preston has been called the most finished orator the South
ever produced, and this not even excepting his maternal uncle, Patrick
Henry."

Major John Neville Hughes

We will copy from a book, The Merriwethers, pages 148-9—"Ann

Merriwether, a great-granddaughter of Nicholas Merriwether, married Major John Neville Hughes, who was of Welsh descent. Tradition says they have the blood of ancient kings of Britain; however, they have been reconstructed, and, at the present day, are good Democrats. He was born in Powhatan county, Virginia, Aug. 11, 1763. At the age of fifteen he left Hampton-Sydney College and enlisted in the Revolutionary army, serving until the close of the war. At the age of twenty he married Ann Merriwether; and they had many children, fourteen of whom arrived at maturity.

Major John N. Hughes, an adventurous spirit, came West in 1786. He served again in the war of 1812. He died on his farm on the Ohio river, six miles below Louisville, Kentucky, Dec. 11, 1842. He survived all of his children except five. Major Hughes was a great-grandfather of Miss Martha Hughes of Jefferson county, Kentucky. Major John N. Hughes is, we think, buried in Nicholasville, Jessamine county, Kentucky.

George Walton

The mother of George Walton, the signer of the Declaration of Independence, was Sally Hughes, of Powhatan county, Virginia (see page 154, North Carolina Register, Vols. 1-2, 1900-1901).

The above mentioned George Walton was reared and educated by his uncle, George Walton, who married Martha Hughes (see original county records of Hughes in this book). He was born in Prince Edward county, Virginia. We have proved above that he was a grandson of Jesse Hughes, of Hughes Creek plantation, in Powhatan county, Va. We are told that some of the Jesse Hughes branch lived in Prince Edward county, Va. (American Ancestry, Vol. 4, 1889, pages 77-78). The writer has in her possession, among old family papers, one showing that her great-grandfather, Colonel Archelaus Hughes, owned valuable land in Prince Edward county, Virginia. This land, consisting of two hundred and thirty acres, lying on Spring Creek, in 1779 sold for two thousand pounds, "current money of Virginia." This was something like ten thousand dollars, which must have been considered a good price in 1779 for 230 acres.

We find the Hughes, Daltons, Waltons, and Martins, all of the same family connection, together in eastern Virginia, and later some of them in Fairfax county, Virginia, and in Albemarle, whence they moved to Southwestern Virginia and to Georgia. Some moved to Charleston, S. C. George Walton, on leaving Virginia, settled in Savannah, Georgia, whither Samuel Dalton (1619-1802) had gone in early manhood; but returned to Virginia—as he thought—but on the North Carolina side of the boundary line.

In 1777 George Walton married Dorothy Camber, daughter of an English nobleman, who resided in Chatham county, Georgia. He later lived at Augusta, Georgia. Here his old home, "Meadow Garden," is now the property of the D. A. R. We are glad to say that "Old Glory" chapter, D. A. R., at Franklin, Tennessee, of which the writer is a charter member, contributed to the purchase of "Meadow Garden."

George Walton, the uncle and educator of the signer of the Declaration of Independence, whose wife was Martha Hughes, in his latter years moved to Wilks county, Georgia. Here some of the daughters of Daniel Frame lived after marriage. The writer has letters among old family papers showing this.

The writer has in her possession a deed of gift of land from George Walton to Daniel Frame.

The year after his marriage we find George Walton leading his regiment in defense of Savannah. Here he was desperately wounded and taken prisoner by the enemy. General Robert Howe addressed him a letter of sympathy and commended him for his bravery. In a letter written by Walton at this time to his young wife with the probabilities of death threatening him, he says "Remember that you are the beloved wife of a man who has made honor and reputation the ruling motive of every action of his life." He was Georgia's first Governor; and was again made Governor in 1789. Walton was six times a representative to congress. He was in U. S. senate 1795-96. He was four times Judge of the Supreme Court, and was Chief Justice of the state of Georgia. In 1791 we find him living at "Meadow Garden," Augusta, Georgia. This was his home until the year of his death, 1804. Under its hospitable roof was entertained the best, the bravest, the most cultured in the land. George Washington was George Walton's guest at "Meadow Garden" when he visited Augusta in May, 1791. When the Marquis de Lafayette was in Augusta, in 1824, he visited "Meadow Garden" because it had been the home of his "valued friend, George Walton" (see American Monthly Magazine for June, 1899, pages 1216-17).

Madame Octavia Walton Le Vert

Madame Le Vert was a granddaughter of George Walton. She wrote a fascinating story of her travels abroad. In the publishers preface to "Souvenirs of Travel," by Madame Le Vert, Vol. I, it is said "Her social position at home, and an extensive acquaintance with the highest circles abroad, gave her familiar access to scenes and personages and conditions of life not ordinarily within the reach of the foreign traveler. The mystic veil, which hides the penetralia of courtly and aristocratic society, was lifted for her eyes. The gifts of personal loveliness were hers in a very high degree; but in her intelluctual accomplishments, and the perpetual sunshine of a gay and joyous spirit, always amiable, kind, and considerate, gave to their possessor her chief charm." She was the wife of Dr. Henry S. Le Vert, a learned and eminent physician, of Mobile, Alabama. She would playfully call him "M. D."

Among her most intimate friends was Lady Emiline Stuart Wortly, a daughter of the Duke of Rutland, and of the household of Queen Victoria; another friend was Frederika Bremer, the gifted novelist of Sweden. In 1853 she visited Belvoir Castle of the Duke of Rutland, a noble old baronial structure.

In 1855 Madame Le Vert made another visit to Europe. She also tarried a few weeks in the brilliant city of Havana, Cuba.

Old people in the South are still (1914) fond of recounting the social triumphs of Madame Le Vert. One old lady, Mrs. Childress, who was a Nashville girl at the time, tells with pride of having danced in Mobile, Ala. On one occasion she danced in a set with Madame La Vert, Mrs. Walton, her mother, and the daughter of Madame Le Vert. Three generations were represented. Madame Le Vert often when dancing wore anklets.

Mme. Le Vert was a member of the Mount Vernon Ladies' Association, which was founded in 1853. The object of this association was to preserve for all time America's chief shrine—the home and tomb of Washington.

Hughes

Orlando and Leander Hughes, brothers, who came to Virginia from Wales about 1700, had, as we have proved, grants of land in Powhatan and Goochland counties. Orlando made his home in Powhatan county, Va. His wife's name was Elizabeth, as shown in his will. His sons were Anthony, Josiah, and Leander. He also had a daughter who married John Maney. Orlando Hughes, in his will made Leander and his son-in-law, John Maney, executors. This will was proved Sept. 26, 1768.

The will of Leander, son of Orlando, was proved June 26, 1775. His legatees were his sons, Powell, Stephen, John, and Archelaus. John Hughes, son of Leander, son of Orlando, is spoken of as the offspring of intermarriage between the Hughes'family of Welsh blood and the Jesse Hughes branch of Huguenot blood. That these two Hughes branches intermarried, see pages 77-78, American Ancestry, Vol. 4, 1889, Muncell's sons, publishers. See also Frances Cowles.

This Major John Hughes married Ann (or Nancy) Merriwether, of the well known Virginia family. We have already given a sketch of this man as copied from a book, The Merriwethers, pages 148-9.

This man's son, John Hughes, married Anne Moore, a daughter of olutionary fame. In fact he was only six years old when Col. Archelaus Hughes married Mary Dalton in 1769. John Hughes was a member of the Loyal Land Company of Southwestern Virginia. This company was composed of forty-two gentlemen. Samuel Dalton (1699-1802) was also a member of the Loyal Land Company. See History of Southwestern Virginia by Thos. Preston Somers. The elder James Madison, father of President James Madison, was a member of the Loyal Land Company.

This Loyal Land Company consisting of forty-two gentlemen, had two grants of land, one grant of a hundred and twenty thousand acres, and another of eight hundred thousand acres, making in all nine hundred and twenty thousand acres of land. In Thomas Preston Somer's History of Southwestern Virginia there is recorded a toast given by John

Hughes at some gathering of this company.

This man's son, John Hughes, married Ann Moore, a daughter of Matthew Moore, and his wife, Letitia Dalton (see Moore). Mrs. Susan Letitia Rice Clotworthy of Hillman, Georgia, has the will of Matthew Moore, who was her great-great-grandfather. This will is nine pages on foolscap paper. In the will Matthew Moore mentions his "daughter Anne, wife of John Hughes" and he also left a sum of money to educate her son, Archelaus Hughes. There are many John and Archelaus Hughes. Of course the name came from his uncle Archelaus Hughes of the Revolution. Among the children of Matthew Moore, one son married a sister of General William Martin, of Williamson county, Tennessee. One son married a sister of General Edmund Pendleton Gaines.

Colonel Archelaus Hughes

Archelaus Hughes, son of Leander, son of Orlando who came to Virginia from Wales about 1700, was born in Goochland county, Virginia, in 1747. His father, Leander Hughes, was born and reared in Powhatan county, Va. After his marriage he lived in Goochland county. Here his children were born.

When quite young, Archelaus Hughes went to Pittsylvania county, Va., to live. He was married to Mary Dalton, daughter of Samuel Dalton (1699-1802), of Mayo, Sept. 25, 1769. We have given a sketch of Mary Dalton, daughter of Samuel Dalton, of Rockingham county, N. C., under head "Dalton." Among old family papers which have come down to the writer from her grandfather, Captain John Hughes (1776-1860), who administered on the estate of his father, Col. Archelaus Hughes, is a paper showing that "Archelaus Hughes and John Wimbish of Virginia" paid for a bill of goods bought from John Lidderdale, of London, England, in 1769. These goods, bought in London, contained wedding toggery.

After this marriage Archelaus Hughes lived in what is now Patrick county, Va. This had been cut off from Pittsylvania county as Henry county, named in honor of Patrick Henry, whose home was here, and then another division was made; and the part in which Col. Archelaus Hughes lived was called Patrick county, also in honor of Patrick Henry.

Their home was called "Hughesville," and was the first frame house built in what is now Patrick Co. It was about ten miles from the home of Samuel Dalton on Mayo river. In calling their home "Hughesville" they were following an old Saxon custom. A single farm house in Scotland is still called a town (see page 54, Leading Facts of English History by Montgomery). The first Saxon settlements were called towns or tun, meaning a fence or hedge, because they were surrounded by a rampart of earth, set with a thick hedge. One or more houses might constitute a town. Possibly the custom of sometimes having the suffix "ville" to the names of some Southern homes lay in the fact that here not only was the house in which the master lived but also the Negro quarters and other accessories of the old-time plantation. Indeed, an old-time Southern plantation was like a little commonwealth. We know from old family papers that at Hughesville was a blacksmith shop and a country store. Col. Archelaus Hughes had large landed estates, but he seemed to like to add to his income through merchandise. He operated seven stores in different localities. "Hughesville," a house of ten rooms, still stands (1912), and is in a very good state of preservation.

All of the children of Col. Archelaus Hughes and his wife, Mary Dalton, were born at "Hughesville." We like to feel certain of our assertions. The writer holds an old letter written by their son, Leander, in his old age, to his brother, Captain John Hughes, in which he speaks of living in the "old home in which they were both born and grew to manhood." This letter was written in 1859.

On the twenty-seventh day of Sept., 1775, Archelaus Hughes was appointed, by the Committee of Safety, captain of a company of militia in Pittsylvania county, Va. (see American Monthly Magazine for June, 1912, page 255). Here quotation is made from original county records. Later he was made colonel of a Virginia regiment (see page 415, Vol. IX, Virginia Magazine of History and Biography).

"Hughesville" was situated on the regular stage and mail route. It was a home of large hospitality. Many friends from different parts of the country on their way to White Sulphur Springs would make it a point to visit "Hughesville."

Col. Archelaus Hughes and his wife are buried at "Hughesville." Indeed the old family graveyard here is full of Hughes graves.

Dr. Robert Hunter Dalton, the family chronicler, who was born and reared in Rockingham county, N. C., which is near Patrick county, Va., was often at "Hughesville." He speaks of attending the wife of Col. Archelaus Hughes as a physician, "Aunt Mollie Hughes." Dr. R. H. Dalton says that Col. Archelaus Hughes held some civil office under George Washington's administratioin as President. This office called him to Philadelphia. He said that in Philadelphia society Mary Dalton Hughes proved herself an attractive and cultured woman. She had had the honor of knowing George Washington in his home at Mount Vernon when she would visit her uncle, John Dalton, at Alexandria. We have shown elsewhere of the association of John Dalton and George Washington (see Dalton).

We learn from old family papers that Col. Archelaus Hughes was an extensive land owner. Some tract of land belonging to him in Patrick county, Va., is spoken of as joining Fontaine's and Walton's line. He owned valuable land in Prince Edward county, Va. This county was the old home of George Walton. He also owned land on Snow Creek, Stokes county, N. C. In 1794 he bought land from Samuel Walker in Surry county. He owned property about Leaksville. Jeancy (Hughes) Fulkerson and her husband, Col. John Fulkerson, sold land in

Lee county, Va., "of the estate of Col. Archelaus Hughes." Jeancy Fulkerson was a daughter of Col. Archelaus Hughes.

In 1796, Archelaus Hughes settled a family account with Henry L. Biscoe. This included "Linen sheeting and 16 yards black bombazet, 3 papers gilt pins, 1 yard swansdown, 1 pair knee buckles, pewter dishes," etc. For these he paid in L. S. D. His family accounts show that much linen sheeting was bought by him.

If the writer should record all names on business papers belonging to Col. Hughes it would convey a good idea of all people who lived in this section at that time.

Mary (Dalton) Hughes wrote a splendid hand. It is thin Italian. Her husband, Col. Hughes, wrote a fine bold hand. When we come to their children the penmanship is still good. The writer has John Hughes' (1776-1860) signature as witness on one of his father's notes, when he was sixteen years old. It is written in splendid hand. But when we reach the grandchildren many of them show carelessness in writing. To this rule, however, there are exceptions. Rachel Jane (Hughes) Henderson, the mother of the writer, received at school a card of merit for good penmanship.

Some of the Hughes family became converts of Mr. Whitfield, and later were known as Methodists. We quote from Thackeray: "Mr. Whitfield had come into Virginia where the habits and preaching of the established clergy were not very edifying. Unlike many of the neighboring provinces, Virginia was a Church of England colony: the clergy were paid by the state and had glebes allotted to them; and there being no Church of England bishop as yet in America, the colonists were obliged to import their divines from the mother country. Such as came were, naturally, not of the very best, or most eloquent kind of pastors. Nobleman's hangers-on, insolvent parsons who had quarreled with justice, or the bailiff, brought their stained cassocks into the colony in hopes of finding a living there. No wonder that Mr. Whitfield's great voice stirred the people."

After the death of Col. Archelaus Hughes in 1798, his wife still lived here, and dispensed Southern hospitality in a lavish way until her death in 1841. At the time of her death she was in her ninety-third year. Dr. Robert Hunter Dalton, the nephew, who knew her well and loved her, said that his aunt, although she lived to be so old, never had any wrinkles in her face like most old people. Every one of the connection who remembered her said that she was bright and cheerful always.

Children of Colonal Archelaus Hughes and his wife, Mary Dalton

We do not know the order of their births.

1. Leander Hughes, died unmarried, aged ninety-seven years, at "Hughesville."

2. Archelaus Hughes, married Nancy Martin, daughter of Captain (and Rev.) Wm. Martin and his wife Rachel Dalton.

3. William Hughes, married, first, Moore; second, Alice (or Alsey) Carr, of N. C.

4. Jeancy Hughes, married Col. John Fulkerson of Lee county, Va.

5. John Hughes, born Aug. 3, 1776; married Sally Martin, daughter of Captain (and Rev.) Wm. Martin and his wife, Rachel Dalton, Feb. 7, 1798. He died Dec. 26, 1860.

6. Samuel Hughes, died a bachelor, aged sixty-eight. He served in Virginia senate, etc.

7. Reuben Hughes.

8. Nancy Hughes, married Brett Stovall.

9. Madison Redd Hughes, married three times; first, Moore; second, Mathews; third, Sally Dillard.

10. Sally Hughes, married Col. Joseph Martin, of Henry county, Va., son of General Joseph Martin.

11. Matilda Hughes, married Gen. John Dillard, son of Capt. John Dillard of the Revolution.

I. Leander Hughes

Leander Hughes, son of Col. Archelaus Hughes and his wife, Mary Dalton, was born at "Hughesville." Leander Hughes inherited this old place, and at his death gave it to his niece, Mary (Martin) McCabe, eldest daughter of Col. Joseph Martin and his wife, Sallie Hughes. She had lived with him in his old age and made life pleasant for him.

Mary (Martin) McCabe left "Hughesville" to her son, John McCabe, and he, in turn, left it to the widow of Tom McCabe, a Hughes relative. The widow of Tom McCabe had been twice married. Her first husband was Tom Staples, brother of John Staples. John Staples was one of Virginia's best lawyers. Staples lived at "Hughesville" and took an interest in keeping up the place. He made his home here with the McCabe family. He was a bachelor.

II. Archelaus Hughes

Archelaus Hughes, son of Col. Archelaus Hughes, who commanded a Virginia regiment during the Revolutionary war, and his wife, Mary Dalton, was born about 1771. Archelaus II. married Nancy Martin, daughter of Wm. Martin and his wife, Rachel Dalton. Two brothers, Archelaus and John Hughes, married sisters, and these sisters were their first cousins.

Archelaus Hughes was born at "Hughesville" in Patrick county, Va. This family had a penchant for legislative assemblies. He served in the Legislature of Virginia; and was a cultered gentleman.

Nancy Martin, his wife, was a daughter of Capt. (and Rev.) Wm. Martin and his wife, Rachel Dalton. She was a niece of Gen. Joseph Martin; and of the brave old patriot of "Rock House," Col. Jack Martin. Elsewhere we copy a letter written by Nancy (Martin) Hughes to her son, Archelaus M. Hughes, in Williamson county, Tennessee. This letter was written in 1831 from the home of her mother, Rachel (Dalton) Martin, in Stokes county, N. C. She said in her letter that she would stay with her daughter, Letty, while Colonel Winston was off attending the legislature at Raleigh. This daughter was Letty (Hughes) Winston, the wife of Col., afterward General, Joseph Winston, who lived at the ancestral home of Major Joseph Winston, hero of King's Mountain. This son, Joseph, inherited the home through his father's will, which is given elsewhere.

This letter proves Nancy (Martin) Hughes to have been a cultured, refined and warm-hearted woman, this being characteristic of the family. Her sisters, Sally (Martin) Hughes and Susan (Martin) Moore, were of this type; and Col. Wm. Martin, of Williamson county, Tennessee, is said to have been "a man of warm heart and courtly manner."

Children of Archelaus Hughes and His Wife, Nancy Martin

1. Matthew Hughes.
2. Polly Hughes, married a Mr. Dobson.
3. ———— Hughes, married ———— Banner, of Stokes county, N. C. They were parents of John Banner.
4. Nancy Hughes, the youngest child, married, 1837, late in life.
5. Archelaus M. Hughes, married and lived in Tennessee. He ran for congress against Davy Crockett. He had six children; one being named William Martin Hughes, another Brice Hughes, who was the father of Mrs. Lizzie Fowlks, of Dyersburg, Tenn.
6. Letitia Hughes, married Gen. Joseph Winston, son of Major Joseph Winston, of Stokes county, N. C. They lived, first, in Stokes county, N. C., later moving to Missouri. We give her descendants in full elsewhere.

General Joseph Winston and his wife Letitia, or Letty, as she was called by the family, were cousins. The wife of Major Joseph Winston, of King's Mountain fame, was a sister of Rachel (Dalton) Martin, grandmother of Letty Hughes. Gen. Joseph Winston moved with his family to Platte county, Missouri, in 1839. She died in Nov., 1855.

Patrick Henry, who lived at one time in Henry county, Va., and whose descendants have intermarried extensively with this family connection, was himself of this Winston family. His mother was Sarah Winston. His only brother had no children; but they had many sisters, all of whom left descendants. Elizabeth Henry's first husband was Gen. Wm. Campbell, hero of King's Mountain, and ancestor of the Preston's of South Carolina; also an ancestor of Mrs. James S. Pilcher of Nashville, Tenn. Anna Henry, sister of Patrick Henry, was the wife of Gen. Christian. Mrs. Wood, sister of Patrick Henry, was the grandmother of Gen. Joseph E. Johnston. Mrs. Madison was the ancestor of many of the Lewises. Among the descendants of Letitia Hughes and her husband, Gen. Joseph Winston, which we give in full elsewhere, will be found many distinguished names of men and women in Missouri and elsewhere of Hughes-Winston-Woodson, etc., connection. Something of their genealogy can be found in the History of Platte county, Missouri.

Archelaus M. Hughes III.

Archelaus M. Hughes III., son of Archelaus Hughes II., and his wife, Nancy Martin, came to Tennessee to live when a boy. He first made his home in Williamson county with his uncle, Gen. Wm. Martin. Gen. Martin lived in the old house in which, later, the writer was born and reared. His coming to live with his uncle, who was a bachelor, was hailed with delight. Gen. Martin wrote back a letter to the family, in which he says: "Archelaus seems a part of myself." While in Williamson county, Tenn., the letter we record elsewhere from the mother, Nancy Martin Hughes, was written to him in 1831. From Williamson county he went to Dresden, Tenn., to live, and, while living here, became a candidate for congress. His opponent was Davy Crockett. Archelaus M. Hughes wrote to his uncle, Gen. Wm. Martin, of Williamson county, from Dresden, Tenn., Aug. 30, 1837, in which he says: "I was badly beaten for congress by young Crockett. No man could have beaten him at this time. I knew it, but as I was first out, I would not back down." In his old letters the names Wm. E. Anderson, of Nashville; Wm. H. Johnson, of Dresden, his kinsman; Robert E. C. Daugherty; W. H. Hunt; and his cousin, Brice F. Martin, are spoken of familiarly. Archelaus M. Hughes died Aug. 25, 1838.

We will quote from a letter, written at the time of his death by Wm. H. Johnson, whom Archelaus Hughes had spoken of as his "particular friend and relation." He speaks of Johnson also as "State Senator from this district." Johnson wrote General Martin from Dresden, Tenn., Aug. 26, 1838: "I have the very unpleasant intelligence to communicate to you, the death of Archelaus M. Hughes. He departed this life yesterday after an illness of ten days with congestive fever. He had as good medical aid as there is in the district, but his disease baffled their skill, and our county has lost one of its most worthy citizens, and his family one of the kindest husbands and the most tender parents." He left six children. He had just received the appointment of cashier in a bank in Kentucky carrying a splendid salary; and he was to have charge of this business the very day he died. "How uncertain is the dispensation of Providence," Wm. H. Johnson adds.

III. Sally (Hughes) Martin

Sally Hughes, daughter of Col. Archelaus Hughes and his wife, Mary Dalton, was born at "Hughesville," their homestead, in what is now Patrick county, Virginia.

After her marriage to Col. Joseph Martin, son of Gen. Joseph Martin, April 27, 1810, they built a splendid home in Henry county, Va. This home has always been known as "Greenwood." It was near "Leatherwood," the old home of Patrick Henry. Also it was near "Belmont," the home of Gen. Martin. This home of Gen. Joseph Martin had been purchased from Benjamin Harrison of Berkley (Virginia Magazine and Biography, Vol. —— in article on Gen. Joseph Martin).

Sally Hughes Martin was one of the most remarkable women of her day. She was possessed of rare personal beauty and great intelligence.

"Greenwood" was for fifty years the center of old-fashioned hospitality; and "she was the queen of the household, the light of the home." Their circle of friends and relatives extended over many states.

She was for sixty years a member of the Baptist church. She survived her husband twenty-three years; and at the time of her death was in her ninety-second year, and was the ancestor of one hundred and fifty descendants. Among the children of Col. Joseph Martin and his wife, Sally Hughes, the girls were noted for their beauty and attractiveness, and the boys were worthy men. Their children were given the finest educational advantages. Under head "Martin" we give sketches of their children.

IV. Captain John Hughes (1776-1860)

John Hughes, son of Col. Archelaus Hughes and his wife, Mary Dalton, was born at "Hughesville," the family homestead in Patrick county, Va., Aug. 3, 1776. Here he grew to manhood.

The year 1798 was to him a memorable year. On Feb. 7, 1798, he was married to his cousin, the lovely and graceful Sally Martin, daughter of Capt. (and Rev.) Wm. Martin and his wife, Rachel Dalton, of Snow Creek, Stokes county, N. C. John Hughes was a member of the Virginia legislature at the time of the passage of the famous "Madison Resolutions of 1798." He spoke on these resolutions and voted for their passage. Everybody knows that these resolutions led up to Nullification and Secession.

In 1798, his father, Archelaus Hughes, died, and John Hughes was made administrator of his father's estate. In this way many valuable old family papers of Col. Archelaus Hughes have come into the hands of the writer. Among these papers are grants of land signed by Thos. Jefferson and Patrick Henry in 1768, 1769, etc. She has a deed of gift of land from George Walton to Daniel Frame, a kinsman of this man. She has letters from Daniel Frame after he moved to Kentucky.

In Annals of Platte County, Missouri, by Wm. M. Paxton, page 57, can be seen something of Frame-Hughes marriage. Here, we are told, Andrew S. Hughes' mother was Margaret Frame, born 1758, a daughter of David Frame. Andrew S. Hughes was born in Kentucky on Feb. 9, 1789; died in Plattsburg, Dec. 3, 1843. He married Rhoda Metcalfe in 1829 in Fayette county, Ky. Later he moved to Clay county, Missouri. We are told that the "Metcalfe family is one of the most distinguished families of Kentucky." "A volume would be required to record their honors in civil and military life." Descent is from—

I. Francis Metcalfe, of Yorkshire, England.

II. John Metcalfe, who came to Virginia in 1760.

III. John, his son, born in Fauquer county, Va., came to Kentucky in 1784. His children were: Thomas Metcalfe, the old "Stone-hammer" Governor of Kentucky, Bela, Sarah, Rhoda D., married Gen. Andrew Hughes.

This Platte County History was published in 1903. The author lived to be over ninety years old.

Since the close of the war between the States the name of the county seat of Patrick has been changed from Taylorsville to Stuart, in honor of General J. E. B. Stuart, of Confederate memory.

In Virginia, tobacco seems to have been one of the chief sources of revenue. We find John Hughes making large sales of tobacco to Wm. King of Abingdon, Va., in 1806. In 1796, when only twenty years of age, John Hughes had an account with Buckanan, Dunlop & Co., at Petersburg, amounting to 2,913 pounds. We can see that he did business with men in Lynchburg, Petersburg, and Richmond. Later he had dealings with men in Mobile and Huntsville, Alabama. He and other members of his family would often visit the home of Gov. Gabriel Moore, a first cousin of John Hughes, near Huntsville. The families had been reared together in Virginia and were very intimate. Also John Hughes had dealings with men in New Orleans and in Nashville. Sometimes he would exchange his produce for groceries in Mobile and New Orleans.

A friend in Madison, N. C., sends a letter by "Capt. Dalton's" hand to John Hughes, in which he speaks of Mr. Dandridge giving him property. John Hughes was of Dandridge descent.

On April 5, 1834, John Hughes sold sixty-two bales of cotton in New Orleans for $2,370.28. He often sold cotton after moving to Tennessee. He also sold tobacco in New Orleans and Mobile. We are glad to say that this man had dealings with James Robertson, "the father of Tennessee."

In 1826 John Hughes gave a note to Thos. Henderson, promising to pay him nineteen hundred dollars. This was witnessed by Hon. B. G. Killingsworth. He promised to pay this "in the circulating medium of the State of Tennessee." The writer has Thos. Henderson's autograph, written March 1, 1827. One old account shows that John Hughes sold in different lots ninety-eight bales of cotton, forty-six and sixty-one bales.

In an account book we see this entry: "July 22, 1819—This day left with Capt. Campbell of the agency in Leaksville, $23 for interest—my bond to be renewed the twenty-second day of September, next for fifteen hundred dollars." Under his Leaksville accounts we see that James Martin owed him two thousand dollars in 1821. In May, 1821, he sent two of his boys, Leander and Brice Martin Hughes, to school in Leaksville. This was in order that they might be near their mother's relatives.

He sometimes sold tobacco raised in Virginia to Henry Daggett of Mobile, Ala. In early life Capt. Hughes had dealings with Grenville Penn. Also with a firm—Fontaine and Dandridge, and, a little later with Brett Stovall, George S. Clark, Samuel Dalton, Joseph Martin, Samuel Martin and Archelaus Hughes. He often speaks intimately of the Penn family. There were several intermarriages between Penn and Hughes families.

John Hughes (1776-1860) was a Mason. Captain T. P. Henderson, a descendant, has the charter of a Masonic lodge, the Way of Happiness Lodge No. 71 in Patrick county, Va., made to John Hughes as master of this lodge in 1803. The writer has a record of some of the meetings of this lodge. In April, 1804, they met at the courthouse in Patrick county. Members' names are called as follows: John Hughes, Master; John Hanby, Charles Foster, John Hanby, Jr., James McCampbell, Samuel Hanby, Robert Scott, John Patterson, Brett Stovall, John Roseland, Jol W. Campbell and John Dabney, visitors. On Oct. 25, 1804, at a meeting of the Way to Be Happy Lodge No. 71 in Patrick county, Va., of which John Hughes was Worshipful Master, Charles Foster and Brice Martin were chosen to represent the lodge in the next grand lodge of Virginia. Nathaniel H. Claiborne was a visiting brother, Matthew Sandfer and Abraham Sandfer petitioned for admission to membership. John Hanby, Jr., was treasurer.

John Hughes bought large tracts of land in what is now West Tennessee from Thos. Henderson about 1820. His taxes on this land were often paid at the hands of his brother-in-law, Gen. Wm. Martin, of Williamson county, Tennessee, when he would make visits to this part of the country. The tax receipts show that Gen. Martin would sometimes carry his nephew, Leander Hughes (1804-1828), with him.

It looks as if John Hughes (1776-1860) "went all the gaits." He bought lottery tickets; and owned an interest in a horse that was valued at sixteen thousand dollars. This, of course, was a race horse. He was a well educated man, having learned to speak the French language. He used to tell us, his grandchildren, that in traveling once he stopped at an inn. In the evening two girls were conversing in French, thinking he did not understand. One of them, referring to him, said that she was in love with him. He arose, and with all the eloquence at his command, declared his love for her, in the French language. Covered with confusion, the girls fled from the room.

Business often called Capt. Hughes to Abingdon, Va. Then, too, he visited relatives there. At one time he was there with his sister, Jeancy Hughes. Jeancy was engaged to be married to John Fulkerson, of Lee county, Va. Her family opposed the match, preferring another suitor of more wealth, a Mr. Lacey. Jeancy was in distress because the engagement had been broken off. John Fulkerson came to see her; and the brother, seeing them together, read his sister's heart. He said in confidence to her, "Jeancy, if you love John Fulkerson, go on and marry him." Soon after John Fulkerson and Jeancy Hughes were married; and Fulkerson became a favorite with the entire connection. This is attested by the fact that the name John Fulkerson is handed down in the families of Jeancy Hughes' brothers and sisters. Capt. John Hughes named one of his first boys John Fulkerson. Many descendants of John and Jeancy (Hughes) Fulkerson live in Missouri and Tennessee, and add luster to the name.

The trumpet call is in the blood, the family has given soldiers to every war of our country. Captain John Hughes enlisted under Col. Samuel Staples in the war of 1812, but later hired a substitute. Perhaps his business was such that he felt it imperative that he should stay at home. We find this old paper—

"Patrick county, Aug. 9, 1814.
"David Colston is received as a substitute of John Hughes, Esq., who was of the No. 3 in 8 Banks Company,
            "SAMUEL STAPLES, Col. Comd."

Thus we see that John Hughes (1776-1860) was an enlisted soldier during almost the whole war of 1812. We have his colonel's written word.

On Nov. 24, 1814, W. Banks writes from Wilkes county, Georgia, to John Hughes (1776-1860) in Patrick county, Va. On this letter fifty cents postage is paid. Banks speaks of Samuel Dalton's executor, and of his sending some vouchers which Judge Gilbert promised "to lodge at your mother's in Patrick county, Va."

He tells something about the militia, enlisting under Andrew Jackson, and going to Mobile, where he "expected they would have stirring times," etc. He speaks of Major Carter. Major Carter's daughter married a Hanby, a cousin of John Hughes. He speaks of George and Gabriel Penn and of David Perkins. He speaks of writing to Major Carter, but doubts whether he would receive the letter or not. He said his handwriting was well known in Patrick county, and that his most secret letters had been intercepted. This shows something about the trouble with mail delivery in those days. An old letter of older date (May 7, 1832) makes us appreciate the frequent mails of today. The name signed to this letter looks like Sandfer; the paper is torn. He writes from Patrick county, Va., and says: "The western mail only comes here once a fortnight (on Wednesday)."

At this time John Hughes had a case in court against Hanby. Mr. Sandfer says something about notifying Mrs. Hanby, and wrote to Jonesville, N. C., taking Col. Kelley's deposition. He says Major Carter attended taking of the deposition, to cross examine. He speaks of Mrs. Hanby being Major Carter's daughter. He then says: "It is far from me to wish to be the instrument of promoting or increasing differences between connections and once confidential friends. On the contrary, my desire is now, and always has been as far as my feeble efforts would extend, to endeavor to conciliate." He signs himself, "Your sincere and devoted friend." He says "Everything we have here for market is very low indeed—corn 716 per barrel; bacon 6¼ cents per pound."

John Hughes (1776-1860) was a large land owner. He moved with his family from Patrick county, Va., to Williamson county, Tenn., in the fall of 1828. A body of land belonging to him extended for several miles along the Big Harpeth river. He lived most of the time in Williamson county, Tenn., in the old home from which his bachelor brother-in-law, Gen. Wm. Martin, went out to the war of 1812. For several years he occupied the two-story brick house, which he bought from Mr. Nichols on Big Harpeth river. He gave this house to his son, Dr. Brice Martin Hughes. Here his lovely granddaughter, Mrs. Sallie (Hughes) Ewing, one of the purest types of Southern womanhood, and her brothers, were born and reared.

After Capt. John Hughes (1776-1860) had given off land to his many children, when he died at the age of eighty-four, his will at the courthouse in Franklin shows that he still owned valuable land in several counties, Weakley, Gibson, etc. Business papers show that he owned the site of Dukedom, a small town on the Kentucky border. In 1828 he paid taxes on two thousand four hundred and eighty acres in Gibson county, Tenn. In 1834 a receipt for taxes is signed by M. McLairine, Sheriff. He owned many slaves.

John Hughes was, as we have said before, a stockholder in the Roanoke Navigation Company. On Oct. 10, 1825, E. T. Brodnax writes to him a receipt of money "on account of his stock in the Roanoke Navigation Company." Other old family papers show him to have been a stockholder. His intimate friend, Archibald Stuart, who, by the way, was the father of Gen. J. E. B. Stuart of honored Confederate memory, writes from Patrick county, Va., to John Hughes in Williamson county, Tenn., May 1, 1829. He writes a long and friendly letter. In this letter he speaks of having paid the fifth installment in the Roanoke Navigation Company. He goes on to say "the Dismal Swamp Canal is opened and large boats adapted to the navigation of the same are towed by small steamboats, and trading briskly between Weldon and Norfolk. You cannot imagine what a spur has been given to everything on the Roanoke and its waters by this event." He says the convention, that is the Constitutional Convention of 1829-30, "seems to engross public attention to the exclusion of every other subject." He also says: "there are eight or nine candidates for this Senatorial district, of whom four are to be elected. There is one candidate in Franklin (H. Calloway), one, Col. Martin, in Henry, one (your humble servant) in Patrick, and all the balance in Pittsylvania."

We know Col. Joseph Martin of Henry county, Va., was elected a member of the convention. He was the husband of Sally Hughes, a sister of John Hughes (1776-1860). In later years the son of Col. Joseph Martin, Joseph by name, married a cousin of Gen. J. E. B. Stuart. Gen. Stuart graced the occasion of their wedding by his presence in his West Point regimentals.

It may be of interest to recall something of the effort to drain the Dismal Swamp. He organized the company which dug a narrow canal, designed to carry away the waste water. Among the subscribers to the

Dismal Swamp canal in 1791 where Patrick Henry, Benjamin Harrison and James Madison (see page 432, North Carolina Register). A second canal was dug later, and part of this is now used for the inside passage of vessels from Norfolk to Albemarle Sound. John Hughes subscribed to this second canal.

May 1, 1829, M. Sandifer writes from Patrick county, Va., to John Hughes. Among other things he says "I am sorry, dear Hughes, that you left this county." He regrets the loss of his society "which was at all times more agreeable to me than that of any other person who lived in this section of the country. And I feel more disconsolate on account of your absence than I ever did on a similar occasion in my whole life.'

John Hughes (1776-1860) was very intimate with Gen. John Sumner Russwurm. The General's wife's mother was a sister of John Hughes' wife. In 1837 Gen. Russwurm writes John Hughes that they are well pleased with their move. They have moved from near Triune, Tenn., to six miles from Murfreesboro. He purchased a spinning factory in Murfreesboro, and also a factory store. He speaks of Samuel Clark, who lived on Red river, having raised eighty bales of cotton that year. The writer has many letters from Gen. Russwurm to her grandfather.

An old business entry shows that John Hughes in 1796, when only twenty years old, made a personal purchase of "1 man's hat, L. 1, S. 2, and plaid hose," etc. Whether or not this indicates a fondness for dress, he always took pride in his personal appearance. He was tall and slender. His son, Leander Hughes, writes him from Transylvania college, Lexington, Ky., where he was at school about 1827, that Henry Clay was at home from Washington and that he, John Hughes, looked very much like Mr. Clay.

John Hughes' descendants, no doubt, would like to know something of the old home where he lived, for many years, and died, and was buried. This old home, a part of which still stands (1915), overlooks a beautiful little stream—Five Mile creek. From this old home Gen. "Buck" Martin went out to the war of 1812. Later he left it as a member of the State Legislature, in 1815-21 (see page 791, History of Tennessee, The Goodspeed Publishing Co.) This old brick house now looks as if it might be the abode of the bat and owl, but when we remember that when this house was built many homes in the Cumberland settlement were only log huts, it bears very favorable comparison.

The house, originally, consisted of eight rooms, besides the two little rooms in the roof now standing (1915). It seems to have been built with an eye to making a good appearance from the public road, being long and narrow. Some old English homes were built this way. A "brick passage" joined one part of the house to the other. This passage was about twenty feet square. The floor was made of brick set up on end. This "brick passage" had banisters at front and back. To the left of the passage was the parlor, which is still standing, then a hall and family room. Above these rooms there is a half story. To the right of the brick passage was what was known as "grandpa's room" and the "Buck Martin" room. This last, after the death of Gen. Martin, was used as a guest chamber. Above these two rooms were two very nice rooms with ceilings high enough to justify fireplaces. One of these upstairs rooms the writer remembers as a cozy, well lighted room, when occupied by her brothers, Judge John H. Henderson and Dr. Samuel Henderson, when boys, soon after the war between the States. The windows of this room were, however, higher from the floor than windows are to-day. Then the kitchen and diningroom stood some feet from the rest of the house, but in a line with it. This, like the main body of the house, was built of brick and had a porch extending the length of both rooms. This dinningroom overlooked the creek, on whose bluff were many eglantine roses growing. These, when in bloom, filled the air with most delicious fragrance. The writer remembers that a flock of geese were always swimming on the water. This old place was owned by her brother, Dr. Samuel Henderson (1852-1913), at the time of his death, and now by his heirs. A visit here brings back to the writer a flood of memories. Almost every foot of ground here is marked by some tragedy of the Civil war. Three skirmishes were fought on this place. Here dear ones were buried. In the graveyard, which is literally covered with boxvine, lie the bodies of grandfather and grandmother, uncle "Buck" Martin, whose memory we were taught to love, and those of a little brother and sister who died in infancy—the first, little Samuel, who died before Dr. Samuel Henderson, Jr., was born and Levisa, who, by the way, was named for father's oldest sister, who was born about 1789 and was named "Levisa" for the old name given to the Kentucky river on which Boonsboro was founded by her uncle, Judge Richard Henderson, of North Carolina. This man's father, Nathaniel, having been at Boonsboro with Judge Richard Henderson (see diary of Richard of Henderson, kept while on his way to found Boonsboro).

Over this old place hovers sweet memories of childhood, under the care of "the best father in the world," a loving grandfather, and the rosetint of a mother's caressing love still brightens life's early dawn. Then, the hopes and aspirations of the six brothers and sisters, the affectionate devotion, the sharing of each other's joys and sorrows, make sacred the very atmosphere of the old place.

The writer remembers perfectly every piece of furniture in her grandfather's room. There was a tall fourposter bed, a chiffonier which held his wearing clothes, and an elegantly shaped candle stand One could turn it back on hinges. He also had a large pendulum clock, but not the floor clock. The bedsteps, which were never used by him because he was a tall man and athletic until helpless old age came on him, when he was lifted to and from his bed, were only for grandmother's use. The sentiment of this man never suffered these bedsteps to be taken from the room although his wife died eighteen years before he did. We remember that these bedsteps were a favorite seat for the grandchildren. On his candle-stand rested a candlestick, and his Bible. Often there were newspapers upon it, as he always, until the day of his death, in fact, kept up with current topics. Among old family papers are receipts for subscriptions to leading newspapers of the South.

After the marriage of his youngest child, Rachel Jane Hughes, to Dr. Samuel Henderson (1804-1884), in 1844, his widowed daughter Mrs. Mary Matilda Webb, made her home with her father at this old place, called by him "Rural Plains." Dr. Henderson first carried his wife to Bethesda, where he was practicing medicine. Here they lived in the home of one of his best friends, Rev. Henry C. Horton. Later Dr. Henderson came to Franklin to live and bought Dr. Mayfield's home here. This house was afterwards the home of the highly honored and much loved Dr. John Park. It is now the home of Mr. Alex H. Ewing.

After the marriage of Mrs. Mary Webb to Mr. Wm. H. Harrison, Dr. Henderson and his wife came back to her father's home. Rachel Jane Henderson died in June, 1858. One and a half years later her father died. The circumstances of his death were very sad. Dr. Henderson, who was president of the Nashville and Franklin turnpike, had gone in his buggy to Nashville, twenty-three miles away, on this cold, short, winter day, to collect money from the toll-gates. He reached home about dusk, and, being tired and cold, did not go to the room of the invalid before supper was announced. When a negro woman carried supper to "Old Master," as they always called him, she found that in chunking the big open wood fire he had fallen from his chair onto the hearth, and was badly burned, so badly, in fact that he lingered only two days. Beside his chair there was a cord which he might pull and ring a bell on the outside for his man servent. Of course in falling he could not reach this bell cord. He died Dec. 26, 1860.

We will copy the obituraty of Capt. John Hughes, which was written by Mr. C. W. Callender, president of the Tennessee Female College in Franklin, at that time, and published in the local paper. This clipping from the newspaper was preserved by his granddaughter, Mrs. Sallie (Hughes) Ewing, and pasted in her scrap book:

"Obituary of Capt. John Hughes (1776-1860)

"By C. W. Callender

"John Hughes, the subject of this notice, was born in Patrick county, Va., Aug. 3, 1776. He was married to Sally Martin, Feb. 7, 1798; removed to Tennessee in 1828, and died near Franklin on the 26th day of Dec., 1860, in the eighty-fifth year of his age. He was buried with Masonic honors, and his mortal remains repose by the side of his faithful wife, the partner of his youth and the companion of his old age, who preceded him to the spirit land some years ago.

"We believe him to be the oldest Mason in Tennessee, having been a member of that ancient and honorable order more than sixty years. He had in his possession at the time of his death a charter of some Virginia lodge which was made to him as master thereof bearing date 1803. Born amid the exciting struggle for our National independence, he early imbibed that patriotism pecular to the heroes of '76, and the love of liberty and independence, then implanted in his bosom, glowed and burnt with steady flame 'til quenched by the hand of death.

"When but a youth and scarcely eligible for office, he was elected a member of the Virginia legislature, and such was his honesty, intergrity and patriotism that he was again and again the recipient of that high honor from a grateful and appreciative constituency. It is more than probable that he was the last surviving member of that distinguished body which passed the far-famed resolutions, so well known as the Virginia Resolutions of 1798; he on that occasion speaking and voting with the Republican party.

"After his removal to Tennessee he more than once held offices of honor and trust in his adopted state. He was a man of fine ability, of strong passions and prejudices, tempered with a keen sense of justice and right. Endowed with great energy of character, he was positive and firm; even obstinate and unyielding in his positions when once taken and sanctioned by his judgment, which seldom erred. He was a high-minded, honorable old Virginia gentleman, a ·devoted friend and indulgent parent, an affectionate husband and a devoted Christian. He was a member of the Methodist Episcopal church about thirty-six years. From bodily infirmity he has been confined almost entirely to his room for the last ten or twelve years, but notwithstanding his great energy and untiring industry and active business habits for more than three quarters of a century, he bore his long confinement with examplary resignation and submission. With his Bible as his constant companion, and its rich promises as his solace and comfort, he calmly waited, like a ripe sheaf, to be gathered to the harvest of immortality. He retained the vigor of his intellect, not preceptibly impaired until a short time before his death.

> "Of years, of honors and affection full,
> He laid him down and died."

We have given a sketch of Sally Martin, wife of Capt. John Hughes (1776-1860), under head "Martin."

Children of Capt. John Hughes (1776-1860) and His Wife, Sally Martin

Note: We will copy from their old family Bible:

"John Hughes was born August 3, 1776, and was married to Sally Martin on the 7th day of Feb., 1798.

"Their issue is as follows:

"Archelaus Powell Hughes, born the 7th day of Jan., 1799.

"William Madison Hughes, born the 5th day of Nov., 1800.

"John Fulkerson Hughes, born the 10th day of Nov., 1802.

"Leander Hughes, born the 7th day of Oct., 1804.

"Brice Martin Hughes, born the 22nd day of Oct., 1806.

"Samuel Carter Hughes, born the 11th day of April, 1808.

"Albert Gallatin Hughes, born the 17th day of April, 1812.

"Mary Matilda Hughes, born the 15th day of Jan., 1816.

"Rachel Jane Hughes, born the 27th day of Feb., 1818.

Major Archelaus Powell Hughes

Archelaus Powell Hughes, son of Capt. John Hughes and his wife, Sally Martin, was born in Patrick county, Va., Jan. 7, 1799. When a boy he spent some time in Tennessee with his bachelor uncle, Gen. Wm. Martin, of Williamson county, Tenn.

A. P. Hughes was elected major of militia in 1827. He married Polly Webb, of Williamson county, Tenn. After their marriage they lived a while in Gibson county, and later in Maury. Their children were—

James Hughes.

Henry Hughes.

Fanny Hughes, married Col. Wilkinson of Giles county. One of their daughters, Fanny, married a cousin, Leander Hughes, a successful business man and politician of Dallas, Texas. Another daughter married a Mr. Witt.

——————— Hughes, married Mr. Cannon.

——————— Hughes, married Mr. Scales.

Archelaus Powell Hughes, died July 10, 1873.

William Madison Hughes. we think never married.

John Fulkerson Hughes

John Fulkerson Hughes, son of Capt. John Hughes and his wife, Sally Martin, was born Nov. 10, 1802, in Patrick county, Va. He came with his father to Williamson county, Tenn., to live in 1828. He married Jane Baldwin, a niece of Mrs. Logan Douglas, by whom she was reared.

Their children were:

Mary Hughes, who married Mr. Lee.

Sallie Hughes.

John Hughes, married Mary Rowlet.

Ann Redd Hughes, married Sneed.

Martha Hughes.

Rachel Hughes, married her cousin, John Hughes.

Matilda Hughes.

Laura (Hughes) McEwen.

Bettie (Hughes) Henderson.

Leander Hughes

Leander Hughes, son of Capt. John Hughes and his wife, Sally Martin, was born Oct. 7, 1804. He was an unusually bright boy, and grew to brilliant manhood. He and his brother, Brice Martin

Hughes, two years younger than himself, entered school in Leaksville, N. C., in May, 1821.

In 1823 Leander and Brice Hughes entered the University of North Carolina at Chapel Hill. In one of his letters home from the University, Leander says: "I board at Mrs. Mitchel's and room with a Mr. Prince, a class-mate of mine whom I esteem and respect. In one of my letters I stated that I roomed with M. Moore, but preferring Prince, and he appearing equally anxious, we decided to room together."

"M. Moore," spoken of by Leander, was of the Maurice Moore branch. This Hughes family was related to both the Maurice Moore branch, and the Matthew Moore branch, first of Albemarle county, Va., and later of Stokes county, N.C. We have written this up in full under head "Dalton and Moore." The "M. Moore" spoken of by Leander Hughes, who was at school at the University at Chapel Hill at this time, was a son of Alfred Moore, and lived in Orange county, N. C., whence they had moved from Brunswick county, N. C. Alfred Moore was a son of Alfred Moore, Sr., of Brunswick county, N. C., who was a son of Judge Maurice Moore, who always signed his name "M. Moore." M. Moore, Martin Howard and Richard Henderson constituted the Judicial Bench, the Supreme Bench of North Carolina, when the Revolution shut up the courts.

This branch of Moore is an illustrious line. Judge Maurice Moore's grandfather, Sir Nathaniel Moore, was governor of the two Carolinas in 1705. James Moore, of this family, had married a daughter of Sir John Yeamans, who established the city of Charleston, and was the governor of the two Carolinas in 1670. Judge Maurice Moore was lenially descended from James Moore and his wife, who was a Miss Yeamans. Judge Maurice Moore, Wm. Hooper, Richard Caswell, Robert Howe, and Joseph Hewes were a committee to address the citizens of the British Empire on the wrongs of America, and the oppression of England (see Wheeler's History of North Carolina, Series II, page 101; also Stokes county, pages 47, 48, 49; Series III, etc.).

Leander Hughes writes his father from Chapel Hill, where he was still in college in 1825, that he preferred studying medicine instead of law. He seemed to think the practice of medicine "more lucrative" than that of law and he "feared he might not distinguish himself as a lawyer." In one of his letters, written in 1824, he speaks of "Mr. Scales and R. Gentry having been pierced by 'Cupid's Dart.'" Then he adds: "It seems my friend, E. Thomas and Miss Mary are to be sacrificed at Hyman's alter."

His reports while at school at Chapel Hill were fine.

In a letter written Oct. 2, 1824, he speaks of some members of the faculty, Mr. Mitchell as president, Mr. Bittner, and of Mr. Sanders.

Leander and Brice Martin Hughes attended the Transylvania University, at Lexington, Kentucky. Leander, in a letter written to his father, Nov. 15, 1826, says: "I have engaged board with Mrs. Cook, including eating, lodging, washing, candles, firewood; and a servent to attend to my room, all of which is afforded for one hundred and twentw dollars a year." He adds "I room with R. H. Dalton (this was Dr. Robert Hunter Dalton whose manuscripts we quote elsewhere) and a Mr. Watkins, of Virginia. Cousin Robert and myself are well and you can inform Mr. Scales that Walker also is well.   I have not taken a private ticket of any of the professors. By being very saving we sometimes are losers." He went on to express great admiration for Dr. Dudley. Later he did become a private student of this celebrated man. Dr. Dudley, everybody knows, made Transylvania University illustrious. Leander gives his father a summary of the cost of his tickets, viz: "To Dr. Dudley for private pupilage, including his tickets this summer and next winter, $80; for Caldwell's ticket, $15; Short's, $15; Blythe's $15; Richardson, $15; library ticket,$5; for my diploma, $25; for invitation into the medical society and a diploma from the same, $3.50; Cook's ticket, $15." He sends his best love to his mother, a kiss to Mary and Jane, his little sisters, his best respects to his granamother and to Gen. Dillard.   Then he speaks of him as "Uncle Dillard, and my worthy little friend, Hughes Dillard." Leander writes from Lexington: "Last evening Mr. Scales, Mr. Galloway, and Mr. Gentry arrived at this place." In one of his early letters he speaks of "my friend, Mr. Gentry," who was there.

In May, 1826, Leander Hughes went from his home in Virginia on business to what was then called the Western district, that is West Tennessee. He writes his father from Williamson county, where he had gone to visit his uncle, Gen. Wm. Martin, May 5, 1826: "I have just returned from the Western district where I have secured an occupancy which adjoins your thousand-acre tract in Gibson. The mosquitoes were terrifying after we crossed the Tennessee for several days and nights. There is a kind of fly which the inhabitants call Buffalo Gnat, which is very destructive to horse and terrifying to the man." He goes on to tell his father about having been honorably released from a love affair. He adds: " At this I rejoice. I now feel myself honorably liberated from the thralldom of love and uneasiness. Nothing shall ever induce me to renew that engagement which youth and inexperience prompted me to make."   He asks his father if Brice expects to take a regular course through college.

The whole time Leander is in Transylvania University his letters are full of Dr. Dudley. Sometimes he speaks of him as "my beloved and unrivalled preceptor, Prof. Dudley." In April, 1827, we find Leander again in Tennessee. They did not seem to think a trip from Lexington to Williamson county, Tennessee, much of a trip; but now his health was beginning to fail, and he says Dr. Dudley advised him much riding exercise.   So he came leisurely to Tennessee, being more than two weeks on the road. He tells his father that he expects to ride horseback to Virginia, and says, "I have been living for some time on mush and milk." Then he speaks in the most affectionate terms of his mother, and says "Tell her that I hope she will have a plenty of rye meal when I arrive, as I think that rye mush and milk would be conducive to my health." We suppose that this "rye meal" was our oatmeal of to-day.

One feels indeed glad that Leander made this visit home to Virginia in 1827. He was anxious to complete his course at Transylvania in the spring of 1828, notwithstanding his failing health. Early in 1828 Capt. John Hughes visited his boys, Leander and Brice, in Lexington. Leander's messages to his little sisters, Mary and Jane, are always sweet. January 6, 1828, he writes from Lexington, "If I do not regain my health entirely by spring I shall return to Virginia." He says that Dr. Dudley approves this. Leander says "Brice has an idea of returning to Franklin (Tenn.) and reading medicine with Dr. Dickinson." In this letter he wants to find out from Mr. Lacey where Mr. Overton lives, somewhere about Lexington. He says, "You must not infer from anything I have written that I am very unwell," but he goes on to say, "I have moved my boarding house and now live in about twenty steps of the Medical Hall. Brice is still at Chipley's. I am rooming with Mr. Penn, and find him a very agreeable roommate. Inform his friends that he is well." This boy was a member of the Penn family who lived near his father in Patrick county, Va. Col. Gabriel Penn lived here and other members of the family. This family intermarried extensively with the Hughes connection. Some of their decendants enter patriotic orders through William Penn.

It may seem that I am off at a tangent, but I want to include as much family history as I can. Matilda Dillard, daughter of Gen. John Dillard and his wife, Matilda Hughes, married Shelton Penn; also several members of Col. Joseph Martin's family married Penns. Now Col. Joseph Martin's wife, Sally Hughes, and Gen. John Dillard's wife, Matilda Hughes, were both sisters of Capt. John Hughes (1776-1860). The Penn family were people with a good deal of money; several of them went to Danville, Va., and engaged in the tobacco business as manufacturers, making large fortunes. Some of them moved to North Carolina. While some of the members of the Penn family lived in Patrick county, Va., one branch of the Penn family drifted from Pennsylvania to Carolina county, Virginia. Here John Penn, one of the signers of the Declaration of Independence, was born on May 17, 1741. John Penn read law with his kinsman, Edmund Pendleton. He moved to Granville county, N. C., in 1774, and was a member of the Continental Congress at Philadelphia, 1775-79. He died in 1788. (see Wheeler's History of North Carolina, Granville county.)

In Virgina Magazine of History and Biography, Vol. IX, page 415, is said: "March, 1780, Archelaus Hughes, Esq., is advanced to office of Colonel and Abraham Penn, Esq., to office of Lieutenant Colonel."

Then on page 417 we see that John Dillard is appointed Captain in 1780.   Capt., later Colonel, John Dillard was the father of Gen. John Dillard.

We will copy an extract from the St. Louis Republic, Sunday, Sept. 18, 1910:

"Southampton, England, Sept. 17.—American tourists in Britain this summer have found their way in increasing numbers to Portland, for they have discovered that there the grandson of the founder of Pennsylvania built a lordly home for himself.   Pennsylvania Castle, as it is called, is situated on a secluded spot on the Dorset coast, overlooking the English channel.   The grounds boast of the only grove of trees in Portland.   This English home of the famous American family was built about 1790 by John Penn, a friend of George III.   Knowing that the family had suffered greatly during the War of Independence, the English monarch of that day made John Penn a Justice of the Peace and Governor of Portland.   The appointment was a soft snap, for it carried a salary and no official duty.   This is the way the lovely site for the castle was chosen: One day George III. and John Penn were riding across Portland.   They came to the particular place on which the mansion stands.   'What a magnificent site for a house,' said the King.   John Penn replied: 'Your Majesty, it shall be done.'

"The builder carried out the royal hint, and the imposing turreted structure was in due time erected and opened by Princess Elizabeth, George's daughter.   Ultimately 'Pennsylvania Castle' became the only residence of the Penn family.   It contains several relics and family potraits of particular interest to Americans.

"George III. gave John Penn the old ruin, 'Rufus Castle,' which stands like a bird on a crag in the grounds overlooking Church Hope cave.   The direct line of Penns has died out (of course that means of this particular branch) and the castle is now occupied by J. Merrick Head, a Britisher, who is a jealous custodian of the building and its contents." (from the Weiner Agency, Ltd.)

We will return to Leander Hughes after our digression.   His health seemed to grow steadily worse, and, after he graduated in medicine, in 1828, at Transylvania University, we find him still following the idea that horseback riding would benefit him.   So he started for his home in Virginia in May, but first went to Williamson county, Tennessee, to visit his uncle, Gen. Wm. Martin, and rest a while, later going to Patrick county, Va.   An affectionate letter was written him by his friend, Jas. M. Cortes, from "Burbon," May 10, 1828.   This letter was directed to Leander in Patrick county, but Leander never reached Virginia.

August 11, 1828, Gen. Wm. Martin writes his father that there is no hope of Leander's recovery.   He tells him that Dr. Steith is very attentive.   Aug. 25, he writes to Capt. John Hughes, saying "I never yet have performed a duty, which I have to do, with so much reluctance as on the present occasion.   And I must tell you this disagreeable truth at once—that your precious little boy Leander is no more." He tells him what a comfort "good old Douglas" was to Leander. This was Thos. Logan Douglas. He speaks of Leander's beautiful death, then says "He is buried here by his own request, under a mulberry tree, not more than two hundred yards from the house. Great respect was paid to his interment, and it was done as decently for him as for any who have gone before him." T. L. Douglas and Thos. D. Porter were the ministers who officiated at his burial

While Capt. John Hughes had expected to bring his family to Williamson county, Tennessee, Leander's death and burial at this time seemed to hasten his coming. In the fall of this year, 1828, we find him living in the house where Leander had died. Gen. Martin, who was a bachelor, still made his home there with his sister's family. Leander's mother was buried at his side. Her body rests between that of her husband and Leander. Gen. Wm. Martin's body is near. "They were lovely and pleasant in their lives, and in their death they were not divided."

Brice Martin Hughes

Brice Martin Hughes, son of Capt. John Hughes (1776-1860), and his wife, Sally Martin, was born Oct. 22, 1806, in Patrick county, Va.

He and Leander attended school together at Leaksville, N. C., in 1821. While there they made their home with Col. James Martin's family. In 1823 these two brothers entered college at Chapel Hill, North Carolina. While Leander left here in 1826 to enter Transylvania University at Lexington, Brice, the younger of the two boys, continued one year longer at Chapel Hill. In Jan., 1825, Brice writes from Chapel Hill as "this charming and enlightened place." He says he expects Leander to graduate with credit.

Brice spent a while in Tennessee studying medicine under Dr. Dickinson. He was attending Transylvania University at Lexington, Ky., during the winter of 1827-28. Nov. 28 he writes his father from Lexington, saying that he was not boarding with his old friend Chipley because "he had his number when I arrived," but he went on to add that he was simply delighted with his new quarters. His father had friends about Lexington and Brice tells of visiting them. He says: "I stayed with the General. and when bedtime came on he would have me sleep with him in his single bed. It was not so pleasant; nevertheless I did so." Who the "General" was we do not know. Brice does not call his name in the letter, writing as though his father understood.

About the time his father moved from Patrick county, Va., to Williamson county, Tenn., in 1828, Brice writes: "You will find society as good as in Virginia, and land more productive." He says to tell his "Aunt Susan Moore not to be in too great a hurry to return to the barren hills of North Carolina." She lived at Snow Creek, N. C.

Dr. Hughes was a public spirited man. The Nashville and Decatur railroad, as it was then called, now known as the Louisville and Nashville, was projected in 1851.   The railroad company was organized in July, 1851, and work on the road between Nashville and Franklin was begun Nov. 26, 1852 (I know this from the diary of my father, Dr. Samuel Henderson, (1804-1884).   Dr. Henderson was one of the original stockholders, and was one of the railroad directors until it was merged into the L. & N. railroad.

We quote from Dr. Hendersons's diary: "Feb. 14, 1853.   The railroad was located through Franklin.   Dr. Brice Hughes and myself have undertaken to graduate and do masonry on the railroad through Franklin,   March 3, 1853.   We first began to move dirt, etc."

So these two men, brothers-in-law, put their negro men to work on the railroad.

Dr. Brice Hughes aided in building Douglas church.   On the completion of this church, his lovely daughter, Sally Martin Hughes, presented a handsome red silk velvet cushion for the large old-fashioned pulpit.

An entry in Dr. Henderson's diary is: "June 5, 1846, Dr. B. M. Hughes received the Royal Arch degree of Masonry."   We find them winding up the estate of the late Gen. Wm. Martin.   Among other negroes, we see that "Lewis, about forty-seven years old, and Anderson; twenty-two, were delivered to John Hughes (1776-1860) in Dec., 1843."   I speak of these two negroes who belonged to Gen. Martin because of the old adage "Like master, like servant."   Lewis, who seemed to imbibe something of his master's spirit of independence and aggression, was the negro who, during the Civil war, when Governor Johnson. afterward President of United States, was addressing the negroes in Nashville, stepped to the front.   Governor Johnson, warming to his subject, exclaimed "Would there were a Moses to lead my people out of bondage!"   Then Lewis cried: "You shall be our Moses, Governor!"

Dr. Brice M. Hughes, after his marriage to Elmira Fleming, lived in a home given him by his father on the Big Harpeth river.   This home they called "River View."   It is a commodious two-story brick building with large rooms and presses let in the wall just as at the "Hermitage," Andrew Jackson's home.   An office was down in the yard, such as was seen in all old Southern homes for the boys.   Their plantation was added to by Mr. Fleming, his wife's father.   The family lived in affluence.   The writer remembers well their handsome carriage of which old Lewis, spoken of above, was the driver.   She remembers, too, that after the cruel war was over, under the pressing needs of the time, the carriage had been sold.   One night she was at a young people's entertainment at "River View" and her aunt, Mrs. Hughes, told her that she had been out to take a look at her former carriage, in which some guests had driven out from Franklin.   It had been sold to a liveryman.

A marauding party of pretended Federal soldiers went to this home one night after the death of Dr. B. M. Hughes, and pretended to be looking for guerrillas. Mrs. Hughes followed them into the dining room and took her handsome solid silver castor from the center of the table, carrying it in her hand the whole time these men were in the house. Strange to say, they did not snatch it from her; and in this way she saved this valuable piece of silver. This silver castor now belongs to their grandson, Mr. Alex Hughes Ewing.

Dr. Brice Martin Hughes died in 1862. His wife lived through the days of reconstruction, and by skillful management succeeded in hold-on to their landed estate.

Children of Dr. Brice Martin Hughes and his wife, Elmira Fleming.

1. Leander Hughes, died a soldier in Civil war.
2. Sallie Martin Hughes, born 1841, married H. S. Ewing.
3. John Thompson Hughes, married Rachel Hughes.
4. Susie Hughes, born 1852; died 1857.
5. William Hughes.
6. Brice Martin Hughes, died 1888, unmarried.

1. Leander Hughes, the oldest child, was named for his father's much loved brother. This was the name, too, of-one of the earliest American ancestors: and we are glad it is still to be found in the family. In this branch of the family, however, it has passed into the names of girls: Susie Lea (Ewing) McGavock and Susie Lea (Roberts) Briggs.

Leander enlisted in the Confederate army at the opening of the Civil war. After one year's service he was brought home sick and died in 1862, being unmarried. He was a boy of graceful manner; and, had he lived he would probably have fulfilled the ambitions of his family.

2. Sallie Martin Hughes, daughter of Dr. Brice Hughes and his wife, Elmira Fleming, was born in 1841. She was a beautiful, attactive girl, and grew to loveliest womanhood. Indeed she was one of the purest types of the ante-bellum Southern woman.

When quite a child, she attended school at "Henderson's Academy," while Mr. Brewer was principal. She would ride from home on horseback with her brothers every day, except when it rained; then she would drive over in the carriage. She entered the Academy for Young Ladies, in Nashville, when very young. Dr. D. C. Elliott had charge of this school. It is claimed that this was the first chartered woman's college in America.

As a girl she was fond of dress. Perhaps this was because she was given "carte blanche" by an indulgent father. She left school in 1858, and was married to Mr. Hubbard Saunders Ewing, March 10, 1859. Mr. Ewing was a son of Alexander Ewing. His grandfather served on the staff of Gen. Nathaniel Greene during the Revolutionary war. After their marriage, they went to live at the old Ewing ancestral home, which was on the original military grant of land to his grandfather. This house, although across the river, is in sight of Franklin. Here their children were born and reared.   It was here that Mrs. Ewing died March 3, 1907.   She was to the writer, and her brothers and sisters, like an older sister after the death of their mother in 1858.

Her children are Alexander Hughes Ewing, Susie Lea (Ewing) Mc-Gavock, and Sallie (Ewing) Roberts.   All live in Franklin.   Their beautiful homes are clustered together on Maple avenue.   A. H. Ewing was married to Gertrude Wallace, daughter of Dr. Wallace and his wife, Fanny Park.   Fanny Park was the daughter of Dr. John S. Park, a high-ly esteemed man, and sister of Col. John Park of the U. S. army.   For several years before the World war, Col. Park was millitary attache at the court of Belgium.

Their children are Alex. Hughes Ewing, Jr., and Fannie Park Ewing.

Susie Lea Ewing married Winder McGavock, son of Col. John Mc-Gavock and his wife, Carrie Winder.   Carrie Winder was the grand-daughter of Felix Grundy.   He built and lived in the grand old home in Nashville, which was later the home of President James K. Polk, now Polk Flats (1916). *married Haynes Agnes of Springhill, Tenn. Sarah,*

Their children are Hattie McGavock, who was noted for her fine voice, died in 1911; Martha McGavock, who died young; Winder Mc-Gavock, who volunteered in the American army in 1917; John Mc-Gavock, who married Mary Gillespie.   Their children are John and Martha McGavock.

Sallie Ewing, daughter of H. S. Ewing and his wife, Sallie (Martin) Hughes, married Walter A. Roberts in 1890.   Mr. Roberts' Revolutionary ancestor, through whom members of the family enter patriotic orders, was Lieutenant Hendricks.   Mr. Roberts is a successful business man, and is chairman of the board of stewards of the Methodist church.   He went overseas in Y. M. C. A. work July 1, 1918.   Their children are Susie Lea Roberts, a graduate of Randolph-Macon Woman's College, married George Briggs, one child, Sarah Ewing; Ewing Roberts, married John Green, and they have one child, Walter Roberts; and Sarah Roberts.

3.   John Thompson Hughes, son of Dr. Brice M. Hughes and his wife, Elmira Fleming, was eager to enlist in the Confederate army when little more than a child.   But his father, who was bowed with sorrow at the loss of Leander, restrained the boy.   But the "trumpet call" is in the blood, and John T. Hughes served during the last year of the war be-tween the states.   He married his first cousin, Rachel Hughes.   Their children are Wallace, Brice, and Brown Hughes.

4.   William Hughes, son of Dr. Brice Martin Hughes and his wife, Elmira Fleming, was born 18—.   William is a man of generous nature. He has never married.

5.   Brice Martin Hughes, son of Dr. Brice M. Hughes and his wife, Elmira Fleming, chose his father's profession, studying medicine in New Orleans.   After graduation he practiced in the hospitals of New Or-leans for several years.   Later he made his home in Birmingham, Ala., where he had a large and lucrative practice.   Aside from his practice, he was a successful business man for some years.   He invested his patri-

money in real estate in Birmingham just before a wonderful boom in prices. Later, however, real estate declined in value and he lost heavily. He died in 1888, unmarried.

Samuel Carter Hughes

Samuel Carter Hughes, son of Capt. John Hughes and his wife, Sallie Martin, was born in Patrick county, Va., April 11, 1806. After his marriage he lived on a plantation of his father's in what was then called the "Western District," that is, in West Tennessee. We find this entry in the diary of Dr. Samuel Henderson (1804-1884): "April 29, 1847. The children of Samuel Hughes were brought here by Mr. Webb. They are: Sally Ann, Brice, Leander and Samuel."

Sally Ann Hughes, after her marriage to Mr. McLelland, went back to West Tennessee to live. Brice and Leander both became successful physicians. Dr. Brice Hughes married and lived in northern Alabama. Dr. Leander Hughes served as a Confederate soldier. Samuel married in West Tennessee and reared a family.

Albert Gallatin Hughes

Albert Gallatin Hughes, son of Capt. John Hughes and his wife, Sallie Martin, was born in Patrick county, Va., April 17, 1812. After growing to manhood, he kept "Bachelor Hall" at what was then known as the "Red House" on his father's estate in Williamson county, Tenn. Here he died.

Mary Matilda Hughes

Mary Matilda Hughes, daughter of Capt. John Hughes and his wife, Sallie Martin, was born in Patrick county, Va., Jan. 15, 1816. When she was twelve years old her father brought his family to Williamson county, Tenn., to live. She conned her first lessons at school in Virginia. We learn from old family papers that a Miss Taliaferro taught them at Harpeth Academy. These two sisters attended school at Harpeth Union Female Academy, near Triune, Tenn. While here at school they made their home with their kinsman, Gen. John Sumner Russwurm. Their mother's sister, Virginia (Martin) Clark, was the mother of Gen. Russwurm's wife. These two sisters also attended school at Hines Academy, in Franklin, Tenn. This was a large old-fashioned brick building where is now the home of Mr. C. R. Berry.

A letter from her uncle, Gen. John Dillard, of Virginia, makes it appear that Mary had an ardent suitor by name of Hairston, from Virginia. She first married Dr. Wm. Webb of Williamson county, Tenn. The writer holds an old letter to him from his brother, Jas. Webb.

William Webb was a man of affairs. One of his business papers shows that he had an account against Wm. W. Smith, Jeremiah Vardeman and Britain Smith, in Holmes county, Miss., for $12,854 in 1838. Dr. Webb died, leaving his wife and one child, Wm. Leander Webb. We find this entry in Dr. Samuel Henderson's diary: "Mr. William Harrison and Mrs. Mary M. Webb were married Oct. 3, 1845." Wm. Harrison was also a man of independent fortune. He owned many negroes.

The Harrison home, where her children were born and reared, is a commodious two-story brick house on the Columbia pike about three miles from Franklin. This house has passed out of the hands of the family. Mary Harrison was a thorough-going housekeeper. Her house was always immaculate, and the grounds beautifully kept. In each corner of the front yard was an office, after traditional Southern custom. Her garden, with its wealth of old-fashioned flowers, was one of the finest in the state. She was a woman of kind heart. After the death of her only sister, she often played the part of fairy god-mother to her children, giving to them and doing things for them which only a mother could think of. She died July 8, 1873, in the fifty-eighth year of her life. Her body rests in the old family burying ground on the Columbia pike beside that of her husband, Wm. Harrison. Here her daughter, Sallie Martin Harrison, who died at the age of fourteen years, also is buried. Wm. Leander Webb, son of her first husband, is buried at the old Hughes graveyard. His grave is marked by a tombstone. At the time of Leander Webb's death his mother had only one child by her second husband, John Hughes Harrison. So the property of Wm. Leander Webb was divided between his mother and this brother; and when John H. Harrison became of age he was one of the wealthiest young men in Williamson county in his own right. The children of William Harrison and his wife, Mary M. Hughes, were:

1. John Hughes Harrison, who married Bettie Scruggs, merchandized in Franklin for many years. He inherited the family homestead. Their children were:

    a. William Harrison, who married ———— Buchanan.

    b. Dora Harrison, who married Mr. Black. They have one child, Robert.

    c. Florence Harrison, married Mr. Frank Davis, and lives in Chattanooga.

    d. John Hughes Harrison, Jr., married Louise Henderson, daughter of Dr. Samuel Henderson (1852-1913). John H. Harrison belonged to U. S. census department and proved himself a competent man. His home was Los Angeles, Cal., when taken with his last illness. He died Dec. 30, 1914. They have one child, Samuel Henderson Harrison.

2. Sallie Martin Harrison, daughter of Wm. Harrison and his wife, Mary M. Hughes, born in 1850; died in 1864.

3. Matilda Harrison, daughter of Wm. Harrison and his wife, Mary M. Hughes, was born in 1852. She married George Briggs, of Franklin, in 1870. Their children are:

    a. Annie James Briggs, married William Winder Campbell.

    b. Willie May Briggs, married Walter Jones.

    c. Elizabeth Briggs, married Whit Winstead.

    d. Tillie Briggs, married John Whitfield.

    e. Mattie Briggs, married Harold Henderson.

    f. George I. Briggs, married Susie Lea Roberts.

Annie James Briggs was adopted by her uncle, Mr. James Harrison, and his wife, Annie Briggs, who had no children. She married Wm. Winder Campbell, a successful merchant of Franklin. Mr. Campbell's father was Scotch-Irish; his mother was Louise Winder, a granddaughter of Felix Grundy, the statesman. Felix Grundy's home in Nashville was sold to Jas. K. Polk, President of the United States.

Annie James Campbell served as secretary of "Old Glory" chapter, D. A. R., 1914-1916, and was elected State secretary at Nashville, Nov. 1917. She was Williamson county's chairman for Woman's committee for Liberty Loan bonds, doing splendid work. Mrs. Campbell was delegate to the League of Woman Voters, which met at the capitol in Nashville, Tennessee, in May, 1920. She has served as president of the Woman's Missionary society of the Presbyterian church in Franklin. The children of Wm. Winder Campbell and his wife, Annie James Briggs, are: James Harrison Campbell and Stewart Campbell.

Willie May (Briggs) Jones is a member of the Woman's Missionary Council of the Methodist Episcopal church, South, and is a splendid church worker. She, also, is a member of "Old Glory" chapter, D. A. R.

Mattie Briggs married Harold Henderson, who was born and reared in Murfreesboro, Tenn.; out, since their marriage, Birmingham, Ala., has been their home. They have one child, Martha.

Elizabeth Briggs married Whit Winstead, who is a professor in a Southern college.

George I. Briggs was the president of a college in Rome, Georgia; and is now assistant in the Baylor school in Chattanooga, Tenn. He has one child by his first wife, Jane Briggs. His second wife is Susie Lea Roberts. They have one child, Sarah Ewing Briggs.

Rachel Jane Hughes

Rachel Jane Hughes, daughter of Capt. John Hughes and his wife, Sally Martin, was born in Patrick county, Virginia, Feb. 27, 1818. Her first years at school were in Virginia. After coming to Tennessee to live, her father placed her and her sister in school at Harpeth Union Female Academy, which had been established in 1828. While here at school, they made their home with their kinsman, Gen. John Sumner Russwurm. In 1828 a deed to grounds for this academy "was made by Governor Newton Cannon to Samuel Perkins, W. S. Webb, T. D. Porter, John Bostick and Newton Cannon, as trustees for the academy. This school was managed with success for many years. In 1837, lot No. 134, in Franklin, was purchased and the foundation laid for the Franklin Female Academy.

These two sisters also attended school at Hines Academy, in Franklin. This old brick building stood where is now (1903) the residence of C. R. Berry. The girls studied music and art; they had an old-fashioned piano, a spinet, with six beautifully carved mahogany legs. After her marriage, Mary, the elder daughter, came in possession of this instrument. Both sisters kept up their music as long as they lived. The writer, however, remembers their music not such as would thrill a modern audience. Some specimens of their paintings, which have come down to us, are very tasteful in their simplicity. A card of merit given in school to Jane for "excellent parsing" and another for good penmanship have been preserved. An essay on "Gratitude," written by Rachel Jane Hughes, is preserved by the writer in the family album. This proves her to have been a girl of high ideals.

We will copy one of Rachel Jane Hughes' invitations, because the ball was given on a patriotic day, Jan. 8, the anniversary of the Battle of New Orleans, and because it bears many Nashville names of the '30ties:

"Society Ball

"We respectfully solicit the pleasure of your company at a ball to be given at Mr. Gowdey's new Ball Room, on Thursday evening, January 8.

"Members

"Josiah Nichol
Thos. G. Moss
W. S. Pickett
John P. Tyree
R. R. Rice
Frank Williams
J. W. Butler
J. W. Bacon
L. E. Johnson
A. D. Berry
Hugh Kirkman

"J. Robinson
C. C. Daviess
J. Grimes
Alex. McIntosh
Patterson B. West
Chas. F. Berry
Thos. R. Jennings
Wm. Crockett
Thos. W. Earskine
Jas. Bankhead

"W. O. Harris
Henry Dickinson
Charles Symes
John Kirkman
Ralph Martin
Jno. N. Esselman
Charles Nichol
Robert W. Greene
Samuel Park
V. S. Stephenson
J. T. Collinsworth."

There may have been other names; the paper is cut off.

Rachel Hughes was married to Dr. Samuel Henderson (1804-1884) March 14, 1844.

The writer remembers following her mother through the negro quarters when she would go to look after sick negroes. She was a kind mistress. Always she would give the regular cook a holiday on Sunday, when some woman from the quarters would come and take her place. Throughout the South in those days so many negroes were kept about the house, that they must have sat much of the time with folded hands. The negroes were allowed to have garden plots for themselves.

Other women used to spin and weave cloth for their clothes; very often mother would reel this thread with four cuts to a hank. I think spinning a hank of four cuts was considered a good day's work for one woman. A separate hand did the carding.

We always played with the negro children. While we enjoyed this, it must have been elevating to the little negroes, for they were not allowed to use any low language in our presence. We suppose they were well instructed by their mothers in regard to this, for vile language I cannot remember having heard from them. Of all the negroes, we loved our "Black Mammy" best; and "Aunt Charlotte" was simply devoted to her children, as she called us. I remember her as a woman of good figure; she always looked tidy in her kerchief and turbaned head. After mother's death, in June, 1858, Aunt Charlotte seemed, if possible, more tender toward us than ever.

During the Civil war several skirmishes were fought on our place. Capt. Freeman, of the artillery, and four men were killed here. Alston, a negro driver, who happened to have his team out on the place, was ordered to carry their five bodies to Spring Hill. My brother, Judge John H. Henderson, then a manly boy of thirteen, of his own accord, jumped into the wagon and went to Spring Hill with them in order, as he said, to bring back the wagon, horses, and driver. In those days the army was too apt to consider whatever was available as belonging to them. Several years before his death Judge Henderson wrote for the Confederate Veteran of June, 1911, his little experience of camp life. Our soldiers at Spring Hill treated him as one of themselves, and made him feel just like a soldier, too. But father grew very restless about his boy; and walked across the woods to Mr. Frank Hardeman's, a friend of his, seeking his help about getting his boy home. After reaching Mr. Hardeman's house with his oldest daughters, he was taken violently ill and was compelled to remain over night. Some northern soldiers came to our home, went into the smoke house, and took hams; then started toward the house. Our "black mammy" hustled off in a great hurry with my little sister Sue and myself; and rushed across the fields to Mr. Jefferson's. There is so much of tragedy connected with war. After brother John reached home safely with the wagon, team, and driver, the day after the skirmish, while the horses were being unhitched from the wagon, some Northern soldiers came and carried them off. This boy had struggled nobly for what he was not permitted to enjoy.

In the days before the war when the negroes married, if it was summer time, they would always stand on the green grass under the shade of the tree in the master's yard. If at night, there were always the younger friends of the bride to act as "candle holders." These stood on each side of the negro preacher who performed the ceremony. Mother would pin on the veil for the bride. I have a vivid impession of the marriage of Logan, Grandpa Hughes' body servant, to "Sal," one of the house girls, at Uncle Brice Hughes'. Aunt Elmira Hughes had a long table spread in her basement in the form of an L. The table groaned under all kinds of good things to eat. Pickles were brought in in great trays, etc. The marriage ceremony was performed in Aunt Elmira's dining room. The "candle holders" attracted my attention. The custom of having "candle holders" prevailed in the South among the negroes until recent years. Martha, a faithful servant to me in Alabama, married in 1888, and on this occasion had "candle holders."

When Logan and "Sal" married, the merry-making lasted all night long. I, in company with all the other children of the family, spent the night at Uncle Brice's. To us it seemed indeed a joyous occasion.

My mother was very fond of flowers. The beautiful old-fashioned gardens belonging to her and her sister are among the sweetest of my early memories. Mother's garden had flowers that lingered as a monument to her memory, beautifying the lives of her children long after she had been gathered to her father. Here was found the snowball, purple lilac, althea, sarynga, hyacinths, sweet-william, brilliant peonies, blue-bottles, the four o'clocks, and innumerable daffodils. All of these were on borders of the squares of vegetables.

I have a fond memory of the war connected with my "black mammy" and this garden. It was surrounded by a hedge, which, like everything else, was neglected during the war, and grew up high and wild, so much so that all soldiers were afraid to enter the garden, fearing "bushwhackers" might be hidden there.

One day, when in the garden with "Aunt Charlotte," she took me to a corner, where high weeds had grown. Pushing these weeds aside, she showed me her chest of clothes, which she had placed there for safe keeping. In the chest, among her own clothes, she had put things belonging to us which she knew we children prized. It seemed to me she was always thinking of the happiness of "her children."

The people of the South loved their "black mammy" so much I will copy a tribute made by the New York Sun during the movement to erect a monument to the "Black Mammy" of the South. The New York Sun agreed that this monument should be made national by placing it at Washington:

"Southerners, whether we refer to those still living South, or to the countless thousands who are distributed over the North, East, and West, hers is a name to conjure with. White aproned, turbaned, always devoted and alert, she nursed a strenuous and proud race through the ailments and vicissitudes of childhood. They went to sleep to her cradle tales and chants. They lolled upon her humble, patient breast. She comforted them in their hours of infantile affliction. The Civil war, with its dread epilogue of terror, touched "old mammy" not at all. She was unconsciously sworn to the family. She performed her simple, but incalculable duty; few members of her class survive; the race is surely dying; but if there were heroes and martyrs who deserved immortal celebration, the old "Negro Mammy" is among them; and not far from the head of the list, either."

My mother was one of the purest and best of Christians. I remember how I loved to sit beside her at church: there was a sweet joy in it that I could not define. Her life and death were both inspiration to her children. When dying she had her children called to her bedside and gave each a parting message. She had us to promise to meet her in heaven. Since I am the last surviving child, I can testify to the fact that I feel assured they are all united in the Happy Land. This promise to his mother impressed Judge John H. Henderson profoundly. He spoke of it during his last illness and in his dying hour.

Adam Riggs, a most excellent man, a Methodist preacher, who lived near, was often with mother during her illness. He officiated at her burial. The text from which he talked is the last verse in Daniel:

"But go thy way to the end: for thou shalt rest and stand in thy lot at the end of the days."

Her father, Capt. John Hughes (1776-1860), who, at the time of his daughter's death, was an invalid in this home, survived her two and a half years. She died in June, 1858; he died in the home of his son-in-law, Dr. Samuel Henderson (1804-1884), Dec. 26, 1860. A sketch of Dr. Henderson is given elsewhere in this record. See "Henderson."

Children of Dr. Samuel Henderson and his Wife, Rachel Jane Hughes

1. Samuel Henderson; born 1845; died in infancy.
2. Sallie Martin Henderson; born Sept. 14, 1847; married Capt. George Smithson.
3. Mary Jane Henderson; born Jan. 17, 1849; married Rev. Wm. R. Warren.
4. John Hughes Henderson; born Dec. 18, 1849; married Lizzie Ewin Perkins.
5. Lucy Matilda Henderson; born Jan. 14, 1851; married Henry Claiborne Horton.
6. Samuel Henderson; born June 22, 1852; married, first, Florence Morton; second, Bettie Hughes.
7. Susan Virginia Henderson; born June, 1855; married Meredith P. G. Winstead.
8. Levisa Henderson; born 1857; died in infancy.

The two children who died in infancy, Samuel and Levisa, are buried in the old Hughes graveyard, where Capt. John Hughes' (1776-1860) body rests.

V. Col. Samuel Hughes.

Samuel Hughes, son of Col. Archelaus Hughes and his wife, Mary Dalton, was born at "Hughesville," the family homestead, in Patrick county, Va. He died at the age of sixty-eight. Col. Hughes was of the highest type of the old Virginia gentleman. For many years he was a member of the Virginia senate. We have letters written by him while a member of the legislature in Richmond to his brother, Capt. John Hughes, who at that time lived in Patrick county. Aside from this he was fond of visiting Richmond; for he enjoyed the social life of the capital, having many relatives and friends there. Here came to him the great tragedy of his life at the time of the terrible theatre fire in 1811. On this occasion the Governor of Virginia lost his life, as did many others. A monument to them stands in the church built on the site of the theatre. People who visit Richmond can look on the tall old iron fence which enclosed the theatre in 1811.

The fiance of Samuel Hughes lost her life in this theatre fire. We know not whether he accompanied her or not. Possibly he did, and the thought that he escaped and she was lost added poignancy to his grief; and, yet, knowing this man's character as we do, he must have made his utmost effort to save her. How futile the effort to save anyone is brought out in Virginia Historical Magazine, Vol. 5, 1897-98, page 460.

He always cherished this love, and never married. However, he seemed to bestow a double portion of love on his mother. The devotion of mother and son was something beautiful. The tradition of this has been handed down in the family, and to this good day (1912) the pictures of Samuel Hughes and his mother hang side by side in some of our homes. He outlived his mother only a few years. She lived to be ninety-three years old; and when she died he seemed to be inconsolable. His sister Sallie, wife of Col. Joseph Martin, of Henry county, Va., tried to comfort him. He said to her: "You have a companion; I have none.'

We will copy a letter written by Samuel Hughes, then a member of the Virginia senate, to his brother, Capt. John Hughes:

"Richmond, Dec. 29, 1811.

"Dear Brother:

"I sit down to inform you of the fortunate escape that I made from the late conflagration of the theatre in this place. I was prevailed upon to accompany some of my acquaintances to the play. The evening on which that memorable catastrophe happened, from the pleasantness of the evening and the probability of a good play, we had an unusually full house. I happened myself to be in the pit, not far from the door, when the alarm of fire was announced by one of the actors. I, at that moment, discovered the fire through the scenery. It is said that it caught from one of the lights against which some of the canvas scenery was thrown, which was so very combustible as to be almost instantaneously communicated to the roof of the theatre, and which in a very few moments wrapped the whole house in flames.

"In consequence of my being so near the entrance of the pit, and flying to it immediately, I was enabled to get to the outer door before the greatest crowd reached it. For the more correct description of the scene I will refer you to the Inquirer, where you will not only see the account of the memorable catastrophe, but also a list of those who perished, amongst whom you will perceive there are some of the most distinguished citizens in the Commonwealth. The members of the legislature have all escaped without the loss of a single life, though many were wounded in the flight from windows. But there is no one hurt from our part of the country, and none but what are likely shortly to recover.

"The business of this session has been mostly of a local nature, as you will perceive from the Inquirer, which is a good journal of our proceedings. The Senate having adjourned at an early period of session. there has, of course, been no law of a general nature yet acted upon. It appears to be generally concluded that Barbour, since the loss of the late Governor, probably without opposition, will be appointed the Chief Magistrate.

"I wrote you in a letter to my mother the prices of hides, which remain plenty and at the prices quoted. I am well. Mr. Fontaine and I have taken a room together, whom I find to be most agreeable.

"I will not make any further comments on our prospects, our proceedings, and that of the general Government. I must refer you to the direct information of your paper that accompanies this letter. Pray write me immediately as I am extremely anxious to hear from home. Have not as yet received one word since leaving there. Am in hopes the few articles I was enabled to get have all come on safe, and that my horse has by this time arrived. By Capt. Penn I sent Matilda some things which she requested me, that I did not get when wagon was here."

"I am, dear brother, yours with fraternal affection,

"SAMUEL HUGHES."

In this letter to his brother delicacy kept him from mentioning the fact that his fiance perished in the fire; but we see that he sent a newspaper bearing all names of those who were lost.

In the early years of the nineteenth century people wrote important words beginning them with a capital letter.

We will copy another of Samuel Hughes' letters while a member of the Virginia legislature in 1807. In this he speaks of the embargo, of laws regarding slaves, etc. Then, too, we see that he took an interest in foreign news, as well as domestic. This, according to Thomas Nelson Page, was a class test: "This interest in foreign affairs, and was handed down from father to son in the Old South."

"Richmond, Dec. 30, 1807.

"Dear Brother:

"After informing you of having no doubt of you making this in your way from Petersburg, you will no longer wonder why I did not write you then. Having, agreeable to your request, inquired of Messers. Harris and Bisco the price of those screws and where they could be procured, am informed that they are not to be had without sending to New York or some other port for them. Those gentlemen inform me that they would not recommend the screws to you as a country manufacturer, that they conceive the press with the beam much the best. The screw, getting the smallest injury, is irreparable, and a good one difficult to get.

"Mr. Bisco says if you think proper to try them he will, at your request, write on to New York for as many as you want, that the prices of such as would answer your purpose would be from thirty to forty dollars. Should have written by the last mail, but not being apprised of the prices. Hour of its departure was disappointed in getting my letter. But am sending you the Inquirer; I am persuaded that it has given every information of Domestic as well as Foreign intelligence that I could have transmitted, it being so complete a journal. Shall only here mention the Bill to amend the slave law, admitting the reception of slaves into the State by will or marriage. And also the Bill for establishing a Superior Court of Law and Equity in each county, and abolishing the present district Courts of Law and district Courts of Equity. It is rather thought this Bill will pass.

"There have been more than the usual number of Bills of a local nature presented to the Legislature, and from lengthy discussions of unimportant points produced by the young lawyers in the House, who are numerous, it is thought we shall have a long Session.

"On arrival of the news from Washington of the embargo on the vessels in our ports, produce has fallen to a very low price. It is said Tobacco could not be sold for three dollars; flour very dull. Hemp alone retains its price. War with one of the belligerent powers of Europe is thought quite probable, with which power we are at a loss to determine.

"I have since in this place enjoyed a tolerable share of health, and hope this will find you and all the family favored with a like blessing Nothing more at the present, but must subscribe myself, with fraternal affection, yours, Samuel Hughes."

We find in Dr. Robert Hunter Dalton's chronicles of the family that Col. Samuel Hughes went to Richmond and employed council to prosecute a lawsuit, seeking to recover money involved in business of the Loyal Land Company, an issue between his grandfather, Samuel Dalton (1699-1802), and elder James Madison, father of President James Madison.

This man enjoyed the devotion of his family, and had many warm friends.

VI. Matilda (Hughes) Dillard.

Matilda Hughes, daughter of Col. Archelaus Hughes and his wife, Mary Dalton, was born at "Hugesville," the family homestead in Patrick county, Va. From old family accounts we infer she was fond of dress. Her brother, Col. Samuel Hughes, in writing home from Richmond in December, 1811, to Capt. John Hughes, speaks of sending Matilda some things by Capt. Penn. The "things" he sent were swansdown trimming and lace. She married General John Dillard. Gen. Dillard served in the war of 1812 with distinction. He was a son of Capt., later Col., John Dillard, of the Revolutionary war (see his obituary following; also Virginia Magazine 7, 1899, page 4).

We have a letter written by Matilda (Hughes) Dillard to her brother, Capt. John Hughes, in Williamson county, Tenn., after she had had a visit from Dr. Samuel Henderson (1804-1884) and her brother, Madison Redd Hughes, of Tennessee. Dr. Henderson had visited all of his wife's (Rachel Jane Hughes) relatives in Patrick, Henry, and Pittsylvania counties, Va. This is a most affectionate letter. She speaks of having enjoyed Dr. Henderson's and M. R. Hughes' company "to the fullest extent," and says "I felt really sad for several days after they left," adding that she is "anxious to see those brag children of whom the the Doctor speaks so much." She had contemplated a visit to Tennessee, but says: "Since the death of my beloved Peter (her son) I cannot leave home with much satisfaction." Peter Dillard had married a Miss Redd, of the same family into which, Wm. Ballard Preston married. Wm. Ballard Preston was Secretary of the Navy, 1849-50. He was U. S. Minister to France during the Buchanan administration. He was also a member of the Confederate congress at the time of his death, 1862. His wife was Lucinda Redd. Col. Peter Dillard, Gen. John Dillard's brother, married Elizabeth Redd. Both of these women descended from Major John Redd of the Revolutionary war. He is the author of The Redd Narrative, included in the celebrated Draper manuscripts in the Wisconsin State library. Major Redd accumulated vast wealth.

Three of the Redd sisters and brothers married grandchildren of Patrick Henry by the name of Fontaine. Overton Redd married Martha Fontaine; Polly Redd married Rev. John T. Fontaine; Edmund Redd married Sarah Ann Fontaine. This Redd family was not the same one to which Anne (Nancy) Redd, wife of Samuel Dalton (1699-1802), belonged. Nancy Redd was a descendant of Sir Wm. Lionel Rufus de Redd.

The Dillard family were originally Church of England people. On page 15, Vol. II, Old Churches and Families of Virginia, by Bishop Meade, it can be seen that Thomas Dillard was vestryman of Camden parish, Pittsylvania county, Va. This same family took part in Colonial wars (see page 84, Gleanings of Virginia, and Henning's Statutes).

Mr. John Lea Dillard of Portsmouth and Columbus, Ohio, has in his posession a record from Williamsburg, Va., showing that Capt. James Dillard was allowed so much money for paying off his troops after an Indian campaign. This, of course, was in colonial days. He also has a dictionary which belonged to the same Captain, later Major, Jas. Dillard; and some of his writings dated 1703. The penmanship is fine.

There were many Penn and Dillard intermarriages. Some of this Penn family lived in Patrick county, Va. Here in colonial times "Penn's Store" was, and still is, a postoffice. We have papers which prove this. In old family papers there is constant reference to members of the Penn family. Abraham Penn was made Lieutenant Colonel at the same time Archelaus Hughes was made Colonel (see page 415, Vol. IX, Virginia Magazine of History and Biography). One branch of this family lived in North Carolina. Perhaps the best known of the North Carolina branch was John Penn, of Granville county, N. C., who signed the Declaration of Independence. He was, however, born in Caroline county, Va. (see Wheeler's History of Granville county, N. C.). He studied law under his kinsman, Edmund Pendleton.

Mr. John Lea Dillard, of Ohio, is related both to the Penns who lived in Virginia and those who lived in North Carolina; indeed they are one and the same family. An aunt of his, Martha Richie Dillard, married William Joseph Penn, a son of Capt. Charles Penn. Capt. Penn's wife was

Nancy Skeller, whose father was an aide to Gen. George Washington.
Mr. Dillard, when a boy, often visited the old Penn home, "Springwood,"
and remembers having seen these letters signed by Gen. Washington and other well known men of the day. Both Gen. Dillard and
Col. Peter Dillard had sons with Penn in their names.

We are told that numbers of this Penn family have entered patriotic orders through Wm. Penn, founder of Pennsylvania. In early days
people often drifted from place to place, along lines of least resistance.
Valleys between mountains easily led from Pennsylvania to Virginia
and North Crolina.

Matilda Hughes Dillard married a Penn of the North Carolina
branch. Their descendants are very wealthy people at the present
time (1918) and live in Virginia and North Carolina. She was a daughter of General John Dillard and his wife, Matilda Hughes.

Archelaus Hughes Dillard, son of Gen. John Dillard and his wife,
Matilda Hughes, was born March 17, 1817; died Aug. 21, 1901.
Archelaus Dillard married his cousin, Martha Ann Dillard, daughter of
Col. Peter Dillard and his wife, Betsy Redd. They were both granu-
children of Major John Redd and his wife, Mary Walker. A. Hughes
Dillard was educated at the University of Virginia, and became a bril-
liant lawyer. He served, as did many of the family, in the Virginia
legislature, but was defeated by Gen. Jubal Early for a seat in the
secession legislature. Dillard ran on the secession ticket, however
He educated all of his sons well. John Lea Dillard was a cadet at
V. M. I. He served with Gen. Lee's army until the end of the war after
the cadet corps were disbanded. He studied law at the University of
Virginia, and was Judge of Henry county, Va., at the time of his death,
at the age of twenty-seven.

Peter H. Dillard, father of John Lea Dillard, of Ohio, studied law
at the University of Virginia, and is now (1918) Judge of the Circuit
Court of Franklin and Bedford counties, Va. A. Hughes Dillard II. is
Commonwealth Attorney for Pittsylvania county, Va., and has held this
position for thirty years or more. This family seems wedded to the
practice of law: the four sons of Peter H. Dillard were all lawyers.
Only three of them, however, are living. Carter Lea Dillard died in
1909. Hughes Dalton Dillard is now a member of the Virginia legislature (1918). He was educated at the University of Virginia. H. D.
Dillard was born two months before his great-grandmother, Matilda
(Hughes) Dillard, died. She claimed the privilege of naming him for
two branches of the family, Hughes Dalton Dillard. He was born at
Rocky Mount, Va., Jan. 28, 1875. Two brothers in this family were
educated at Washington and Lee University. John Lea Dillard, the
other brother, is a civil engineer and is also a railroad contractor. J.
L. Dillard graduated from V. M. I. He served in the war with Spain.
He is a son of Judge Peter Dillard, of Rocky Mount, Va., and great-
grandson of Gen. John Dillard and Matilda Hughes, his wife. In the
present World war (1918) the family is represented by John Dillard.

son of Hughes Dillard, of Chatham, Va., and by Brigadier-General Wil_
liam Chamberlain, son of Wm. Chamberlain, attorney-at-law, and his
wife, Mattie Dillard, who is daughter of A. H. Dillard. John Dillard is
Second Lieutenant in the Coast Artillery. Gen. Wm. Chamberlain is
of the regular army. He was in command of artillery at Chateau Theiry
in the World war. When he graduated at West Point his grandfather,
A. Hughes Dillard, thought he should have a family heirloom, which
had been handed down to men of the same name. This was the sword
worn by Col. John Dillard in the Revolutionary war, and by Gen. John
Dillard in the war of 1812. It came into possession of Mr. John Lea
Dillard, of Ohio, from his uncle, John, but, at the grandfather's request, the historical sword was given to Gen. Wm. Chamberlain. Archelaus Hughes Dillard, his grandfather, is buried at Chatham, Va. Gen.
Chamberlain's sister, Annie, is the wife of Major-General Frank Coe.

To make reference more easy, we will insert some Dillard genealogy:

Major James Dillard

Children of Major James Dillard:
1. Capt. Thomas Dillard.
2. George Dillard.
3. Captain, later Col., John Dillard.

Children of Colonel John Dillard

a. General John Dillard; married Matilda Hughes, daughter of
Col. Archelaus Hughes and his wife, Mary Dalton.
b. Col. Peter Dillard; married Elizabeth Redd, daughter of Major
John Redd and his wife, Mary Walker.
c. James Dillard; married Lucy Mooreman.
d. Ruth Dillard; married Mr. Spencer.
e. Pattie Dillard; married Mr. Shelton.
f. Jane Dillard; married first, Mayo; second, Cheatam.

Children of General John Dillard and his Wife, Matilda Hughes

1. Samuel; died unmarried.
2. Archelaus Hughes; married Martha Ann Dillard, daughter of
Col. Peter Dillard and his wife, Elizabeth Redd.
3. Peter F.; married ———— and left two sons and one daughter.
4. John Lea; married Isabel Jones.
5. James Madison; died unmarried.
6. Dr. George Penn; married Miranda Brooks.
7. Matilda Hughes; married Shelton Penn.
8. Mary Dalton; died unmarried.
9. Jane; married Mr. Watkins.
10. Annie; married Richard Watkins.

Captain, later Major, James Dillard, served his country in the French and Indian war. He went out to this war from Halifax county. This county joins Pittsylvania. Captain James Dillard was paid for his services during the French and Indian war (see page 84, Gleanings of Virginia, and Henning's Statutes.)

The French and Indian war, which lasted from 1754 to 1763, was the American phase of the Seven Years' war, and the culminating portion of the struggle between France and England for the possession of North America.

Mr. John Lea Dillard, of Portsmouth and Columbus, Ohio, a lineal descendant of Capt. James Dillard, has some of this man's relics, an old book bearing the date 1703. He has, too, several specimens of this man's writing. The penmanship is fine. He has a record of service of some of his colonial ancestors, among them Capt. James Dillard, from Williamsburg, who was allowed so much money for paying off his men after some campaign.

Captain Thomas Dillard, his son, was of the Continental line of the Pittsylvania county regula s. On pages 255-257 of the American Monthly Magazine, of the Daughters of the American Revolution, for June, 1912, where quotation is made from original county records, we see something of the services of these Dillard brothers in the Revolution. George Dillard, who was the grandfather of Mrs. Ella (Hughes) McKinney of Nashville, Tenn., served in his brother's (Capt. Thos. Dillard) company. On page 256 we see that Capt. Thomas Dillard in June, 1776, with Lieutenant Jesse Heard and Ensign Robert Dalton, commanded a company of minute men under Gen. Andrew Lewis, and they marched against Gwynne's Island. These men were called "Shirt Men," because they wore hunting shirts. "This company under Captain Thomas Dillard marched from Pittsylvania through the counties of Halifax, Charlotte, and Dunwiddie to the town of Petersburg, crossed James river at Cobhams, and proceeded by way of Jamestown and Clever's tavern until Gwynne's Island was reached. Here they were stationed five or six weeks under Gen. Lewis and took part in the battle of Gwynne's Island, fought July 9, 1776." On page 257 we find: "In Jan., 1778, Captain Thomas Dillard and Lieuetnant Chas. Hutchings commanded a company of militia that marched direct from Pittsylvania to Isaac Riddles' house, twelve miles above the Long Island of Holston river; thence on to Boonsboro, Kentucky, where they were stationed three months. Later, some of Capt. Thomas Dillard's company, among them his brother George, serving under Colonel George Rogers Clark, marched into the country known as the Illinois, of which they took possession." In the Spring of 1778 Captain John Dillard (another son of Capt. James Dillard) marched with his company to the frontier. The writer, Lucy Henderson Horton, has interesting autograph letters written by Gen. John Dillard, a son of Capt. John Dillard, to her grandfather, Captain John Hughes, brother-in-law of Gen. Dillard.

Gen. John Dillard of Henry county, Va., had a son, Archelaus Hughes Dillard (see page 4, Virginia Magazine 7, 1899).

The Watkins family was from Appomattox county, Va.

John Lea Dillard married a second time, and moved to Missouri. Matilda, daughter of Dr. George Dillard, with her brother George, went west to live.

Matilda Dillard married Shelton Penn. Some members of Gen. Joseph Martin's branch also married into the Penn family.

Mary, daughter of General John Dillard, was never married. When a young girl she was considered a beauty, and was engaged to be married to a young gentleman; but her family oppposed the match because he was poor. He went to Louisiana to live, and became one of the leading men of that state. Mary Dillard lived to be quite old. A nephew lost what money she had; and when she died she was utterly penniless.

Jane (Dillard) Watkins lived at the old Dillard home. Ann (Dillard) Watkins lived at Farneville.

We will copy the obituary of General John Dillard as published in a Richmond, Va., paper at the time of his death:

"Patriot, Soldier, and Christian gone to Rest. Died, on the ninth of January, 1847, at 'Fonthill,' his residence, in the county of Henry, General John Dillard, in the sixty-fourth year of his age. The deceased had been for many years suffering at intervals, most acutely from chronic inflammation of the tongue and pharynx, which, though it impaired his general health, was yet insufficient to repress the energy and vigilance which eminently distinguished him in every pursuit of his life, until the o'er informed tenement of clay crumbled under the workings of the indwelling spirit. Few men in his sphere of action have descended to the tomb followed more unaffectedly by the regrets, not only of relatives and friends, but of a very extended circle of acquaintances. Born of highly respected parents, yet reaching manhood with no particular advantage of education, and a very humble patrimony, by an energy of character which no adverse circumstances could retard, and a native vigor of intellect that supplied by profound observation of men and things the deficiency of early mental culture, he very soon laid the foundation of an ample competency, while he secured the esteem and confidence of all who approached him by the kindness and courtesy of his manners, and a high-toned, unimpeachable integrity, showing out in every transaction of his life.

"Honored at an early day by the almost unanimous suffrages of his fellow-citizens of Henry, he repeatedly represented them in the House of Delegates. It was while he held that relation to them, in 1812, that, on the call of his country, then invaded by a powerful and relentless foe, he flew to her standard, at the head of a gallant company of volunteers, and during his service at Norfolk and its vicinity, evinced those high qualities of head and heart, that, in the event of a protracted war, would have inevitably advanced him to a prominent command in the army of his country. No man knew better how to temper the inflexible exactions of the most rigid discipline with the kindness and paternal solicitude which win the heart and increase the efficiency of a citizen-soldiery. His purse and his advice were freely resorted to by his men, while his strict attention and firmness in exacting from a negligent and badly organized commissariat department wholesome and adequate supplies for his soldiers, are believed to be the principal cause of the very small loss which his command sustained amidst the unparalleled destruction of life that attended the quartering of the mountain troops in that miasmatic region. There remains not one of the gallant men whom he led on that occasion who would not seal with his life's blood, if needed, his attachment to his chief.

"At the close of the war the necessity of attending to his private affairs caused him to decline a continuance in the public service, but the eyes of his fellow-citizens were upon him, and unsolicited, perhaps then scarce desired, such honors as were compatible with his private pursuits were in rapid succession heaped upon him. The Legislature, upon the first vacancy occurring, conferred upon him, by a nearly unanimous vote, the rank and office of Brigadier General; and, in the same discharge of the duties appertaining to that appointment, while he extended his acquaintance, and made many friends, he left the impression on all that approached him that, in any emergency which might arise, he was equal to the requirements of his high station. As a magistrate none were more active—none discharged the delicate and sometimes painful duties incident to the office with more singleness of purpose, and none with more entire reliance of those interested, on his judgment and impartiality. Indeed, so abiding was this belief that he was universal umpire among all classes of his neighbors, and often .by his interposition, in that way, prevented litigation and reconciled friends," etc.

John Dillard Spencer, descendant of Gen. John Dillard, lived in Modesto, California. Here he was editor of the Evening News. He was a democrat, and his paper was democratic. His great-uncle, Moses Spencer, of Henry county, Va., lost an eye at Brandywine. We will quote from the Evening News an article which was copied by a Danville, Va., paper some years ago in regard to Captain, later Colonel, John Dillard of the Revolutionary war: "The career of Col. John Dillard of Henry county, Va., in the Revolution was full of work and incident. He was severely wounded through the lungs at Princeton in 1777 under General Washington, and rendered incapable of field service afterwards. In fact he never recovered from his wound, though he lived to a good old age. Like his friend Spencer, he was always a democrat. He frequently represented the county of Henry in the Legislature of Virginia during the administration of the elder Adams and Thomas Jefferson, and though admiring Gen. Washington almost to adoration, he opposed some of his measures as inconsistent with the true democratic spirit of our constitution. After his wound had partially healed, he was detailed and furnished with a detachment of disabled patriots like himself to get up provisions and horses in the mountains of his state and North Carolina for the Continental army.

"Col. Dillard retained his military spirit all his life, and when the war with Great Britain begun, in 1812, he saw one of his sons, John Dillard, Jr., go into the service, the captain of an artillery company of volunteers and come out a general of brigade; who became one of the most useful, eminent, and wealthy citizens of his day in his part of upper Virginia."

VII. William Hughes

William Hughes, son of Col. Archelaus Hughes, of the Revolution, and his wife, Mary Dalton, was born at the family home, "Hughesville," in Patrick county, Virginia. He married first his cousin, Susannah Moore, by whom he had no children. His second wife was Alice Carr. This family always seemed fond of calling names in old Welsh form; so Alice Carr Hughes was familiarly known as "Alsey" Hughes. She came of the well-known family of Carr, represented in both Virginia and North Carolina.

After his marriage to "Alsey" Carr, William Hughes moved to Stokes county, North Carolina. In 1828 he brought his family to live in Maury county, Tennessee.

Children

Judge Archelaus Madison Hughes, born Nov. 21, 1811.

Rev. John Fulkerson Hughes.

Rev. William Hughes.

Maria Hughes, married Wm. Doss.

Judge Archelaus Madison Hughes (1811-1898)

Archelaus Madison Hughes, son of William Hughes and his wife, Alice Carr, was born in Stokes county, North Carolina, Nov. 21, 1811. When seventeen years old he came to Maury county, Tenn., with his father; this being his home until his death in 1898. He was principally educated in Henry county, Va., at the Patrick Henry Academy. After leaving school he engaged in teaching at Cedar Springs, now in Marshall county. He always intended that law should be his profession, even while in business carrying on the study of law; however, later he devoted his entire time to studying law in the office of Madison S. Frierson; and was admitted to the bar at the age of thirty-five by Judge Dillahunty. He commenced practice in Columbia, which was ever after his home. In 1847 he was elected Attorney General for Columbia Judicial circuit, and re-elected in 1853. A year and a half after this the constitution was changed, and he was thrown out of office; but was re-elected in 1860, holding the office altogether for thirteen years. He was elected Judge of the same court in 1866, presiding there until 1870, when the adoption of the revised constitution of that year again turned him to private practice.

From 1873 to 1877 he was United States District Attorney, under appointment from President Grant.

Judge Hughes became a Mason at Columbia, Tenn., about 1837. For many years he was a Knights Templar. He served several terms as Grand Master of Tennessee. He was twice Grand High Priest of the State of Tennessee. This is the only secret organization to which he ever belonged.

In the practice of his profession Judge Hughes was financially successful, having built up a handsome fortune by his own unaided exertion. He gave his children fine education, which he considered the best fortune he could give them.

His methods in the conduct of life, as pursued by himself, and enjoined upon his children, were strict veracity and the avoidance of dissipation. He never made anything by speculation, or by any other means than the practice of his profession. The highest fee he ever received was fifteen hundred dollars.

While Attorney General he did his best to convict the guilty; but he never used his influence to prosecute anyone, believing it to be as much his duty to let the innocent go free as to convict the guilty. In one instance a female indicted on a criminal charge was, as he thought, insufficiently defended, and, believing her innocent, instead of continuing the prosecution, he addressed the court in favor of her discharge, which was granted by Judge Dillahunty with a high compliment to the Attorney General. He was an able and forceful speaker, and most courteous in debate. He was a man of superior mentality; of decided views; but never obtrusive.

We will relate an incident which proved the intergrity of this man's life: Soon after the war (1861-1865) he found it necesssary to foreclose a mortgage which he held upon a large landed estate, and, much to his surprise and regret, the property only brought the amount of the debt. The sale was confirmed and the courts made a clear title. of the property to Judge Hughes; thus he was in possession of one of the finest estates in the State for less than one-fourth of its value. The debtor asked the privilege of redeeming it; and the request was granted. In less than a year it was done, and Judge Hughes gladly returned the deed. This man of wealth upon his dying bed enjoined his children never to forget Judge Hughes' kindness. He charged them if ever misfortune befell Judge Hughes, if he should need financial aid, they must stand by him.

The possession of this land would have meant to Judge Hughes large wealth. Being asked by one of his friends if he did not find it hard to part with the property when he might hold it by law, he replied: "I will die with a clear conscience and leave to my children a far richer inheritance—a good name."

In politics Judge Hughes was a republican; and in the State Convention of 1881 he was voted for as a candidate for governor.

His home was a commodious two-story brick house in the West End of Columbia, surrounded by large grounds which were always beautifully kept. Here were found the giants of the forest in pristine beauty, filled with sweet singing birds, which no one was allowed to molest. Here squirrels were often seen to dart from tree to tree.

Arch M. Hughes was twice married. His first wife was Sarah G. Mosley, of Bedford county, whom he married Oct. 11, 1836. She died in 1842. His second wife was Mattie B. Neill, daughter of Col. John L. Neill, of Bedford county. Col. Neill distinguished himself at the Battle of New Orleans. He was one of the prominent men of the state. In fact, the family has been prominent in the affairs of the nation since its early history. Both of the wives of Judge Hughes were descendants of Abram Martin, some of whose descendants are buried at old St. Micheal's church, Charleston, S. C. The names of his descendants adorn many a page in history. Mattie B. Neill was married in 1844. A few years after her marriage they moved to this home in West End, which at that time was a small house; but she always said that she was as happy as a queen. Here she lived for fifty-seven years, and died June 11, 1909. She and her husband were both members of the Presbyterian church. They lie buried in the beautiful Rose Hill cemetery at Columbia. His interment took place with Masonic honors. Children by first wife:

1. Rebecca M., born July 30, 1838; died April 18, 1851.

2. Sarah G., born Dec. 21, 1842; married Gideon W. Grifford Jan. 16, 1866.

Captain G. W. Gifford was born in New York Oct. 9, 1842, and died at his home in Nashville, on West Greenwood avenue, in 1914. He was connected with the postoffice at Nashville, being superintendent of mail carriers, appointed in 1898. He was a captain in the Union army during the Civil war, holding several important commissions. At the time of his death he was secretary of the local Civil Service board.

Captain Gifford was a member of the Moore Memorial church, Nashville, serving both as deacon and elder. He was a man of deep piety.

Arch M. Hughes' second marriage was to Mattie B. Neill, Dec. 12, 1844.

Nine children were born to this union, but only five reached maturity.

3. Col. Archelaus M. Hughes, Jr., a lawyer, was Internal Revenue collector through one administration. He was Lt.-Col. of a volunteer regi-

ment during the Spanish-American war. Col. Hughes married Elizabeth T Smoot, Oct. 6, 1867.

4. Captain William Neill Hughes of U. S. regular army 13th Infantry, which showed great gallantry at San Juan Hill, was later a retired Major. He lost his health in the Cuban campaign. Capt. Hughes married Annie R. Murphy, June 3, 1875. During the great World war Major W. N. Hughes did magnificent work as recruiting officer. He loves his flag with a perfect devotion; and has written an interesting and edifying article on "Old Glory."

Captain W. N. Hughes, Jr., son of Major, later Colonel, W. N. Hughes, was born and reared in Maury county,, Tenn., near Columbia. He received commission as 2nd Lieutenant in August, 1899, in the Thirteenth Infantry, serving in the Philippine Islands. It was at this time that the islands were most disturbed by the insurrections fermented and led by Aguinaldo. Capt. Hughes fought in a number of minor engagements, capturing a number of Insurrectos, supplies, ponies and money.

He was commissioned 1st Lieutenant in 1901. Later he graduated . at Fort Leavenworth. For two years after this he was aide-de-camp to Major-General J. Franklin Bell, later becoming Chief of Staff under this officer.

In 1908, Captain Hughes returned to the Philippine Islands, where he served as chief of the signal, first in the department of Mindanao and later in the department of Visayos. He later served with the maneuver division on the Mexican border. After this service he received his commission as Captain in the Seventh Infantry, being stationed at Fort Leavenworth again. In 1913 he went to Galveston in the division mobilization there. For about six months Capt. Hughes served at Vera Cruz as cable censor, being appointed by General Funston. He served for some time in Tennessee, his native state, as recruiting officer and August 21, 1916, he left Nashville for service in Washington, D. C. He became Chief of Staff of the 42nd, or Rainbow Division during the World war. He was decorated by General Pershing with the Distinguished Service Medal; and since this has been decorated three times.

Brandon F. Hughes, a grandson of Judge A. M. Hughes, belonged to the 15th Engineers during the World war. Arch. A. Hughes, grandson of Judge A. M. Hughes, was of the 161st Infantry. Both of these men belonged to the 41st, or Sunset Division; and they served on the Mexican border, both being volunteers.

5. General James W. F. Hughes, of Topeka, Kansas, married Nina Clark, Oct. 6, 1886. he at one time commanded the Kansas State Guard as Brigadier General. At one time he was mayor of Topeka.

6. Edmund Dillahunty Hughes lives near Mt. Pleasant, Tenn. He is engaged in farming. Under McKinley's administration he served as postmaster at Mt. Pleasant. He married Tennie B. Dickson, May 17, 1885. He had a son in the World war.

7. Alice A. Hughes married James B. Smith, of Columbia, Dec.

16, 1875. Since the death of her mother, she makes her home with her two daughters, Mrs. Eldrige Watts Poindexter (Lena B. Smith), of Roanoke, Virginia, and Mrs. Eugene Tavenor, of St. Louis.

Mr. Tavenor is a graduate of Peabody College, and studied five years at Columbia University, N. Y., from which he graduated, getting his P. H. D. in Latin at the latter place. He was born at Petersburg, West Virginia, of English parentage. He is a member of the Baptist church. In 1919, Mr. Tavenor became a member of the faculty of Washington University at St. Louis, occupying the chair of Latin and Greek. In the Summer of 1919 he taught Greek at Columbia University. He is a gifted musician.

Mr. Poindexter is of English and French descent. He was born in Bedford county, Virginia. He is a graduate of the law department of Washington and Lee University. Mr. Poindexter is a Methodist, and is head of the firm of Poindexter, Hopwood & Poindexter, in Roanoke, Va., with his brother and brother-in-law. He has been quite successful.

Rev. John Fulkerson Hughes.

John Fulkerson Hughes, son of Williamson Hughes and his wife, Alice Carr, was born in Stokes county, N. C.

He was an influential minister in the M. E. Church, South, and filled many posts of honor. He was a man of polished manner. His children were: Mrs. Pink Hine, Mrs. Silas Hine, of Columbia, Tenn., later of Birmingham, Ala., Jim Hughes, Ada Hughes, and Mary Anna Hughes.

Rev. William Hughes

William Hughes, son of William Hughes and his wife, Alice Carr, was born in Stokes county, North Carolina, and came with his father's family to Tennessee to live in 1828. He married Zuluka ——————, near Mt. Pleasant, Tenn. Soon after his marriage he went to Texas to live, settling near Dallas. The town of Dallas grew out and took in a good deal of his large farm here. This made him a man of ample wealth.

After the death of his mother, he came back to Tennessee to look after his father in his old age. He was a minister in the M. E. Church, South, and filled many positions of honor. While in Tennessee he had charge of the churches in Pulaski, Lebanon and Gallatin. He was a man who easily won his way to the hearts of his people; and he was a man of independent nature. His children were: Eliza Hughes, married Mr. Oliver, Leander Hughes, married Fanny Wilkinson, of Tennessee; they moved to Dallas, Texas, where Leander filled an important political office; William Hughes.

Maria Hughes Doss

Maria Hughes, daughter of William Hughes and his wife, Alice Carr, was born in Stokes county, North Carolina. Some of the ancestors of this family have been converts of Whitfield when his eloquence and persuasive force swept the Atlantic seaboard. This branch of family furnished many ministers of the gospel. Maria Hughes married Wm. Doss, a minister of the M. E. Church, South. She was a woman of strength and beauty of character. Their children are Rev. Wm. Doss, of the Tennessee Conference, who was stationed in Nashville, etc.; Alice Doss.

VIII. Madison Redd Hughes

Madison Redd Hughes was born at "Hughesville," and lived to be ninety years old. He was the youngest of a large family. The home in which he grew to manhood was indeed a happy one, surrounded by plenty in a most charming social atmosphere. He had good educational advantages.

This family seems to have had a "penchant" for law-making bodies. Madison R. Hughes was for some time a member of the Virginia legislature. In the fall of 1828, he, in company with two of his brothers, Capt. John Hughes (1776-1860) and William Hughes, moved to Tennessee to live. This man settled on a large landed estate near Eagleville. When Madison Hughes decided to move to Tennessee, his mother remonstrated, telling him that he was her youngest child, and that he should live near his mother in her old age. He promised her that as long as she lived he would come to visit her in Virginia every year. This promise he kept to the letter. For fourteen consecutive years he made a happy pilgrimage to Virginia each year. This was in the days before railroads. His trips were made on horseback.

About the time these men came to Tennessee to live, people seemed to have the "Western fever." Many people went West. Mr. Stone, a kinsman of Madison R. Hughes, went to Missouri from Virginia to live. The field is still pointed out on the old Madison Redd Hughes estate, where tents were pitched for his one hundred and fifty negroes to occupy during a visit of the Stone family on their way west. Hughes was fond of riding horseback. When very old he would mount his horse and ride to Nashville or Franklin. He was three times married. By his first wife he had one daughter, who married a Mr. Jordan. Their children were Rev. John Jordan; Tom, who died young; Eliza Jordan, who married a Mr. Bostick.

The second wife of M. R. Hughes was Martha Matthews. Children by this marriage were: Dr. William Hughes, who was born Feb. 25, 1825, and died Jan. 29, 1891. He was educated at Chapel Hill, N. C., and took his degree of medicine at Transylvania University, Lexington, Kentucky, He married Mary Jane Henning, who died Jan. 30, 1891. Husband and wife were buried in the same grave. The wife was first taken sick, and when it was found that she could not live, the devoted husband seemed to lose a hold on life, and died one day before his wife did.

The children of Dr. William and Mary Jane Hughes were:

a. Madison Redd Hughes; married Susan F. Bright, daughter of Wm. Bright and his wife, Elizabeth DeMoville.

b. Josephine; married Robert Ogilvie; no living children.

c. Sallie B.; married E. H. Murray.

d. Alice Bell; married W. I. Bright.

e. Pattie; married Burns Petway, Sept. 25, 1878.

f. Henning; married Hollie Jones, Nov. 25, 1891.

g. Ella; married Dr. Tulloss; died Sept. 20, 1892.

h. Kate; married Will Tulloss; Feb. 17, 1891; died April 4, 1893.

Children of Madison Redd Hughes and His Third Wife, Sallie Dillard, of Virginia

1. Ann; married Dr. James Williams.   Children:

a. James Madison; married Jennie Hicks, of Nashville, Tenn., daughter of Alfred Hicks.   J. Madison Williams is a well known citizen of Davidson county. He was born on his father's plantation near Truine, Tenn., in 1849. His father, Dr. J. Williams, was a brother of one of the founders of Nashville. "Matt" Williams, as he is familiarly called, entered the real estate business in 1887, and has conducted a large and sucessful office. He is now (1912) senior member of the well known concern, Williams & Hayes Company.   He is a public-spirited. man.   Mr. Williams is one of the originators of the National Real Estate Association.   His interest in public welfare is handed down to his children. His daughter, of Chicago, when the United States entered the World war, offered to her country her farm, including house, etc., for service.

b. Sallie; married Rev. P. A. McFerrin of the well-known family of this name in Tennessee, a gifted man. Their children are: Matt McFerrin and Annie Porter McFerrin Fulton (Mrs. Overton Fulton). They have one child, McFerrin Fulton.

c. Ella Williams; married Leonidas Bell.

d. Robert Williams; died young.

2. Arch; was born May 20, 1833; died Aug. 27, 1891; married Jemima Scales, daughter of Elsworth Scales, of Triune; Tenn.   Their children were:

a. Elsworth; married Orgay Fleming.

b. David.

c. Matt Dillard; died unmarried.

d. Margaret; married a Mr. Johnson and moved to Louisiana.

e. Bowen.

3. Mattie Hughes; married Robert Work.

Children of Robert Work and his wife, Mattie Hughes:

a. Hughes, who married ————————, is a sucessful business man.

b. William.

c. Sallie; married Robert Ogilvie.

4. Sallie Hughes, daughter of Madison Red Hughes and his wife, Sallie Dillard, married Thomas Rone.

5. Pattie Hughes; married Wilis Wilhoit. Their children are:

   a. Luella.

   b. Sallie.

   c. Mattie.

   d. Wilis.

   e. Young, who after his marriage to Rena Douglas, moved to California.

6. Ella Hughes, daughter of Madison Redd Hughes and his wife, Sallie Dillard, married Beverly McKinney, of Nashville. Their children were:

   a. Rena, married G. A. Puryear.

   b. Beverly, married Emma Beard, of Lebanon, Tenn. (Emma Beard was the daughter of Judge Beard, of Lebanon, and a niece of Judge W. D. Beard; chief Justice of the Supreme Court of Tennessee).

   c. Sallie; died unmarried.

7. Virginia Hughes; married Frank Ogilvie. Their children were:

   a. Sallie; married a Mr. McQuitty.

   b. Annie; married W. H. Ogilvie.

   c. Ida; married Robert Lee.

   d. James; married Martha Bogle.

   e. Hughes; married Alice Hailey.

8. Lou Hughes; died young.

9 George Dillard Hughes, son of Madison Redd Hughes and his wife, Sallie Dillard, married Mary McKinney, a daughter of Beverly McKinney, Sr., of Nashville; Tennessee. The McKinney family date back their ancestry to the early Virginia colonist. The McKinney home was a surburban home of Nashville. The house was commodious and stood in a magnificent grove of trees.

George Dillard Hughes was educated at the University of North Carolina. He also attended Randolph-Macon College in Virginia. He was an educator; and was for many years principal of the Hughes and Mimms school for boys at Nashville, Tenn. Before his death he was president of a large school in Greenville, Ala. His children are:

   a. Lou; married Preston Barnes, and lived in Louisiana.

   b. Randolf.

   c. Georgia.

   d. Ella.

   e. Carrol.

   f. Mary, married Mr. Sharp.

Sallie Dillard Hughes
(The third wife of Madison Redd Hughes)

Sallie Dillard Hughes was a daughter of George Dillard, who was born in that part of Pittsyvania county, Va., which in 1776; was cut off

from Pittsylvania and called Henry county. George Dillard was an uncle
of General John Dillard, whose wife was Matilda.   He was a brother of
Capt. Thos. Dillard of the Continentinal line of of the Pittsylvania county
Regulars. On pages 255-257 of the American Monthly Magazine, of the
D. A. R., for June, 1912, where quotation is made from the original
county records, we learn something of the services of these Dillard
brothers in the Revolution (see also in this book "Matilda Hughes Dillard").   George served in his brother's (Capt. Thomas Dillard) company.

IX. Fulkerson.

Jeancy Hughes, daughter of Colonel Archelaus Hughes, of the Revolution, and his wife, Mary Dalton, was born at the old home, "Hughesville," in Patrick county, Virginia.   She is said to have been a most
charming and popular girl.   She was engaged to be married to John
Fulkerson but her family opposed this marriage because he was poor,
favoring Mr. Lacey.   So she broke off her engagement with Fulkerson.

She and her brother, Capt John Hughes, were visiting relatives near
Abbingdon, Va., when John Fulkerson came to see Jeancy. The brother,
seeing them together, read the heart of his sister and said to Jeancy
privately, "Jeancy," if you love John Fulkerson, go on and marry him."
The marriage of Jeancy Hughes and John Fulkerson was a most happy
one. He became a favorite in the family. Captain John Hughes named one
of his daughters, the mother of the writer (Lucy Henderson Horton),
Rachel Jane.   The "Jane" was for this much-loved sister.

Col. John Fulkerson and his wife, Jeancy Hughes, went out into the
wilderness to live a long, happy, and useful life.   They lived in Lee
county, Va.   Here they reared a large and splendid family.

(This woman always signed her name "Jeancy". I have some of
her papers that were in the hands of my grandfather (her brother), show-
in this. This form of the name "Jeancy" shows a combination of
French (Huguenot) and Welsh.)

John Fulkerson in the war of 1812 was lieutenant in the company
of his brother, Capt. Abram Fulkerson of the 105th Virginia Regiment.
John Fulkerson's son-in-law, a Mr. Neill (husband of Mary Dalton Fulkerson), was a private in the company of Capt. Graham. This company wintered near Norfolk. They took part in the battle of Craney
Island; and were marched to Richmond, where they were mustered out,
March, 1814.

John Fulkerson was born in 1774, and died in 1846.   He was the
son of James Fulkerson, who was born June 22, 1737; and died Sept. 6;
1799. James Fulkerson married Jan. 18, 1764, Mary Van Hook, who was
born Sept. 19, 1747, and died July 12; 1830.   James Fulkerson was

captain in Col. Campbell's regiment, and fought at King's Mountain (see page 539 in Who's Who in Tennessee—Paul & Douglass).

Children of James Fulkerson and His Wife, Mary Van Hook

Peter; born 1764; died 1847; married Margaret Craig.
Dinah; born Jan., 1766; died 1769.
Jacob; born Dec., 1766; killed by Indians.
Hannah; born 1769; died 1844; married Sharp.
James; born 1771.
John; born 1774; died 1846; married Jeancy Hughes.
Isaac; born 1776; married Steel.
Frederick; born 1779; died 1841; married Bradley.
Caty; born 1783; died 1840; married Hanby.
Thomas; born 1786; married Bradley.
Abram; born 1789; married Margaret Vance.

This last, Captain Abram Fulkerson, married Margaret Vance on Nov. 21, 1815.   A son of his, James L. Fulkerson, married Alice Armstrong.   Alice (Armstrong) Fulkerson, when a widow, married Major F. S. Heiskell, of Knox county, Tennessee, in 1853.   Margaret Vance Fulkerson, daughter of James Fulkerson and his wife, Alice Armstrong, married B. W. Toole; and their daughter, Nellie Toole, married A. G. Story.   Albert Junius Toole, of this same family, married Hattie Horton, of Franklin, Tenn.

James Fulkerson (1737-1799) was a Major in the Revolutionary war from Washington county, Va.   He was also an early justice and public benefactor.   His wife, Mary Van Hook, was of a noted family of Long Island Patroons, as was he (see records of old Lennent church, New Jersey).

In a list of of the personal property, or inventory of the estate of the progenitor, Judge Lawrence Van Hook, 1720, is "One copy of Dalton's County Justices," and we wonder if this might not have been compiled by Samuel Dalton (1699-1802).

The granddaughter of this Judge Van Hook married James Fulkerson in Virginia.   From this branch of the Fulkersons are descended the noted families of which General Frelinghuysen and Henry Van Dyke are representatives.

Dr. James Fulkerson was a nephew of Col. John Fulkerson. Dr. James Fulkerson married Fannie Patterson, sister of General Patterson, of the Union army.   She, however, was an uncompromising Southerner. One of their sons, Peter Graham Fulkerson, was a Confederate soldier. This is one illustration of how families in the border states were divided during the war between the states.   Peter Graham Fulkerson's first wife was Emma V. Glenn.   He became Attorney-General of Tennessee a few years after the close of .the Civil war.   One of his daughters married Judge Hughes, of Tazewell, Tenn. Margaret Fulkerson, sister of Dr. James Fulkerson, married James Patterson, brother General Patterson, of the Northern army.   James Patterson was graduated at West Point.

They had one son, Robert, a lawyer-preacher; address, Cumberland Gap. A member of this connection is Miss Lucy Patterson, who has been prominently urged for President-General D. A. R.

Children of Col. John Fulkerson and his wife, Jeancy Hughes.

1. Sarah Ann; married William Smith Ewing, of Virginia and Tennessee.

2. Martha; married John Ransom, of Tennessee. She died in St. Joseph, Missouri.

3. Margaret; married Benjamin Jordan Woodson, of Kentucky; died in St. Joseph, Missouri.

4. Mary Dalton; married Stephen T. Neill. Mrs. Annie Neill Todhunter is their daughter.

5. John Jr.; married Henrietta Ewing, cousin of Dr. Joshua Ewing and Rev. Finis Ewing.

6. Catherine; married Dr. Joshua Ewing. Judge Joshua Caldwell, of Knoxville, Tenn., was their grandson.

7. Matilda; married Wm. Sheath, of Virginia. She died in St. Joseph Missouri.

We are sorry that we cannot give full genealogy of this Fulkerson branch of the Hughes family. Members of this family drifted to Missouri. Joshua A. Graham, attorney-at-law of St. Joseph, Missouri, is a son of Jane Hughes Ewing, who was a daughter of William Smith Ewing and his wife, Sarah Ann Fulkerson, daughter of John Fulkerson and his wife, Jeancy Hughes, a daughter of Colonel Archelaus Hughes. This makes descendants in this line eligible to membership in Sons and Daughters of the American Revolution. They might also enter these orders through Major James Fulkerson (see page 539 of Who's Who in Tennessee—Paul & Douglass Company). Their eligibility to colonial societies comes through Mary Van Hook and her husband, Major James Fulkerson. They both sprung from noted families of Long Island Patroons (see records of old Lennent church, New Jersey).

Mr. Joshua A. Graham married Sarah Yeatman, of Nashville, Tenn., in 1906. She is a grand niece of Col. H. C. Yeatman, of Maury county, Tenn. His wife's mother was Margaret Webster. The Yeatman and Webster are two of Tennessee's most noted families.

The Graham branch of the Hughes family has a most interesting history. They trace back to the Grahams of Sir Walter Scott's Ellen Graham. In a letter written to me July 14, 1911, by Mrs. Annie Neill Todhunter, I am told that "they still own part of the old estate in Scotland and visit there."

Col. John Fulkerson and his wife, Jeancy Hughes, lived as we have said, in Lee county, Virginia. This county borders on east Tennessee. Some of their descendants live in that part of Tennessee. Judge Joshua

Caldwell, grandson of Catherine Fulkerson and her husband, Dr. Joshua Ewing, lived in Knoxville, Tennessee. Beautiful Ellen Graham, his cousin, was reared near Rogersville, Tenn. She had a most romantic history. Although she was an ardent Southern sympathizer, she married a Northern man. It came about in this way: Ellen Graham was banished from the South because she slipped a file, hidden in an innocent loaf of bread, to Confederate prisoners. This file was used as a means of reaching freedom. On leaving Tennessee, she went to Pennsylvania to make her home with relatives by name of Patterson. While here in the home of General Patterson, her kinsman, she met and married Thomas R. Patton, a Northern man of vast wealth. She died after one short year, and the Masonic Temple in Philadelphia is a monument erected to her memory by her devoted husband.

Judge Joshua Caldwell, of Knoxville, Tenn., was a grandson of Catherine Fulkerson and her husband, Dr. Joshua Ewing. Dr. Ewing was a double cousin of General P. G. Fulkerson (see page 539, Who's Who in Tennessee). Judge Caldwell entered the order of Sons of the American Revolution through the services of his ancestor, Col. Archelaus Hughes, of Virginia. In this organization he filled offices of honor. He, on patriotic occasions, was called to New York and Washington to make public addresses. This he did in most felicitous style.

He was born in Athens, but was reared and educated in Knoxville, Tennessee. He was trustee of University of Tennessee, of the Tennessee Deaf and Dumb school, and of the Lawson McGhee library. For eight years he was city attorney, and the last years of his life he was referee in bankruptcy. Judge Caldwell was one of most prominent attorneys in the state, and at the time Mr. Eward W. Carmack ran for the United State Senate, the friends of Judge Caldwell wanted to place him in the race. But his eyesight was failing him and he declined. He was the author of the "Constitutional History of Tennessee," and of the "Bench and Bar of Tennessee." The second edition of the former came out in 1907. In this he illustrates the rise of modern democracy. He shows how the government of the Watauga Association, the little backwoods settlement in which Anglo-Saxon political principles had for the first time full scope, where the government derived its power from the unanimous consent of the governed, every freeman having signed the compact, created a true democracy. He brings in the history of the Cumberland and Franklin settlements, and the compacts under which they were governed. He tells us of the tradition that General Andrew Jackson suggested our state name, Tennessee. His treatments of Secession and Reconstruction are perhaps the most comprehensive account yet written of the singular and pathetic position in which Tennessee found herself in 1860.

Judge Caldwell died at Knoxville, Tennessee, Jan. 18, 1909, aged fifty-three years, after an illness of one week. All courts adjourned here out of respect of his memory. He left one brother, John D. Caldwell, one sister, two daughters and one son.

Children of Stephen Thomas Neill and His Wife, Mary Dalton Fulkerson

Catherine.

Jeancy.

Arthur Leander; died in Arizona.

Henry; married Sallie Elliot.

Matilda.

Mrs. Annie Neill Todhunter of Lexington, Missouri, is a daughter of Henry Neill and his wife, Sallie Elliot. Henry Neill was a son of Stephen Thompson Neill and his wife, Mary Dalton Fulkerson. Mary D. Fulkerson was a daughter of John Fulkerson and his wife, Jeancy Hughes.

Stephen Thompson Neill was a son of Major William Neill, of the Revolutionary war, from Virginia, and his wife, Bathsheba Harrison. Bathsheba Harrison was a daughter of Robert Harrison and his wife, Bathsheba Bryan. The latter was a member of the Benjamin Harrison family.

Stephen Thompson Neill was born in Lee county, Va., April 9, 1795. When eighteen years old he enlisted in the war of 1812. He entered as a private in Lieut. James Graham's company of infantry, 94th regiment of Virginia militia. Later he was transferred to Capt. Francis Moore's company of riflemen, the 5th Regulars of Virginia militia. He took part in the Battle of Craney Island, and for some months was in a camp to the rear of Fort Norfolk. In memory of the soldiers who fought and died in the Battle of Craney Island, a monument is to be erected by the Dorothy Payne Madison Chapter of Richmond, Virginia. Stephen T. Neill and a chum walked from Richmond to Lee county after they were discharged from the army.

He was married to Mary Dalton Fulkerson in Lee county, Virginia, Sept. 3, 1821. She was a daughter of John Fulkerson, who entered the war of 1812 as lieutenant in his brother's (Capt. Abram Fulkerson) company, the 105th regiment of Virginia militia from Washington county. In 1829, Stephen Neill, with his wife and six children and their slaves, moved to Missouri. They went by the "Wilderness Trail" to St. Louis, and thence by boat to Lexington. He was a Mason. He and his wife became members of old Tabo Presbyterian church. He was a Whig. Stephen Neill was in Virginia legislature 1821-22-23-25-26; and served in the Missouri legislature of 1844 and 1854. He was a man of genial humor. His home was noted for its hospitality. Among his descendants are: Judge Stephen Neill Wilson, Mrs. Ryland Todhunter, Dr. Stephen T. Neill, Lee Fry Wilson and Mrs. Lee Hawkins (see the Lexington (Missouri) News of Nov. 6, 1919).

Mrs. Catherine Dalton Neill Wilson, eldest sister of Mrs. Todhunter's father, Henry Neill, was reared in Lee county, Va., and died in Lexington, Missouri, in 1904. She loved to recount to the younger members of her family her knowledge of the Virginia and North Carolina branches of the family. She would sometimes dwell on her visits in the home of her kinswoman, Letty Winston, wife of Gen. Joseph

Wins,on, of North Carolina.   Gen. Joseph Winston inherited the home
of his father, Major Joseph Winston, of King's Mountain fame. This
we have already proved by his father's will, given under head of
"Winston" in this book.   We have already proved this also by an old
autographed letter, in the hands of the writer, written from the home
of Letty Winston by her mother, Nancy (Martin). Hughes.

Mrs. Wilson would tell of the full length potrait of Major Joseph
Winston in epelettes and full uniform, which hung in the Winston
home of North Carolina.   This portrait was carried by the family
of General Joseph Winston to Missouri, and in the home here of General
Joseph Wintson the portrait of his father hung above a table on
which were placed two swords crossed.   One of these swords was
given to Major Joseph Winston by the Legislature of North Carolina.
By the swords on the table were placed a pair of gauntlets with
gold fringe, worn by him during the Revolutionary war.   This portrait
later became the property of his descendant, Mrs. Frederick Flower, of
New York.

Mrs. Annie (Neill) Todhunter was reared by this aunt, Mrs. Catherine Wilson. She says in a letter written April 27, 1910: "After my
grandfather removed from Virginia to this county some of the Winstons
and Frosts, who married into the Hughes families, also removed from
North Carolina, and located in Platte county, Missouri, about one hundred miles from my grandfather. Dr. Charles Macey married a daughter
of Letty Hughes Winston in 1848 in Platte county. She died soon after,
and Dr. Macey married Jeancy (Hughes) Neill, a cousin of his first wife,
and my father's sister. Dr. Macey died within fifteen months of this
marriage and his wife returned to her father's home with a son two
months old, Charles Winston Macey.   Later his wife married Mr.
Samuel Wilson, of Lexington, Missouri, a man of high standing and
of vast wealth before the war. Charles W. Macey was sent to college
in Kentucky to induce him to give up joining the Confederate army. He
was the only child of my aunt, and she and his stepfather adored him.
But he and half the school joined the army; and this fine fellow was
killed at Perryville. I was reared by his mother, who, as stated, was my
father's sister. She died six years since and her portrait resembles that
of Mary Dalton Hughes (1748-1842)."

Besides the Fulkersons, Grahams, Caldwells, Pattersons and Ew-
ings, already mentioned, Mrs. Todhunter is related to the Vance and the
Houston families of North Carolina. Col. Ryland Todhunter, her husband, is related to the Watkins, the Polk, the Barnett and the Hines families of Tennessee.

Mrs. Todhunter is an enthusiastic Daughter of the American Revolution. She has served as Regent of the Lafayette-Lexington Chapter
in Lexington, Missouri. When the patriotic organization was interested
in having a State highway, she spoke to this end before the Governor
and an immense audience.

Col. Ryland Todhunter at the Battle of Franklin acted as Adjutant-
General of Ector's Texas brigade. He was wounded at the Battle of

Nashville, and here he had two horses killed under him. Col. Todhunter was born in Lexington, Kentucky. He moved to Lexington, Missouri, in 1870. He is a grandson of Jacob Todhunter, who served in the Revolutionary war from '78 to '83. Col. Ryland Todhunter entered the Confederate army in 1862 at Lexington, Kentucky, as aide to Gen. T. J. Churchill, commanding a division of Gen. Kirby Smith's army. After the Battle of Murfreesboro, Tenn., Jan. 16, 1863, he was commissioned by President Jefferson Davis as Captain and Assistant Adjutant-General, being assigned to Ector's Texas brigade. He served in that capacity and in that brigade in all its battles and skirmishes until April 20, 1865. He was then at Meridian, Miss., and was appointed by Lieut. General R Taylor, commanding department of Georgia, Alabama, Mississippi and eastern Louisiana, Colonel of the first and only regiment of supernumerary officers of the Confederate states. He served in many battles: Richmond, Ky., Perryville, Murfreesboro; Jacksonville; Chickamauga; he fought against Sherman from Dalton to Atlanta. On retreat his brigade was ordered to Mobile, Ala. During the war he was wounded five times, and five horses were shot under him.

He has always been interested in thoroughbred horses. "Star Wilkes," one of his horses, sold for.$10,000; another; "Idol," sold for $10,000 also; "Lady Thorn," $5,000, "Ashland Chief," $2;500; etc. His only son, Neill Todhunter, is a cotton planter in Oklahoma, and a breeder of Hereford cattle and trotting horses of finest stock. One of his horses, "Allie Brook," is now winning on the Grand Circuit (1919) (see The Lexington (Mo.) News for Nov. 6, 1919).

The family has taken much interest in reunions of Confederate veterans, and in conventions of the Daughters of the Confederacy. During the reunion of Confederate veterans in 1911' the guests in the Todhunter home were: Judge Woodson, of Liberty, Missouri, and Hon. Richard Gentry, of Kansas, both distant cousins of Mrs. Todhunter through her father; Mrs. Allen Partee, of Kansas City, who had been her daughter's chaperon at the Little Rock reunion; and Dr. S. A. Cunningham, editor of the Confederate Veteran.

Children of General Ryland Todhunter and His Wife, Annie Neill

Neill.
Elliot.
Catherine Ryland.
Emory Parkes.

The two younger girls are graduates of Randolph-Macon Woman's College in Virginia. Elliot is a reader of note. She acquired her technical training under the personal instruction of Leland T. Powers, interpreter of plays, at the Leland Powers School, Boston. She has been accorded every honor at the hands of Confederate veterans, from sponsor of her State to maid of honor for the South.

Gen. Bennet Henderson Young of Louisville, Ky., Commander of Confederate veterans, a life-long friend of Col. Todhunter, appointed his daughters to posts of honor at Confederate reunions. These two men were school-mates at Transylvania University. Many honors have come to this family from other sources. Catherine graduated from the Conservatory of Music in Atlanta. Emory is a violinist. These three sisters, when in Atlanta, ran down to Florida for the Christmas holidays. Here they met Wm. Dean Howells and his daughter at a hotel, The Monson, in St. Augustine. He seemed much interested in these girls, and, to entertain him, they gave a concert. He was so pleased with Elliot's reading that he arranged one of his one-act plays for her. While in Atlanta, for it was the winter of 1917, they frequently gave concerts for our soldier boys at Camp Gordon. Indeed, they did their part toward helping win the war by helping to keep up the morale of our men. They gave programs of violin, voice, and reading in camps and cantonments of Southeastern and Central war departments. They had been notified that they would go overseas and were expecting to sail when the armistice was signed. Even after the signing of the armistice they did much work in camps. Just before Christmas, 1918, they spent a week at Camp Funston, on call from the Y. M. C. A., giving seventeen concerts; and in Feb., 1919, they were notified to come again to Camp Funston for a week of concerts, and to Ft. Leavenworth for three days. Elliot has one hundred and sixty boys in her classes of public speaking at the Wentworth Military Academy. Emory teaches violin at both W. M. A. and Central College.

When Elliot Todhunter at one time gave a program from Days of the Old South, Polk Miller, author and impersonator, said: "I enjoyed your stories very much. The naturalness with which you did your work, and the good negro dialect combined to make your characters most charming. You didn't over do it, as so many do, and I know of no one who is your equal in that line, for your impersonations are inimitable and their delicate humor bewitching."

We will quote from the Atlanta Journal: "An appreciative audience assembled in the palm room of the Georgian Terrace on Tuesday evening to hear Miss Elliot Todhunter, of Lexington, Missouri, official drama reader for the Daughters of the American Revolution, at the Drama League. Miss Todhunter chose 'L'Aiglon, Rostand's famous drama, and her interpretation of the play was so finished, so perfect, so sympathetic, as to charm all who heard her."

DALTON

Dalton Coat of Arms

Arms-Az., a semee of cross-crose-crosslets, or, a lion rampant; arg., a chief bary ne bulee of three of the last and sa; crest, a dragon's head with wings displayed vert., the outside of the wings or, garged with a collar, nebulee of the last.

Motto: "The character of the just shall stand."

Authorities on Dalton: Vols. I and II, Ancestral Records and Portraits, which contain the pedigree of persons composing the first chapter of Colonial Dames in America (John Dalton's record is taken from one of these books); the works of A. G. Salley, Jr., Secretary of Historical Commission of South Carolina (Columbia, S. C.), whose works comprise many volumes under head of South Carolina Historical Collection. There are numerous pages in several volumes under heads of Land Grants; Letters of John Dalton; Warrants for Land, etc., referring to Dalton family; Dr. Robert Hunter Dalton's record filed in the library of the Missouri Historical Society at St. Louis; Meade's Old Families and Churches of Virginia; Burke's Landed Gentry; Burke's Peerage; Original Fairfax County, Va., Records; old family papers in the hands of the writer; Daughters of the American Revolution Magazine for October, 1916, pages 239-245.

We refer people interested in tracing ancestry of American families to a collection of ninety folio volumes of more than four hundred pages each, compiled by Col. Joseph Lemuel Chester. These volumes are extracts from parish registers. The English were so grateful to Col. Chester for his genealogical work in compiling "The Marriage, Baptismal and Burial Registers of the Collegiate Church, or Abbey of St. Peter, Westminster" that they made Col. Chester one of the four Americans to whom they have placed memorials in Westminster Abbey.

The name Dalton in the days of William the Conqueror was written D'Alton. Yorkshire fell to the lot of Count D'Alton, one of the henchmen of William the Conqueror. From Count D'Alton the American family of Dalton descends (see Dr. Robert Hunter Dalton's family record filed in the library of the Missouri Historical Society in St. Louis).

Records of the Dalton family Bible, formerly belonging to Catherine Dalton, daughter of Capt. John Dalton and his wife, Jemima Shaw, of Alexandria, Virginia: and wife of Wm. Bird. This Bible was destroyed during the Civil war. It carried the pedigree back to a younger branch of the family of which Sir John Dalton was the head, and was long established in England.

Investigations by Hon. William L. Yancey (grandson of Catherine Dalton and her husband, William Bird), who was familiar with the Dalton Bible; and later research by others of the family, substantially ratify these Bible records, and show that John Dalton and Wm. Dalton, first of the name in Virginia, were of the younger branch of the Dalton family of York county, England; and that the elder line had become extinct during the life of John Dalton, the colonist.

The head of the Daltons in Hanxwell county, York, was Colonel John Dalton, fifth in descent from John Dalton who was settled in Kingston-upon-Hull in 1458; and was a son of Sir William, who was Knighted at Whitehall April 28, 1629 (see Burke's Landed Gentry). Sir William Dalton died in 1649, and was buried in York Minster. Col. John Dalton married Hon. Dorothy, daughter of Sir Conyers Darcy, under whom Dalton was Lieutenant Colonel. He was wounded July 5, 1643, while conducting Queen Henrietta Maria from Birdlington to Oxford. He died of his wound in July, 1644, and is buried at York Minster. The elder line of his descendants became extinct in 1792 upon 'he death of Francis, his great-grandson, and the title reverted to one of the younger sons of Col. John Dalton.

We throw in, by way of parenthesis, the statement that in 1844 John Dalton of this house married a young daughter of Sir Charles Dodsworth (see Burke's Landed Gentry).

The colonists, John and William Dalton, brothers, came to America between 1685 and 1690, settling first in Gloucester county, Va. Some of this family later settled in Westmoreland county Va., before 1722, and still later we find that they shared the restless spirit of the day, some of them settling in the vicinity of Goochland county, Virginia. A kinsman of these two men, Philemon Dalton by name, had come to America in 1635 and settled in New England at Dedham.

We have some record of Tristram Dalton, a descendant of Philemon Dalton, who came to Dedham in 1635. Philemon Dalton had four or five children, John, William, Michail, Margaret; etc. Tristam Dalton, son of Michail Dalton and his wife, Mary Little Dalton, was born at Newbury, Mass., May 28, 1738. He graduated in the class at Harvard with John Adams.. He studied law in Salem; and revised the public school system in Newbury. In 1774 he was delegate to the Provincial Congress; in 1776 was elected Representative of the court. He supported Continental Government in Revolutionary war. In 1815 he was surveyor of the Port of Boston. He married in 1758 Ruth Hooper, daughter of a rich merchant of Marblehead. They had five children. He died at Boston, May 30, 1817. He had had the honor of being on the committee to receive George Washington when he was first inducted into office as President of the United States. A son of this man, who bore his father's name, Tristram Dalton, was induced by George Washington to invest in property about what is now Washington City. This did not prove for him a successful financial venture. Tristram Dalton was chosen vestryman of Fairfax Church, Fairfax Parish, Fairfax county, in 1789 (see page 268, Vol. I, Meade's Old Families and Churches of Virginia).

Old family papers prove that Samuel Dalton (1699-1802) of Mavo river, Rockingham county, North Carolina, and John Dalton (1722-

1777), of the firm of Carlyle and Dalton in Alexandria, Va., were brothers. They were children of William Dalton, the colonist, who came first to Glouchester county, Virginia. Another son of Wm. Dalton was Robert Dalton; and a daughter of Robert was Agatha Dalton, who married James Mitchell, Nov. 25, 1768 (see Wm. and Mary Quarterly, Vol. VI, page 86; also Vol. IX, page 136).

Captain John Dalton (1722-1777)

John Dalton was the youngest child of William Dalton, of Glouchester county, Va., who died sometime before 1733. John Dalton's oldest brother was Samuel Dalton (1699-1802), of Rockingham county, North Carolina (see Dr. Robert Hunter Dalton's Manuscript).

John Dalton was a member of the firm of Carlyle and Dalton. They did an extensive business, and both built homes which still stand, landmarks in old Alexandria, Va. (1917). John Carlyle's house is what is now familiarly known to us as the Braddock House. John Dalton's home stands a few steps from the Carlyle home. These two houses were among the most imposing residences in colonial Virginia. The Dalton-Herbert home is four stories high, as is also the Carlyle house. The Dalton-Herbert home is so called because the house was inherited by John Dalton's daughter, Jennie, who married William Herbert. We will say in passing that they were parents of Noblet Herbert, whose two children are buried at Mt. Vernon. This old Dalton-Herbert home is now (1917) known as the "Anne Lee Memorial Home for the Aged." It is a memorial to the mother of General Robert E. Lee. Jennie Dalton was married to Wm. Herbert some time between 1760 and 1790. The Dalton-Herbert home is commodious. The building is now (1917) in colonial yellow with white trimmings and when all improvements are completed, it will accommodate twenty to twenty-five inmates.

About 1909 the "women of Alexandria, moved by a desire to commemorate the virtues of the mother of our beloved Gen. Robert E. Lee, formed an association—'The Anne Lee Memorial Association.' " It's president was Mrs. L. Wilbur Reid, later president of the Seventeenth Virginia Regiment Chapter U. D. C. To-day (1917) on the ground floor of this house is a beautifully furnished reception room, the gift of the Seventeenth Chapter. In this house General Robert E. Lee's mother was born. It was in Alexandria in the yard of Old Christ Church, of which he was at that time a member and vestryman, that Gen. Lee announced his determination to cast his lot with his native state in the pending conflict, stating his purpose to leave the next day to join the army of the Confederacy.

Hon. William L. Yancey was a grandson of Catherine (Dalton) Bird; and we will say in passing that Mrs. Susan Letitia Rice Clotworthy, of Hillman, Georgia, historian of family, who was a lineal descendant of Samuel Dalton, of Rockingham county, North Carolina, knew intimately the family of her kinsman, Hon. William L. Yancey.

John Dalton, of Alexandria, Virginia, was born in 1722 and died in 1777. He was one of the founders of the town of Belhaven. He was a vestryman of Old Christ Church, serving with George Washington, John Shaw, and John Carlyle. The latter was his partner in business (see page 4, Daughters of the American Revolution Magazine for January, 1917).

John Dalton was a member of the Fairfax County Committee of Safety, 1774-1775, when George Washington was chairman of this committe (see page 239, D. A. R. Magazine for October, 1916, in which county records are copied). On page 240 of the same magazine it can be seen that the Fairfax County Committe of Correspondence in November, 1775, consisted of George Mason, John Dalton, Ramsay, Kirk, and Carlyle. To this committe John Muir was added.

John Dalton was one of the founders of Alexandria in 1749 (see page 242 of magazine above quoted) as was also Carlyle. The wife of John Carlyle was Sarah Fairfax, daughter of William Fairfax, who was grandson of Lord Culpeper (see page 5, D. A. R. Magazine for January, 1917), and who was closely related to Lord Fairfax. John Carlyle built the Carlyle residence (Braddock House). He also completed Christ Church when the contractor defaulted. Among his descendants is Mrs. Burton Harrison, whose delightul Belhaven Tales give so true a picture of Alexandria life during the first half of the nineteenth century. In 1774 the city Alexandria was the most important port in northern Virginia.

John Dalton was chosen vestryman along with George Washington on March 28, 1765. In Meade's Old Families and Churches of Virginia, page 270, where copy is made from Sparks' Life of Washington, we find Fairfax vestry, chosen March 28, 1765, the following, with votes given: John West, votes 340; John Alexander, votes 309; William Payne, votes 301; John Dalton, votes 281; George Washington, votes 274, etc.

After John Dalton's death in 1777. John Carlyle was the guardian of his two daughters (see Shaughter's Truro Parish). These two daughters, Catherine and Jennie Dalton, made their home, after their father's death, with their guardian, John Carlyle.

The public now (1917) have access to John Carlyle's old home as an antique shop and teahouse. Here one may drop in for a cup of tea and a chance to think over the changes these old walls have seen since the days of 1755, when Braddock and the council of governors met here to plan the campaign which was to carry his Majesty's arms to Fort Duquesne. It was this house that, on invitation of the owner, Major John Carlyle, Commissary of the Virginia Militia, Gen. Edward Braddock made his headquarters preceding his disastrous campaign. Here Braddock met the five Governors in council. This meeting lasted for three days, April 14-16. 1755, and one can imagine the brilliancy of the gathering that seated themselves around the council room, or gathered at dinner around the mahogany table. The hostess, a typical Colonial Dame of high degree, daughter of a former Chief Justice of the Bahama Islands and president of the Council of Virginia, great-granddaughter of a former governor of Virginia, Lord Culpeper, is described by a contemporary as "a lady of most amiable character, endowed with excellent qualities." The Hon. Augustus Keppel, brother of Lady Caroline Kepple, who wrote Robin Adair, and son of the Earle of Albemarle, "General and Commander of all and singular our Troops and Forces, Edward Braddock. The staid and troubled Governors, who could not raise funds to fight, and could not fight without funds; the gay young aides and naval officers, and the galaxy of girls of old Belhaven and lower Fairfax county, that must have gathered for social relaxation after the strain of the Council was over" (see page 5, Daughters of the American Revolution Magazine for January, 1917).

John Dalton, his wife, and two daughters, Jennie and Catherine, shared in these festivities. John Dalton's wife died in 1765.

The old Dalton-Herbert home was purchased by the United Daughters of the Confederacy in 1916 as a memorial to the mother of Gen. Robert E. Lee. This is, as we have said before, known as the "Anne Lee Memorial Home for the Aged" (see pages 52-53, Confederate Veteran for February, 1917).

For further statement in regard to the Herbert family we refer again to Vol. I, Ancestral Records and Portraits. Jennie Dalton, daughter of John Dalton and his wife, Jemima Shaw, married William Herbert. Two of their grandchildren were taken suddenly ill while on a visit to Mt. Vernon and died there. Tradition says they died of diphtheria. Both were quite young. These two Herbert children were buried at Mt. Vernon. Their father was Noblet Herbert. He married again, in 1819, Mary Lee Washington, who died in 1827. She was the fourth child of Corbin Washington, the son of John Augustus Washington and Mary Ball.

The only other surviving child of John Dalton and his wife, Jemima Shaw, was Catherine Dalton, who married William Bird in 1781, the wedding taking place at "Cameron," near Alexandria, as stated in the family Bible.

Bird

One of the sons of Wm. and Catherine (Dalton) Bird, James Wilson Bird, was born in Alexandria, Va., in 1787. He died in 1868 near Sparta, Virginia. James W. Bird married Feb. 1, 1820, Frances Pamela, the daughter of John and Pheloclea (Edgeworth) Casey, who was born in 1789, and died in 1855, then living in Savannah, Georgia. Their son was William Edgeworth Bird. He was born July 21, 1825, and died Jan. 11, 1865. W. E. Bird resided in Hancock county, Georgia. He was Captain of Co. E, 15th Georgia Volunteers, C. S. A. He was later Major on the staff of Major-General Benning, and was wounded at the second battle of Manassa. He married February 24, 1848, Sarah C. Baxter, the daughter of Thomas W. and Mary (Wiley) Baxter, of Athens, Georgia, who was born March 26, 1828.

Children

(1) Saida Bird, who married Nov. 16, 1871, Victor Smith (see Baxter, Harris, Alexander, Shelby, Wiley, Barnett, and Spratt families).

(2) Wilson Edgeworth Bird, who married Imogene Reid.

Saida Bird Smith and Sally Bird are members of Chapter I Colonial Dames.

Yancey

William L. Yancey (1814-1863) was a grandson of William Bird and his wife, Catherine Dalton. William L. Yancey was a son of Benjamin Cudworth Yancey and his wife, Caroline Bird, a daughter of Colonel Wm. Bird of "The Aviary," Warren county, Ga. Col. Wm. Bird was the son of William Bird and his wife, Catherine Dalton, daughter of John Dalton 1722-1777), of Alexandria Va., and his wife, Jemima Shaw.

Four Welsh brothers named Yancey came to Virginia with Sir Wm. Burkley in 1642. A son of one of these, Louis Davis Yancey, married into the wealthy Kavanaugh family, and thereby came into possession of a large landed estate in Virginia.

Wm. L. Yancey descended from James Yancey of the Lewis. Davis, Yancey stock, who was a major in the patriot army of the Revolutionary war, and went with Gen. Nathaniel Greene to South Caolina. He married Miss Cudworth of Charleston. His son, Benjamin Cudworth Yancey, married Caroline Bird, a daughter of Col. Wm. Bird of "The Aviary," Warren county, Ga. Of this union was born William Lowndts Yancey.

Hon. Wm. L. Yancey was born in 1814, and died in 1863. He represented Alabama in the U. S. congress as a democrat from 1844 to 1847. He was a leader of the extreme party in the South. He proposed the formation of Committees of Safety in the Southern States "to fire the Southern heart." He made a tour through the North and West during the campaign of 1860, urging the rejection of the republican candidate. He was a most brilliant and impassioned orator. Hon. W. L. Yancey was a Confederate Commissioner to Europe, 1861-1862, when he became a member of the Confederate senate (see Life of Wm. L. Yancey by DuBose).

Mrs. Susan Letitia Rice Clotworthy, of Aikin, S. C., and Hillman, Ga., has in her possession many valuable family records. She is considered an authority on family history. Added to this, Mrs. Clotworthy knew the Yancey family intimately. She says that William L. Yancey, who figred so conspicuously in the South at the opening of the Civil war, was a kinsman of Col. Archelaus Hughes of Revolutionary fame. There was so much intermarriage in old Virginia families.

When Wm. L. Yancey was Confederate Commissioner to Europe, in 1861, he was authorized by both the Samuel Dalton and John Dalton branches of the family to investigate the Dalton estate in Great Britain, but found that the time limit for inheritance had expired.

Samuel Dalton (1699-1802)

Samuel Dalton was the oldest child of William Dalton of Glouchester county, Virginia, who died some time before 1733. The youngest child in this family was John Dalton (1722-1777) who lived in Alexandria, Va.

The colonist, John Dalton, and his brother, Wm. Dalton, came to America between 1685 and 1690, settling first in Glouchester county, Virginia. Some of this family later settled in Westmoreland county before 1722, and still later we find that they showed the restless spirit of the day and had settled in the vicinity of Goochland county, Va. Samuel Dalton was of an enterprising nature, and, after his marriage to Anne Dandridge Redd, he moved to Orange county, Va., and "lived, when a young man, in the vicinity of the elder James Madison, father of our President," we are told in manuscript written by Dr. Robert Hunter Dalton, a great-grandson of Samuel Dalton (1699-1802). Dr. R. H. Dalton was born at the home of Samuel Dalton (1699-1802) several years after the death of his great-grandfather. I will later give Dr. Dalton's manuscript in full. Dr. Dalton says that Madison and Dalton were intimate friends; and that this was proved by the many old letters from the elder Jas. Madison to Samuel Dalton, which Dr. R. H. Dalton had read. These letters belonged to Dr. Dalton's aunt, Mary (Dalton) Hughes of Patrick county, Va., a daughter of Samuel Dalton (1699-1802).

Jas. Madison, Sr., was Lieutenant of Orange county. He inherited land here from his father, Ambrose Madison. To this land he added from time to time. This was the estate which subsequently was known as "Montpelier." Here Mr. Madison, the President, spent his life (see page 5, Life of James Madison, by Caillord Hunt).

Samuel Dalton and the elder James Madison were members of the Loyal Land Company, and invested extensively in lands in Western Virginia and North Carolina (see History of Southwestern Virginia). By referring to page 48, etc., of History of Southwestern Virginia, by Thos. Preston Summers, it can be seen that this was first called The Loyal Company in 1749; and that later on it was known as The Loyal Land Company. This land company consisted of forty-two gentlemen. Samuel Dalton (1699-1802) and John Hughes, a brother of Col. Archelaus Hughes, were members.

The Loyal Land Company had two grants of land, one of one hundred and twenty thousand acres and another grant of eight hundred thousand acres, making in all nine hundred and twenty thousand acres of land.

Another member of this family connection was a member of this Loyal Land Company, John Hughes, a brother of Col. Archelaus Hughes, of Patrick county, Va. This John Hughes married a Miss Moore. Mrs. Susan Letitia Rice Clotworthy of Hillman, Ga., has the will of this man, John Hughes, which is quite a lenthy paper.

Col. Archelaus Hughes and his wife, Mary (Dalton) Hughes, named one of their sons John Hughes for this brother. This last John Hughes (1776-1860) and his wife, Sarah (Martin) Hughes, were grandparents of the writer, Lucy Henderson Horton.

Samuel Dalton saw the light of three centuries. He was born in

1699, and died at his home on beautiful Mayo river in Rockingham county, North Carolina, in 1802.

Before finally settling down in Rockingham county, this man had been lured by the possibilities of Georgia, and carried his family to what is now Savannah, Ga., then simply in its incipiency as a town. Here he lost a bright child, and there was much sickness in his family. Afraid of the miasma, he retraced his steps, thinking to return to Virginia. Dalton built a commodious house, which for many years we know was painted in Spanish-brown, overlooking the beautiful Mayo river, above its juncture with the Dan river and near where is now Madison, N. C. He thought he was in Virginia, but when the boundary line was made, his home fell in North Carolina. Other members of this family connection moved to Wilkes county, Georgia, Waltons, Clarkes, etc. The writer holds letters written by some of them and a note written by Samuel Dalton (1699-1802) himself. The penmanship is so good that "he who runs may read." This note is written to his son-in-law, Col. Archelaus Hughes, and the father assures Col. Hughes that he and his son, John Dalton, will see that the money is paid back. The business paper reads as follows:

"We, Samuel and John Dalton, do agree to pay to Archelaus Hughes, or his assigns, the amount of a Bond due from Wm. Dalton to the said Hughes, on or before the 25th day of December.

"Witness our hands this 9th June, 1796, Samuel Dalton, John Dalton."

This note was written by men whose "word was as good as their bond." The writer, in studying the descendants of Samuel Dalton (1699-1802), finds many men and women of whom this may be said. We agree with Burns when he says that "An honest man . . . is King of men."

Dr. Robert Hunter Dalton in his manuscript says that Samuel Dalton (1699-1802) was the wealthiest man in all the Piedmont region of Virginia and North Carolina. His home, in which his sons and daughters grew to manhood and womanhood, was noted for its hospitality. Here congenial spirits met. Here was lived that life which Thos. Nelson Page says "is believed by some to have been the sweetest, purest and most beautiful life ever lived." We quote again from the same authority in describing the old-time Southern hospitality: "The constant intercourse of the neighborhood, with its perpetual round of dinners, teas and entertainments, was supplemented by visits of friends and relatives from other sections, who came with their families, their equipages, and personal servants to spend a month or two, or as long a time as they pleased. A dinner invitation was not so designated. It was with exactitude termed 'spending the day.' On Sundays everyone invited everyone else from church, and there would be long lines of carriages passing in at the open gate."

One wonders what formed topics of conversation. Our same authority says: "The conversation was surprising. It was of the crops,

the roads, politics, mutual friends, including the entire field of neighborhood matters, related, not as gossip, but as affairs of common
interest, which everyone knew, or was expected or entitled to know.

The fashions came in, of course, among the ladies, embracing particularly 'patterns.' Politics took the place of honor among the gentlemen, their range embracing not only state and national politics, but
British as well, and to which they possessed astonishing knowledge,
interest in English matters having been handed down from father to
son as a class test."

The social life of the home may be judged by that of families in
this and adjoining counties, into which the Dalton family married for
several generations, and of the families of their relatives. Mary Dalton
married Colonel Archelaus Hughes of Patrick county, Va., an adjoining
border county. Rachel Dalton, another daughter of Samuel Dalton
(1699-1802), married Captain Wm. Martin, who was born in Albemarle
county, Va., and when a young man lived in Pittsylvania county, later
moving with his family to Stokes county, North Carolina, in order to
be near his brother, Col. Jack Martin, of "Rock House." A daughter
of Samuel Dalton was the wife of Major Joseph Winston of Stokes
county, N. C. He was a hero of King's Mountain, his name being on
the imposing monument placed by the government on this battlefield.
Later his son, Gen. Joseph Winston, lived in this ancestral home. His
wife was Letitia Hughes, a daughter of Archelaus Hughes and his wife,
Nancy Martin. Letitia Hughes, a daughter of Archelaus Hughes II. and
his wife, Nancy Martin, was grandaughter of Col. Archelaus Hughes
and of Capt. William Martin. Another daughter of Samuel Dalton maried Jonathan Hanby, who is spoken of in history as "Francis Marion's
right hand." They lived, however, in Charleston, S. C., for some years.
Samuel Dalton's son, Samuel, married a Miss Ewell. She was a relative of the father of Gen. James Ewell Brown Stuart. The writer has a
letter written by Archibald Stuart, father of Gen. Stuart. This letter
was written to Capt. John Hughes in 1829. Governor Alexander Martin
was a neighbor of Samuel Dalton (1699-1802). We are told that he
entertained most lavishly. We know that Dr. Robert Hunter Dalton
was a lineal descendant of Samuel Dalton and of a brother of Gov.
Martin, through marriage into the Henderson family of Granville county,
N. C. The colonial judge, Richard Henderson, who was at the head of
the Transylvania Company, was a representative of this family. Judge
Henderson's wife was a daughter of an English Nobleman (see Archibald Henderson).

Samuel Dalton's (1699-1802) daughter, Letitia, married Matthew
Redd Moore, a son of William Moore, of Albemarle county, Virginia,
a family noted in early Virginia history.

The writer has in her possession old business papers of William
Moore, of Albemarle county, Virginia. These papers are dropping apart
with age.

William Moore was a son of Bernard Moore, who married Ann

Catherine, daughter of Governor Alexander Spottswood. Gov. Spottswood lived in Orange county, Virginia, which adjoins Albemarle. Another son of Bernard Moore was John, who married Ann Dandridge. This Ann Dandridge was closely related to Ann Dandridge Redd, who married Samuel Dalton (1699-1802).

Samuel Moore maried a kinswoman, Elizabeth Gaines, sister of Edmund Pendleton Gaines, hero of Lake Erie. Susan Martin married a brother of Samuel Moore. The writer has some of her letters to her brother, Gen. William Martin. Peter Perkins and Jas. S. Gentry, James Taylor and Henry Scales lived near this place of Samuel Dalton (1699-1802). The Dalton family was related to Gen. Joseph Martin's family of Henry county, Va., and often enjoyed the hospitality of the Leatherwood home and of "Greenwood," the beautiful home of Col. Joe Martin. Everyone knows that Patrick Henry lived in this vicinity for some years. His descendants intermarried extensively with this family connection.

Samuel Dalton in 1740 married Anne Redd, or, as she was often called "Nancy," which is another form of the name Anne. She was so called in order to distinguish her name from her mother's name—Anne (Dandridge) Redd.

Anne (Dandridge) Redd, mother of Nancy (Redd) Dalton, was a daughter of Sir William Lionel Rufus de Redd and his wife, Catherine Moore. Sir Wm. Lionel Rufus de Redd came to America with Alexander Spottswood. He renounced his title, dropping the "de" from his name, and married Catherine Moore, a kinswoman of Gov. Spottswood. Anne Dandridge Redd was a cousin of Anne (Dandridge) Moore, whose husband was John Moore, a son of Bernard Moore and his wife, Anne Catherine, eldest daughter of Gov. Alexander Spottswood. Alexander Spottswood's wife was a niece and ward of James Butler, Duke of Ormand (see pages 703 and 704, Prominent Families of Virginia, by Dubellet, Vol. 2).

Bernard Moore was a member of the House of Burgesses in 1744. He was one of the "Knights of Golden Horseshoe," who went over the Blue Ridge Mountains in 1716. There have been many intermarriages between the descendants of Bernard Moore and the Dalton and Hughes families. The writer has autograph letters written by Susan (Martin) Moore, whose husband was a brother of Elizabeth Gaines' husband, to her brother, Gen. William Martin (17—1843) of Williamson county, Tenn. These letters prove her a cultured and smypathetic woman, a devoted sister. Her husband was a son of Matthew Redd Moore and his wife, Letitia (Dalton) Moore. She, herself, was a granddaughter of Samuel Dalton (1699-1802) through his daughter, Rachel Dalton Martin.

Major John Hughes, brother of Col. Archelaus Hughes, married a Miss Moore. He was the ancestor of Judge Woodson, of Missouri. He was one of the members of the Loyal Land Company, which colonized a large part of Southwestern Virginia (see History of Southwestern Virginia, by Thos. Preston Somers).

Some further information can be gained of this family connection from American Ancestry, Vol. V, 1890, Muncells Sons, Publishers, Albany, N. Y.

Some members of the Redd family, to which Samuel Dalton's wife belonged, lived in Goochland county, Va., notably Jesse Redd, who married Mary Woodson in Goochland county, Nov. 21, 1785 (see page 160, Virginia County Records, 1909). There have been intermarriages between the Dalton, Hughes, Woodson. and Winston families in every generation since colonial times.

Sarah Hughes, a sister of Orlando and Leander Hughes, married a Woodson. William Jordan Woodson, a great-great-grandson of this Sarah Hughes Woodson, married Margaret Fulkerson, a granddaughter of Jeancy (Hughes) Fulkerson. This is one of many intermarriages. Margaret Fulkerson's grandmother was a daughter of Col. Archelaus Hughes of the Revolution. Mrs. Ryland Todhunter, of Lexington, Missouri, is a granddaughter of Margaret's sister, Mary Dalton (Fulkerson) Neill.

Samuel Dalton married Anne Dandridge Redd in 1740.

Children

David; lived in Stokes county, North Carolina.

Samuel; lived in Rockingham county, North Carolina; married Nancy Kenner.

Robert; lived in Campbell county, Va.

William; lived in Virginia.

John; lived in North Carolina.

Mary; born 1748, married Col. Archelaus Hughes, of Patrick county, Va., in 1769; died Feb. 22, 1848.

Letitia; married Col. Matthew Moore, of Stokes county, N. C.

Rachel; married Capt. (and Rev.) William Martin; lived at Snow Creek, Stokes county, N. C.

Jane; married Major Joseph Winston, of Stokes county, N. C., March 24, 1769.

Matilda; married Capt. Jonathan Hanby; lived in Charleston S. C.

Virginia; married Capt. Hanby's brother.

The daughters of the home on Mayo river all married men who became soldiers in the Revolutionary war. They were officers in the American army.

Mary Dalton, daughter of Samuel Dalton (1699-1802), and his wife, Ann Dandridge Redd, of Rockingham county, N. C., was born in 1748, and died in 1841. She was married to Col. Archelaus Hughes of Pittsylvania county, Sept. 25, 1769.

Among old family papers which have come down to the writer from her grandfather, Captain John Hughes (1776-1860), who administered on the estate of his father, Col. Archelaus Hughes, is a paper showing that Archelaus Hughes and John Wimbish, of Virginia, bought a bill of goods from John Lidderdale of London, England, in 1769. Of course these goods included wedding toggery.

After the marriage of Mary Dalton and Col. Archelaus Hughes they lived in what is now Patrick county, Va. This had been cut off from Pittsylvania county. Their home was called "Hughesville," and was the first frame house built in Patrick county. This house of ten rooms still stands (1912), and is in very good state of preservation. The writer has an old letter written by Leander Hughes in 1859 to his brother, Capt. John Hughes (1776-1860), from this old homestead. In this letter, Leander, a very old man, speaks of them both having been born and reared here.

"Hughesville" was situated on the regular stage and mail route. It was a home of large hospitality. Many friends from different parts of the country on their way to the White Sulphur Springs would make it a point to visit "Hughesville." Here all the children of Col. Archelaus Hughes and his wife, Mary Dalton, were born. Indeed, the old family graveyard at "Hughesville" is full of Hughes graves.

On the twenty-seventh day of September, 1775, Archelaus Hughes was appointed, by the Committee of Safety, captain of a company of militia in Pittsylvania county (see American Monthly Magazine for June, 1912, page 255). Here quotation is made from the original county records. Later he was made Colonel of a Virginia regiment (see page 415, Vol. IX, Virginia Magazine of History and Biography).

Mary (Dalton) Hughes was a woman of buoyant nature. Cheerfulness characterized the whole of her long life of ninety-three years. Her youngest child, Madison Redd Hughes, whom the writer knew long and well, said that she was always addressed and spoken of as "Madame Hughes." We find this to have been the case with a family connection of later date, Octavia Walton LeVert was always spoken of as "Madame LeVert."

Mary Dalton Hughes had a good deal of pride, and was given to playful banter. On one occasion the elder Wade Hampton was visiting in her home, and a flock of guineas were making a great noise. Mr. Hampton said: "Madame Hughes; order those fowls killed." In a playful way he continued: "I who command am a Congressman of the United States." With a proud toss of the head she rejoined: "I who refuse am Madame Hughes of 'Hughesville.'" Wade Hampton was connected with her family through the Winstons. This assertion is made by Senator Pettus, of Alabama, and it may be seen in the genealogy of the Winston family. Wade Hampton (1754-1835) represented South Carolina in Congress, 1795-97, and from 1803 to 1805, commanding on the northern frontier from 1813 to 1814. He was the father of Gen. Wade Hampton, who served during the war between the States as commander of a force known as Hampton's Legion of Cavalry. In 1876 he became Governor of South Carolina, and served in the United States Senate 1879-91. It may be interesting to note the fact that the elder Wade Hampton owned three thousand slaves (see page 289, Dictionary U. S. History, by Jameson). I note this fact in order to make the statement that throughout the South one hundred, or even fifty slaves were considered a goodly number for one man to possess.

Miss Josephine Robertson, of Statesville, North Carolina, who, as a child, spent many happy days at "Greenwood" in Henry county, Va., the home of her grandfather, Col. Joe Martin, and his wife, Sally Hughes, who was a daughter of Mary (Dalton) Hughes, says, "fond memories cluster about 'Greenwood' of the visits of Mary (Dalton) Hughes. She always brought a wealth of cheer with her."

Robert Hunter Dalton, who knew the family intimately, and was very fond of his aunt Mary Hughes, tells us in his family chronicles that Col. Archelaus Hughes held a position in Philadelphia during Washington's administration, and that his wife was with him here; and proved herself in Philadelphia society an attractive and cultured woman. Judge Joshua Caldwell of Knoxville, Tennessee, a writer of note on legal subjects and a man many times honored by the Sons of the American Revolution, was always interested in family history. He is a descendant of Col. Archelaus Hughes; and he once told the writer that Col. Hughes was appointed to some office of trust in Philadelphia by Washington. We wish we could state just what this office was. We know that, aside from other things, Mary Dalton Hughes had the honor to know George Washington in his own home while on visits to her uncle, John Dalton, at Alexandria.

The writer has a letter written by Mary (Dalton) Hughes in 1829 to her son, Capt. John Hughes, of Williamson county, Tenn. Capt. John Hughes was the grandfather of the writer, Lucy Henderson Horton. Her penmanship is thin Italian. The language is chaste and elegant:

"Patrick County, Virginia, June, 12, 1829. My Dear Son: Some days since I received a letter from you bringing the welcome intelligence of the health of your family, as well as that of my other children, and friends in your section of the country. The welfare and happiness of my children bring the chief source of my pleasures. You must know that I could but be delighted at that part of your letter. . . . .

"I find myself declining under the hand of time with great rapidity, my earthly enjoyments are now but few, and must ere long end forever. Would to God I could make that important preparation for futurity which you so strongly and earnestly recommend. I am not insensible of the great necessity of a change on my part.

"You mention that you remember me in your prayers. This is to me, my dear son, a source of great pleasure to believe my distant and pious children should remember their unworthy Mother in their supplications to our great and good God.

"I wish I had something of importance to communicate to you. I suppose many little occurrances have taken place among the acquaintances in this section that you would like to know, but as I know but little of the passing events of the day, I shall content myself by telling you that your relations in this part of the country are all well, and in tolerable good health, except Reuben's wife. There has been no material change in her situation since you saw her. She is sometimes better than at others, but I think there is no hope of her recovery. Strange to tell, your sister Stovall is entirely relieved, and is now more fleshy and cheerful than she has been for many years.

"Will you be so kind as to remember me to your wife in the most tender and particular manner?   Tell her that her dutiful and affectionate treatment of me has been so uniform and kind that I was almost insensible of the strength of my attachment to her until since I ha·e been deprived of the pleasure of seeing and conversing with her.   Tell her that I shall only cease to love and admire her with the end of my own existence.   Tell her to write to me.

"I will now close by tendering my love to you and all my dear grandchildren, individually, as well as all relations and inquiring friends in your part of the country, and to none more than to Billy Martin.   Your affectionate Mother, Mary Hughes.

"P.S. Tell Susan Moore her relations are all well here, that her negroes are well, and her affairs are all doing well in this part of the country as far as I know. M. H."

Madison Redd Hughes, youngest child of Mary (Dalton) Hughes, told the writer that his mother always sat bolt upright in her chair, never leaning back.   This possibly came of the stilted age in which she lived.   He said she always bathed her face before going to bed at night, and rubbed back the wrinkles.   Her face was wonderfully smooth, even in extreme age.

We will next copy the obituary of Mary (Dalton) Hughes (1748-1841).   This obituray was given me by Joshephine Robertson:

"Obituary of Mary (Dalton) Hughes (1748-1841).

"Departed this life on the 30th day of December, 1841, at her residence in Patrick county, Virginia, of chesmber rheumatism, the venerable Mrs. Mary Hughes, relict of Col. Archelaus Hughes, in the ninety-fourth year of her age.   Apart from the extreme age to which it pleased Kind Providence to prolong the life of Madame Hughes, she may truly be said to have possessed very many of the most remarkable and excellent traits of the human character.

"Her life began before the existence of this Government, and consequently she witnessed in its most destructive ravages the horrors of the Revolutionary war, and felt its effects on her immediate circle. The brave old soldier, with whom she had linked her earthly fortune, was absent in that momentous struggle in his country's service, and while his safety was the dearest object of her solicitation, the glory and success of her country's arms were never lost sight of.   During the struggle she imbibed a spirit of patriotism, which to the last day of her existence, like her other personalities, of the highest, was not in the slightest degree diminished, and which to her many admirers has been a source of peculiar interest.

"Kind to the human family with almost a universal benevolence. she dispensed alms in the true spirit of charity.   From her lips no account of self-claimed merit was ever heard.   To speak of her and to do her justice is the delight of her many relatives and friends who thronged around her and sweetened the gloom of her declining years. To portray adequately the cardinal virtues of her remarkable character is more than at present I shall attempt to do.

"As a mother we may safely say no woman could excel her. As a mistress she was humane and kind, devoted to the comfort of her servants, giving every necessary attention. As a friend the high regard in which she was held by her neighbors sufficiently attest the hospitality of her soul. As a woman she united to the greatest energy of character, the most refined and cultured tenderness of disposition. Ready to give the frailties of her sex, she raised for herself an elevated standard of female excellence, up to which she most exactly came, discharging every duty which, in her estimation, was proper to be practiced by the female portion of society. She was sick but a few days, and it seemed that her disease had been arrested, when, after the return of apparent convalescence and in very cheerful spirits, she discoursed the morning she expired. She thus may be said to have retained, to the day of her exit from time to eternity, that hilarity of feeling with which her long years had been characterized. The number of her descendants is almost three hundred."

While Mary (Dalton) Hughes was a devoted mother to all of her children, there was something especially touching about the devotion of son and mother in the case of Col. Samuel Hughes. This son had had a sorrow which he could never forget. His fiance lost her life in the famous theatre fire in Richmond in 1811. After this great sorrow he seemed to lavish a double portion of love on his mother. Their devotion was a thing so beautiful that to this good, day some of the family still hang on their walls the pictures of mother and son, side by side.

It is generally conceded that the Welsh family of Hughes of Powhatan and Goochland counties, Virginia, were of royal descent. Dr. Robert Hunter Dalton in his family papers says that Samuel Dalton (1699-1802) was the brother of an English lord. We know that it is a well-founded tradition that Samuel Dalton's wife was known as "Lady Dalton" among her descendants in Virginia and the Western States. We quote Judge Arch M. Hughes of Columbia, Tenn., as one authority for this assertion. Judge Hughes was born in Stokes county, North Carolina near the home of his lineal ancestor, Samuel Dalton (1699-1802), of Rockingham county, N. C.

History tells us that in colonial days younger sons of noblemen came to America. Thackery in the Virginians corroborates the statement. He says, "The resident gentry was allied to good English families." In writing of Virginia during the period which embraced 1756, Thackery says: "Never were people less republican than those of the great province which was soon to be foremost in the memorable revolt against the British Crown. The gentry of Virginia dwelt on their lands after a fashion almost patriarchal. . . . their hospitality was boundless. No stranger was ever sent away from their gates. The gentry received one another and traveled to each other's houses in a state almost feudal." Again he says, "E're the establishment of Independence there was no more aristocratic country in the world than Virginia." Thackery says it was a custom in old families at that time to have a little servant assigned to each boy at his birth. This custom prevailed in the South up to the time of the Civil war. The writer's brother, Judge John H. Henderson, who was only eleven years old at the, time the war began, used often to say laughingly that he was a slave owner in his own right. His grandfather, Capt. John Hughes (1776-1860), for whom he was named, gave him at the time of his birth a negro boy, Manuel. He made a deed of gift of this negro boy to his grandson, John Hughes Henderson (1849-1915).

Children of Mary Dalton and Her Husband, Col. Archelaus Hughes

1. Leander; died unmarried, aged ninety-seven, at "Hughesville."

2. Archelaus; married Nancy Martin, daughter of Wm. and Rachel (Dalton) Martin.

3. William; married first his cousin, Susannah Moore; second Aisey (Alice) Carr.

4. John; born Aug. 3, 1776; married Sally Martin, daughter of Wm. and Rachel (Dalton) Martin.

5. Samuel; died a bachelor, aged 68 years.

6. Reuben; married a daughter of Gen. Joseph Martin.

7. Jeancy; married Col. John Fulkerson. Lived in Lee county, Va.

8. Sallie; married Col. Joseph Martin, son of Gen. Joseph Martin.

9. Matilda; married John Dillard, General in war 1812

10. Nancy; married Brett Stoval.

11. Madison Redd; married first, Moore; second, Matthews; third, Sallie Dillard.

Children of Rachel Dalton and Her Husband, Captain (and Rev.) William Martin.

1. Nancy; married Archelaus Hughes, son of Col. Archelaus Hughes and his wife, Mary Dalton.

2. Sally; married Captain John Hughes, Feb. 7, 1798, a son of Col. Archelaus Hughes and his wife, Mary Dalton.

3. Col. James, of Leaksville, North Carolina.

4. Brice; died rather young, leaving two daughters.

5. Virginia; married Samuel Clark, who was born in Albemarle county, Va.

6. Gen. William; (17 ?-1843) of Williamson county, Tenn., never married.

7. Susan; married ———— Moore, son of Matthew Redd Moore and his wife, Letitia Dalton.

8. ———— Martin; married Charles Banner. He was member of

the House of Commons in Stokes county, N. C., 1797-1802 (see Wheeler's History of N. C.).

9. Polly; married Daniel Hammock. He died in 1829.

10. Mary; married ———— Moon; lived at Snow Creek, N. C., Stokes county.

This branch of the family is written up under the head "Martin."

The family of Samuel Dalton's daughter, Letitia, is written up under the head "Moore."

An extended sketch of the family of Samuel Dalton's daughter, Mary, is written up under the head "Hughes."

Samuel Dalton's daughter, Matilda's, family comes under the head "Hanby."

The family of Samuel Dalton's daughter, Jane, is written up under the head "Winston."

Dr. Robert Hunter Dalton, who was born on the estate of his ancestor, Samuel Dalton (1699-1802), in Rockingham county, N. C., was always interested in family history, and wrote a paper in 1868 which was filed in the archives of the Missouri Historical Society in St. Louis by Mary L. Dalton, his granddaughter. She was librarian of the Missouri Historical Society. Mary Louise Dalton served a term as State Historian N. S. D. A. R: of Missouri: She was also honored by her home town, Wentzville, Missouri, which named their local chapter of the Daughters of the Confederacy for her.

Dr. Robert Hunter Dalton grew to manhood in Rockingham county, N. C. Later in life he made his home for some years in St. Louis, Missouri. He, like his great-grandfather, Samuel Dalton, lived to be very old. Dr. Dalton died in Tacoma, Washington, in 1901. One of the sons of Robert Hunter Dalton and his wife, Jane Martin Henderson, who, by the way, was a niece of Gov. Alexander Martin of North Carolina, also lived in Tacoma, Washington. This was Wm. Robert Inge Dalton, whose residence was 815 North Fifth street, Tacoma, Washington, and another residence of his was 101 Convent Ave., New York.

In 1832 Dr. Robert Hunter Dalton was married to Jane Martin Henderson, a daughter of Alexander Henderson and his wife, Mary Wallace. Alexander Henderson was a son of Thos. Henderson, who was a son of Samuel Henderson (1700-1783), of Granville county, North Carolina. This Thomas Henderson was a brother of the colonial Judge, Richard Henderson, president of the Transylvania Company. Jane Martin Henderson was a niece of Gov. Alexander Martin, whose home was at Danberry, Rockingham county, N. C. Gov. Martin in his will makes bequest to this family.

The writer, also, descends from Samuel Henderson, of Granville county, N. C. In Southern families there have been so many intermarriages. This, we suppose, is because there was never the influx of immigrants in the South as we find elsewhere.

We will copy extracts from Dr. Dalton's paper: "The name Dalton is Norman-French. The English progenitor is said to have come over from Normandy with William the Conqueror. . . In time it came to be an extensive family in both England and Ireland, and now many branches are living in America."

Dr. Dalton speaks of a Lord John Dalton, a dissolute man, who was an uncle of his great-grandfather, Samuel Dalton (1699-1802). He speaks of two brothers coming to America. These brothers were William and John. One brother, he says, settled in New Jersey and the other in Virginia. William Dalton, we know, settled in Gloucester county, Va. He speaks of one of Samuel Dalton's brothers settling in Alexandria, Virginia. This was John Dalton of the business firm Carlyle & Dalton.

This record says again:

"Samuel Dalton (1699-1802) lived for many years in the vicinity of the elder Jas. Madison, and had much to do with the family, as I have seen by reading over a large bundle of papers in possession of Aunt Mary (Dalton) Hughes of Patrick county, Va., whom I was in the habit of visiting in my boyhood, and after I became a physician.

"From Virginia he moved to Georgia and settled the very place now occupied by Savannah, but after living there a few years and finding the country very unhealthy, having lost several of his family, he was on his way back to Virginia, when he was induced to purchase a large body of land on Mayo river, Rockingham county, North Carolina, about ten miles above the present village of Madison at the junction of Mayo and Dan rivers, where he lived during the balance of his life, one hundred and six years. He became the wealthiest man in all the country, and raised a large family of children and owned a great many negroes.

"I was born and reared within five miles of his residence, and I well remember, not only the large plantation, which he cultivated, but the very house in which he lived in his latter days. It was a large frame house on a hill, overlooking the beautiful Mayo river. He died but a short time before my birth. He was active and erect as long as he lived, and in his latter days generally walked with his hands behind him. For many years before his death he refused to ride horseback or in any vehicle, and sometimes during the year in which he died he walked five miles to my father's, and back again, without any very great fatigue or injury.

"When a child, I remember the great respect and reverence with which the old people spoke of him. He had several sons of whom I knew: David, a man of large wealth in Stokes county, North Carolina; Robert, of Campbell county, Virginia; and William, who also lived somewhere in Virginia. He had many daughters of whom I well remember Mary Hughes, of Patrick county, Virginia, wife of Colonel Archelaus Hughes, a distinguished man; Letitia (Letty) Moore, wife of Colonel Moore, of Stokes county, North Carolina, who were the father and mother of Gabriel Moore, once Governor of Alabama and later a senator in congress; Matilda Hanby, wife of Capt. Hanby, one of Marion's right hand men, whose name is mentioned honorably in history;

Virginia Handby, wife of Capt. Handby's brother, and two or three others whose names I have forgotten, one of these was the wife of of Col. Hughes' brother, and lived and died in Surrey county, North Carolina; another, a Col. Moore, who lived and died near Ward's Gap, Patrick county, Virginia; and one who married a man named Winston in Stokes county, North Carolina (a marginal note says that Matthew Hughes of Surrey and Col. Moore near Ward's Gap belonged to the next generation).

"All of these left large posterity, many of them of whom I have seen and many of whom have been dear to me as relatives. And right here I will take occasion to say, in all truth, that in the immense posterity of Samuel Dalton, of Mayo, I have never known or heard of scarcely any crime or racality committed by any of them equal to families generally.

"The third son of Samuel Dalton, of Mayo, was Samuel Dalton, my grandfather, who lived and died, at the age of thirty, on Beaver Island, where I was born. He died from the effect of a rattlesnake bite. His death when so young was much regretted by his family and friends, as he was a very promising, energetic man; and without accident was likely to live to great old age, like his father who lived to be one hundred and six years old. In 1835 I saw Aunt (Mary Dalton) Hughes at her own house, at the age of ninety-eight, when she was as young looking as average women are at forty, and she scarcely had a wrinkle in her face. Her mind was then active and vigorous. She was straight and her gait was like that of a girl. In fact, she looked handsome, except that her eyes had a hard, unearthly appearance. The other long-lived sisters were healthy looking, but quite wrinkled."

Dr. Dalton did not have the age of Mary (Dalton) Hughes exact. She was born in 1748, and died in 1841.

We will copy a letter written by Dr. Dalton in 1896 to his niece, Mrs. Bettie Kennedy of "Daltonia Farms," Houstonville, North Carolina. This letter gives us information of Samuel Dalton's (1699-1802) immediate descendants:

"304 N., 11th St., Tacoma, Washington, Jan. 28, 1896.

"My Dear Bettie: Our genealogy is a matter that has always interested me very deeply, but since I have been quite old and so far separated from any of my relations of my generation, and indeed of the succeeding one, I seem to have lost interest in it. However, my memory of facts is by no means impaired.

"Generations beginning with Samuel Dalton (1699-1802): Samuel Dalton, of Mayo, died about the beginning of the present century, perhaps in 1801 or '02· . . He settled on a plantation adjoining the elder James Madison and lived here for several years, during which time, I learned by perusing papers, left by him in possession of his daughter, Mary Dalton Hughes, of Patrick county, Virginia, that he had many important transactions with Mr. Madison. They were both members of the once celebrated Loyal Land Company, with thirty-eight others, who were granted a large territory over the Blue Ridge, embracing many counties. And when he sold out and went to the Georgia territory, he assigned his stock to Mr. Madison, as a mere agency, as seemed very probable, inasmuch as the land at that time had assumed little or no value, nor did it improve during his life. But while I was a young physician in Guilford county, North Carolina, happening to read in 1828 an advertisement in the Richmond Inquirer calling on heirs of the stockholders to assemble to make good their claim; and seeing the name of Samuel Dalton as one of the forty gentlemen, I rode up to my father's with the paper, and soon after Col. Samuel Hughes (he was a son of Mary (Dalton) Hughes) and your father went to Richmond and employed Chapman Johnson to bring suit as the transfer of stock was not for 'value received.' We lost, as the 'onus probendi' rested with us. But yet our worthy ancestor did become a very great 'land grabber,' for, while on the way back to Virginia from the swamps of Georgia with his sickly family, he halted at Mayo, North Carolina, and took up a homestead, where he prospered and finally was the owner of the best lands around in every direction, so that my father, his grandson, inherited two thousand three hundred (2,300) acres, and a number of likely negroes. These rich Hairstons bought their land of him; and every one of his children was endowed with very large tracts. He was probably the largest land holder in all the Piedmont region of Virginia and North Carolina.

"The children of Samuel Dalton, who died at the age of one hundred and eight years (the writer thinks he was one hundred and three years old) were four sons and six daughters: David, Robert, Samuel, William, Letitia, Matilda, Mary, Rachel, Jane, and a daughter whose name I forget, the mother of Gen. Wm. Martin of Tennessee (nicknamed Buck, who distinguished himself at the Battle of New Orleans).

(Note by the author: General William Martin (17—1843) was a son of Rachel Dalton and her husband, Capt., later Rev., Wm. Martin, who was born in Albemarle county, Va., enlisted in the American Revolutionary army in Pittsylvania county, Va., and later lived and died on Snow Creek, Stokes county, North Carolina. The writer, who is a grandchild of his sister, Sally (Martin) Hughes, was born and reared in the old house in Williamson county, Tennessee, in which Gen. Wm. Martin (1787-1843) lived and died. Then, too, Dr. Robert Hunter Dalton (1804-1901) himself said in record written by him in 1868, which is filed in archives of Missouri Historical Society in St. Louis, that one of these sisters was the wife of Major Joseph Winston, of King's Mountain fame. We think her name was Jane).

We resume Dr. Dalton's record:

"Second Generation: David Dalton, son of Samuel Dalton, of Mayo, inherited the rich lands up and down Fawn Fork in Stokes county, North Carolina, where he reared his family, all known to me when a boy, and all went to Tennessee before I was grown, excepting David, whose posterity are there yet.

"Second Generation: Robert, son of Samuel Dalton (1699-1802), settled on a large tract of land on Mayo river, adjoining his father, where he reared a son, Thomas, who reached the age of ninety-six; Elizabeth, who married Col. Critz, of the Revolution, and perhaps other children I have forgotten. A son of Thomas, ninety-one years old, is now living (1896).

"Second Generation: Samuel Dalton, son of Samuel Dalton (1699-1802), of Mayo, màrried a Gelihu. (Note: Dr. Dalton's daughtei, Mrs. Brodnax, genealogist, and his granddaughter, Mary Louise Dalton, affirm that this Samuel Dalton married a Miss Ewell. She was closely related to the ancestor of Gen. Jas. Ewell Brown Stuart. The writer has an autographed letter written by Archibald Stuart, father of Gen. J. E. B. Stuart, to her grandfather, Capt. John Hughes 1776-1860). This letter was written in 1829).

"Samuel Dalton, after marriage, settled on Beaver Island Creek, where I was born. Aunt Molly Hughes always spoke of him as the most sprightly of her father's sons, and even at her age of ninety-eight years she seemed to grieve at his untimely death, from the effects of a snake bite. His sons were John, Nicholas, William, Samuel and Ewell. His daughters were Nancy, Elizabeth and Mary.

"Third Generation: John Dalton, son of Samuel Dalton, married a Gentry, and had a son, Madison, and two daughters whom I knew when we were small children before they went to Tennessee to live (see History of the Gentry family by Richard Gentry for further account of Meredith Poindexter Gentry, who was a nephew of above).

"John Dalton was a tall and well-proportioned man, the noblest-looking man I ever saw. (He was Mrs. Bettie Kennedy's grandfather).

"Third Generation: Nicholas, son of Samuel Dalton, II., my father, was five feet, eleven inches high, and a man of gigantic strength. He lived a life of ease and comfort and died of paralysis in 1868, while I was living in Alabama. He left a large estate to twelve of his children, I being disinherited on account of my absence, I suppose, and the influence of nurses over his weakened mind. But I never held him accountable for the deed. On the contrary, I have ever regarded him as the best specimen of humman character I have ever known. He never had an enemy in all his life, and all his neighbors seemed to worship him. As the senior magistrate of Rockingham, he held the county courts as judge as long as he lived. His children were: Samuel S., Jane H., Mary H., Charlotte G., Ewell G., Leander, Robert H., Nancy K., Elizabeth, John, Nicholas, Susan S., and Pleasant H.

"I will now return to the second generation, children of Samuel Dalton (1699-1802), of Mayo. I have already mentioned David, Robert, Samuel, and his posterity.

"Second Generation: William, I think, settled in Kentucky territory and founded a family there, prominent to this day, two of whom I know, Dr. Samuel Dalton of the U. S. army and his brother, William, a commission merchant of New Orleans. Dr. Samuel and I could not determine whether the Kentucky William, his ancestor, was a son of

Samuel, of Mayo, or his brother who settled in the Winchester Valley, while the third brother lived at Alexandria, Virginia, and was the great-grandfather of William Yancey, the prominent lawyer and politician of Alabama when the Civil war begun in 1861.

"Second Generation: Letitia was the wife of Col. Moore, of Stokes county, North Carolina, and the mother of Gabriel Moore, Governor of Alabama, a very wealthy farmer. Gabriel was a senator in congress in 1825, or '26· He removed to Texas, where he died. Aunt Letitia reared a large family of sons and daughters, all of whom were highly respected and most of whom I knew.

"Second Generation: Matilda, daughter of Samuel Dalton (1699-1802), of Mayo, was the wife of Capt. Hanby, of Patrick county, Va., or just over the Stokes line in North Carolina. He was General Marion's right-hand man during the Revolution, and became an historical character.

"Second Generation: Jane Dalton married the Captain's brother, living in the same neighborhood. They had no children. (Note by author: Dr. Robert Hunter Dalton in his paper, which was written in 1868 and filed in the archives of the Missouri Historical Society in St. Louis states the fact that one of Samuel Dalton's (1699-1802) daughters was the wife of Major Joseph Winston, of King's Mountain fame. The writer has much proof that this was true. She thinks the name of Major Joseph Winston's wife was Jane).

"Second Generation: Mary Dalton, daughter of Samuel, of Mayo, was the wife of Colonel Archelaus Hughes, of Patrick county, Virginia. Col. Hughes carried his wife to Philadelphia, where he held a government position under General George Washington. Here she figured in the best society, proving herself a most accomplished woman.   When I left North Carolina in 1835, where I had been her doctor for several years, she was ninety years old and, but for the "arcus senile" (white spot in the eyes), she seemed not to be more than seventy years old. Every one of the four sisters lived to be nearly one hundred years old, and all were wealthy but one. That generation of the Hughes family were numerous, and all were sprightly and intellectual. I was much among them until I was a practicing physician, and left the country.

"I will now revert to the heirs of Samuel Dalton, my grandfather. Samuel was next to my father, a man of ordinary size, with short, powerful arms and wonderful agility. He was periodically intemperate. And in those times of fisticuff manhood, when he went to a public gathering, he was very apt to tackle some notorious bully and come off badly bunged up, but always victorious, his adversary having cried out 'Enough!' I witnessed his last fight at Jennings, when sleet was covering the ground.   His antagonist was Len Joice, a tall, powerful bully, who had never cried 'Enough.' They began at the yard gate, twenty yards above the store, and struggled for half an hour or more down the slope.. The man cried out: 'Take him off!' when his eyes were nearly gouged out, and his shirt being scraped off by the ice. His back was skinned and covered with blood and icy mud. Uncle Sam was lifted to Jenning's house, where he laid a week before he could go home. He married a Scales and reared a family of worthy children. At the age of forty-seven he abandoned whiskey, married a second wife, a widow Moore of Stokes, but lived only a few more years. When sober, he was really a model of fine manhood, and a most excellent gentleman; and, although occasionally intemperate, he was always full-handed and independent. Uncles William and Ewell both went to the Mississippi territory before I was born. The former reared a family of children, but the latter had none. This must be nearly a correct history of our ancestry on the Dalton side, from Samuel of Mayo to our own period.

"I have an abundance of legendary evidence showing conclusively that the Daltons in England, from the time of William the Conqueror, have accomplished much and occupied respectable, and some of them very honorable, standing in Yorkshire and other parts of Britain.

"The records left with Aunt Molly Hughes, which I carefully read, show that the English law of 'primo geniture' was the cause of three junior sons coming to America. The estate in Yorkshire fell to John, the eldest son, who was a dissolute, heartless bachelor. So the younger brothers left the home of their father to seek their fortune in America. Finally the besotted bachelor, occupant of Dalton Hall, soon ran his race, leaving the estate escheated to the crown.

"A large number of Yorkshire Daltons colonized Ireland about the 12th or 13th century, and held their own well until they were subdued by King William of Orange.

"I perceive that I have omitted to notice my father's sisters. Nancy wife of Absolem Scales, had a large family of sons and daughters, and they lived on Mayo, occupying the same place, a beautiful situation, where Samuel Dalton, of Mayo, had lived so long. They went to Tennessee in 1815. Their children were sprightly. (Note by author: One of this name, Alfred M. Scales, was Governor of North Carolina, 1885-87).

"Elizabeth, the wife of Vaul Martin, of Surry county, N. C., had several children. I knew her son, Samuel, a clever boy, but never saw her. My older brothers and sisters knew them well.

"Mary, married a Mr. Harbor and went to Louisiana territory before I was born, making a large fortune, and rearing a large family, of whom I often heard but have never seen any of them. By the way, the father of this Mr. Harbor married my father's widowed mother, and they, also went to Louisiana.

"Our family went by the name of D'Alton for a long time after the advent of William the Conqueror, and Yorkshire fell to the lot of Count D'Alton, one of his henchmen."

Those who care to look further into the Dalton English records will find much information in Burke's Landed Gentry, as well as in Burke's Peerage. We note that Sir William Dalton, who was Knighted at Whitehall. April 28, 1629, lies buried in York Minster. We see, too, that Dalton Hall, spoken of by Dr. Robert Hunter Dalton, near Burton,

Westmoreland, which adjoins Yorkshire, is in possession of someone
whose name is not Dalton.

Samuel Dalton (1699-1802), because of his vast estate in lands and
slaves, was known as "Samuel Dalton of Mayo." Dr. Dalton always
designates him by this title.

We will copy a notice of the death of Dr. Robert Hunter Dalton
(1806-1900) from whom we have aid in our family history. This little
sketch was published in the Tacoma Evening News, Washington, Jan.
22, 1900:

"Passes on to His Last Rest

"Death of Dr. Robert Hunter Dalton (1806-1900). Close of a brilliant and remarkable career, extending over seventy years. The day
before his demise, at the age of ninety-three years and eleven months,
he penned his own epitaph:

> 'All you who come my grave to see
> Just as I am so you must be,
> Once I lived and moved in space,
> And felt the joys that charm our race,
> But now I lie beneath the sod,
> My body dust, my soul with God.'

"The day before his death, at nearly ninety-four years of age,
Dr. Dalton, a retired physician who resided a number of years in Tacoma, penned these lines, and then awaited the call that he felt was
coming.

"Mrs. Alexander Smith, a daughter of the deceased with whom he
was making his home, saw that he was not feeling strong yesterday
morning and insisted that he breakfast in his room. The Doctor insisted that he was able to be up and about. He had partaken of a portion
of his breakfast, and when a servant went back to him with his coffee,
she found him sitting in front of the fire with a smile on his face, dead.

"Dr. Dalton was in many respects a remarkable man. For more
than sixty years he had pursued a brilliant and active professional life,
and up to within a few weeks of his death was engaged in writing articles
which had been accepted by prominent medical journals to which he was
a constant contributor. Graduating from the medical college at Lexington, Kentucky, at the age of twenty-two years, he took a course at
Philadelphia and then entered on the active practice of medicine.

"During the Civil war he joined the army and held high positions
during a number of campaigns. After the war he practiced in St.
Louis and later in California. At sixty-nine years of age, Dr. Dalton
sustained a severe injury through accident that made him less active
of body in later years; but his mind never wavered even at an age when
the allotted span of life is over, and those who survive it usually fall
into second childhood.

"His papers on various medical branches and on hypnotism were
sought by prominent periodicals. Dr. Dalton was born in North

Carolina, his ancestors being among men of national fame, and heroes of the Revolutionary war. One of them, Col. Hunter, was so much a thorn in the side of the British that a price was placed on his head.

"Dr. Robert Hunter Dalton leaves a son in San Diego, his daughter, Mrs. Alexander Smith, and grandchildren. He leaves six children. One grandson, Hunter Dalton, resides in Seattle. The funeral will be held tomorrow afternoon at Trinity church at two o'clock. Interment in Tacoma cemetery. Family residence 304 N. 11th St., Tacoma, Wash."

This obituary notice was furnished us by Mrs. P. B. Kennedy (Bettie D. Kennedy), "Daltonia Farms," Houstonville, North Carolina, R. F. D. No. 1. Dr. Robert Hunter Dalton was an elder brother of the father of Mrs. P. B. Kennedy. .

Dr. R. H. Dalton attended Transylvania College at Lexington, Ky., at the same time that the two brothers of the writer's mother were there, Leander and Brice Hughes. We have and old letter written by Leander Hughes from his school in 1827, in which he says that his room-mate is Robert H. Dalton. This was the first school of higher learning west of the mountains. Robert H. Dalton used to speak of himself and Leander Hughes as Damon and Pythias.

Children of Dr. Robert Hunter Dalton and His Wife, Jane Martin Henderson.

A. H. Dalton, of North Carolina.

Mrs. Mary Lou Brodnax, of New York, who died in London England.

Capt. H. H. Dalton, of St. Louis, Mo.

R. H. Dalton, of San Diego, Cal.

Dr. H. C. Dalton, of St. Louis, Mo.

Dr. W. R. Dalton, North Carolina.

Mrs. K. H. Smith, of Tacoma, Washington.

Robert P. Dalton, of Lambert's Point, Norfolk, Va., who was reared near the old Dalton place in Rockhingam county, North Carolina, tells us that Beaver Island, the home of Samuel Dalton, son of Samuel of Mayo, is still in possession of the family. This place was always in possesion of some one by the name of Dalton until the death of Lea Dalton, father of Mrs. John Price, the present owner (1913). Mrs. Price was the only child of Lea Dalton.

Beaver Island was a part of the estate of Samuel of Mayo. It was about four miles from the residence of Samuel Dalton (1699 1802), and was the home of his son, Samuel, who lived and died there; his son, Samuel, Jr., lived and died there also; and his son Nicholas, lived and died there; and his son, Leander, lived and died there. Leander had only one child, a daughter, who married John H. Price.

Beaver Island is now the home of John H. Price and family (1911), the place having been in the Dalton family for six generations.

Judge Richard Cardwell, of Hanover county, Va., is a member of this branch.

Mr. R. P. Dalton, when questioned in regard to his family, said,

"We are scattered from Dan to Bersheba, or rather from London to Los Angeles, and it is very hard to get together even in a book." He had seen the old graveyard at "Hughesville," in Patrick county, Va., where Col. Archelaus Hughes and his wife, Mary Dalton, and many others of the family are buried. Some of the older members of the Dalton family are buried near the Seuratown mountain in Stokes county, N. C. The old Dalton home on Mayo river is about ten miles from "Hughesville," in Patrick county, Va.

Some of the vast landed estate of Samuel Dalton, of Mayo, is still in the hands of his descendants. "Daltonia Farms," an estate of about five thousand acres, is the home of Mrs. Bettie (Dalton) Kennedy, near Houstonville, N. C. "Hughesville," in Patrick county, Va., formerly the home of his daughter, Mary Dalton Hughes, is still owned by a descendant.

The fortunes of the family have been varied. Mrs. Mary Lou Brodnax, a brilliant and lovely woman, was a well-known genealogist. After her son lost their fortune on Wall Street, N. Y., she made her living tracing genealogy for people who were willing to pay her for her work. She died in London, England, in 1911, where she had gone to search archives.

As a family they like to preserve traditions. Miss Ada Dalton, of Winston-Salem, North Carolina, who descends from the Dandridge-Custis family on the maternal side, and throught the Dandridge on the paternal side, helps to preserve traditions. Ethel Dalton, a daughter of R. P. Dalton, on graduation from college, had a watch presented her bearing the Dalton crest. Descendants of Samuel Dalton, of Mayo, in Williamson county, Tenn., of the Henderson and Harrison branches. have family coat-of-arms framed and hanging on their walls. We are mindful of what William E. Gladstone said: "No greater calamity can befall a people than to break utterly with their past." Mrs. Caddie Sparrow Dalton (Mrs. Frank Dalton) of Greensboro, North Carolina, uses a die. The Henderson, Harrison, and Briggs branches in Tennessee and the Todhunter family in Missouri have a family die.

Samuel Dalton (1699-1802) first met Anne Dandridge Redd, whom he later married, at Williamsburg, Virginia, when Williamsburg was the center of social life. Here had been founded William and Mary College in 1693. This, next to Harvard, is the oldest of American colleges. An institution of learning always gives tone to society. Besides, Williamsburg was at this time the capital of Virginia, and was through winter months the resort of Virginia planters.

We will give a partial genealogy of Samuel Dalton's, of Mayo, branch. We are sorry not to be able to give complete genealogy:

Generation I—Generation I in America: William Dalton.

Generation II—Samuel Dalton (1699-1802), of Mayo, married Anne Dandridge Redd in 1740.

Robert Dalton, whose children settled in Kentucky.

John Dalton (1722-1777), of Alexandria, Va.

Generation III—Children of Samuel Dalton (1699-1802) and his wife, Anne Dandridge Redd:

David; lived in Stokes county, N. C.

Samuel; lived in Rockingham county, N. C.

Robert; lived in Campbell county, N. C.

William; lived in Virginia.

John; lived in North Carolina.

Mary; born 1748; married Col. Archelaus Hughes; lived in Patrick county, Va.

Letitia; born May 15, 1742; married Col. Matthew Moore in 1757; lived in Stokes county, N. C. She died Feb. 22, 1838.

Rachel; married Capt. (and Rev.) William Martin; lived first in Pittsylvania county, Va., later on Snow Creek, N. C.

Jane; married Major Joseph Winston of Stokes county, N. C.

Matilda; married Capt. Jonathan Hanby, March 24, 1769; lived some years in Charleston, S. C.

Generation IV—Children of David Dalton: Isaac, Jonathan, David. This branch of the family were all wealthy. Isaac Dalton was vastly rich, and was an elegant gentleman. He often represented his county in the legislature. They lived in Stokes county, N. C. Jonathan moved to Tennessee to live.

Children of Samuel Dalton III: Nicholas; lived at Beaver Island, Rockingham county, North Carolina, where his father and grandfather had lived.

John; moved to Tennessee.

William; lived on the Mississippi river. He became wealthy.

Samuel, IV.; married a Miss Scales, lived in Rockingham county, N. C.

Ewell; lived in Mississippi with his brother, William.

Mary; married a Mr. Harbor; and lived in Louisiana. They were wealthy people.

Elizabeth; married Vaul Martin, of Surry county, N. C.

Nancy; married Absolem Scales, moved to Tennessee.

Generation V—Madison Dalton, son of John Dalton, who moved to Tennesse, married a sister of Meredith P. Gentry.

Madison Dalton, son of Samuel and his wife, ——— Scales, lived in Louisiana.

Nicholas, of Beaver Island, had seven sons and five daughters. His son, Leander Dalton, lived at Beaver Island, N. C. One of his daughters married———Cardwell, and they were parents of Judge Richard Cardwell,

Nicholas was the father of James, Robert Hunter, P. H., and another who was the grandfather of W. W. Gladstone. Most of the five daughters and seven sons of Nicholas Dalton, of Beaver Island, left large families.

Generation VI—In this generation comes Mrs. John H Price, of

Beaver Island, Rockingham county, N. C., a daughter of Leander Dalton.

Rev. P. H. Dalton had a son, Robert Frank Dalton, of Greensboro, N. C., who married Caddie Sparrow.   Jas. had a son, Nicholas Dalton. In this generation is Judge Richard Cardwell, of Hanover C. H., Va.

Generation VII—In this generation is Mary Louise Dalton, St. Louis; Robert P. Dalton, son of Nicholas. lives at Lambert's Point, Norfolk, Va.; W. W. Gladstone lives in Danville, Va.; C. J. Price lives in Los Angeles, Cal.

Generation VIII—In this generation is Major J. W. Dalton, son of Robert P. Dalton. Hunter Dalton, of Seattle, is a grandson of Dr. Robert Hunter Dalton (1806-1900), born in North Carolina and died in Tacoma, Washington.   J. W. Dalton has a son Lawrence.

Children of R. P. Dalton, of Lambert's Point, Norfolk, Va.

R. L. Dalton, San Antonio, Texas.

Major J. W. Dalton, Winston-Salem, N. C.

Ethel Dulton.

Robert Frank Dalton, son of Rev. P. H. Dalton, is president of a large lumber company in High Point, the largest manufacturing plant there. He stands at the head of the business world in his community.   His home is in Greensboro, North Carolina.   He was educated at Bingham School and Davidson College.   His father was a Presbyterian minister.

Mr. Dalton married Miss Caroline Fowle Sparrow.   They have two sons, Carter Dalton and Thomas Sparrow Dalton.

Carter Dalton was known in school for brilliant scholarship.   He graduated from the High School with first honors and won the State University Scholarship.   He studied law at the State University, after graduation, and then attended Harvard Law School, where he took his degree.   He afterwards practiced law in Greensboro for two years, then moving to High Point he became a partner of Mr. Westcott H. Robinson.   The Robinson-Dalton law firm is eminently successful. He was elected to the Legislature in 1918; but refused reelection because he wanted to devote his time to law practice.   He married Mary Drew Land and has three children: Mary Drew, Caddie Sparrow, and Frank, Jr.

Thomas Sparrow Dalton is a man of winning personality.   He is beloved by all who come in contact with him, regardless of position or color.   Dalton was educated at Bingham School and at the State University at Chapel Hill.   Here he was a star on the football team. He married Elizabeth Landon of New York State and has one child, Caroline Landon Dalton.   His home is in Wilkes county. It is a palatial residence, made very beautiful by shrubbery, flowers, terraces, and fountains.   His apple orchards are far-famed, known as "Gold Medal Orchards," the largest in Wilkes county.

Dalton Record

(As dictated by Mrs. John Bell Crockett, nee Nancy Dalton Sayers)

The Dalton family in North Carolina was related to the Ewell, Redd and Kenner families.

John Dalton; married Elizabeth Gentry.

Mary Dalton; married Mr. Harbor.

Children of John Dalton and His Wife, Elizabeth Gentry

Theodocia; died unmarried.

Matt; died unmarried.

Charlotte Henry; married Samuel Scales.

Ewell Harbor was the son of Mary Dalton and her husband, ——— Harbor.

(This family lived in Louisiana. They were wealthy. In writing a sketch of the life of Gen. William Martin (———1843) of Williamson county, Tennessee, we have copied a letter written to him by his nephew, Samuel Clark, who lived on Red river. This letter was written from New Orleans, whither Samuel Clark had gone to lay in plantation supplies, and to enjoy the social life of the city. He speaks of seeing "Cousin Polly Harbor and her son Ewell," etc. They always kept up social intercourse with their Tennessee relatives.)

Children of Nancy Dalton (1773-1840) and Her Husband, Absolem Scales (1769-1835)

Charlotte Gelihu; died single.

John Scales had three wives: Lucy Fields, Sally B. Sayers, Rebecca Ladd.

Joseph; married Fannie Webb.

Samuel; married Charlotte H. Dalton.

Nicholas; married Eliza Cody.

Jane; married John Bellanfont.

Nancy Kenner; married David Sayers.

Absolem; married Eliza Morton. Left no children.

Noah; married Mary B. Sayers.

Children of John Scales and His First Wife, Lucy Fields

Nathaniel Fields; married Anne Webb.

Nancy; married Hamilton Crockett.

Mary; married Samuel A. Dalton, of Rockingham county, N. C.

Children of John Scales and His Second Wife, Sally Sayers

Robert.

John; married Bettie Sayers.

James.

Noah.

Sayers.

Children of John Scales and His Third Wife, Rebecca Ladd, whose Mother was a Miss Dalton

Ewell.
Charlotte.

Children of Joseph Scales and His Wife, Fannie Webb

William; died single.
Absolem; married first, Eliza Lavender; second, Eliza ——————.
James, married Mary Morton.
John; married ———— Westover.
Mildred; married Dr. Fields.
Charlotte; married Mr. Wilson.
Joseph; married Miss Elliot.
Samuel; married Miss Hughes.
Henry.
Ewell; married Miss Young.
Nancy; died single.
Fannie; married Alfred Wallace.
Bettie; married Mr. Williams.
Noah; married Laur Phillips.
Laura; died in infancy.

Children of Samuel Scales and His Wife, Charlotte Henry Dalton
(They were first cousins.)

Elizabeth.
Ann; married Crockett Sayers.
Ab. Watt, M. D.
John Russwurm.
Tabitha; married Joe Billie Scales, M. D.
Fannie; married Henry Sherrod.
Mary Dalton.

Children of Nicholas Scales and His Wife, Eliza Cody

Nancy Jane, married Abner Sayers.
Charlotte, married Mr. Drew.
Eliza.
Jo Ab.

Children of Jane Scales and Her Husband, John Bellanfont

Lucy; married Mr. Winn.
Absolem.
John.
Nicholas.
Nancy; married Mr. Seay.
Charlotte.
Joseph.

Children of Mary Kenner Scales and Her Husband, David Sayers

(Mary Kenner Scales was born Oct. 28, 1806; died Sept. 10, 1866.

She married David Sayers, who was born April 14, 1805; died Aug. 3, 1870).

Nancy Dalton; married John Bell Crockett, M. D.

Robert Absolem.

Mary Charlotte; married Andrew James Crockett.

Sarah Jane; married Col. Thos L. Yancey.

David.

Joanna.

Josephine.

Samuel.

James Kenner.

Children of Noah Scales and His Wife, Mary Beatty Sayers

(Noah Scales was born Sept. 28, 1804; died Sept. 22, 1859. He married Mary Beatty Sayers, who was born Jan. 4, 1809, and died Nov. 7, 1870).

Absolem, M. D.; died single.

Nancy Dalton; married first, Rufus A. Crockett, M. D.; second, B. H. Paschall, M. D.

Mary Jane; married J. K. Womack.

Charlotte Gallihue.

Robert Scales; died single.

Robin Sayers and Nancy Crockett, his wife, were both reared in Wythe county, Virginia. (The writer chances to know that they were related to Mrs. Maggie (Grayson) Williams, wife of Judge and General Samuel W. Williams, of Wytheville, Va. Samuel W. Williams served as Attorney-General for the state of Virginia, being elected in 1907 to this office. Gen. Williams is also a descendant of Mary (Dalton) Hughes (1748-1841).

Children of Robin Sayers and His Wife, Nancy Crockett

Sallie Elliot.

David.

Mary Beatty.

Crockett.

Abner Sayers was a cousin of this family.

Miss Annie Bell Crockett goes on to say: "One of my Crockett records says that Joseph Crockett married Mrs. Eliza Moore Woodson, the daughter of John and Mary Moore, of Albemarle county, Virginia. This Mary was a daughter of Matthew Jowett. The Jowett family were Huguenots. Mary Jowett Moore was a great aunt of Matthew Jowett, the eminent Kentucky artist.

Polly Crockett, the daughter of Joseph Crockett and his wife, Elizabeth Moore, married Bennett Henderson. Their daughter, Josephine Henderson, married Mr. Young, and they were parents of Gen. Bennett H. Young, of Louisville, Ky., who was Commander-in-Chief of Confederate veterans.

General Bennett Henderson Young descends from Thomas Henderson, who came to Jamestown, Va., in 1607. (See Henderson).

Miss Annie Bell Crockett says also that she has a family record which shows that Martha Martin, a niece of Gov. Alexander Martin, married Alfred Moore Scales, who was a nephew of Absolem Scales and the uncle of Gov. Alfred Moore Scales, of North Carolina.

James Scales Dalton

James Scales Dalton, son of Samuel A. Dalton and his wife, Mary Scales, was born not many miles from Madison, in Rockingham county. North Carolina, Aug. 1, 1835. At the beginning of the Civil war he enlisted and helped organize a company of infantry from Rockingham county, being later elected Lieutenant, and finally Captain. This was known as Company G., 45th North Carolina regiment. He served with honor and distinction at the Battle of Malvern Hill and at the Battle of the Wilderness besides other engagements. He was taken prisoner at the Battle of the Wilderness, and was imprisoned at Fort Delaware, where he remained until the close of the war.

After the war James Dalton settled at Reidsville, North Carolina, where for many years he was engaged in the manufacture of tobacco.

He married Maggie Reid, a daughter of John J. Reid and Margaret Winchester Reid, on Jan. 28, 1875, and lived in Reidsville, N. C., until his death in 1906. They had three children, Maggie Reid Dalton, who was born in Reidsville, Feb. 14, 1876; James S. Dalton, born Feb. 28, 1878; and William Reid Dalton, born July 20, 1884.

Maggie Reid Dalton married James Campbell Womack, April 25, 1894. From this union there was only one child, Margaret Rebecca Womack, born in Reidsville, North Carolina, Jan. 22, 1899. James C. Womack was the son of John Archibald Womack and his wife, Rebecca Brown. He was born at Pittsboro, N. C., and died July 26, 1901. Later, on Nov. 8, 1905, Maggie Reid Dalton married Dr. George W. Brittain, a druggist of Reidsville, N. C., where they now live (1919). They have no children.

James S. Dalton, born Feb. 24, 1878, died at Reidsville in 1904. He was never married. He was educated at Reidsville and at Oak Ridge Institute in Guilford county, N. C.

William Reid Dalton, son of James S. Dalton and his wife, Maggie Reid, was educated at Reidsville and at the University of North Carolina. Here he was an academic student until his brother's death in 1904. At that time he returned home. He worked in the insurance office of Mr. Francis Womack, of Reidsville, until January, 1909, when he returned to the University of North Carolina at Chapel Hill where he commenced a course in law. In the Spring of 1910 he passed successfully the examinations of the University Law School as well as those of the Supreme Court of North Carolina at Raleigh, and was admitted to the practice of law in 1910. He settled in his home town of Reidsville, N. C., where he at once formed a co-partnership with Mr. Julius Johnston of Yanceyville, N. C.,.and Mr. Allen D. Ivie of Leaksville, N. C., for the practice of law under the firm name of "Johnston, Ivie & Dalton," which continued until the death of Mr Johnston in 1914, after which William Reid Dalton practiced alone. He has served as City Attorney for several years, and he is local counsel for the Southern Railway Company since 1910.

He married Emma Mebane Staples, of Roanoke, Va., June 26, 1915. She is a daughter of Abram Penn Staples, Dean of the Law School of Washington and Lee University at Lexington, Virginia. He was formerly a prominent attorney at Roanoke, Virginia.

Two children have been born of this union, Wm. Reid Dalton, Jr., born Feb. 2, 1917; and Sarah Staples Dalton, born Aug. 24, 1918.

Reid Ancestry

Hugh Reid married Jemima Carmin, who lived in Pennsylvania. Their son, John Reid, was born in Baltimore, Md., Jan. 10, 1777; died July 3, 1844. He married Jane Dilworth, of Rockingham, N. C.

John Reid and his wife, Jane Dilworth, had a son, John Jackson Reid, born Jan. 15, 1817; died Aug. 14, 1853. He had only one child, Maggie Reid, who married James S. Dalton, and they were the parents of William Reid Dalton, attorney-at-law in Reidsville, N. C.

MOORE

Moore Coat of Arms

Argent, a moorcock sable, combed and wattled, gules. The crest is: On a tuft of grass, vert, a moorcock sable, combed and wattled, gules. The motto is: "Nihil utile quod no honestum."

This is the coat of arms as used by James Moore of Charleston in 1700. It is also the coat of arms of the Bernard Moore branch, which signifies that there is at least a remote connection between these two branches, of the family of Virginia and that of Charleston, S. C., of which Maurice Moore of North Carolina, in Colonial and Revolutionary times, was a representative. A sketch of his life can be found on page 47 (Brunswick) Wheeler's History of North Carolina. He came of illustrious ancestry. Maurice Moore served as Colonial Judge of North Carolina along with Martin Howard and Richard Henderson.

Generation I (In America)

Bernard Moore married Ann Catherine, eldest daughter of Governor Alexander Spottswood. Governor Spottswood lived in Orange county, Virginia, which adjoins Albemarle county. Bernard Moore was a member of the House of Burgesses in 1744. He was one of the "Knights of the Golden Horseshoe." They went over the Blue Ridge mountains in 1716.

Alexander Spottswood's wife was a niece and ward of James Butler, Duke of Ormand.

Generation II

Children of Bernard Moore and His Wife, Ann Catherine Spottswood:
William Moore, of Albemarle county, Va.

John Moore; married Anne Dandridge; died in Louisa county, Va., in 1777.

There may have been other children.

William Moore lived in Albemarle county, Va. His brother, John Moore, married Anne Dandridge (see pages 703, 704, Vol. II, "Prominent Virginia Families" by Dubillet). Since we are trying to carry in mind family connection, we state the fact that Anne Dandridge Redd, the wife of Samuel Dalton (1699-1802) was an own cousin of Anne Dandridge, wife of John Moore.

Mrs. Susan Letitia Rice Clotworthy, of Hillman, Ga., a descendant of Samuel Dalton and his wife, Anne, or, as she was often called, Nancy, which is another form of the name Anne, Anne Dandridge Redd; and also a descendant of Wm. Moore of Albemarle county, Va., through his son, Matthew Redd Moore, tells me that she has the will of John Moore and that he died in Louisa county, Va., in 1777.

We are told in the "Life of James Madison," by Caillard Hunt, on page 21, that at the christening of James Madison, our President, "John Moore, a kinsman of the young mother, was one of the sponsors." James Madison was born in 1751. The writer has old business papers of William Moore, of Albemarle county, Virginia. These papers are dropping to pieces with age.

Generation III

Children of William Moore, of Albemarle county, Virginia:

a. John; married Mary Jowett, a daughter of Matthew Jowett His son John married Martha, eldest daughter of John Harvie and his wife, who was a Gaines. This John Moore was the first clerk of the Superior Court of Oglethorpe county, Ga., 1793 (see "Georgians," by Gov. Gilmer).

b. William; married Mary Marks, of Albemarle county, Va.

c. Frances; wife of John Henderson.

d. Edward.

e. Matthew Redd; married Letitia Dalton.

f. ——— (Moore) Martin; of the Martin-Chiles-Page line.

g. ——— (Moore) Bullock.

h. ——— (Moore) Crockett.

i. ——— (Moore) McAlley; wife of Andrew McAlley.

John Moore McAlley, son of Andrew McAlley and his wife, ——— Moore, served in congress at the same time his cousin, Gabriel Moore, son of Matthew Redd Moore and his wife, Letitia Dalton, served in the Senate from Alabama, 1829-1835. Gabriel Moore was also Governor of Alabama.

Frances Moore, daughter of Wm. Moore, of Albemarle county, Virginia, married Captain John Henderson, whose Revolutionary service has been verified by the D. A. R. Her daughter, Lucy Patterson Henderson, married Thomas Lewis Gaines, son of Frances and Elizabeth Lewis Gaines. This Francis Gaines was a double first cousin of Capt. James Gaines, father of General Edmund Pendleton Gaines, hero of Lake Erie. Hon. John Wesley Gaines, of Nashville, Tenn., is a great-grandson of Capt. John Henderson and his wife, Francis Moore. John Wesley Gaines served the Hermitage district in Congress. We give later a certified copy of John Henderson's will.

Many Albemarle county records in reference to this Henderson branch are to be found in the Congressional Library at Washington. One of the descendants of Thomas Henderson, who came to Jamestown, Virginia, in 1607, settled in Albemarle county, Virginia. (See Henderson).

One of the daughters of William Moore, of Albemarle county, Virginia, married a Martin. Representatives of this family were Capt. William Martin, who married Rachel Dalton. Capt. John Martin of "Rock House" notoriety. and Gen. Joseph Martin. A living representative is Senator Thomas Staples Martin (1915).

One of the daughters of Wm. Moore, of Albemarle county, married a Bullock; another daughter married a Crockett. These two last are well-known Southern families.

Matthew Redd Moore, son of William Moore, of Albemarle county, was born there in 1738. When nineteen years old he was married to Letitia Dalton, daughter of Samuel Dalton (1699-1802) and his wife, Anne, or Nancy, Dandridge Redd. This marriage took place in 1757 when Letitia Dalton was only fifteen years of age. They settled in Stokes county, North Carolina, at the foot of Sauraton mountain, where he owned a thousand acres of land, including Morris Knob. Samuel Dalton died in 1802 at the home of his grandson, Matthew Moore, Jr., and of his own daughter, Letitia (Dalton) Moore. This daughter, Letitia, died in 1838, aged ninety-six years. They are buried at the foot of Sauraton mountain. Her husband, Matthew Moore, died before she did (see North Carolina Historical and Genealogical Register, J. R. B. Hathaway, Editor, Edenton, N. C., Vol. I No. I; Jan., 1901, page 306; also Vol. 1, No. 3, July, 1901).

Some record is given of Matthew Moore's service in Vol. 10, The Colonial Records of North Carolina, page 251: "From M. S. Records in office of Secretary of State. Proceedings of the Safety Committee in Surry county, Wednesday, Sept. 20, 1775." Among the number mentioned was Matthew Moore.

From M. S. Records. page 255, in office of Secretary of State, Thursday, Sept. 21, 1775:

"Resolved, That for a Committee of Secrecy and Intelligence, this Committee has truly elected John Hamlin, Ch.; Joseph Walton, Joseph Winston. Richard Goode, Jesse Walton, Joseph Phillips, James Doak and Matthew Moore.

In Wheeler's History of North Carolina, page 407, it can be seen that this son of Matthew Redd Moore often served in the Senate of North Carolina.

Wiiliam Moore, of this generation, married Mary Marks, of Locust Hill, Albemarle county, Va. Mary Marks was a daughter of Captain John Marks, whose Revolutionary service is established, and his wife, Mrs. Lucy (Merewether) Lewis, whose first husband was Col. William Lewis, by whom she had Merewether Lewis (see page 75, American Monthly Magazine for February, 1913).

Generation IV

Children of Matthew Redd Moore and his wife, Letitia Dalton:

Samuel; married Elizabeth Gaines, sister of Edmund Pendleton Gaines.

——— Moore; married Susan Martin, sister of General Wm. Martin, of Williamson county, Tenn., and of Sally Martin Hughes.

Gabriel; was Governor of Alabama.

Matthew Redd, Jr.

Mary; married Ambrose Gaines.

There may have been others.

Mrs. Susan Letitia Rice Clotworthy, of Hillman, Georgia, is historian of the family. She is a great-granddaughter of Samuel Moore and his wife, Elizabeth Gaines. Elizabeth Gaines was a sister of Edmund Pendleton Gaines, hero of Lake Erie. Mrs. Clotworthy is of double Gaines blood (see "Gaines").

John Baird Clotworthy was born in Dunover county, County Down, Ireland, Jan. 16, 1842. He married Susan Letitia Rice, Oct. 12, 1869. She was born in Sullivan county, Tenn., Sept 13, 1848.

Children of Susan Letitia Rice and her husband, John Baird Clotworthy:

Charles William; born Aug. 21, 1871, married Mabelle Affleck, of Westfield, New Jersey.

Hugh Alexander; born Jan. 26, 1878, married Salome G. Bell, of Aikin, S. C. No children.

John Baird, Jr.; born at Westfield, N. J., Aug. 21, 1893.

Children of Charles William Clotworthy and his wife, Mabelle Affleck:

Charles Melville; born Dec. 28, 1895.

William Rice; born Dec. 28, 1897.

Russell Gaines; born Feb. 3, 1899.

Leram Affleck; born Jan. 10, 1905.

Virginia; died young.

Mary Esther; born July 14, 1912.

One of the sons of Matthew Redd Moore and his wife, Letitia Dalton, married his first cousin, Susan Martin, daughter of Captain, later Rev., William Martin and his wife, Rachel Dalton, who was daughter of Samuel Dalton (1699-1802), of Mayo. Captain William Martin was born in Albemarle county, Va., but came in early life to Pittsylvania county. Va., and during the Revolutinoary war had his family move to Stokes county, N. C., to be near the family of his brother, Col. Jack Martin, of "Rockhouse." Susan Martin Moore lived at Snow Creek, Stokes county, N. C. The writer has splendidly written letters of this woman. These letters were written to her brother, Gen. William Martin, of Williamson county, Tenn. They prove her to have been cultured, refined and sympathetic. Their mother, Rachel Dalton Martin, lived to be very old. An old letter written from the home of Gen. Joseph Winston in Stokes county, N. C., in 1831, by one of her daughters, Nancy (Martin) Hughes, speaks of Rachel (Dalton) Martin being "very well for one of her age." Capt. William Martin had died in Stokes county, N. C., in 1803.

Gabriel Moore, son of Matthew Redd Moore and his wife, Letitia (Dalton) Moore, had the best educational advantages of the day. He was in college at Chapel Hill, N. C. In Wheeler's History of N. C. it can be seen that he served in the Senate of N. C. He moved to Alabama, near Huntsville. He became Governor of Alabama, and he served in U. S. Senate. He was a wealthy farmer and lived on his plantation near Huntsville, Ala. Later in life, when people had grown wild over the possibilities of Texas, he moved to Texas, and here he died. The writer has many letters which prove the intimacy of Gabriel Moore and the family of her grandfather, Capt. John Hughes (1776-1860). And she has letters which show that Gen. William Martin, of Williamson county, Tenn., her great uncle, was often on visits to Gov. Moore's family.

Matthew Redd Moore, Jr., son of Matthew Redd Moore and his wife, Letitia (Dalton) Moore, often served in the Senate of N. C. (see Wheeler's History of N. C.—Stokes County). Mrs. George C. Goodman (nee Anna Moore Wilfong), of Mooresville N. C., enters the order of Colonial Dames of America through William Moore, Jr., who came from Albemarle county, Va., to North Carolina and became Justice of Quorum in 1769.

Mrs. John L. Cox

Lorena (Butler) Cox is daughter of Matthew Moore Butler and his wife, Mary Taylor Dulaney. Matthew Moore Butler was a son of William Fields Butler and his wife, Elizabeth Gaines. And Elizabeth Gaines was a daughter of Ambrose Gaines and his wife, Mary Moore.

Mary Moore was a sister of Gov. Gabriel Moore, and she was daughter of Matthew Redd Moore and his wife, Letitia Dalton. And Letitia Dalton was daughter of Samuel Dalton (1699-1802), of Mayo, who lived in Rockingham county, N. C.

Ambrose Gaines fought at the Battle of King's Mountain during the Revolutionary war. This establishes Mrs. Cox's eligibilty to membership to National Society Daughters of the American Revolution. The mother of Mrs. Cox, Mary Taylor Dulaney, was a daughter of Dr. William Robert Dulaney and his wife, Mary Taylor. Both her grandfather and great-grandfather Dulaney served in the Legislature of Tennessee. Her grandmother, Mary (Taylor) Dulaney, was a daughter of Gen. Nathaniel Taylor, who was with Andrew Jackson at the

Battle of Horseshoe, and at Battle of New Orleans. Gov. and U. S. Senator Robert L. Taylor was first cousin of Mrs. Cox's mother.

We have already spoken of Gen. Edmund Pendleton Gaines' relationship to this family.

John I. Cox served in the Tennessee Legislature prior to the time he was Governor of Tennessee (1905-1906). He was later again a member of the Legislature. Among other things, while governor, he brought about an immigration convention in Nashville in which governors of other Southern states took part. The writer, Lucy H. Horton, was interested in this convention, because she, at that time, was serving as chairman of the D. A. R. State Committee on Immigration. Governor Cox is now (1920) postmaster at Bristol, Tennessee, and has been for four years. Mrs. Cox owns some valuable family relics, jewelry which was the gift of Governor Gabriel Moore to one of her ancestors. She also has a miniature of Gov. Moore, and a copy of the will of Matthew Moore, which is long and interesting.

Generation IV

Jane Dalton, daughter of Samuel Dalton (1699-1802) and his wife, Anne Dandridge Redd, of Mayo, married Joseph Winston, who afterward became a Major in the American Revolutionary army.

Major Joseph Winston was born in Virginia in 1746, and was distinguished for gallantry in frontier war with the Indians. In 1776 he removed to Surrey county, North Carolina, serving in the campaign against the Cherokee Indians.

Among field officers appointed by the Provincial Congress, which met at Halifax, April 4, 1776, we find Joseph Winston of Surrey county, made 1st Major, and Jesse Walton made 2nd Major (see Wheeler's History of North Carolina, page 81). At the Battle of King's Mountain, Oct. 7, 1780, as Major with Colonel McDowell and Colonel Sevier, Major Winston commanded the right wing in that fierce and bloody battle. Isaac Shelby, also, took a conspicuous part in that engagement.

Major Joseph Winston was in command of a part of Col. Cleveland's men. Cleveland's men were from the counties of Wilkes and Surrey, N. C. No officer in this battle was commander-in-chief. The official report was signed by William Campbell, Isaac Shelby and Benjamin Cleveland.

Benjamin Cleveland commanded more men at Battle of King's Mountain than did Col. Shelby or Lieut.-Col. John Sevier or Col. Mc-Dowell. Col. William Campbell was in command of a larger force than either one of these (see page 389-91, Andrew Jackson and Early Tennessee History by S. G. Heiskel).

Col. Cleveland is buried on his old plantation in North Carolina. One of his children married a child of Gen. Joseph Martin, and one of his daughters married Gen. Thomas J. Rusk, who was U. S. Senator from Texas for ten years. The Congressional Monument at King's Mountain was dedicated Oct. 7, 1909, upon the anniversary of the battle, and bears the names of these patriots.

Joseph Winston was the first Senator from Stokes county after it was cut off from Surry. Stokes county was formed in 1789. He occasionally served in the legislature as late as 1812. He was a member of Congress, 1793-1795, and in 1803-1807. He lived near Germantown, and died in 1814, leaving a large family (see Wheeler's History of N. C. II, pages 148 and 404).

In recognition of his services in the Revolutionary war, he was voted by the N. C. Legislature a sword. This sword passed first to his son, Gen. Joseph Winston, whose wife, by the way, was Lettie Hughes, and later to his grandson, Col. John Hughes Winston, of Platte county, Mo. In Major Joseph Winston's will he gives this sword to his son, Joseph, with the injunction, "Never to use it except in the defense of his country."

In the home of his son, Col. Joseph Winston, later General of Militia, in Stokes county, N. C., hung a full length portrait in oil of his father, Major Joseph Winston, in regimentals. This portrait later hung in the home of Col. John Hughes Winston in Platte county, Mo. Beneath the portrait was a table on which was placed this sword, given by the N. C. Legislature, and another Winston sword, crossed. Beside the swords lay gauntlets trimmed in gold fringe, which were worn by Major Joseph Winston during the Revolutionary war. These things passed into the hands of Mrs. Frederick Flower, of New York, granddaughter of Col. John Hughes Winston. All were placed by her in a building in New York among historical relics. This building some years ago was burned.

Major Joseph Winston died in 1814. His will is dated April 12, 1814. In this will he named the following children:

Robert is given lands and personal property.

Joseph W. gets his homestead, etc.

Sally receives his "precious bureau," etc.

Lewis gets slaves, his watch, etc.

Samuel gets his diamond shoe buckles, etc.

Fontaine gets his gold sleeve buttons, etc.

William is mentioned, and he, with Joseph and Lewis, are made executors. Eight thousand acres of land are to be divided.

He concludes with these lines:

> "My suffering time shall soon be o'er,
> And I shall weep and sigh no more,
> My ransomed soul shall soar away
> To sing God's praise in endless day."

The town of Winston-Salem was named in honor of Major Joseph Winston. His father and his father's brother lived awhile in Albemarle county, Va., near the Martins and Clarkes, among whom later there were intermarriages.

Generation V

Gen. Joseph Winston was the son of Major Joseph Winston, of King's Mountain fame, and his wife, Jane Dalton, who was daughter of

Samuel Dalton (1699-1802), of Mayo, and his wife, Anne Dandridge Redd.

Joseph Winston, Jr., was born in Stokes county, North Carolina, about 1790. He sometimes represented Stokes county in the legislature. He was a member of the legislature in 1831 (see Wheeler's History of North Carolina). His leaving home for Raleigh at this time is spoken of in a letter written by his wife's mother, Nancy (Martin) Hughes, to her son, Archelaus Hughes, in Williamson county, Tennessee. The writer has this old letter (see "Martin").

Joseph Winston was Major in a North Carolina regiment stationed at Norfolk, Virginia, in War of 1812, and served to the end. He was appointed Brigadier General of Militia and advanced to Major-General. He married about 1813, a cousin of his, Letitia Dalton Hughes. She was often called by the family "Letty." She was a daughter of Archelaus Hughes, Jr., and his wife, Nancy Martin. She was granddaughter of Colonel Archelaus Hughes of the Revolution and his wife, Mary Dalton. On the maternal side she was granddaughter of Captain and Rev. William Martin, of the Revolution, and his wife, Rachel Dalton. Rachel (Dalton) Martin was still living in 1831.

General Joseph W. Winston moved with his family from Stokes county, North Carolina, in 1839 to Platte county, Missouri, when this was known as the Platte Purchase. He is supposed to have been drowned in the Missouri river at his town of Winston, above Parkville. He was last seen there. His wife died in Nov., 1855.

Generation VI

Colonel John Hughes Winston, son of General Joseph W. Winston and his wife, Letty Hughes, was born in Stokes county, North Carolina, Jan. 22, 1815. His mother named him John Hughes for a favorite uncle, Captain John Hughes, of Patrick county, Virginia, who afterward moved to Williamson county, Tenn. These two branches were doubly related. Two brothers, Archelaus, Jr., and John Hughes, sons of Col. Archelaus Hughes, married two sisters, Nancy and Sallie Martin—and they were cousins. All were descendants of Samuel Dalton, of Mayo (see "Martin").

John Hughes Winston went to Platte county, Missouri, in 1837 and settled seven miles southeast of Platte City. Dec. 4, 1839, he married Elizabeth, daughter of William S. Debbs and his wife, Lydia Kennedy, who died Dec. 1, 1886. John Hughes Winston was for many years a Major in a Platte county militia regiment, and when the war between the States broke out his Southern enthusiasm and military qualifications pointed him out as the proper person to raise a regiment in Platte county for the Confederate states. In July and August, 1861, a military camp was formed near his residence, called Camp Cain. Here a regiment was organized with companies under command of Captains Chiles, Chrisman, Chestnut, McKennie, Miller and others. They hastened to join Price and took part in seige and surrender of Lexington. This regiment was at Pea Ridge, Corinth and other important fields. In the Spring of 1864, Col. Winston, by order of Gen. Price, returned to his home to raise recruits and to help them on their way South. While on this duty he was arrested by a detail of Federal troops, and was kept a military prisoner until the close of the war, or about twenty months. He was often threatened with death as a spy. He served in the State Senate for four years. He was a man of commanding person, military bearing, sound judgment and unblemished honor. Mrs. Elizabeth Winston was a tall and dignified lady, formal and precise in her address, polite and genial in her conversation, and amiable in her disposition.

Children of Col. John Hughes Winston

II. Lydia Winston was born Aug. 14, 1843; married Feb. 2, 1865, to Milton E. Clark, a banker of Leavenworth, Kansas. She spends much of her time in Massachusetts. Children:

a. Nellie E. Clark was born Dec. 13, 1866, married Sept. 8, 1892, to Lieut. Stephen M. Hadons.

b. Cora Clark; born Aug. 6, 1868, married Mr. Pullion, of New York.

c. Hilda Clark; born Dec. 16, 1873; married Frederick Flower, a banker of New York on Wall Street. He is a nephew of Governor Flower.

2. Cora A. Winston; born Sept. 17, 1844; married May 2, 1864, Judge William H. Woodson, who was born Jan. 16, 1840. She was a woman of rare charm and grace of manner. Her husband was distantly related to her. He is a son of Samuel Hughes Woodson, of Independence, Missouri; was circuit Judge and member of congress; city attorney of Liberty, Mo., 1867; prosecuting attorney of Clay county, 1876-80; and judge of probate, 1884-90. He commenced the practice of law in Platte county, Mo., in 1864, and was soon at the head of his profession. He enlisted early in General Price's army, and was assistant adjutant general of the Missouri state guard. Children:

a. Winston Woodson; born Aug. 29, 1865; died Nov. 18, 1891.

b. Samuel Hughes Woodson; born March 4, 1867; died Oct 7, 1883.

c. Elizabeth T.; born Oct. 17, 1870.

d. William H.; born Feb. 21, 1874.

e. Arch L.; born Jan. 8, 1876.

f. Lydia K.; born Oct. 14, 1877.

g. Joseph L. A.; born May 23, 1880.

h. Everard M.; born Dec. 27, 1882.

3. Harry C. Winston, after graduating at William Jewell College, Columbia Law School, and at Washington, D. C., Law School, settled at Kansas City, Missouri, where he is succeeding at the practice of law.

4. George F. Winston, graduated at Wm. Jewel College and took a course in law. He is practicing in Kansas City, Missouri.

5. Alg. Sidney Winston. On April 10, 1883, married Amanda, daughter of James Duncan and his wife, Sarah Tracy. Children:

   a. Joseph.
   b. Harry.
   c. Bessie.
   d. John.

II. Louisa Winston was born in North Carolina. She married Mr. Frost, who died in North Carolina. She came to Platte county, Missouri, in 1839, bringing with her two children:

1. Elizabeth Frost married Col. John Pitt. Col. Pitt died June 19, 1884. Mrs. Pitt was a handsome and lovely woman, graceful and fascinating in manner. Col. Pitt was a man of genial manners and sparkling wit. He represented his county in the legislature, and the district in a constitutional convention. They left four children:

   (a) James F. Pitt; a leading lawyer of St. Joseph, Missouri.

   (b) Lula; born Sept. 13, 1853; married Feb. 28, 1881, Dr. Guildford Yorkom, who was born in 1844. Children: Helen Yorkom, born Oct. 31, 1882.

   (c) Katie; born 1856, died Dec. 4, 1889. She married George M. Dameron, Sept. 21, 1876. Children:

Warren Dameron.

   (d) Lettie Pitt; married R. Weller. Children:

John C., James, Elizabeth.

2. James E. Frost; married Jennie E. Almond, Dec. 19, 1859. Children:

Addie Frost.

III. Matthew Hughes Winston, born 1830; died March 25, 1864. He never married.

IV. Joseph Winston; died 1864. He went to California to live. He was elected probate judge and died in office.

V. Samuel Winston; married Letitia, daughter of Ed. M. Dobson, March 14, 1878. He served as a captain in his brother's regiment. He was captured by the enemy and served a long imprisonment. His children live in Jackson county, Missouri.

VI. Ann Powell Winston; married Dr. Charles Macey, who died in 1847. They had been married just one year when she died, leaving him with one child, Joseph Winston Macey.

Later Dr. Macey married a cousin of his first wife who had acted as bridesmaid at his first marriage, Jeancy Hughes Neill. Of this marriage there was one issue, Charles Hughes Macey. Charles H. Macey was attending college in Kentucky when the war between the States broke out. He joined the Confederate army and was killed at the battle of Perryville. Joseph Winston Macey, the elder brother, was also a Confederate soldier. He married a Miss Oldham and lives in California.

The second wife of Dr. Macey was an own aunt to Mrs. Ryland Todhunter, of Lexington, Missouri, whom she reared. Mrs. Macey's second husband, Mr. Samuel Wilson, of Lexington, Missouri, was a man of immense wealth (something of Hughes-Winston genealogy can be seen in History of Platte county, Mo.).

We will copy extracts from a book written by Mrs. Elizabeth Winston Campbell Hendrichs, of Washington, D. C., showing further Hughes-Winston connection.

These references were furnished me by U. S. Senator E. W. Pettus of Alabama, in September, 1906.

1. Isaac Winston, the Saxon emigrant; about 1740 he married in Virginia, Mary Ann Fontaine. Their son, Peter Winston, married Elizabeth Powell. Their son, John Winston, married Miss Austin. Their daughter, Mary Ann Winston, married Peter De Noville. Their daughter, Susie Bright, married Mr. Hughes.

2. Sarah Winston, a granddaughter of Isaac Winston, the emigrant, and mother of Patrick Henry, had a daughter named Lucy Henry who married Valentine Wood. And their daughter married Judge Peter Johnston. And their son, Charles Johnston, married Emely Preston. And their daughter, Elizabeth, married Judge Robert Hughes.

3. William Winston, one of the emigrants, about 1730 married Sarah Dabney, who was the mother of Judge Edmund Winston and Sarah Winston, the mother of Patrick Henry. William Winston and his wife, Sarah Dabney, had another daughter named Mary Ann, who married Dr. John Walker. Their son, also named Dr. John Walker, married Susan Christian. Their daughter, Maria Walker, married Dr. M. Spencer. And their daughter, Ann Spencer, married B. Nowlan. And their daughter, Virginia Nowlan, married John Hughes.

We will quote from letter of U. S. Senator E. W. Pettus, of Alabama:

"So far as I am informed, my first known ancestor, on the Winston side, was Isaac Winston, of York, England. Three of his grandsons, Isaac, William and Anthony, settled in Hanover county, Virginia. Isaac Winston, the Saxon, was my first American ancestor and lived in Hanover county, Virginia, before 1700. His son, Anthony, married Alice Taylor, Sept. 29, 1723, and lived in Hanover and had a son named Anthony, born Nov. 27, 1752, and married, and the last Anthony was my grandfather. He moved to Buckingham county, Va., and married Kesia Jones in 1776. My mother was Alice Taylor Winston, and my father was John Pettus, of Fluvana county, Va. My grandfather, Anthony Winston, moved to Davidson county, Tenn., with his family and lived near "The Hermitage." Later in life he followed his children to Alabama.

"Edmund Winston, of Franklin, Tenn., who died last year, was a son of my uncle, Edmund Winston, of Lagrange, Tennessee." Then Senator Pettus adds by way of P. S.—"General Wade Hampton's brother was a Preston, and she was of the Winston stock."

Edmund Winston, of Franklin, Tenn., referred to in this letter, married Josephine Cocke, of Chattanooga, Tenn., who came of a well known Virginia family. His father, Edmund Winston, of Lagrange,

Tenn., was a fine type of the ante bellum Southern gentleman.

Old people in the family often speak of the Winston-Hughes-Hampton connection.

Edmund W. Pettus

Edmund W. Pettus served Alabama in United States senate. He was a man of ability, and his character was such that he held the friendship of Senator Pugh over whom he was elected to the U. S. senate. Indeed, the friendship of Pugh, Morgan and Pettus, and the combined effort of these men for public good, caused them to be spoken of sometimes as "Alabama's great triumvirate."

Pettus was a man who was largely quoted by newspaper men about Washington. He was held in great veneration by them. "But his quaint old-fashioned simplicity, his unfailing good nature, his constant droll humor, terse and frank speech, combined to make him a frequent source of interest, especially to those whose mission it was to supply anecdotes of public men." Sometimes these publications were a bit trying on him, but with his unfailing philosophy he would say, "Well, I suppose I am legitimate prey".

He by no means escaped life's sorrows. His son, Frank Pettus, who was an honored leader among strong men in Alabama, died in the prime of life. His beloved wife, the companion of his youth and old age, passed over the river before him. Only a few months before her death he had spoken of her as "the handsomest 88-year-old girl in the land." Senator Pettus was a man trusted in his larger sphere just as he had at home been honored, trusted and beloved, a man to inspire fresh faith in human nature.

John A. Winston, Governor of Alabama 1853-57, was closely related to U. S. Senator Pettus, of Alabama. Winston county, Alabama, was named for the Governor.

Generation IV.

Matilda, daughter of Samuel Dalton (1699-1802), of Mayo, and his wife, Anne (Dandridge) Redd, married Jonathan Hanby, one of Francis Marion's lieutenants. Hanby is sometimes spoken of in history as Francis Marion's "right hand."

Hanby first joined Marion when he had comparitively few men under his command. Sometimes Marion had 400 or 500 men under his command. Not only had he the British to fight, but the Tories as well. Nowhere in the whole country was the proportion of Tories as large as in South Carolina.

After Gen. Greene succeeded Gen. Gates, Lieut.-Col. Lee and his legion served under Gen. Marion.

Jonathan Hanby and his wife made Charleston, S. C., their home for a time. Here their friendship for Francis Marion was renewed. After Marion was past fifty years of age he married Miss Mary Videau, one of Charleston's most attractive daughters. She, like Marion, was of

Huguenot stock, and was wealthy. We note the fact that Prince Murat, of France, said that he found the "best and most cultured society in Charleston, South Carolina, that he had ever met this side of the Atlantic." We quote this because it gives some insight into Southern culture in the early days (see Confederate Veteran for March, 1915, page 116).

Judge Joshua Caldwell, of Knoxville, Tenn., who was related to this Hanby family, told the writer of a portrait of Matilda (Dalton) Hanby. This portrait was in the home of some family connection in Charleston at the time of Matilda Hanby's death. Several descendants were contending hotly for possession of the portrait when, in jerking it around, a slip of paper fell from the frame. On this paper was written in Matilda Hanby's own handwriting directions about the disposition of the portrait. Judge Caldwell descends from Matilda Hanby's sister, Mary Dalton Hughes.

Generation IV

Virginia Dalton, daughter of Samuel Dalton (1699-1802), of Mayo, married a brother of Captain Jonathan Hanby.

We know from old family papers that some of the Hanby connection lived in Patrick county, Va. The names of several Hanby men are given in the old Masonic Chapter minutes when Capt. John Hughes (1776-1860) was master of The Way To Be Happy Lodge. Capt. Hughes was made master of this lodge when little more than twenty years of age. He moved from Patrick county, Va., to Williamson county, Tennessee, in 1828. We learn by an old letter written to him from Patrick county, Va., by his lawyer—the name is torn, but it looks like Sandfin—that a lawsuit, Hughes against Hanby, was in progress. In this letter Mr. Sandfin says something about notifying Mrs. Hanby, and he ha† written to Jonesville, N. C., and took Col. Kelley's deposition. He says, "Major Carter attended taking of deposition to cross-examine." He speaks of Mrs. Hanby's being Major Carter's daughter. Then he says: "It is far from me to wish to be the instrument of promoting or of increasing differences between connections and once confidential friends. On the contrary, my desire is now, and ever was, as far as my feeble efforts would extend, to endeavor to conciliate." This old letter bears the date May 7, 1832, and is quite a long and friendly letter. One thing he says makes us appreciate the frequent mails of to-day: "The Western mail only comes here once a fortnight (on Wednesday)." And the market of that time was in strong contrast with to-day (1917). He says, "Everything we have for market here is very low indeed—corn 716 per barrel, bacon 6¼ cents per pound."

When the heirs of Samuel Dalton (1699-1802) employed William L. Yancey to look after their interest in the estate of Lord John Dalton in Great Britain, one of the heirs mentioned was Jonathan Carter.

Samuel Dalton was married to Nancy, or Anne (which is one and the same name) Dandridge Redd in 1740, the year in which Gov. Spottswood died.

George Redd married Ann Dandridge. They were parents of Ann Dandridge Redd, wife of Samuel Dalton, of Mayo.

On page 166, Vol. 1, of "Old Churches and Families in Virginia," by Meade, we can see that Gov. Spottswood's daughter, Catherine, married Bernard Moore. Another daughter, Dorothea, married Nathaniel Dandridge. On pages 703-704 of "Prominent Virginia Families" by Dubillet, Vol. 2, we learn something of Bernard Moore's marriage to Ann Catherine, eldest daughter of Gov. Alexander Spottswood; and that Gov. Spottswood's wife was a niece and ward of James Butler, Duke of Ormand. Bernard Moore was a member of the House of Burgesses in 1716. One of their children, John Moore, married Annie Dandridge.

George Redd's wife was Annie Dandridge, a daughter of Nathaniel Dandridge and his wife, Dorothea Spottswood.

George Redd and his wife, Annie Dandridge, were parents of Annie Dandridge Redd, wife of Samuel Dalton (1699-1802), of Mayo.

William Moore, of Albemarle county, Va., and his son, Matthew Moore, who married Letitia, daughter of Samuel Dalton (1699-1802), descend from Bernard Moore and his wife, Ann Catherine Spottswood. In Virginia and throughout the South cousins often married each other

Members of this family of Redd intermarried with the Woodsons of Goochland county, Va. (see page 160, Virginia County Records, 1909). Samuel Dalton (1699-1802) and his wife, Anne, or Nancy, as she was sometimes called, have descendants who have intermarried with the Woodsons since early colonial times.

MARTIN

Coat of Arms

Ancient Arms of Martin.

Ar. two bars gu. Crest-out of a mural crown vert, a talbot's head eared and langued gu. Collared of the first.

Motto: "Sure and steadfast."

The coat of arms of Colonel John Martin and of our immigrant ancestor, Joseph Martin, of Caroline county, Virginia, is: Gules, a chevron between three crescents argent (see page 89, Crozier's General Armory). (In painting, place this beneath the Ancient Arms of Martin.)

In the early years of the eighteenth century two kinsmen, Colonel John Martin and Joseph Martin, came from Great Britain to live in Caroline county, Virginia. The fathers of these two men were brothers.

Col. John Martin

Col. John Martin was a member of the House of Burgesses from Caroline county, Virginia, at the sessions of Nov., 1738, and May, 1740; and for King William county, where he later lived, at the sessions of 1752, '53, '54, '55, and '56. He died in 1756 (see page 198, Virginia Magazine of History and Biography, for October, 1905). From order books of Caroline county court proceedings it can be seen that a deed was recorded October 17, 1752, from George and John Martin, of the City of Bristol, merchants, by John Martin, Jr., gentlemen of Virginia. George and John Martin of the City of Bristol, merchants, were brothers of Joseph Martin, of Virginia (see page 409, Annual Report of the American Historical Association for the year 1893. See also note at foot of page. Col. John Martin and Joseph Martin married into the same family. This we shall prove later.

While Col. John Martin moved from Caroline county to King William county, Va., Joseph Martin moved from the same county to Albemarle county, Va. Of him we shall write later. With him went Thomas Martin. one of the sons of Col. John Martin. We see in the Genealogy of the Lewis Family in America, by William Ferrell Lewis, on page 360, that this Thomas Martin was the father of Major John

Martin, of Albemarle, Va., who married Elizabeth Lewis in 1775.

It can be seen (pages 197, 198, 199, Virginia Magazine of History and Biography, for October, 1905) that Col. John Martin, of Caroline county, and Joseph, brother of George Martin, merchant of Bristol, England, were close... .... Martin, of Withy Bush House, County Pembroke. Col. John Martin is the brother spoken of in Sparks Martin's will. One can see a copy of this will on page 197 of magazine referred to above. It reads as follows:

"All my manor of Pindergast, with all Royalties, Profits, etc., from lands in County Pembroke, Haverfordwest County, Middlesex, City of Bristol, or elsewhere in Great Britain, to my sister, Elizabeth Phelps, for life, subject to charges made upon certain of my estate through the will of my late wife, Martha Martin, to be held in trust by Right Honorable Richard Philipps, Lord Milford of Kingdom of Ireland, and the Right Honorable William (Edwards) Lord Kensington, of Kingdom of Ireland, to preserve to her use the said estates and after her to her son Thomas Phelps, and oldest son in succession, failing him, to John Phelps, second son of my said sister Elizabeth, and his heirs, failing him, to my brother Henry, who went to Virginia in America many years ago, and eldest son in succession, failing him, to my brother, John Martin, who also went to Virginia many years ago. Whoever inherits to take the name and arms of Martin. To my housekeeper, Mary Probert, five pounds a year for life. To Elizabeth Probert, her sister, five pounds a year for life. To Martha Jones, five pounds a year for life. Executrix, Elizabeth Phelps. Witnesses: Thos. Ormes, Junior; Hannah Wills, Joseph Wills, all of Charles Square, Hoxton."

At the time of the American Revolution some, or all, of Col. John Martin's sons were residents of Great Brittain, or were Tories. A petition dated January 12. 1784. from James, Lord Clifden, and Edmund Perry, Esq., Speaker of the Irish House of Commons; and a petition from George Martin, merchant of Bristol England, a brother of Joseph Martin, of Virginia, to the same end, was made to the Virginia House of Delegates in behalf of Lucia, eldest daughter of John Martin, Esq., wife of Lord Clifden, and Patty, youngest daughter of the above mentioned John Martin, wife of Edmund Pery, Viscount Pery, Speaker of the House of Commons of Ireland 1771-1785. This petition was in regard to a certain estate which was escheated.

In the Virginia Gazette for December 8-15, 1738, is advertised a reward for the return of a silver pint cup, fluted on both sides, which had been stolen from Col. John Martin, of Caroline county. It had engraved on it his coat of arms, "a chevron between three half moons" (see also page 89, Crozier's General Armory-Gules, a chevron between three crescents argent).

Col. John Martin married Martha Burwell, a kinswoman of the Page family (see page 220. The Old South, by Thomas Nelson Page).

At "Clifton," in Caroline county, is her tomb with the following inscription (see W. and M. Q., XI, 146; also Virginia Magazine of History and Biography for Oct. 1905, page 199):

> "Interred beneath this stone,
> lies the body of Mrs.
> Martha Martin, wife of Col.
> John Martin, of Caroline
> County, and daughter of
> Lewis Burwell, Esq., of Gloss-
> ter County, who departed this
> life the 27th of May, 1738, in
> the 36th year of her age, and left
> three sons and four daughters."

Col. John Martin's kinsman, Joseph Martin, first of Caroline county, later of Albemarle county, Va., married Susanna Chiles, a descendant of Col. John Page, founder of the Page family in Virginia. Thus we see that these two men married into the same family.

The celebrated English portrait painter, George Romney, who was born in Dalton, on the coast of Cumberland, Dec. 15, 1734, gave to the world gems in his line of work. "He painted many ladies as allegorical subjects. One of his pictures shows Caroline, Viscountess Clifden and Lady Elizabeth Spencer, afterward Countess of Pembroke, as 'Beauty and the Arts.' " The latter was a reigning beauty. Walpole wrote of her, "Lady Pembroke alone, at the head of the Countesses, was the picture of majestic modesty." In this picture Viscountess Clifden is seen sketching a Greek model, while the Countess of Pembroke is playing on a harp. Viscountess Clifden was the mother of Lord Clifden, Lucia Martin's husband.

Origin of Martin

Col. John Martin and his kinsman Joseph Martin, both of Caroline county, Va., who came to America in the early years of the eighteenth century, were descended from the Barons or Cemmæs, or Kemeys.

Eleanor Lexington in the Nashville American of Aug. 28, 1904, tells us that "The first Baron of Cemmæs was Martin de Tours (born 1030), who came over from Normandy with William the Conqueror and made conquest of Cemmæs, or Kemeys, in Pembroke county, England, about 1077. He was also made Lord of Combe-Martin, of Martinshoe, in the northern part of Devon. (His son, Baron Robert Fitz-Martin, married Maud Peverell).

"Martin de Tours founded a monastery for Benedictine monks near Cardegan. This institution was endowed with lands by Robert Fitz-Martin, son of the founder, Martin de Tours, and his sucessors were suummoned to the King's Council as Barons of Cemmæs, and continued to be Lords of the English Parliament. The third Baron married Augharad, daughter of Rhys, Prince of Wales. More than one knight, or man-at-arms, are recorded in the Roll of Battle Abbey as bearing the name Martin."

It is perhaps superfluous to explain of what the Roll of Battle Abbey consisted. On Oct. 4, 1066, A. D., the Battle of Hastings was fought, and William the Norman was seated on the throne of England, under the historic title of William the Conqueror. Close by the field of Hastings, William caused a stately pile to be erected which was named Battle Abbey, in commemoration of his victory. A roll, or catalogue, was prepared in which was carefully recorded the names and titles of the Norman chivalry who had followed William's banner in the enterprise. This was the famous Roll of Battle, or "Battle Abbey." It has been of inestimable service to the herald, the genealogist, and the historian.

Some portions of the Abbey still remain. Battle Abbey was dedicated to St. Martin.

Eleanor Lexington says that "the patron saint of the family is St. Martin, the son of a Roman military tribune, who was born at Sabarda, a city in Hungary, about 316 A. D. The saint attained great celebrity on account of his sanctity. The festival of St. Martin, which occurs Nov. 11, was instituted by Pope Martin about 650 A. D. Upon that day casks of new wine were tapped. Our English ancestors kept the feast by the consummation of roasted goose. The old tradition is that St. Martin hid himself on acconut of his unwillingness to become a Bishop, but his retreat was discovered through a goose. It would be well for Martin descendants in this country to keep this feast by the consummation of roasted goose. The writer herself has celebrated Nov. 11 by having the family enjoy roast goose at dinner.

No less than seven churches in London and Westminster are dedicated to St. Martin.

In the reign of King John, in 1208, the town of Newport was incorporated by a charter granted by William Martin, Lord of Kemes.

Newport Castle, founded by Martin de Tours, is believed to have been completed by his great-grandson, Sir William Martin, son of William Martin, who married the daughter of Lord Rhys Ap Gryffidith, Prince of South Wales. His son and heir, William Martin, was born in 1160. And this last William Martin's brother, "Sir Oliver Martin, who was born at Dartington House about 1165, was the ancestor of the Irish branch of the family; accompanied King Henry II, in 1186, in the conquest of Ireland. In 1193 he accompanied Richard Cœur de Lion to the Holy Land, and shared his captivity" (see pages 495 and 496, Colonial Families of the U. S., by George Norbury McKenzie, Vol. 2.).

Wliiam Martin is a name still honored in Europe. When Germany and the allied powers signed the Treaty of Peace, June 28, 1919, at Versailles, France, William Martin was the Master of Ceremonies. He escorted the German plenepotentiaries to the signatory table, where they signed the Treaty (see Nashville Tennessean for June 29, 1919, page 1).

William Martin, of Bristol, England

William Martin was born at the manor of Pindergast in Pembroke county, England, about the middle of the seventeenth century. This manor and the estate of his father passed to the eldest son, father of Sparks Martin, whose will we have recorded. William, being a younger son, entered the mercantile business in Bristol, England. He carried on an extensive American trade. Seeing that his youngest son, Joseph, was about to contract an undesirable marriage, he sent him as super-cargo to Virginia in the early years of the eighteenth century.

Children of William Martin, of Bristol, England

George; succeeded his father as merchant in Bristol, England.
John.
Joseph, who came to America.
Nancy.

There may have been others. See annual Report of American Historical Association for 1893, in article: "Gen. Joseph Martin and the War of the Revolution in the West," by Stephen B. Weeks.

Generation I in America

Generation I in America: Joseph Martin.

Joseph Martin was the youngest son of William Martin, merchant, of Bristol, England, and brother of George Martin, later merchant of Bristol, Eng. William Martin did extensive business, including much American trade. At this time Bristol was the second city in the Kingdom in size. Seeing that his son, Joseph, was about to contract an undesirable English marriage, William Martin fitted out one of his vessels, called the "Brice," which, by the way, came to be a family name, and sent Joseph, as supercargo, to Virginia. Joseph seems given to the "tender passion," for there he soon fell in love with and married Susanna Chiles, daughter of one of the oldest and most respected families in the province. Joseph Martin is described as "a perfect Englishman, possessing all the arrogance and self-important air, characteristic of them as a nation. He was bold, self-willed, supercilious, with the highest sense of honor." His wife, Susanna, is spoken of as "a most amiable woman" (see Vol. 8, Virginia Magazine of History and Biography. Also report of American Historical Association for the year 1893, pages 409 and 475). After his marriage, Joseph Martin moved from Caroline county, Va., to Albemarle county in the same state.

A lineal descendant of Joseph Martin and his wife, Susanna Chiles, has entered the patriotic order of Colonial Dames through the Martin-Chiles-Page line. This is Mrs. Betty Hairston Ingles, of Virginia. Proofs for her Colonial Dames papers were given by one of Virginia's finest genealogists, Sally Nelson Robins, as follows:

"Colonel John Page, member of the King's Council, was the father of Mary Page, who married Walter Chiles (see Vol. XIX, pages 104, 211, 324, and 437 of Virginia Magazine of History and Biography). For the two Walter Chiles in this line who were both members of the

House of Burgesses, and Susanna Chiles, wife of Joseph Martin, see Ibid. For Martin, see same magazine; see also, Vol. XIII, page 2; also William and Mary Quarterly, Vol. V, page 272, which carries line to Mrs. Betty Hairston Ingles' branch. For offices of ancestors, see Stanard's Colonial Virginia Register."

Lucy Henderson Horton, writer of this family history, is also a lineal descendant of Joseph Martin and his wife, Susanna Chiles, through his son, Capt. William Martin, of Revolutionary fame. Mrs. Betty Hairston Ingles descends from Joseph Martin and his wife, Susanna Chiles, through his son, Gen. Joseph Martin, of Revolutionary fame. We give an extended sketch of Capt. Wm. Martin and his brothers, General Joseph and Col. John Martin of "Rock House," and Brice Martin elsewhere.

Colonel John Page was a nephew of Sir Francis Wyatt. Henry Tylor, ancestor of President Tylor, was also a nephew of Sir Francis Wyatt (see "Vital Facts About Jamestown, Yorktown, Williamsburg, College of William and Mary—prepared by students of the College of William and Mary in honor of the attendance of the President of the U. S. Oct. 19, 1921.")

"Sir Francis Wyatt (1575-1644) was appointed Governor of Virginia in 1621. He brought from England a constitution upon which subsequent forms of government in the colonies were modeled. Trial by jury, an annual assembly convoked by the Governor, an executive veto power, and the concurrance of the Virginia Company and the Colonial Assembly in all acts, were features. He governed from 1621 to 1626 and from 1639 to 1642" (see page 728, Dictionary of United States History by Jameson).

A living representative of the Page family is Thomas Nelson Page.

In Vol. 8, Virginia Magazine of History and Biography, is found a sketch of Gen. Joseph Martin, son of Joseph Martin and his wife, Susanna Chiles. The original of this sketch is found among the Draper Manuscripts in the Wisconsin State Library. The sketch was originally written by Colonel William Martin, of Dixon Springs, Tenn., for Lyman C. Draper in 1842. We will say in passing that there were two William Martins in Tennessee. This Col. Martin, of Dixon Springs, and Col. William Martin, of Williamson county, were grandsons of Joseph Martin and his wife, Susanna Chiles. In this sketch William Martin says:

"My grandmother—that is, Susanna Chiles Martin—was one of the best of womankind. Her parents were of English descent. They raised a large family of children, all highly respectable, and from whom have descended an immense offspring, as the Waller, Carr, Lewis, Markes, Overton, Minor, Terry, Chiles, etc., now spread mostly through the South and West."

We are told that after the death of Susanna Chiles Martin, Joseph Martin married again; was unhappy; took to drink; and died in Albemarle county, Va., in 1760, leaving a large estate.

We are sorry we cannot follow up the lines of descent of the daughters of Joseph Martin and his wife, Susanna Chiles; but they had four sons—

Sons of Joseph Martin and His Wife, Susanna Chiles

(Generation II in America)

(1) General Joseph Martin (1740-1808).

(2) Captain William Martin (1742-1809).

(3) Colonel "Jack" Martin of "Rock House".

(4) Captain Brice Martin.

The daughters married into the Minor, Lewis, Clark, Waller, Overton, Carr and Edward families.   We know the name of only one, Martha Martin, who married Pomfret Waller, Sr., born Jan. 20, 1747. She died June 20, 1813, and is buried at "Belmont," on Leatherwood Creek, Henry county, Va.

General Joseph Martin

Joseph Martin, son of Joseph Martin and his wife, Susanna Chiles, was born in Albemarle county, Va., and died in Henry county, Va., in 1808.   As a boy he was roving in disposition and ungovernable. When a young man he was a boon companion to Sumpter, afterwards of South Carolina, and Benjimin Cleveland, a kinsman, who was reared in an adjoining county, Orange.   Martin had settled in this county after his marriage to Sarah Lucas in 1762.   These three men were imbued with the reckless spirit of the day; gambling was a favorite pastime.   They worked but little, depending on hunting, gambling, and trading for a livelihood.   With maturer manhood they settled down to lives more earnest.

Martin's first contribution to the onward movement of English civilization was his attempt at the settlement of Powell Valley, which included Cumberland Gap.   In 1769, he made a stand twenty miles north of Cumberland Gap, which has become known as Martin's Station. The men put in corn and other field products, but late in the summer Indians broke up the settlement.

Powell's Valley

A second effort to settle Powell's Valley was made by the above mentioned and a company of sixteen others from Henry county in 1774, immediately after his return from the Shawnee war.   Richard Henderson, in his journal kept on his memorable trip from the Holston to the Kentucky river after his treaty with the Indians and the Transylvania Purchase, says that he arrived on the 30th day of May, 1775, at Capt. Martin's in Powell Valley.   In the train were forty mounted riflemen and some slaves.   They remained here until the 5th of June, "making a house to secure their wagons, as they could not clear the road any farther."

Powell's Valley was included in the Transylvania purchase, and Joseph Martin was made attorney and entry taker for this division of the purchase.   After the Transylvania men had gathered under "the divine

elm tree" at Boonsboro and organized a legislative assembly, Judge
Richard Henderson wrote Joseph Martin, on July 20, 1775: "We did
not forget you at the time of making laws, your part of the country
is too remote from ours to attend our convention, but you must have
laws made by an assembly of your own. I have prepared a plan which
I hope you'll approve, but more of that when we meet, which I hope will
be soon."

This post was held with difficulty; and at the beginning of the
Indian war in 1776, the settlement was broken up. In 1783, with tenac-
ity of purpose, a third, and this time a permanent settlement, was made
in Powell's Valley. Martin's new station, established at this time, was
two miles from Cumberland Gap, this being about midway between
the Clinch and Kentucky rivers, furnished a resting place for poor
citizens going back and forth.

The year 1783 was a strenuous one for Joe Martin. He was Indian
Agent for North Carolina, with headquarters at the Long Island of
Holston. He served Virginia as Commisssioner to the Chickasaws,
effected the Powell Valley settlement, as we have said, and he engaged
in an extensive land speculation along with William Blount, Gen. Grif-
fith Rutherford, John Donaldson, John Sevier, Governor Caswell and
others.

Leading Spirit

Of this company William Blount was the leading spirit; and Joseph
Martin made the purchase while on one of his visits to the nation. The
purchase lay on the north side of the bend of the Tennessee river, in
what is now Alabama, then Georgia. It was also claimed by South
Carolina. It included all land in what is now Alabama lying between
the Tennessee river and the Tennessee state line. This extended across
north Alabama. The company secured a charter from Georgia in 1784.

The Commissioners who were also Justices of the Peace, were Lachlan McIntosh, Jr., Joseph Martin, William Downs, Stephen Heard, John
Donaldson, John Sevier and John Morse. The settlement was soon
broken up, owing to the hostilities of the neighboring Indians. But
the spirit of these men was undaunted, for we find that Jas. Glascow,
Secretary of State for North Carolina, went to Georgia in 1787 to have
conveyance made after the Legislature of Georgia had confirmed their
title to the bend of Tennessee.

The settlement was destined to be short-lived. Congress was not
in harmony with Georgia in confirming the title to the bend. Twenty
years before this all purchases by individuals had been inhibited by
royal proclamation of George III. Congress held that this right now
belonged to the general government. Hence the purchase came to
naught; and yet the effort must have contributed something to the
onward movement of English civilization by helping to open up the
way for those who followed.

When the State of Franklin was formed, in 1784, Joseph Martin
was a member of their first convention. He was on the committee to

take into consideration the state of public affairs. He opposed the scheme of a separate government from the first. Many notable Virginians shared his sentiments. He was chosen a member of the Privy Council (see Cal. Va. State paper IV., 31) but refused to serve.

In Henry's Life of Patrick Henry we find a letter to Martin written Oct. 4, 1786, giving reasons why Franklin should be abandoned. This, no doubt, served to confirm Martin in his belief, for the two men were great friends, but his mind had been made up before, as we have seen. In this new State there was discord among its own people, and North Carolina never yielded her claim of jurisdiction over the territory. This created pandemonium.

The influence of Martin is seen by the attitude of Sullivan, the county in which he resided. Sullivan and Hawkins were for the old State. Sullivan sent Martin, as her representative to the North Carolina assembly in 1784, the year in which the State of Franklin was organized, and again in 1787, when he was placed by this body at the head of the militia in what is now Tennessee, being commissioned Brigadier General. His was a most difficult place to fill. The Franklin men stood distinctly for encroachment: they had built houses within two miles of Chota, the beloved town of the Cherokees. Here dwelt Oconostota and Nancy Ward, the prophetess, "pretty woman." Here was the council house of the nation.

Martin writes Gov. Randolph in April, 1788, "I am happy to inform Your Excellency that the late unhappy dispute between the State of North Carolina and the pretended State of Franklin has subsided." Thus Martin, by a wise and conservative policy, ended tumult and violence and prevented what might have been, under other circumstances, civil war. The State of Franklin had died a natural death.

In 1785 Congress, weary of border warfare, caused by encroachment of the whites and retaliations of the Indians by pilfering, resolved to exercise the treaty-making function. To this end Benjamin Hawkins and Lachlan McIntosh, of Georgia; Joseph Martin, of Virginia; and Andrew Pickens, of South Carolina, were appointed commissioners to make a treaty defining boundary lines, etc. James Madison was official interpreter. Besides Choctaws and Chickasaws there were present at Hopewell-on-Keowell almost one thousand Cherokee warriors. Because of his knowledge of the situation, the negotiations were left largely with Joseph Martin.

The Cherokee Hopewell Treaty was a compromise. The Indians laid claims to most of Kentucky and Tennessee, also to a large territory in Georgia and the Carolinas. They were induced, however, to give up the Transylvania purchase, and to leave the Cumberland settlement outside of Indian territory. This Cumberland territory belonged to the whites by virtue of a treaty held Nov. 5 and 6, 1783, at the French Lick on Cumberland river (four miles northwest of Nashville) by Joseph Martin and John Donaldson, representing Virginia and North Carolina (see report of Gov. Harrison in Calendar Virginia State Papers, III, December 16, 1783).

In this treaty of Hopewell, boundary lines were decided upon; prisoners on both sides were to be given up; negroes and other property to be given up. The Cherokees acknowledged themselves under the United States alone.

As late as August, 1790, Washington still talks of enforcing the Treaty of Hopewell. We said that Martin had been placed by North Carolina at the head of the militia in what is now Tennessee. After North Carolina ceded this territory to the United States, Martin went out of office, and the territory went out of the hands of North Carolina.

Martin was urged for the position of Governor of the Southwest Territory (now Tennessee) by Patrick Henry, Lee, Grayson, Bland and others.

Sure and Steadfast

Martin, true to the motto of his house, "Sure and Steadfast," when representing Sullivan county in the Hillsboro Convention of 1788, favored the adoption of the Federal constitution. He was a member of the Fayetteville convention when the constitution was adopted. When returning to his beloved home in Virginia, we find him for a good many years a member of the Virginia assembly. He was a member of the Virginia assembly at the time of the passage of the memorable Madison Resolutions of 1798. We are told that on this occasion "he was Madison's right hand." Here his county town of Henry, Martinsville, was named in his honor.

Martin's chief merit lay in Indian diplomacy. He engaged in many treaties in which he always took conspicuous part because of his knowledge of Indians and of his influence with them. His most lasting, his best service, toward American independence was rendered during the British invasion of 1780-81. It was Martin, who, by his diplomacy, kept the Indians quiet, thus enabling the Watauga men to strike a heavy blow for liberty at King's Mountain. Had it not been thus, they must needs have stayed at home to defend their own firesides. A few months later, after North Carolina had rewarded Shelby and Sevier for gallantry at this time, a sword and pair of pistols, called on them again to take their men into the field for the support of the Union. They were not able to do so, having an Indian war on their hands, and could not leave their homes (Phelan 62).

Since this Battle of King's Mountain marked the turning of the tide of war, it seems that the Revolution hinged on the Indian agent, Joseph Martin.

After his return from Georgia, Martin built a commodious house, which, embowered in green, crowned the summit of a bell-shaped knoll overlooking Leatherwood creek in Henry county, Virginia. Here he spent his declining years with his second wife, Susanna Graves, the happy mother of many children. He left a large estate, consisting principally of negroes and lands in Tennessee and Virginia.

To see further of the Colonial services of General Joseph Martin, turn to page 415 of the Annual Report of the American Historical Asso-

ciation for the year 1893: "August 25, 1774, Lord Dunmore commissioned Martin a captain of the Pittsylvania militia, in Shawnee war. In
1769 Joseph Martin made a settlement in Powell's Valley" (see page
414, Annual report of the American Historical Association for the year
1893). He was attorney and entry-taker for Powell's Valley division
of Transylvania Purchase (see page 418). Additional authorities: Calendar Virginia State Papers; "Life, Correspondence, and Speeches of
Patrick Henry;" Royce; Draper Manuscripts; Roosevelt; "Colonial
Records of North Carolina;" Historical Collections of Virginia; Adair;
Ramsey; Phelan; "Iredell's Revisal."

General Joseph Martin was twice married. He married Sarah
Lucas in 1762. His second wife was Susanna Graves, whom he married
in 1784.

General Martin was born in 1740 and died in 1808.

In an article headed "A Corner in Ancestors" in the Nashville Banner of June 24, 1911, the Graves family is written up first of New England. Then the writer says, "The distinguished Southern family of
Graves descends from William Graves," and she says the Southern family is not related to the New England family of the same name.

Benjamin Cleveland's wife, Mary Graves, was a sister of Susanna
Graves, wife of General Joseph Martin (see page 13, Virginia Magazine
7, 1899). Benjamin Cleveland was born in Prince William county, but
moved to Orange county, Virginia.

General Joseph Martin's daughter, Elizabeth, bon October 13, 1768; died 1805; married Mr. Carr Waller. He was
a son of Thomas Waller and his wife, Susan Dabney Thomas Waller
had a brother, Pomfret Waller, Sr., born Jan. 20, 1747. His wife was
Martha Martin, who died June 20, 1813. She was a sister of General
Joseph Martin. She and Elizabeth are both buried at "Belmont," the
home of General Joseph Martin.

Carr Waller's second wife was Susanna Edwards, a niece of Gen.
Martin. Mr. Brice Edwards, of Washington, D. C., is of this branch.

Carr Waller Pritchett, D. D., who is (1901) president of the Pritchett College, and of the Morrison Observatory attached, at Glascow,
Missouri, is a son of Martha Myra Waller and her husband, Henry
Pritchett, and is a grandson of Carr Waller. He is a fine and learned
old man.

Children of General Joseph Martin by First Wife

Generation III in America:

(1) Susanna Martin, born 1763; married Jacob Burnes.

(2) Col. William Martin, born Nov. 26, 1765; died Nov. 4, 1846.

(3) Elizabeth Martin; married Carr Waller; was born Oct. 13,
1768; died in 1805; left four children.

(4) Brice Martin; born 1770, died Dec. 30, 1856; married Malinda
Perkins, of Smith county, Tenn., in 1811. He went out to the war of
1812 as captain of a company in Col. Bradley's regiment, First Tennessee Infantry. At the Battle of Talladega one of his men, Thomas Saun-

ders, was killed (see booklet gotten out by the Talladega Chapter, D. A R.). At the Battle of New Orleans, Brice Martin was promoted to the rank of Major. He was surveyor of the boundary line between Virginia and Tennessee in 1802. He had five children.

Children of General Joseph Martin and His Wife, Susanna Graves

(5) Colonel Joseph Martin, of Henry county, Va., born Sept. 22, 1785, of whom we will write later.

(6) Jesse; married first, Annie Armistead, and had one son. His second wife was Cecelia Reid. They had eight sons and a daughter. He was a soldier in the war of 1812. Jesse Martin was a farmer of Henry county, Virginia. He died about 1835. Cecelia Reid Martin died Aug. 26, 1875, aged 83 years.

(7) Thomas W. Martin married Miss Carr, of North Carolina. He went to Tennessee to live.

(8) Lewis Martin went also to Tennessee. He married a Miss Rucker. He saw military service. He died in Lincoln county, Missouri, about 1850.

(9) Alexander Martin; died in Lincoln county, Missouri, about 1850. He married Miss Carr, of North Carolina.

(10) ———— Martin; married Wm. Cleveland, son of Col. Benjamin Cleveland, hero of King's Mountain.

Jesse Martin, son of General Joseph Martin and his second wife, Susanna Graves, was the second child of this wife. He served in the war of 1812. He lived on his plantation in Henry county, Va. Martin died about 1835. He was twice married, his first wife being Annie Armistead. They had one son. His second wife was Cecelia Reid. They had eight sons and one daughter. We are sorry we cannot give all the names of his children. A son, Dr. Washington Lafayette Martin, was born in Henry county, Virginia. Dr. Martin was twice married. His first wife was Virginia Morecock, of Halifax county, North Carolina. His second wife was Sarah King, daughter of Dr. Francis King, of Beaufort, N. C. There were seven children by this marriage.

Children of Dr. Washington L. Martin and His Wife, Sarah King

Thomas S.; is in U. S. Navy.

Eva C.; born 1856; married Samuel Buckman in 1880.

Lula; married Earnest Duncan, of Beaufort, N. C.

Don; died a child.

Sallie; married Rev. Edward Hopkins, a Lutheran minister. They live in Grafton, West Virginia.

Edward; married Miss Felton; lives in Beaufort, N. C.

Lillian; married Warren Whitehurst; lives in Laurinburg, N. C.

Eva C. (Martin) Buckman

Eva Martin was born in Beaufort. She takes an interest in patriotic organizations, being a Daughter of the American Revolution and a Daughter of the Confederacy. She fills an official position as Secretary of the Daughters of the Revolution, being thus both a D. A. R. and a D. R.

In 1889 this family moved to Baltimore. They have three children, two sons and one daughter.

Dr. W. S. Martin's wife, Sarah King, was a daughter of Dr. Francis King, a successful physician of Beaufort.

Major George Wythe Martin

Major George Wythe Martin, son of General Joseph Martin and his wife, Susanna Graves, was born July 7, 1805, at Leatherwood, Henry county, Virginia; died at his home, "Meadows," in Rockingham county, N. C., Oct. 27, 1867. He married Oct. 25, 1837, Caroline H: Watkins, a daughter of Col. Benjamin and Susanna Watkins, of Pittsylvania county, Va. She died Dec. 28, 1897.

Children of Major George W. Martin and his wife Caroline H. Watkins:

Susanna Graves Martin; born Dec. 16, 1842. Died April 3. 1847.

William Watkins; born March 7, 1845; was Lieut. in Confederate army and was killed in battle, Oct. 22, 1863.

George W.; born June 3, 1847. Married Hattie F. France, of Henry county, Va, Oct. 14, 1868. Went West and was never heard of again. His one son, George W. Martin, is living at Danville, Va.

Joseph B.; born July 27, 1849; married Alice Gravely, of Henry county, Va., May 24, 1871. Lives at Reidsville, N. C.

John Henry; born July 15, 1851; died May 22, 1853.

Emma; born Jan. 6, 1854; died July 12. 1874. Married John F. Reid, of Henry county, Va., Sept. 1, 1873. No children.

Mary Catherine; born Sept. 19, 1855. Married Wm. B. Stocks, of England, Dec. 3, 1873.

Thomas Henry Martin was born, as were all the children, at "The Meadows," Rockingham county, N. C., Dec. 14, 1859. He married Rosa V. Hickson, daughter of Richard L. Hickson, of Danville, Va., April 27, 1887. He is a leaf tobacco dealer at Kingston, N. C.

Children of Thomas Martin and His Wife, Rosa Hickson

Caroline Hunt; married Julian G. Frasier, Sept. 4, 1911. They live in Richmond, Va.

Rosa Hickson Martin; married Wiley M. Reddill, Nov. 4, 1911. They also live in Richmond.

Richard H.

Susanna.

Maude.

Thomas.

John Calvin Martin was living near Woodbury, Tennessee, March 20, 1842. Martin saw military service. He married a Miss Rucker.

George Martin first married a Miss Sterling. His second wife was a Miss Watkins. He had several children. Martin served in the Virginia legislature. He removed to North Carolina about 1840; died in 1860.

Patrick Henry Martin was taken to Tennessee by his half-brother, Brice, and was educated by Colonel William and Brice Martin. He studied law and was admitted to the bar about the beginning of the war of 1812. He left his practice to join Jackson's army, and died soon after his return from the Battle of New Orleans.

Col. William Martin, of Dixon Springs, Tennessee
(Generation III in America)

William Martin, eldest son of of General Joseph Martin and his wife, Sarah Lucas, was born in Orange county, Virginia, Nov. 26, 1765. He died of pleurisy in Smith county, Tennessee, Nov. 4, 1746. He went on an expedition against the Indians with some of Colonel William Campbell's men in 1781. Martin was in Powell's Valley in 1785 and remained on the frontier for two years. He shared the hardships of the settlers and protected them with the company of rangers under his command. He was sometimes stationed in a fort, sometimes pursuing marauding parties of Indians, sometimes opening up channels of travel by which emigrants could more easily reach the farming settlements (see Ramsey, Tennessee, 477). He was sent to Middle Tennessee, via Kentucky, about 1787, in charge of a company, by the state of North Carolina and continued in command about two years.

This company under Captain William Martin was a part of Evans' battalion. Another company of this same battalion was commanded by Captain Joshua Hadley. Captain, afterwards Colonel, William Martin and Captain Hadley both died in Smith county, Tennessee.

In order to support these men while in the Cumberland settlement, we find that a part of the tax of the county was to be paid in corn, beef, pork, bear meat, venison, etc.

Captain Martin then returned to Virginia; married when twenty-five, and removed to Tugaloo, Pendleton district, South Carolina, in 1791. He was a member of the South Carolina legislature, and lived there until 1798, when he migrated to the Cumberland, settling at Dixon's Springs, Smith county, and remained there the balance of his life.

Martin was a member of the Georgia legislature in 1787. In 1800 he was engaged in surveying the Indian boundary, in 1804 was a Jefferson elector, and a Madison elector in 1808. He was vice-president of the Whig convention in 1844.

In the war of 1812 Martin was elected lieutenant-colonel of the second regiment of Tennessee volunteers. He served in the Natchez campaign and in that against the Creeks. At Talladega, after the wounding of Col. Pillow, Martin took command and was conspicuous for his fine conduct. Owing to a conflict of opinion as to the date of expiration of their term of service, some of the Tennessee regiments, including that of Col. William Martin, undertook to return home after the 10th of December, 1813.

Col. Martin was a fluent and logical writer. We have examples of this in his "Self-Vindication," and in his sketch of his father, General

Joseph Martin, written for Lyman C. Draper. When Col. Wm. Martin attended the great Whig convention in 1844 he kept a short diary. This old manuscript is now in possession of his great-grandson, Judge S. M. Young. History repeats itself. Judge Young was selected to represent the state-at-large in the Presidential convention at Baltimore in 1912.

Extracts from Diary:

"Tuesday, 16th of April, 1844.—Set out for Baltimore to represent the state-at-large in the national Whig convention to be held there on the first day of May ensuing, for the purpose of nominating candidates for President and Vice-President of the United States.

"19th.—Embarked on steamboat Ohio Mail for Pittsburg; off at three P. M.

"22nd.—Arrive at Louisville early this morning. Pretty good run.

"23rd.—Fine morning. Arrive at Cincinnati at four P. M.; go on board the Narragansett for Pittsburg.

"25th.—Pass Point Pleasant early where the great battle was fought on the 10th of Oct., 1774.

"1st of May.—This is the great day. Nominated Henry Clay for President and Freylinghuysen for Vice-President.

"17th.—Dr. Shelby sends me to my brother's.

"18th.—Go to Lebanon; stay at son Williams'.

"19th.—Being Sunday, got home at 2 P. M., after an absence of 32 days. Found my family well and business in good condition."

Dr. Shelby, spoken of in the diary, was Dr. John Shelby, who lived on the east side of the Cumberland river and owned what is now East Nashville. The brother to whom Dr. Shelby "sent" Col. Martin was Major Brice Martin, pioneer, surveyor, and flat boatman of renown. He came from Virginia to Tennessee with Col. Martin, settling first in Smith county, where he remained until 1815, when he removed to Wilson county and located in the western part of the county on, or near, the Lebanon-Nashville turnpike, near Stone's river.

Mr. John H. Bullock, land commissioner of the State of Tennessee in 1901, said that records in his office showed that General Joseph Martin had a land grant of 1,280 acres on Stones' river, 640 acres on each side of the river. Perhaps it was on this land, inherited from his father, that Major Brice Martin lived. The "son William" referred to was the Hon. William L. Martin, of Lebanon, the father of Mrs. Joel Settle, of Spring street, East Nashville.

The writer holds a letter written by Colonel William Martin to her grandfather, Captain John Hughes, of Williamson county, Tennessee. This letter was dated Sept. 15, 1831 at "Bellview." Col. Martin says, "I yesterday returned home from Nashville, opened your kind letter of the 31st, requesting me to use my influence with Major Buford, our Senator, in behalf of my highly respected kinsman, General Martin," etc.

"General Martin" spoken of in the above paragraph, was General

William Martin, of Williamson county, Tennessee, a brother-in-law of
Captain John Hughes. General Martin, whose home was in Williamson
county, was a bachelor. Colonel Martin goes on to say, "You also in
your letter condole with me, on my irreparable loss in the death of my
dear, my much-belovied wife. Oh, my friend, this is to me a loss indeed.
You can only imagine my distress. Such a wife has fallen to the lot
of but few men. If I have any delight, it is in solitude to dwell on the
memory of her who is gone, and with her is gone the best affections of
my heart. Although this retrospection spreads a gloom over my heart,
it leaves a pensive sweetness which I would not exchange for all this
world calls great. During her conflict with the 'last enemy,' she had
the entire possession of her intellect. Among other things she said to
me, 'don't weep.' I told her I could not help it. She calmly replied,
'Be more of a man.' She seemed to be two persons, one living, the
other dying. Once she said, 'What a sweet death' and her last word
was 'Glory,' with an effort to say something else, but her strength
failed. She died as she had lived, one of the best of women. By this
bereavement I am inconsolable; I know not what I am to do. No
object is sufficiently interesting to engage my attention, though Christianity and philosophy combine to teach me not to grieve. I myself
have to carry my own sorrow. So far as consolation may be derived
from the society of children and friends, I might calculate on as much as
any man, but this comes short—infinitely short—of filling the void oc-
casioned by the loss of her who held the highest seat in my earthly
affections. I loved her much in life but, if there is any difference, more
in death. I fear, however, my friend, I shall weary you by talking so
much on a subject which interests myself more than it could interest
anyone else . . . 'Out of the abundance of the heart the mouth speak-
eth.' Give my love to cousin Sally and your children. And for yourself, accept the best wishes of an old friend,   William Martin."

People have sometimes confused the two William Martins of Tennessee who served in the war of 1812. This letter makes it perfectly
plain that there were two William Martins in Tennessee. This man
lived at Dixon Springs. William Martin, who served on the staff of
General Andrew Jackson, with title of colonel at New Orleans, lived in
Williamson county. He is spoken of in this letter as "my highly respected kinsman, Gen. (William) Martin." General Martin had been commissioned Brigadier General of Militia by Gov. Carroll, September 4,
1824, and when Lafayette was in Nashville, and at the Hermitage, in May,
1825, General William Martin, of Williamson county, was in command
of the 9th Brigade militia reviewed by Lafayette and General Jackson.
"Cousin Sally," spoken of in the letter, was the sister of General William Martin. She was the wife of Captain John Hughes (1776-1860).
Captain Hughes and his wife, who lived in Williamson county, were
grandparents of the writer.

Judge Andrew B. Martin, of Lebanon, Tennessee, comes of this
same family. He was born near Gordonsville, Smith county, Tennessee,

December 9, 1836. He is a son of Matthew Moore Martin and his wife, Matilda Crow. He was educated at Lebanon, graduating from Cumberland University in 1858. The degree of L. L. D: was conferred on him in 1887 by Lincoln College, Lincoln, Illinois. During the Civil War he was a lieutenant in the Seventh Tennessee Infantry, later adjutant on the staff of General Joseph Wheeler. He was a member of the Tennessee Legislature in 1871-72, and served several times as special judge. He became a professor of law in Cumberland University in 1878, and has been president of the board of trustees since 1882. He and his colleague, Judge Nathan Green, have been spoken of not only as educators of men but as character builders.

Judge Samuel M. Young is a lineal descendant of Colonel William Martin, of Dixon Springs, Smith county, Tenn. Judge Young received his literary education at Burrett College, subsequently graduating in the law department of Cumberland University. He is a son of Hon. Howard Young, who was a man of wealth and highly regarded. The Youngs have long been prominent both in White and Smith counties. Judge Young was State Senator from the counties of Smith and Wilson in 1893, a member of the State Democratic Executive Committee of the Fourth Congressional District from 1894 to '98, and in 1909 was elected by the legislature a member of the State Board of Elections, of which body he has been president since its organization. He was elected as delegate from the state-at-large to the Baltimore Presidential Convention in 1912.

Children of Col. Wm. Martin (1735-1846) and His Wife, Frances Ferriss

Col. William, Jr.; father of Mrs. Fanny Tate, of Draper, Va.
Sarah; born Dec. 8, 1798; married Thomas Young, July 31,1817.
Brice.
Wilson Y. (1810-1868); was grandfather of Judge Sam M. Young.
Norval Douglas.
————————Martin; married a Mr. Hughes.
Sarah; born Dec. 8, 1798; married Thomas Young, July 31, 1817. Their daughter, Elizabeth Brooks Young, was born in 1827 and died in 1897. She married James Z. George, U. S. Senator from Mississippi, May 27, 1847.

James Z. George was born in 1826; died August 14, 1897. He signed the Mississippi Ordinance of Secession in 1861. He was U. S. Senator from that state for many years, being first elected to this office in 1881. George was one of Mississippi's most brilliant and worthy sons.

Children of Senator James Z. George and His Wife, Elizabeth Brooks Young

1. Fannie George, mother of Mrs. Mary George Barksdale Kincannon. She married, first, Capt. W. R. Barksdale and had three

children, two girls and one boy; married second time, Thomas George. They had three girls.

2. Elizabeth.

3. Kate; married F. M. Aldridge:

4. A. H. George; was State Senator through two terms.

5. J. W. George; served several times in State Legislature.

6. Lizzie George; married Dr. T. R. Henderson, president of a bank in Greenwood, Mississippi. Mrs. Lizzie (George) Henderson served for two years as President General of the United Daughters of the Confederacy, proving herself an efficient officer. She contributed in no small degree to the monumental work of this order.

We find this family devoted Southerners. Mrs. C. B. Tate, Fanny Martin Tate, who is a daughter of Col. William Martin, Jr., has served for many years as Treasurer General, United Daughters of the Confederacy.

Mrs. Kate George Aldrich, daughter of Senator J. Z. George, lives in Greenwood, Mississippi. She has several children, and her charming home is noted for its hospitality.

A. A. Kincannon, husband of Mrs. Mary George Barksdale Kincannon, former chancellor of the University of Mississippi, and president of I. I. & C. at Columbus, Miss., is now (1921) superintendent of city schools, Memphis, Tenn., and president Tennessee State Normal.

Brice Martin, son of Colonel William Martin and his wife, Frances Ferriss, married Susan Cayce, and had four daughters and one son.

(1) Ann.

(2) Elizabeth.

(3) Mary.

(4) Douglas.

(5) J. F. Martin; married Susan Elizabeth Drake. His grandfather, Col. William Martin, was so fond of this boy that he took him into his own home. Here he was reared.

Children of J. F. Martin and His Wife, Elizabeth Drake

(a) J. B. Martin.

(b) J. E. Martin.

(c) William.

(d) Norval Douglas.

(e) Olive. (Was twin sister to N. D. Martin).

(f) Susie.

(g) Lura.

The grandchildren of J. T. Martin now living (1917) are Norval Douglas, Jr., and J. T. Martin.

Norval Douglas Martin and his wife, Hattie C. Thompson, were

The parents of J. Brice Martin, who married Pauline Elliot. J. B. Martin and his wife had four children, all of whom died in childhood.

Nancy Martin married a Mr. Young. Their children are:

(a) Samuel.

(b) Fannie.

(c) Mamie.

Children of William Martin, Jr.

(a) Lee.

(b) Fannie.

(c) Sallie.

(d) Elizabeth.

(e) Andrew.

(f) Emily.

The last two were by his second wife.

Norval Douglas Martin died in young manhood, after fighting in the Florida wars, contracting fever in Florida and dying at the close of the war.

Colonel Joseph Martin (1785-1859)

Colonel Joseph Martin, son of General Joseph Martin and his second wife, Susanna Graves, was born at "Belmont," in Henry county, Virginia. He grew to manhood in this beautiful home. Martin read law under Hon. Wm. A. Burwell of Franklin county, Virginia, but never practiced it. After his marriage to Sally Hughes, daughter of Col. Archelaus Hughes, of Patrick county, Va., on April 27, 1810, he carried his young bride to his commodious home, "Greenwood," in Henry county, Virginia. Here he owned large landed estates and many negroes, devoting his time largely to looking after his plantations.

Col. Martin was always interested in politics. He was for several years a member of the House of Delegates, and eight years in the Senate of Virginia. He was a member of the Constitutional Convention of 1829-30. His life long friend, Archibald Stuart, of Patrick county, Virginia, father of General J. E. B. Stuart, was also a member of this convention. John Tyler, also a personal friend of Martin, said of Martin in connection with the Constitutional Convention, "Though not a speaking member, he was one of the most sensible of that illustrious assemblage of men."

Colonel Joseph Martin was three times successively Presidential Elector. He was on the successful ticket every time, once for Monroe, twice for Jackson. At the time of the war of 1812 he was in command of a regiment of militia, and held himself in readiness to be called into service, but his regiment was never called out.

When Colonel Martin was only fourteen years old, he was with his father, General Joseph Martin, who was one of the commissioners on the part of Virginia to run the dividing line between Virginia and Kentucky.

Colonel Martin did much to promote free schools in Virginia. He worked along the same lines as did Jefferson and Cabell. He was a friend and liberal patron of the early. railroad projects in Virginia. He lived the life of the typical Southern planter, his home being noted for its hospitality. He had four sons and eight daughters. He died in 1859, full of honors and years, being in the 76th year of his life.

Sally (Hughes) Martin

Sally Hughes, daughter of Colonel Archelaus Hughes, of Revolutionary fame, and his wife, Mary Dalton, was born at "Hughesville," their homestead in Patrick county, Virginia. We are told in the Virginia Magazine of History and Biography (Vol. 9) in a sketch of General Joseph Martin, written by his son, Colonel William Martin, of Dixon Springs, Tennessee, that 'IBelmont," the home of Gen. Joseph Martin, was purchased by General Martin from Benjamin Harrison of Berkley.

Miss Josephine Robertson, of Statesville, North Carolina, a granddaughter of Colonel Joseph Martin, through his daughter, Ella, says in a letter to the writer, dated Sept. 19, 1910, "I remember, when a child, how I loved to sit by the high window in the garret at "Greenwood" and look out over the green fields of Virginia. In searching through the useless plunder, one could see a pair of saddle bags, brought home from the Cherokees by General Joseph Martin. How we would look on them in wonder now! My grandfather's knee buckles were given to the children to play with, and were, of course, lost. In this garret was an old-fashioned wooden chest of clothes. In it were dresses of satin and crepe, with the same skirts, and big sleeves and Empire waists of the style of the French Revolution period."

The writer has a picture of Col. Joseph Martin and his wife, Sally Hughes. This was taken in the days of flowing skirts. Her dress is of handsome material and she has on a handsome Vandyke lace collar. He looks the typical Virginia gentleman.

Sally (Hughes) Martin was one of the most remarkable women of her day. She was possessed of remarkable personal beauty and great intelligence. She has been spoken of by one who knew her well as a woman of rare personal attraction. She survived her husband twenty-three years. At the time of her death, in her ninety-second year, she was the ancestress of one hundred and fifty descendants. For fifty years her home, "Greenwood," was the center of old-fashioned hospitality, and she was "the Queen of the household, the light of the home." The circle of friends and relatives extended over many states. The writer's parents, Dr. Samuel Henderson and Rachel Jane (Hughes) Henderson, of Tennessee, delighted in the hospitality of this home.

Sally (Hughes) Martin was a member of the Baptist church for more than fifty years.

One of their sons, Joseph, a brilliant young man, when at Harvard, writes back to his mother that a certain part of the campus "reminds me of the grounds at 'Greenwood.' "

Since this Martin family was first of Caroline county, and later of

Albemarle, in the same State, as we are trying to prove through history their services to their country, we shall record names of this family connection who enlisted in the first company of volunteers during our Revolutionary struggle in Albemarle county. Charles Lewis was captain, William Terrill Lewis was sergeant, as was also John Martin; Thomas Martin, Jr., corporal. Among privates in this company were. Robert Martin, Jr., Ed Hughes, Stephen Hughes, David Dalton, Edward Carter and John Henderson (see page 63, Genealogy of the Lewis family).

Senator Thomas Staples Martin, of Albemarle county, Virginia, upholds the honor of the name.

Descendants of Sarah (Martin) Lewis intermarried in Tennessee with the Claiborne family. Some members of the Clark, Lewis, Martin connection moved to Clark county, Kentucky, among them Major John Martin, who won his spurs at Yorktown. Major Martin was a member of the Methodist church.

Among the children of Col. Joseph Martin and his wife, Sally Hughes, the girls were beautiful or handsome and the boys were worthy men. The writer holds an autographed letter written by Joseph, their son, while studying law at Harvard University to his mother. It is dated February 10, 1847. He has the pen of a ready writer, and proves himself an affectionate son. Although not then twenty-one years of age, he discusses politics with clear insight. All of this demonstrates something of the social life in the South in the ante bellum days. Women must have had political insight. Among other things, Joseph Martin says his father's "favor of the 20th ultimo containing even more that a truly grateful son could have exxpected from the kindest and most indulgent parent. But it is no more that my dear Father will be r·membered for." He speaks of his fine watch and fob chain, the gift of his father, in a most appreciative way. He also speaks of his ambitions as a lawyer. "At present," he says, "you know my youthful age will prevent me from being admitted to the bar in Virginia, not being twenty-one. My wish is to fit myself for the creditable discharge of my duties of a lawyer whilst here, surrounded by so many facilities for doing so, and commence the practice immediately after my return."

Martin goes on to say, "Immediately after my friend (the name looks like Aylett) left for Virginia, another not quite so old, but as true, moved up from a different part of the city to take his stead. But since then we have concluded it would be more agreeable to room together. He is from the same county that young Warsham was, whom you have perhaps heard me speak of as liking so well whilst at college, and he possesses all the characteristics of a gentleman and a student. We have two rooms, a bed' and sitting room on the lower floor, which are the most desirable in the house, with a pretty cedar tree near, similar to those at 'Greenwood.' There are a number of other trees surrounding the house, but none ever so fondly gazed upon by me. Indeed the calmness of the delightful view, together with the pleasantness of my situation, have almost, at particular hours of the day, translated me to the 'big porch' at home; in fact there are no appearances of a town nearer than three or four hundred yards in any direction." Then Martin speaks of Cambridge being scattered over large territory. He speaks of his sister, Ella, writing him that his mother wanted him to spend his vacation at home, and says, "I wish, dear Mother, that circumstances would justify me in going back to my happy home."

Of Joseph Martin, Jr., the father was justly proud. Joseph was educated at Lexington, Virginia, and, as we have said, took his law course at Harvard College, Cambridge, Mass. He commenced the practice of his profession in Pittsylvania county, Va., and, from the first, took a prominent stand. After practicing law a short time in Virginia, Martin was made Commonwealth Attorney for Pittsylvania county.

Joseph Martin, Jr., married Susan Pannell, of Pittsylvania county. She was a cousin of General J. E. B. Stuart. At the wedding J. E. B. Stuart was present in regimentals from West Point. Of this marriage there was one child, Joseph H. Martin. He inherited "Greenwood," living and dying there. On a visit to "Greenwood," in 1855, Joseph Martin, Jr., became ill with typhoid fever and died September 17, 1855. The County Court, held for the county of Pittsylvania, drafted resolutions on his death.

We are told that in the old Martin burying ground at "Belmont," in Henry county, which overlooks Leatherwood creek, there are four Joseph Martins side by side—General Joseph and his son, Col. Joseph; this man and his son, Joseph.

This last Joseph Martin inherited "Greenwood" and the handsome old furniture. He died leaving no children and his widow moved to Baltimore, Maryland. She later married Mr. Schneder, of Baltimore.

Children of Col. Joseph Martin and His Wife, Sally Hughes

1. Mary; married John Staples, of Patrick county, Virginia. He died in 1839.

2. Susan; married Robert Cook, of Pittsylvania county.

3. Col. William; married Susan Hairston, of Henry county, Va.

4. Jane; married John D. Watkins. They had one child, Susan, who married Col. Wm. Wirt.

5. Archelaus Hughes; died in childhood.

6. Ann; married Judge John Dillard of the Supreme Court of North Carolina.

7. Captain Thomas; was killed at Malvern Hill. He married a Miss Pannell, who lived to be quite old.

8. Judge Joseph; married Susan Pannell, of Pittsylvania county.

9. Matilda; married George Stovall Hairston, of Henry county.

They were parents of Judge Nicholas Hardeman Hairston, of Roanoke, Va., and of Mrs. Bettie H. Ingles.

    10. Elizabeth; married Captain Robert Williams, of Danville, V٤.

    11. Sallie; married Col. Overton Dillard, of Henry county.

    12. Ella; married Dr. John Robertson, of Pittsylvania county.

Children of Mary Martin and Her Husband, Col. John Staples

William; married Anne Penn.

Abram: married a Miss Penn.

Martin.

John.

Joseph.

Samuel.

Susan; married Col. Steadman.

Lucinda; married a Mr. Peeler.

Children of Mary Martin and Her Second Husband, Col. Thos. McCabe, of Floyd County, Va.

Thomas.

Sallie.

Mary Martin Staples McCabe, died in 1889, being 78 years of age. She remembered her grandmother, Mary (Dalton) Hughes, well.

Susan Martin, daughter of Col. Joseph Martin and his wife, Sally Hughes, married Colonel Robert Cook, attorney-at-law, of Pittsylvania county. She is said to have been very beautiful and accomplished. She had only one child, Sarah Jane Cook, who was a charming and lovely woman, but who never married. The last sixteen years of her life were spent in the home of Mrs. John Robertson. She lived to be seventy-eight years old.

William Martin, son of Colonel Joseph Martin and his wife, Sally Hughes, was born at "Greenwood" in 1814. He was educated at the University of Virginia. He was a man of talent and distinction. When quite young, Martin was a member of the Virginia Legislature. As an orator, lawyer, a statesman, he was regarded as a peer of any man in Virginia. Martin was several times Congressional Elector, once a delegate to the National Convention. He was once a candidate for congress, but was defeated by only a few votes by Hon. John Goode. Martin was a member of the State Constitutional Convention of 1850-51. He was in the legislature when the convention known as the Secession convention was called. He declined to represent his county in that convention. Martin served as Colonel of a Confederate regiment. After his brother, Captain Thomas J. Martin, was killed at Malvern Hill, Colonel Martin resigned his commission and returned home. He served as commonwealth attorney. He died in September, 1888.

Children of Colonel Wm. Martin and His Wife, Susan Hairston

Sallie Elizabeth; married Dr. Prengle, of Frederick City, Mo.

Louise Hardeman; married Samuel Sheffield.

Samuel Hughes; unmarried.

George.

Joseph.

Jane; married John Watkins, of Henry county, Va.

Susan; married William H. West.

Matilda; married George Hairston, of Henry county, Va. Col. George Hairston represented this district in congress for a number of years. He was the largest land and slave owner in this part of Virginia. The family is said to have owned a gold table service. One of this connection, Louisa Hardeman Hairston, was a niece, and also an adopted daughter, of President John Tyler, and was married in the Gubernatorial mansion at Richmond, Va., while he was Governor of the State.

Children of Matilda Martin and Her Husband, George Hairston

Sallie Louisa; married Mr. Saunders.

Jane; married Mr. Draper.

Elizabeth; married, first, Mr. Hale; second, Capt. Ingles.

George; married Nannie Watkins.

Nicholas; married a Miss Hairston.

Matilda; married Mr. Tate.

IV. Sallie Martin, daughter of Colonel Joseph Martin and his wife, Sallie Hughes, married Colonel Overton Dillard, of Henry county, Va. Children:

Sallie Hughes; married Frank Gravely.

Elizabeth; married Mr. Ready.

Peter; died a bachelor.

John.

Thomas.

Susan Jane; married Samuel Ford.

Anne; married Mr. Arrington.

Ella; married Mr. Griggs.

V. Joseph Martin, son of Colonel Joseph Martin and his wife, Sally Hughes, married Susan Panell, of Pittsylvania county, Va. Their child was Joseph Henry Martin, who married Jane W————. Her second husband is Mr. Schnider, of Baltimore.

VI. Anne Martin, daughter of Col. Joseph Martin and his wife,

Sally Hughes, married Judge John Henry Dillard, of the Supreme Court oı North Carolina. Children:

Lucy Elizabeth; married John Pannell.

Ruffin; married a Miss Moorman.

Anne Martin; married Frank Hall.

John Henry.

Just a word concerning Judge Dillard: ɟ. H. Dillard was born in Rockingham county, North Crolina. He became supreme court judge in his native state. After marriage, he made his home in Greensboro, North Carolina. Here he and his wife both died. They have a son now (1913) living at Murphy, N. C., who is spoken of for judge, and another living in Guilford, N. C., who was a member of the legislature of 1910-11. The son who lives at Murphy, Chewan county, has a hunting lodge in the Indian reservation twenty miles from civilization. He spends his winters in California.

VII. Elizabeth Martin; daughter of Colonel Joseph Martin and his wife, Sally Hughes, married Captain Robert Williams, of Danville, Va. Their children were:

Sallie; married Capt. D. T. Williams, of Danville. They live in Richmond.

Judge, and General, Samuel Williams; married, first, Margaret ˙rayson, home, Wytheville, Va.; second, Mrs. Walker, who was Miss Henry, of Tazewell county, Va.

Judge Martin N. Williams; married Miss Westand, home, Parisburg, Va.

William C.; married Miss Stockton. Home, Roanoke, Va.

Thomas; married Patty Jennings. Home near Chimney Rock.

Mary Alice; married Mr. Colley.

Bettie; married Mr. Dunn.

Kate; married Mr Colley.

VIII. Matilda Martin, daughter of Colonel Joseph Martin and his wife, Sally Hughes, was born at "Greenwood," in Henry county, Virginia. She married Dr. George Stovall Hairston, of Henry county. They were grandparents of Judge Nicholas Hardeman Hairston, of Roanoke, Virginia, a man distinguished in his profession and who has a large and lucrative practice.

Bettie Hairston, the third daughter of Dr. George Stovall Hairston and his wife, Matilda Martin, married first, Major Samuel Hale, whc was killed in 1864 in the Battle of Spottsylvania. C. H. Ten years later she married Captain Lyrus Hyde Ingles, a great-great-grandson of the Mary Draper Ingles, whose capture by the Indians in the pioneer days of South-west Virginia has been written in the history of that section.

Children of Captain Lyrus Hyde Ingles and His Wife, Bettie Hairston

George Hairston; married Mrs. Harriet Curd Greenway.

Bessie Crawford; married Charles W. Watkins after the death of her sister Maud, his first wife.

Mary Lee.

Mrs. Bettie Ingles is a member of the Colonial Dames through John Page and the two Walter Chiles on her mother's side. She also comes into the order on her father's side. He descends from Colonel Francis Epps of Charles City county, Virginia.

IX. Thomas Martin, son of Colonel Joseph Martin and his wife, Sally Hughes, was a captain of a company in the Confederate army. He was a gallant soldier, and was killed in the battle of Malvern Hill, July 1, 1862. He married a Miss Pannell, who survived him many years.

X. Jane Martin, daughter of Colonel Joseph Martin and his wife, Sally Hughes, was born in the family homestead, "Greenwood," in Henry county, Va. She married John D. Watkins. They had one child, Susan Watkins, who married Colonel William Wirt.

XI. Ella Martin, youngest daughter of Colonel Joseph Martin and his wife, Sally Hughes, was born at "Greenwood" in Henry county. She married Dr. John Robertson, April 8, 1852.

The immigrant ancestor of Dr. Robertson settled first in Petersburg, Virginia. Bishop Meade, in his book, "Old Families and Churches of Virginia," speaks of them as in Bristol parish. Of this same family was Chloe Robertson, who married Abraham Shelton in 1760. Dr. John Robertson descends from the Sheltons also. We think James Robertson, the pioneer of Tennessee, was closely related to Chloe Robertson.

Dr. John Robertson was a son of Thomas Robertson and a grandson of Edward Robertson. The first American ancestor came to Virginia from Scotland. The name is one honored in Great Britain.

John Robertson was born February 7, 1825, in Pittsylvania county, Va. He was a student at Washington College (now Washington and Lee), graduating from Jefferson Medical College at Philadelphia. Robertson inherited a large estate from his father, building a beautiful country home upon it, but lost it all in the war of '61-'65.

In 1875, Dr. Robertson moved from Virginia to Statesville, North Carolina, becoming a charter member of the Baptist church there. He died June 29, 1914. In spite of his great age, he was active and took great zest in life until three months before his death. His wife had died in 1899.

In Dr. Robertson's old age his daughter Josephine was ever at his side. Old people are always full of reminiscences, and the Doctor's conversation with his daughter led her to become interested in family history, which, to her, proved a most delightful research. She has aided the writer in her work. She says, "In the colonial days and the years following, when Virginia reached its highest state of development, and was graced by fair women and great men, some of our own played their part in that life."

The youngest son of Dr. John Robertson and his wife, Ella Martin, was Reverend J. D. Robertson, who died in 1899, while pastor at Rock Hill, South Carolina. He was a graduate of Wake Forrest College and the Southern Baptist Theological Seminary.

J. Martin Robertson also made his home with his father. He is a man who takes great interest in the affairs of the day. He is especially interested in the welfare of his county.

Children of Ella Martin. Daughter of Colonel Joseph Martin, of Henry County, Virginia. and Her Husband, Dr. John Robertson, of Pittsylvania County, Virginia

Joseph Thompson.

John Martin.

Josephine Martin.

Ella Chlotilda; married John McLendon.

Eugene Cook; married E. Couch.

Archibald Thomas, L. L. D., married Ella T. Broadus.

Rosalie Maud.

Annabel O'Leary; married Preston Sartin.

John Darrell.

Archibald Thomas Robertson, M. A., D. D., L. L. D.

Archibald Thomas Robertson, son of Dr. John Robertson and his wife, Ella Martin, was born in Pittsylvania county, Virginia, at the commodious Robertson home, which still stands. Born in Virginia, reared in North Carolina, and since manhood making his home in Louisville, Kentucky, he is a true Southerner, but a man of broad sympathies.

A. T. Robertson is Professor of Interpretation of the New Testament in the Southern Baptist Theological Seminary of Louisville. He has written many books, all of which have been bublished, not only in the United States, but throughout Europe. When "The Glory of the Ministry" came from the press, Dr. John Clifford, of London, England, said of it, "The book has been a gift of God to me. It is a breeze from the hills, bracing and life-giving. The exegesis is faultless, the style as clear as an unclouded sky and strong as the best steel, the sentences are short, packed with meaning and radiant with energy. The volume will do incalculable good." David Smith, D. D., of Londonberry, Ireland; James Hastings, D. D., of Aberdeen, Scotland; James Stalker, of the same place; J. H. Rushbrooke, P. H. D., of London, and many other notable men gave to the public their appreciation of this book.

After giving lectures at Chautauqua and at Northfield, Dr. Robertson made an expansion of his lectures in a book entitled "Practical and Social Aspects of Christianity—The Wisdom of James." "He makes use of all the light which the rich findings of papyri throw on the subject."

In 1901 he wrote "Life and Letters of John A. Broadus;" in 1904

"Students' Chronological New Testament;" in 1906, "Key Words in the Teachings of Jesus;" in 1911, "John, the Loyal—Studies in the Ministry of the Baptist;" also his "Commentary on Matthew;" in 1915, "Syllabus of New Testament Study," etc.   But the crowning achievement of Dr. Robertson is his " Grammar of the Greek New Testament in the Light of Historical Research."   This work has had generous and wide-spread acceptance.   It is said that by this work Dr. Robertson will be remembered in the ages to come.   Alfred Plummer, the great British scholar and commentator, speaks of this as a "magnificent work."   In the Scotsman (Edinburg) it is said of this book "It makes the study of grammar interesting, and demonstrates by conspicuous example the importance of the historical method in gramm tical studies."   Professor James Moffat, of Mansfield College, Oxford, England, in the Expositor, says, "Professor Robertson has the credit of having brought out first a complete New Testament Grammar, in the light of modern research, on the lines of Jannavis rather than of Blass. America has outdistanced both England and Germany in this department, and we congratulate the author on his feat. . . We lay down this book with a sincere appreciation of the labor which has gone to its making, with a cordial recognition of its aim, and with a sense of gratitude to the author for the real service he has done for the science of New Testament grammar. . . The hard, true work of this grammar will not be thrown away.   It is a remarkable achievement from whatever angle it is considered."

Dr. Edwin Mayser, of Stuttgart, Germany, says of this book, "It is a veritable repertory of the Hellenistic speech with complete mastery of all problems and of the entire literature."

Professor F. W. Groshiede, Freie University, Amsterdam, Holland, says of it, "For a long time it will be the book that is to be consulted by every student of the New Testament."

While Dr. Robertson has received appreciation in almost all the countries of Europe, he is not a prophet without honor in his own land. Scholarly men all over America and Canada recognize his worth in this grand contribution to learning.   This book of his is in sympathy with the new point of view as a result of the papyric discoveries.   He did research at Oxford, England.   Dr. Robertson is often called to institutions of learning to make a series of lectures, sometimes to Chicago University, Columbia University, etc.

He is patriotic and believes in preserving tradition, being a Son of the American Revolution.   He entered this order through his lineal ancestor, General Joseph Martin.   His colonial ancestry runs back through Joseph Martin, who married Susanna Chiles, to Colonel John Page, founder of the distinguished Page family of Virginia, whose tomb is at Bruton church, Williamsburg, Virginia.   John Page was a member of the King's Council.   He came to Virginia in 1656, dying January 30, 1691 (see Vol. XIX, pages 104, 211, 324 and 437 of the Virginia Magazine of History and Biography; also Obid, also XIII.2; also William and Mary Quarterly, Vol. V-272). The line runs thus: Col. John Page. Col. John Page had a daughter, Mary Page, married Walter Chiles, also member House of Burgesses. They had a son, Walter Chiles, also member House of Burgesses, whose wife was Eleanor. They had a son, John Chiles, who was father of Susanna Chiles, wife of Joseph Martin. They had sons, Gen. Joseph Martin, Captain William Martin, Col. John Martin, of "Rock-House," Brice Martin. Gen. Joseph Martin had a son, Col. Joseph Martin, of Henry county, Va. He had a daughter, Ella Martin, who married Dr. John Robertson. They had a son, Archibald T. Robertson, L. L. D.

Archibald T. Robertson married Ella T. Broadus, daughter of Dr. John Albert Broadus, of Louisville, Kentucky. So their children have in their veins the blood of this truly great and good man. The Courier Journal of April 9, 1916, in a sketch of Dr. Broadus, speaks of him as "The First Citizen of Louisville." He took a deep interest in the social commercial and æsthetic development of the city, as well as in its religious life. Even after becoming president of the Southern Baptist Theological Seminary, he did not relinguish his class-work, but retained the chairs of New Testament Interpretation and Homilitics. Here his chief work was done, as he helped to mould the life of thousands of young men, some of whom stand in the most influential pulpits of to-day; some are found in village churches; many are preaching the "good news" in the jungles of Africa, and some are telling the wondrous story in the streets of Tokio and Pekin and in South America.

Dr. Broadus loved the class-work. Once he was offered $15,000 a year as pastor of the church in New York which John D. Rockafeller attends, but declined the offer. It was in 1888 that Dr. Broadus was made president of the Southern Theological Seminary. He was a man of great learning and eloquence. It was said of him that "he was greater in his simplicity and humility than in his learning and eloquence." He was with General Robert E. Lee as chaplain. They were strong personal friends. Although a true citizen of the reunited nation, Dr. Broadus ever retained a love for the Stars and Bars and walked in line with his fellow veterans of the grey to pay a last tribune to the humblest comrade who had answered the final roll call.

Children of Archibald T. Robertson and His Wife, Ella T. Broadus

Eleanor; married John A. Easley, Jr., of Manning, S. C., 1921.
Charlotte; died 1917.
John.
Carey.
Archibald.

Charlotte Robertson, who died when seventeen years old, was a girl of unusual mentality. Her teacher, Grace W. Landrum, wrote a biography of her in which she said: "I have written a little biography of the most brilliant young girl I ever knew. Her seventeen years were spent in an environment both charming and distinctive.

"Of all my students, even of all my class-mates at Radcliffe and
the University of Chicago, she was the only one whom I thought destined
to fill among her generation the place of an Alice Freeman Palmer."

Judge and General Samuel W. Williams

Samuel Williams, son of Robert Williams, of Danville, Virginia,
and his wife, Elizabeth Martin (who was a daughter of Colonel Joseph
Martin, of Henry county, Va.) was born and reared in Pittsylvania
county, Va.

When a mere boy Williams enlisted in the Confederate army during the closing years of the war. His gather's family, as was the case
over the entire Southland, suffered reverses of fortune during the war.
So Williams, early in life, was thrown out on his own resources.
He went to Wythville, Va., and began the practice of law. He was one
of Virginia's most distinguished lawyers, serving on the bench and later,
in 1907, was elected attorney-general and collector for the State of
Virginia, in which capacity he made a brilliant record.

He loved with a perfect devotion the Southland and the Confederate cause. At all reunions of United Confederate Veterans, General
Samuel W. Williams was found. He had posts of honor in this body.
He was on General Stephen D. Lee's staff when the Confederate reunion was held in Richmond, Virginia, in 1907.

General Williams married Margaret Grayson, of Bland county,
Va., a daughter of Captain Andrew Grayson and granddaughter of
William Grayson. The old home in Bland couunty, in which Mrs.
Williams was born and reared, is a splendidly built old house, large
and spacious, as were most Virginia houses of that day. The elaborate
carving is hand-work. The nails used were all hand-made. The house
was built when Virginia was a colony of England, and is still occupied
by the family (1907). It is spacious, consisting of fifteen rooms, and
is called "Green Meadows," reflecting something of the past days of
Virginia, being one of the old land-marks.

Margaret Grayson Williams' Crockett ancestors were among the
first settlers about Draper's Meadows, Southwestern Virginia. Some
information may be found of them in "Gleams of Virginia," by Boocher.

Judge Samuel Williams and his wife, Margaret Grayson, had ten
children, seven sons and three daughters.

Judge Williams married a second time, a Miss Henry.

Annie Ruffin Williams, only child of Sally W. Williams and Capt.
D. T. Williams, was born in ———, Virginia. She married Riley
Miles Gilbert, of New York City, having met Mr. Gilbert at White Sul-
phur Springs, Virginia. They have a summer home on Lake George.
She is a brilliant woman and he is a man of affairs.

Of the Hairston connection is Mrs. Marv Moore Barksdale (Mrs.
G. J.), of Marks, Miss. She is daughter of Edward S. Moore and his
wife, Alice Elizabeth Hairston, and granddaughter of Richard Edward
Moore. An aunt of hers, Mrs. Bettie Hairston, lives in Martinsville, Va.

We will give an incident which illustrates the uncertainty in finan-

cial affairs after the close of the World war: A kinsman of Mr. Barksdale, Mr. Selwyn Jones, owned a plantation of 17,000 acres in the
Mississippi delta, near Greenwood. In 1919, when prices of land were
soaring, he was offered one and a half million dollars for this land with
all improvements, but refused the offer. The price. of cotton fell and
labor was still high. In 1921 this place was in the hands of a receiver.

Captain William Martin (1742-1809)

William Martin, son of Joseph Martin and his wife, Susanna Chiles,
was born in Albemarle county, Virginia, in 1742. He died in Stokes
county, North Carolina, in 1809. William Martin was reared in that
part of Pittsylvania county which was cut off and made Patrick and
Henry counties.

He married Rachel Dalton, daughter of Samuel Dalton, of Mayo
river, Rockingham county, North Carolina. This home is about ten
miles from "Hughesville."

Captain Martin is buried at "Hughesville" in the old family burying ground in Patrick county, Virginia.

Captain Martin's wife, Rachel Dalton, lived to be quite old. She
was born in 1746 and died in Stokes county in 1836.

Pittsylvania county, Va., had been cut off from Halifax county in
1767, and named in honor of the great English statesman, William Pitt,
the friend of the American colonies. Captain Martin's postoffice was
"Penn's Store." Here he had settled some of the family of William
Penn. This Penn family intermarried extensively with the Martin and
Hughes families. Some of the Penns later settled in Danville, Va., and
engaged in the tobacco business. Danville, we know, is the largest
loose leaf tobacco market in the world.

Before the opening of the Revolutionary war, William Martin was
county lieutenant. In looking over old Pittsylvania records, we find in the
appointment of officers, by the Committee of Safety, on Wednesday,
the twenty-seventh of September, 1775, many family names. Some of
the captains appointed at this time were this man, William Peters
Martin, and his brother, Joseph Martin, who was later General; and
Archelaus Hughes, who was later colonel of a Virginia regiment. Colonel Hughes and Captain Martin had married sisters. Jonathan Hanby,
who married another of the Dalton sisters, was also made captain on this
day. We see that Captain John Dillard, another family connection, in
the Spring of 1778, marched with his company to the frontier. All
of the Pittsylvania militia was ordered to the assistance of General Nathaniel Greene after General Gates' defeat at Camden, when Greene was
given command of the Southern army. In Henry county is preserved
the original "General Order," issued March, 1781, ordering them to
the assistance of General Green. The Pittsylvania men took part in
the Battle of Guilford Court House. This included Captain William
Martin and his company. In the Summer of 1781, after Cornwallis had
entrenched himself behind the fortifications at Yorktown, the Governor
of Virginia ordered the militia of the various counties to the siege of

York. The following item from the Claim Records tells us of the Pittsylvania order: "To Richard Todd, Riding Express, for giving the
militia officers notice and finding himself four days in consequence of his
Excellency, the Governor's order, to order one-fourth of the militia to the
siege of York" (see pages 255, 256, 257, 258 and 259 of the American
Monthly Magazine of the Daughters of the American Revolution for
June, 1912. Here quotation is made from original county records).

Thus we see that Captain William Martin bore his part in the
Revolutionary struggle. Another evidence of his service is the fact
that he had a grant of land from North Carolina at the close of the
continental war. His family had moved to North Carolina during the
war. North Carolina, at the close of the war, made grants of land to
her soldiers in payment for gallant service in time of battle. William
Martin received a grant of 1,280 acres of land. This land was in
Tennessee, which was then a part of North Carolina, being in what is
now Wilson county (see page 841, Goodspeed History of Tennessee).

Perhaps it is well enough to bring in here some other family names
and their Revolutionary service which we find in county records referred to above. In June, 1776, Captain Thomas Dillard and Ensign
Robert Dalton commanded a company of minute men. They marched
from Pittsylvania through the counties of Halifax, Charlotte and Dunwiddie to the town of Petersburg, crossed James river at Cobham's,
proceeding on by way of Jamestown and Cleve's old tavern until
Gwynes Island was reached. Here they were stationed for five or six
weeks under General Lewis, and took part in the Battle of Gwynes
Island, fought July 9, 1776. In 1778 we find that Captain Thomas
Dillard commanded a company that marched direct from Pittsylvania
to Isaac Riddle's house, twelve miles above the Long Island of the Holston river, thence on to Boonsboro, Kentucky, where they were stationed three months.

Samuel Dalton (1699-1802), of Mayo, the father of Rachel Dalton
Martin, we are told in the old family chronicle written by Dr. Robert
Hunter Dalton and filed in the archives of the Missouri Historical Society, "was the wealthiest man in all the Piedmont region, both of Virginia and North Carolina." William Martin himself was a man of
wealth.

After Martin had gone to war, this family moved to Stokes county, North Carolina, upon inherited land estate in order to be near Colonel Jack Martin, his brother, of "Rockhouse."

Captain William Martin was a man of culture and refinement, being
much given to studious habits. After the close of the Revolutionary war
he became a minister of the gospel. His wife had all the advantages
of the period in which she lived. The Dalton sisters all married soldiers of the Revolution. Mary Dalton married Colonel Archelaus Hughes,
Matilda Dalton married Captain Jonathan Hanby, who is spoken of
in history as "Francis Marion's right hand," and another sister was the
wife of Major Joseph Winston, hero of King's Mountain.

These sisters had the honor of knowing George Washington in

his own home. John Dalton, a brother of their father, lived in Alexandria, Va. He was a member of the firm Carlyle & Dalton. These sisters often visited their uncle in Alexandria. On pages 268 and 270 of Meade's Old Families and Churches, Vol. II, it can be seen that vestrymen chosen from St. Mark's parish March 28, 1765, included the following names, together with the number of votes received: John West, 340; Chas. Alexander, 309; Wm. Payne, 304; John Dalton, 281; George Washington, 274; John Pasey, 222, etc.

We suppose John Dalton received more votes than did George Washington because of his age.

John Dalton's home still stands in Alexandria. It is a house of four stories and is now a home for the aged. This house, Dalton-Herbert home, is only a few steps from the Carlyle house, the old home of his partner in business.

John Dalton and George Washington were good friends, and this speaks well for Dalton's character.

In Stokes county, North Carolina, Captain William Martin and his family were near his brother, Colonel Jack Martin of "Rock House." They were also near the home of Major Joseph Winston. The wives of Captain Martin and Major Winston were sisters. Many others who lived in this section at that time made history illustrious. Thus we see that the social atmosphere of the homes was desirable.

We can learn something of the mother of Captain and Reverend William Martin in Vol. 8, Virginia Magazine of History and Biography. Here is copied a sketch of William Martin's brother, General Joseph Martin. This sketch was written for Lyman C. Draper in 1842. The original of this sketch may be found in the Draper Manuscripts in the Wisconsin State Library. The sketch was written by Colonel William Martin, of Dixon Springs, Tennessee, a son of General Joseph Martin. He says: "My grandmother, that is Susanna (Chiles) Martin, was one of the best of womankind—her parents of English descent. They raised a large family of children, all highly respectable and from whom has descended an immense offspring, as the Waller, Carr, Lewis, Marks, Overton, Minor, Terry, Chiles families, etc., now spread mostly through the South and West."

Children of Captain William Martin (1742-1809) and His Wife, Rachel Dalton

1. Nancy Martin married Archelaus Hughes, a son of Colonel Archelaus Hughes of Patrick county, Va., and his wife, Mary Dalton.

2. Sally Martin married Captain John Hughes, February 7, 1798, a son of Colonel Archelaus Hughes, of Patrick county, Va., and his wife, Mary Dalton.

3. General William Martin (1781-1843), of Williamson county, Tennessee, whom we shall mention later.

4. Brice Martin, died rather young, leaving two daughters.

5. Virginia Martin married Samuel Clark, who was born in Albemarle county, Virginia.

6. Susan Martin married ———— Moore, a son of Matthew Moore and his wife, Letitia Dalton. Her husband was a brother of Governor Gabriel Moore, of Alabama. He was also a brother of Samuel Moore, who married a sister of Edmund Pendleton Gaines.

7. ———— Mart'~ married Charles Banner. He was a member of the House of Commons in Stokes couunty, North Carlina, 1797-1802. Their son, John Banner, was a member of this body in 1829 (see Wheeler's History of North Carolina).

8. Polly Martin married Daniel Hammock, who died in 1829. She was still living in 1840. The writer has old letters written by Daniel Hammock. He lived near Huntsville, Alabama. In these letters he speaks of Governor Gabriel Moore living near him. This was when Daniel Hammock was a boy.

9. Mary Martin married ———— Moon, who was a native of Albemarle county, Virginia. They lived at Snow Creek, North Carolina, and had a large family. They were both living in 1838. Senator Thomas Staples Martin is of this branch through both the Martin and Moon connections.

John Banner, in a letter to his uncle, General William Martin, of Williamson county, Tenn. and dated Snow Creek, N. C., January 24, 1838, says at the close of the letter, "Virginia joins me in tendering our best respects to you, to Uncle Samuel and family and to Uncle John Hughes and family. Also to Aunt Virginia. Your sister Mary, and Esquire Moon and family, and Aunt Susan Moore wish also to be re-m·mbered to you and all the connection."

Then he adds, by way of postscript, "I forgot to say to you that Matt C. Moon was lately married to Miss Mary Ann McHenry of Sullivan county, Tenn. She is a granddaughter of old Uncle Ambrose Gaines."

In this letter John Banner speaks of having sold some of Gen. Wm. Martin's land in Stokes county, N. C., to Mr. John Chandler and took his bond for. payment of same, with Absolem Scales and Andrew Martin as securities. Then he goes on to speak of the New York elections, expressing his gratification, and adds, "I hope by this time you are convinced that the little Van does not suit the best interests of the American people as their Chief Magistrate." He further says, "Your old friend and relation, Nicholas Dalton, of Rockingham county, is no more. He departed this life about three weeks ago. Your cousin, Sam'l Dalton, Sr., is also dead. I think he expired on June last. A very serious occurrence on Saturday last in Patrick county: Mr. Gabriel Penn, the youngest son of Col. Green Penn, accidentally shot himself dead," etc. Mary Martin Moon, spoken of above, had married her cousin. He was of the same family as Judge Schuyler Moon, an uncle of Senator Thomas Staples Martin, of Albemarle county, Virginia.

General William Martin (1781-1843)

William Martin, son of Captain William Martin and his wife, Rachel Dalton (1746-1836), was born in Stokes county, North Carolina, in

August, 1781. He died in Williamson county, Tennessee, in 1843. He was never married.   During the Revolutionary war his father's family moved from Virginia to Stokes county, North Carolina, to be near his uncle, Colonel Jack Martin, of "Rock House," also near the home of Rachel Dalton's father, Samuel Dalton, of Rockingham, N. C. Here Captain William Martin and his wife both died. She lived to be ninety years old.

When quite a young man, the West seemed to lure the son, William. In 1806 he came to live in Tennessee, in Williamson county. His own cousin, William Martin, son of General Joseph Martin, had come to Dixon Springs, Smith county, Tenn., to live, in 1798. The two men have often been confused by students of history; both were born in Virginia, both came to Tennessee to live early in life, both went to the war of 1812 and bore the title of colonel. The writer, who served as State Historian United Daughters of 1812, wrote for the order a sketch of the lives of these two men: Colonel William Martin, of Williamson county, Tennessee, and Colonel William Martin, of Dixon Springs, Smith county, Tenn. The writer was born and reared in the old home in which William Martin had lived and died. She has among letters by Colonel William Martin, of Dixon Springs, one to Captain John Hughes, with whom Colonei William Martin, of Williamson counuty, made his home. In this letter the Dixon Springs Martin asks to be remembered to "my highly respected kinsman, General (William) Martin."

Much of the correspondence of the Williamson county Martin came into the hands of the writer, letters which throw light on his life. He had correspondence with many men of note. There are lettters from Lewis Cass, while Secretary of War during Jackson's administration, messages from Sam Houston, letters from John Bell, Governor Cannon, Adam Henderson, etc.

In the war of 1812, William Martin, of Williamson county, at Pensacola, served as Major, distinguished himself in the battle. At the Battle of New Orleans, two months later, he was in command as Major, and also was detailed for service on General Jackson's staff, with title Colonel. "Here," the old Dalton chronicle says, "he covered himself with glory." In the library of the Missouri Historical Association at St. Louis is filed valuable manuscript written by Dr. Robert Hunter Dalton. Dr. Dalton was born in Rockingham county, North Carolina, in 1806. He was a near kinsman of William Martin, and was thirty-seven years old when General Martin died. These men were reared in the same locality and were intimate friends. We will say by way of parenthesis that Dr. Dalton was a surgeon in the Confederate army, with post at Danville, Virginia. In this record Dr. Dalton says: "General Willim Martin, or 'Buck' Martin, as he was familiarly called, of Tennessee, fought with General Andrew Jackson in the Indian wars, and covered himself with glory at the Battle of New Orleans."

Robert Hunter Dalton's records are also to be found with his daughter, Mrs. Kate Henderson D. Smith, Concord, Contra Costa county, California, and with his niece, Mrs. Bettie Dalton Kennedy, of "Dalto-

nia Farms," Houstonville, North Carolina. The writer has the old red
sash worn by Colonel William Martin, of Williamson county, at the
Battle of New Orleans. When she was young this sash was for a long
time in the rooms of the Tennessee Historical Society in Nashville,
Tennessee, and bore the label showing that it was worn by Colonel
William Martin, of Williamson county, at the Battle of New Orleans.

The writer not only has some of this man's correspondence, but she
possesses some of his business papers, extracts from public speeches,
etc. Another evidence that he was with General Jackson at the Battle
of New Orleans is found in a letter written him by a friend, Littleberry Griggs, from Sparta, Georgia, October 11, 1840. In this he says,
"Our election is over, and news enough has reached us to satisfy us
that Democracy is defeated. Whigism has triumphed, but it is destined to be short lived." He goes on to say: "It has been asserted here
by the Whigs that General Jackson was not at the battleground at
New Orleans, but was three miles off at the time the battle was fought.
This declaration may astonish you, but to us who witness the course
pursued by our opponents, such statements are not surprising. I shall
take it as a favor if you will inform me what you know about the fact so
explicitly as to leave no grounds for quibbling. There are but few of
Jackson's soldiers in this section of the country, and I write to you because it will be in your power to obtain testimony from many of those
who were our comrades in arms on that occasion. This testimony I
wish to accompany your own in whatever form you may think best."

Miss Roseline Russwurm, of Rutherford county, Tennessee, a
daughter of General John Sumner Russwurm and niece of General William Martin, says. "General Martin was in the battles of Talladega, Tallahatchie, Horseshoe Bend, the Battle of New Orleans," etc.

Standing so near Andrew Jackson, the brilliancy of the chief threw
into the background minor officers. Both at New Orleans and at Pensacola Martin was renowned for dash and bravery. At the
Battle of Pensacola, which was fought November 6, 1814, William
Martin was Major. Jackson was here at the head of 4,000 men. He
advanced from Fort Montgomery and demanded from the Spanish governor possession of the forts at Pensacola. This was refused, although
Spain claimed to be neutral; so Jackson stormed the town. The forts
were surrendered, and the British driven from the harbor. Here, we
are told, "Major William Martin performed a signal service to his
country, as well as a brave and fearless act, in carrying the cannon
into the very face of the enemy, to play upon their ranks" (see Resolutions upon his death and published in his county newspapers).

After Colonel Martin's return from the war we find that he represented Williamson county in the legislature from 1815 to 1821 (see
page 791, History of Tennessee, Goodspeed Publishing Company). In
1833 he was again a member of the legislature (see Mr. Park Mrshall's
sketch of Tennessee history).

In 1825 Martin represented Williamson county in the legislature.
This year he writes to his brother-in-law, Captain John Hughes, who

then lived in Patrick county, Virginia, telling him of the campaign, and of his election. He was elected over a strong opponent, Perkins.

In a speech later in life, made before his constituents when running for some county office, he said: "I have served you in various stations of life, sometimes when duty was easy and agreeable of performance. At other times when hardships and privations were to be borne. . . . I have contended for your rights and privileges in the trying scenes of life when there was danger in almost every step."

On September 4, 1824, Governor Carroll commissioned William Martin Brigadier General of the Ninth Brigade of state militia. His commission reads as follows: "State of Tennessee, To all who shall see this presents, greeting. Know ye that reposing special trust and confidence in the Patriotism, Valor, Conduct, and fidelity of William Martin of the county of Williamson, we do commission him Brigadier General of the Ninth Brigade of the militia of the State, and do authorize and empower him to execute and fulfill the duties of Brigadier General of the said Brigade during good behaviour, with all the power, privilege, and emoluments thereto of right appertaining. And the said William Martin is hereby required to obey his superior officers, lawful orders and commands, and all officers and privates under his command are to be obedient to him as aforesaid. In witness whereof we have caused the Great Seal of the State to be herewith affixed. Witness William Carroll, Esq., our Governor, and Commander in Chief, at Murfreesboro, the 4th day of September, 1824, and in the 49th year of the independence of the United States. By The Governor, Wm. Carroll. Daniel Graham, Secretary of State."

The writer holds this commission, which bears the State Seal. The commission was eagerly sought by four candidates, for it carried with it the additional honor of being in command of the militia when General Lafayette, the idol of America and hero of two continents, should reach Nashville on his tour of the States.

An old letter written August 4, 1824, by Archl. Hughes from Williamson county, Tennessee, to his father, Captain John Hughes, of Patrick county, Virginia, shows that Colonel Lewis, Colonel Brady, Colonel Parish and perhaps others, were candidates for Brigadier General at this time, William Martin being chosen for the position. In this letter the death of Judge Trimble, of Nashville, "a few days since," is told of. The writer has in her possession a picture of General William Martin as he appeared before General Lafayette during his visit to Nashville in 1825. In this picture he is in regimentals, in a General's uniform.

The Marquis de Lafayette arrived in Nashville on May 4, 1825. During his stay here he reviewed the millitia which had gathered to do him honor.

Napoleon Bonaparte paid tribute to the men who had fought under Jackson. When shown some of the crude weapons with which our men won the day at New Orleans, he exclaimed, "With such men at my command, I could promenade across Europe!"

In 1842, W. B. Gordon, who had married a niece of General Martin, writes to him from his home in New Orleans. Gordon had been to Texas, and had seen Martin's old friend, Governor Sam Houston. He tells his uncle that Houston spoke of the high place he occupied in his estimation, and that he wanted to appoint him to some office of trust in Texas. He intimates a possible appointment in his cabinet, but adds that suspicion was abroad in Texas that he would fill all worthy offices with U. S. citizens, and Houston had resolved to disappoint their conjectures.

General William Martin, of Williamson county, Tenn., was a man of warm heart and courtly manner. He enjoyed the social side of life, and, never having married, visited much among his relatives. Old family papers prove that he was frequently in the home of Governor Gabriel Moore, of Alabama. Governor Moore lived near Huntsville. Martin was often in the home of General Joseph Martin in Henry county, Va., and at "Greenwood," the home of Colonel Joseph Martin, of Henry couunty. Colonel Joseph Martin's wife was Sallie Hughes. General Martin was often at "Hughesville," in Patrick county, Va. This was the home of Col. Archelaus Hughes, of the Revolution. He was a frequent guest at "Rockhouse," the home of his father's brother, Col. Jack Martin, of Stokes county, N. C., and in Major Joseph Winston's home. The wife of this hero of King's Mountain was a sister of William Martin's mother. Afterwards his old home passed into the hands of General Joseph Winston, whose wife, Letitia Hughes Winston, was a niece of General William Martin. There was so much of intermarriage between these families. General William Martin was a cousin of General Edmund Pendleton Gaines and the two men were very intimate. Then a sister of Gen. Gaines and Susan Martin, a sister of General Wm. Martin, married brothers of Governor Gabriel Moore. Again, Colonel Joseph Martin, of North Carolina, a son of Colonel John Martin, of "Rock House," married Hetty Gaines, a sister of General Edmund Pendleton Gaines.

General E. P. Gaines was a son of Captain James Gaines and his wife, Elizabeth Strother. (See Virginia Magazine of History and Biography, 12, 203, —4, which reads as follows: "Captain James Gaines was a soldier and a statesman much honored in North Carolina, where he settled (Surrey county) soon after the Revolution, and died in Sullivan county, Tennessee." He was a nephew of Judge Edmund Pendleton. His father, William Gaines, married Isabella Pendleton (and Mary, her sister, married James Gaines, a brother of William).

General Edmund Pendleton Gaine's father, Captain James Gaines, commanded a company of volunteers and did good service (see "Daring Deeds of American Generals").

General Gaines and General Martin were near the same age, General Gaines dying six years before General Martin.

William Martin enjoyed life in New Orleans. As we have said before, "he won his spurs" at the Battle of New Orleans. When his chief, General Jackson, was feted here, he, as a member of Jackson's staff, enjoyed the triumph. A nephew of his, W. B. Gordon, lived in the Crescent City. The mother of Edmund P. Gaines' last wife was a Creole, Zumile Carrier des Granges Clark. This gave General Martin entre into Creole society.

It seems that later in life General Martin fell a victim to Cupd's dart. We gather this from a letter written him by his nephew, Sam Clark, from New Orleans, dated March 26, 1836. Samuel Clark lived on Red river and, as many planters did in those days, he would go to New Orleans to plan his business affairs, to lay in plantation supplies, and, incidentally, to enjory life. Here he met with their kinswoman, Mrs. Polly Harbour, to whom, it appears, General Martin had lost his heart. We will quote the letter in full: "New Orelans, March 26, 1836. Dear Uncle Billy: I landed at this great city on Monday last, having left my bachelor cabin on the preceding Thursday. I came here to lay in supplies and to make some monied arrangements for future operations. I have had but little difficulty in arranging my business, and am now ready to start home. I shall be off tomorrow on the same boat that I came down on (steamer Cumberland). I have met with many acquaintances here from Tennessee and elsewhere, among them your old friend, Jack Bradley. He made numerous inquiries about you and the rest of the family—sent his best respects to you and all. He requested me to say to you that he had cut a very pretty orange stick from the battleground below this city and had sent it to you a short time since by an acquaintance whose name I have forgotten, but who promised fatbfully to give it to you. He wishes you to accept it as memento of his regard for his old friend. Jack lives in Texas, Davidson and Jalsey in Long Prairie, Arkansas, near Red river, above the raft. Jalsey has eight children only, and her husband is rich. , Davidson is doing only so-so; takes his liquor too freely. The old lady died last fall. Last evening the steamer Bayuo Sarah arrived, and who should be aboard but my Aunt Polly Harbour. She is accompanied by her sister, Mrs. Kenney, her daughter, Charlotte (the widow Richardson), and her son, Ewell. She was delighted to see me, of course, and I assure you, sir, I was very much pleased to see them. We had a great deal of talk about Tennessee and Tennessee folks, though your name has not been mentioned yet. I shall take occasion to do so if opportunity offers for conversation when there is not as much company as I have heretofore met in her rooms. She is going to Philadelphia this Spring with Ewell, who goes there for the purpose of attending the medical lectures. I have been persuading her with all my might to go through Tennessee. Sometimes she is willing to go if she can get off in time, but she always winds up by putting some difficulty in the way. I think she will not come through Tennessee. I proposed to call at her house on my way up and gallant her to Tennessee, if she'd go, and be responsible for company back in the Fall (which charge, I have no doubt, you would take off my hands with a great deal of pleasure), but I fear it won't all do. However, I have got Cousin Charlotte on my side, and if we succeed in getting the old lady to go, I will write you again. Time has worsted the old

lady a little, though she laces up and looks pretty spruce, notwithstanding. She says nothing about marrying, but she looks like she
would do it, provided always, she could meet with an opportunity to
suit her. I think if you would come down here and make a set at her,
you could trip her up. Jane has married a Mr. Williams, who was
reared about ten miles from them. He is a few weeks younger than
Jane. I cannot gather from the old lady whether she is pleased or
not. I asked her why she let Jane marry—that I was expecting to go
there this Spring on purpose to court her. She replied that she could
not keep her single always. Please let mother know that you heard from
me, and remember me to her and the family. Truly yours, Sam Clark."

There are other letters to General Martin from this nephew, Sam
Clark, which throw some light on the prosperity of Southern planters
in those days.

There are many letters from General John Sumner Russwurm,
whose wife was Sally Clark, a sister of Sam Clark and of Martin Clark,
the Methodist preacher. She was a daughter of General Martin's sister, Virginia Martin Clark.

Among General Martin's notes of his public speeches is a short
extract in which he seems to be defending General Jackson's position
in his wife's divorce case.

To give some idea of General Martin's style of letter-writing, we
copy one of his letters to his brother-in-law, Captain John Hughes:

"20th March, 1824. Captain John Hughes, Patrick County, Virginia. Dear Sir: I am now in Nashville. It is a late hour: the foot-
steps of passengers are heard no more on the pavements, and the
noise of the busy world has all died away with the late hour of the
night. I sit solitary and alone at my table to offer up a few moments
at the holy shrine of friendship before I lie down, but my pen is not
able to do justice to that subject when in so feeble a hand. I never
think of my native neighborhood and friends in it but with the most
tender reflections and doting regret, and an opportunity to renew with
them again the exercise of that friendship, which would be the zest
of all my enjoyments. I have often thought it a pity that I could not
spend my whole life in a society of select friends and acquaintances
with sentiments fully according to my own, of which you would make
one, secluded from the miseries and distresses of the world, shut out
from the angry and ambitious strifes which daily torture the bowels of
society, aloof from the stratagems of iniquity and of factions, interest,
and dupes in the human character that are daily deceiving the honest
heart and rendering man odious to his fellow man. This is a doleful
picture that this world presents to our view, and we are not permitted
to remain the idle spectators of the scene. Our wants and necessities
force us to mingle in the tragedy, and snatch our humble boon from
the gaping multitude, having but a moment now and then to enjoy
social virtues. While we thus act our part in the drama of human life,
it affords consolation to the friendly heart to receive a line from his
absent friend, containing a history of the times and subjects that inter-

est himself. Thus the absent companion can see the life of his fellow pictured to his view, he views his scroll as the type of his mind; and while he reads his history of occurrences, he figures to his mind the personal visage of his friend, becomes interested in the narrations, patrticipates in the feelings expressed, and thus he enjoys real and positive communication, this is the friendship I enjoy with you. As respects myself, I have done no good since I took that fatal appointment. It marred all my peace and happiness, and hung a gloomy cloud over me for months; but a ray of peace and hope has at length shone along my dreary way, and I begin to hope for better times. Archelaus arrived here in good health and appears to be tolerably well satisfied. He will add much to my comforts. I am highly pleased with his principles: he appears to be an immediate piece of myself (Note by the Author: This was Archelaus Hughes, his Sister Nancy's son, and brother of Lettv (Hughes) Winston). I went to Doctor Sandery to see about his tobacco. It has arrived safe, but I could not expect a sale. I think it will be a bad article in that State in consequence if so much being taken there from Kentucky. It is Archelaus' opinion that it had better remain here until you come yourself. My best respects to Sister; tell her I hope her last days will afford her much pleasure; hope her many sons will be an ornament to her and her connection, and her little daughters will comfort her in her old age; and when she has received all the enjoyments allowed for her below, she may be received in the mansion above, where the wicked cease from troubling and the weary are at rest, is the wish of her affectionate brother. Accept for yourself my best wishes for your welfare here and hereafter. I must lie down; the watchman has passed my door and cried the hour of twelve. Wm. Martin."

We will copy an article from the county newspaper, The Western Weekly Review, published at Franklin, Tenn., October 6, 1843, a few days after Martin's death:

"As a mark of respect for the memory of General William Martin, whose death is deeply regretted by all who knew him, the following preamble and resolutions were adopted unanimously at the last quarterly term of the County Court of Williamson. They will be read with interest by his numerous friends and acquaintances throughout the county, as embodying a brief but correct history of one who has rendered essential services to his country in a military, political and civic capacity:

"The State of Tennessee, Williamson County Court, October term, 1843. The death of General William Martin, county trustee of this county, being announced, the following testimony of respect for his memory and worth, is ordered to be entered upon the minutes of this court: General William Martin was born in the county of Stokes, in the state of North Carolina, in the year 1778, and emigrated to the

State of Tennessee about the year 1812 or '13 (Note: He came in 1806), settling in the county of Williamson, where he resided up to the day of his death, which occurred on the 28th day of September, 1843. . . He commenced his career of usefulness in the early stages of the Creek war under General Andrew Jackson. He was an efficient officer in the battles of Talladega, Tallahatchie and Horse Shoe Bend. At the Battle of New Orleans he commanded a company, many of whom are still living, who can testify to the skill and bravery he exhibited on that occasion. At Pensacola he acted as Major and performed signal service to the country, as well as a brave and fearless act in carrying the cannon into the very face of the enemy to play upon their ranks. On his return home, his fellow citizens, grateful for the services he had rendered his country, elected him from the county of Williamson to the State Legislature, which place he filled on several successive occasions. As the strongest proof of their confidence and esteem, he was never refused the suffrage for any office he asked at their hands. In 1842 he was elected to the office of County Trustee, which office he held up to his death, the duties of which he performed, as he had all others in the various relations of life, with honesty, fidelity, and integrity.

"Upon motion of Richard Alexander, Esq., seconded by John Marshall, Esq.—

"Resolved that, in the death of General William Martin, the county has sustained the loss of an efficient, faithful, public officer, and the community at large one of its most worthy members.

"Resolved, that as an evidence of our high respect and esteem for the memory and worth of William Martin, the members of this court all wear the badge of mourning for thirty days.

"Resolved, that a copy of these resolutions be signed by the Chairman and Clerk of the Court, and forwarded to the relations of the deceased, and published in the Western Weekly Review."

General William Martin was buried, with Masonic honors, beside his sister, Sally (Martin) Hughes, in the family graveyard. Here, too, rests the body of his brother-in-law, Captain John Hughes (1776-1860). Here is also the body of Leander Hughes, M. D., the brilliant young son of Captain John Hughes, and two infant children of Dr. Samuel Henderson and his wife, Rachel Jane (Hughes) Henderson. These children's names were Samuel and Levisa Henderson. Here also lies the body of William Leander Webb, son of Dr. William Webb and his wife, Mary Matilda (Hughes) Webb. Later, Mrs. Webb married William Harrison.

II. Nancy Martin, daughter of Captain and Reverend William Martin (1742-1809) and his wife, Rachel Dalton (1746-1836), married her first cousin, Archelaus Hughes, a son of Colonel Archelaus Hughes, of the Revolution, and his wife, Mary Dalton.

Generation

Children of Nancy Martin and her husband, Archelaus Hughes:
    Letitia; married General Joseph Winston.
    Archelaus; moved to Tennessee.
    Nancy; married William Lummis.
    Polly; married ———— Dobson.
    Matthew Moore Hughes; married ———— ————.

Letitia, or "Letty," as she was often called, married Joseph Winston, son of Major Joseph Winston, one of the heroes of King's Mountain, about 1813. We see that Major Joseph Winston in his will left his homestead in Stokes county, North Carolina, to this son. So the old Winston home was theirs until General Joseph Winston moved his family to Missouri to live.

In their home in Stokes county hung a full length oil portrait of Major Joseph Winston, in regimentals. We willl copy a letter written by Nancy (Martin) Hughes to her son, Archelaus Hughes, in Williamson county, Tenn., at that time. She writes from Stokes county, N. C., where she was then spending some time at her mother's, Rachel Dalton Martin, and in the home of her daughter, Letitia (Hughes) Winston:

"Stokes County, North Carolina, November 15, 1831. Dear Son: I am not willing to suffer a favorable opportunity of writing you pass without giving some evidence of that mother-love and affection that should dwell in the breast of every mother. Though it may be possible for some children to forget, in a measure, the breast that nurtured them and the lap that lulled them in infancy, it can never, no, never be the case with the mother. As she watches over the slumber of her innocent babe, so does she watch over the prosperity of her offspring when grown to maturity, and when by fate far removed from them, as is your case, she often prays to the Ruler of the Universe both for their present and eternal happiness. This I have often done for you, and that you could but see the beauties of religion, the deformities of vice, that you would but seriously reflect on death, judgment and eternity. Ah, death! thou dreadful, pleasing theme, dreadful and terrible to the unconverted, when the dread summons comes to call him before the bar—to him the dreadful bar—of a holy and sin-avenging God, to hear that unwelcome summmons, 'Depart, thou'. But on the other hand how different to him whose treasures are not of this world. He can view unmoved the hideous monster. He can leave without a sigh the world and all its vanities, because he is confident he is to enjoy immortal felicity. He is but waiting to hear those consoling words, 'Come, ye beloved, of my Father, inherit the kingdom prepared for you from the foundation of the world.' He is then able to cry out, 'Oh, Death, where is thy sting. Oh, grave, where is thy victory.' Could I but hear you had obtained that pearl of great price it would be to me a pleasure that words cannot express. I must now conclude this excuse for a letter by letting you know that I and most of your relatives are well. I am at this time at your grandmother's (Note:—This was Rachel Dalton Martin, widow of Captain Wm. Martin. She lived to be 90 years old), who is as well as could be expected of one of her advanced age. I expect to go to Colonel Winston's in a few days and remain with your sister, Letty, until the Colonel returns from Raleigh. Your sister, Nancy, will stay with your sister, Polly, until Dobson returns. They will start in a few days, as the Legislature will convene on the third Monday of this month. Let Patsey Hughes hear from her mother, who is not entirely well. Your brother Matt's wife is in better health than she has been for some time past. I must now bid you an affectionate adieu by subscribing myself your affectionate Mother. May the perpetual smile of Heaven be yours. Nancy Hughes. P. S.—You must, if possible, come and see me, but if you cannot do so, send some of the children by the first opportunity."

This letter bears the color of the times in which it was written. That Colonel Joseph Winston, her son-in-law, was a member of the Legislature in 1831, as spoken of in this letter, is proved by Wheeler's History of North Carolina, II, page 407.

This son of Nancy Martin Hughes, Archelaus Hughes, after coming to Tennessee to live, made his home for some time with his mother's brother, General William Martin, of Williamson county, Tenn. General Martin, who was a bachelor, was made very happy by the coming of his nephew. He writes back to Virginia, "Archelaus seems a part of myself." Later on Archelaus Hughes made his home at Dresden, Tenn. Here, in 1837, he ran for congress against Davy Crockett, but of course was beaten. He says in a letter written to his Uncle William Martin, dated August 30, 1837: "I was badly beaten for congress by young Crockett. No man could have beaten him at this time. I knew it, but as I was first out, I could not back down."

We will copy this letter of Archelaus Hughes in full:

"Dresden, Tenn., Aug. 30, 1837. General William Martin; Sir: I have written to you several times of late but have received no answer, and I had concluded that you had left the country, or become a recluse among the hills, and an enemy to all social intercourse amongst your fellow men, until on yesterday morning I received a letter from Wm. E. Anderson, Esq., of Nashville, informing me that it was more than likely that you would be a candidate for the engrossing clerkship to the Senate at the meeting of the Legislature. If you intend being a candidate, why did you not let me know it? My particular friend and relation, Wm. H. Johnson, Esq., of this place, is the Senator from this district. Major Robert E. C. Daugherly, your old friend, is the Senator from the Carrol district. Cousin Brice F. Martin wrote me some time ago that he would be candidate for the engrossing clerk of the Senate. This is what I would dislike to see, for I think him a very deserving, clever kind of a man; but you know that I could not and would not go for any man living against you. I am certain he will not run if you do, but if he does you can certainly beat him. I know Johnson will vote as I want him to, and you can manage Daugherly and Bradford.

" Anderson writes me that W. H. Hunt is candidate for principal clerkship of the Senate, and, as he is a constituent of his, he will have to vote for him, but that if he has to make a second choice, he will go for me. I have but little doubt that I can beat Hunt. You can be of service to me with Marshall, Mitchell, Lowry, Guild and Carothers, and I know that, if you can, you will. I will be up a week or two before the election, or rather the meeting of the Legislature. And if you can be found I will call and see you. The Senator from Rutherford will go for me strongly. I heard from him the other day. I was badly beaten for Congress by young Crockett. No man could have beaten him at this time. I knew it, but as I was first out, I would not back down. My family are in good health, and your namesake grows finely and learns very fast. My youngest sister, Nancy Amanda, got married a few days since to a right clever, hardworking man by the name of William Lummis. Excuse bad writing, but I have a very poor pen and am in a great hurry. I am your friend, A. M. Hughes."

Wm. H. Johnson, who A. M. Hughes speaks of as his "particular friend," writes just one year later to General Wm. Martin, telling of the death of Archelaus M. Hughes. He says: "He had just received the appointment of cashier in a bank in Kentucky, for which he was to get $1,500 per year as salary, and was to enter on the business of his appointment on this day. How uncertain are the dispensations of Providence."

These letters prove to us that Archelaus Hughes left six children. He speaks of one of his children being named William Martin Hughes. One child was named Brice Hughes. This was the father of Mrs. Lizzie (Hughes) Fowlkes, a refined and lovely woman, who died leaving no children. Her husband was a brother of the wife of General Henry A. Tyler, of Hickman, Kentucky, one of the most widely known men in his state. He was one of the first volunteers in the Confederate army, entering April 2, 1861, as captain of Company A, Twelfth Kentucky Regiment. He served under Nathan Bedford Forrest throughout the four years. His dash as an officer at the Battle of Bryce's Cross Roads is spoken of by General Bennett H. Young in the following words: "His assault on the flanks and his charge on the rear of the enemy were noble and superb exhibitions of the highest courage." General Tyler was a man of large wealth and philanthropy. He took special interest in Confederate veterans and reunions. At these reunions he entertained many of his old comrades, always having reserved for his old friends a dozen or more rooms at the leading hotels, and in a number of instances having 300 horses for the old soldiers to ride in the parade, and making it possible for many to attend who were financially unable to do so. General Tyler died April 26, 1915. Robert A. Tyler is his only surviving son.

Some of the Dalton, Martin, Winston, Moore and Henderson connection drifted to Alabama, and several members of these connections became Governor of that state.

Gabriel Moore was the fifth Governor of Alabama. He served 1829-31.

John A. Winston was Governor of Alabama 1853-57.

Joshua L. Martin was Governor of Alabama 1845-47.

Charles Henderson was elected Governor of Alabama in 1914.

We have already noted the fact that Alfred M. Scales was Governor of North Carolina in 1885-89.

III. Sally Martin, daughter of Captain and Reverend William Martin (1742-1809) and his wife, Rachel Dalton (1746-1836), married her first cousin, Captain John Hughes (1776-1860), February 7, 1798. John Hughes was a son of Colonel Archelaus Hughes of the Revolution and his wife, Mary Dalton. Thus we see that children of Sally Martin and those of her sister, Nancy, were double cousins.

Sally Martin spent much time at the home of her grandfather, Samuel Dalton, on Mayo river in North Carolina. The beauty of this river was early recognized. In 1728, when Colonel William Byrd, of Westover, in company with William Dandridge, William Mayo, for whom the river was named, and other commissioners to draw the boundary line between Virginia and North Carolina, Colonel Byrd speaks of this as a "crystal stream." He also says they pitched their tents "on the western bank of the Mayo, for the pleasure of being lulled to sleep by the cascade" (see The Westover Manuscripts, page 76, Vol. I, Cyclopedia of American Literature).

Some of the Dandridge family later settled at Madison on Mayo river. The writer has letters proving this. They were related to Samuel Dalton's family. We have already spoken of the Dalton home on the Mayo river and its refining influence, under head "Dalton." "One day in those sweet, tranquil homes outweighed a fevered lifetime in the gayest cities of the globe."

Sally Martin had all the advantages in an educational and social way the times could give, and grew to lovely and graceful womanhood. William Martin, her father, was born and reared in Albemarle county, Virginia, but, when a young man, went to Pittsylvania county to live. From this county he went out to the Revolutionary war. After the outbreak of the war this little family felt unsettled; and Martin had his wife go back to Albemarle county, temporarily; and in Albemarle county Sally Martin was born, in 1777. William Martin's family, soon after, settled permanently in Stokes county, North Carolina, going there during the Revolution to be near the family of Captain William Martin's brother, Colonel Jack Martin, of "Rock House." Then, too, they were in easy reach of her grandfather's home on Mayo river. The newspaper notice of her younger brother, General William Martin's, death shows that he was born in Stokes county, North Carolina. Sally (Martin) Hughes was a woman adored by her husband and children. Her negro slaves looked on her as their best friend. They would often appeal from the overseer to her. "She was the keystone of domestic economy, which bound all the rest of the structure, and gave it strength and beauty."

After her marriage to John Hughes (1776-1860), she lived in Patrick county, Virginia. Here all of her children were born, seven sons and two daughters. When the youngest child, Rachel Jane Hughes, mother of the writer, Lucy Henderson Horton, was ten years old, Captain Hughes moved his family to Williamson county, Tennessee, to live. This was in the Fall of 1828. The death of an idolized son here and his grave being here no doubt influenced the mother's determination to come. Leander Hughes, the son, had graduated in medicine at Transylvania University, Lexington, Kentucky, coming from that university to visit his uncle, General William Martin, in Williamson county, Tenn. Here he died and was buried under a large mulberry tree, several hundred yards from the house. The loss of this brilliant young son was the greatest sorrow of Sally (Martin) Hughes' life. Her brother, General Martin, had written in heart-broken terms, telling her of the end and as it came to "your precious boy," as he phrased it. He tells her that "followed by a large concourse of friends, they had laid him to rest." In this letter General Martin also speaks of "good old Douglas," and his loving care. This was Thomas Logan Douglas, for whom Douglas church, in that vicinity, was named, an eminent Methodist divine, who lived in the house now occupied by Mr. Henry Reams (1913).

Sally (Martin) Hughes died here September 10, 1842. This was the home in which the writer was born and reared; and she remembers perfectly the beautiful bed steps of cherry, which her grandfather, Captain John Hughes, never suffered to be taken from his room even after he was helpless and did not need them himself. She remembers the old-fashioned chest of drawers, chiffonier, the four-poster bed, and tall mantle clock. · She owns an old-fashioned candle stand, inherited from her grandfather. This was all in cherry wood, beautifully polished. Captain Hughes never suffered his furniture to be changed after the death of his wife. Her clothes were stored away in an old-fashioned chest, together with the many family papers, some reaching back to colonial time. It is from these papers that I, Lucy Henderson Horton, draw largely in writing sketches. Sally Hughes (1777-1842) was very fond of different shades of purple, or violet. The lovely tints at sunset often remind the writer of ribbons and dresses seen in this chest of her grandmother's clothes. A "Treasure Casket," which Sally M. Hughes and her husband prized very highly, is now also in the possession of the writer. It came to the Hughes from a common ancestor, Nancy, or Anne (as the name was sometimes called), Dandridge Redd, wife of Samuel Dalton (1699-1802), of Mayo. This casket was given to their youngest child, Rachel Jane Hughes, on the anniversary of their marriage, Feb. 7, 1838. In the top of the casket is written in Rachel Jane's own hand-writing her name and the date of the gift to her.

This old "treasure casket" is not of intrinsic value. It is made of

Norway spruce, the material from which the best violins are made. The top, bottom and the sides are each made of one piece, the side ends lapped over each other, both being fastened with wooden pegs, driven from the outside. The colors in which the casket is painted are dark green and a faded-looking yellow. On the top is a star within a star. The writer knows of nothing similar to this casket other than a treasure casket deposited in the museum of the Daughters of the American Revolution at Washington, D. C., under letter of authority from Mrs. Matthew T. Scott, President General Daughters of the American Revolution. For account of this casket, see American Monthly Magazine for July, 1910, pages 18 and 19. The owner of this casket lived in France. The casket of the writer is round in shape and is one of the most prized of family relics. These old things are called in Simple Life "vestiges of the souls of our ancestors." We have an old cap which was worn by Sally Hughes (1777-1842).

In this old chest was placed the old, faded, red sash worn by Colonel William Martin, of Williamson county, Tennessee, on the battlefield of New Orleans in 1815.

We will copy the obituary notice of Sallie (Martin) Hughes as published in the Western Weekly Review, of Franklin, Tenn., at the time of her death, September 16, 1842:

"Obituary Notice: Departed this life at her residence in Williamson county, Tennessee, on the 10th of September, 1842, Mrs. Sarah Hughes, the amiable and exemplary consort of John Hughes, Esq., in the seventieth year of her age. This lady, venerable for her years and for her unexceptional conduct through life, as a mild and tender mother and a most affectionate and faithful wife, whose virtues were in every way worthy of imitation, was born in Albemarle county, State of Virginia; married her surviving husband in the year 1797, and migrated to Tennessee in 1828 with her husband and family. They had nine children, two of whom were dead at the time of her death. Her manners were characterized by candor and courtesy, and her heart ever open to impulses of benevolence and humanity, not only sympathetic with human misery and misfortune, but always alleviated such sufferings to the full extent of her means and power. "Without making a boastful parade of her piety and religious sentiments, she not only performed the duties of a vital christian, but embraced in the warmth of a noble heart and highly cultivated sensibilities the God-like sentiment of universal benevolence, the highest attribute of true christianity.   Charles Cassedy."

We will copy also her epitaph, written by the same man: "If those pure virtues, by but few possessed, which give us strength to bear the ills of life, Can found a claim in future to be blessed, Then thou art happy, tender, faithful wife! And if religion of celestial birth, a foretaste gives of Heaven's almighty love, Naught was committed to its kindred earth, But what shall join thee in the realm above."

Sally (Martin) Hughes is buried beside her husband in the old family burying ground in Williamson county, Tennessee, along with General William Martin and others. An oil portrait of this woman be-

longs to her grandson, Judge John Hughes Henderson. Another por_
trait is in the possession of Mrs. H. S. Ewing, and another belongs to
J. H. Harrison.

Children of Sally Martin and Her Husband, John Hughes (1776-1860)

Archelaus Powell; born Jan, 7, 1799; married Polly Webb.
William Madison; born Nov. 5, 1800.
John Fulkerson; born Nov. 10, 1802; married Jane Baldridge.
Leander; born Oct. 1804; died 1828.
Brice Martin; born Oct. 22, 1806; married Elmira Fleming.
Samuel Carter; born April 11, 1806.
Albert Gallatin; born April 17, 1812.
Mary Matilda; born Jan. 15, 1816; married first, Wm. Webb; second,
Wm. Harrison.
Rachel Jane Hughes; born Feb. 27, 1818; married Samuel Hender-
son.

Lineage, in Martin Line, of Sally Martin (1777-1842), Wife of Captain John Hughes (1776-1860).

Sally Martin was a daughter of Captain (and Reverend) William
Martin and his wife, Rachel Dalton. William Martin was a son of Joseph
Martin and his wife, Susanna Chiles. Joseph Martin was a son of
William Martin and his wife ———————————. This William
Martin was a merchant of Bristol, England, who, being a merchant of
means, engaged extensively in the American trade   (see Annual Re-
port of the American Historical Association for the year 1893, page 409).

William Martin, merchant of Bristol, England, was descended from
the Barons of Cemmeas, of Pembroke county, England, whose ancestor
was Martin de Tours who came to England with William the Conqueror,
and was in command of his fleet. That William Martin was closely related to Sparks Martin, of "Withy Bush House," County Pembroke, has
been proved in these pages (see Martin). William Martin's oldest son,
George Martin succeeded him in business in Bristol, England. William also had a son John (see also page 350, Vol. 8, Virginia Magazine
of History and Biography).

Lineage of Sally Martin (1777-1842), Wife of Captain John Hughes (1776-1860), in Chiles-Page Line.

Sally Martin was a daughter of Captain (and Reverend) William
Martin and his wife, Rachel Dalton.   William Martin was a son of
Joseph Martin and his wife, Susanna Chiles. Susanna Chiles was a
daughter of John Chiles, who was a son of Walter (2nd) Chiles and his
wife Eleanor.   This Walter Chiles was a member of the House of Bur-
gesses, and he was a son of Walter (1st) Chiles and his wife, Mary
Page. This Walter Chiles was the immigrant ancestor (see Obid; also
Vol. XIII, 2; also William and Mary Quarterly, Vol. V, 272).   He was
speaker of the House of Burgesses.
For the two Walter Chiles and Susanna Chiles see Obid; for Mar-

tin, see same Magazine; also Vol. XIII, 2. For offices of ancestors, see Stanard's Colonial Virginia Register.

Mary Page was a daughter of John Page, founder of the noted Page family of Virginia (see Vol. XIX, pages 104, 211, 324, 437 of the Virginia Magazine of History and Biography).

John Page was a member of the King's Council. He came to America in 1656; died Jan. 30, 1691. His tomb is at Bruton church, Williamsburg, Virginia, and bears the Page court of arms.

Colonel John Page was a nephew of Sir Francis Wyatt, made Governor at Jamestown, Virginia, in 1621 (see "Vital Facts About Jamestown, Yorktown, Williamsburg, College of William and Mary," published in honor of President of U. S. visit Oct. 19, 1921).

Authorities: Annual Report for the American Historical Association for the year 1893, page 409; also "Two Old Colonial Places," page 217, by Thomas Nelson Page; Stanard's Colonial Virginia Register.

John Page was one of the vestrymen at the old Bruton church in Williamsburg, Virginia. He gave the land on which the old church is built. Here he is buried. On the tomb is the following inscription: "Here lieth in the hope of a joyful Resurrection the body of Colonel John Page, Esq., of Bruton Parish—one of their Majestys' council, in the Dominion of Virginia, who departed this life on the 23rd of January, in the year of our Lord 1691; aged 65."

(Note: Mrs. Bettie Hairston Ingles, a granddaughter of Colonel Joseph Martin and his wife, Sally Hughes, was admitted to membership in the Colonial Dames Society through this line. Her papers were prepared by Sally Nelson Robins.)

John Page, founder of the Page family in Virginia, was known as "Colonel Page." He came to Virginia in 1656, "from the pretty little village of Bedford, Middlesex, where the Pages had for generations been lords of the small manor of Pate, and where they lie buried in the chancel of the quaint little Norman church.... He gave the land on which is built the old church in Williamsburg; and a fragment of his tombstone, recording his virtues, used to lie across the walk doing service as a paving flag until a few years ago, when it was removed by a pious descendant to the interior of the church and a monument was erected to his memory." John Page was a member of the King's Council (see page 217—"Two Old Colonial Places," by Thomas Nelson Page).

IV. Virginia Martin, daughter of Captain (and Reverend) William Martin and his wife, Rachel Dalton (1746-1836), married her cousin, Samuel Clark, who was born in Albemarle county, Virginia.

Samuel Clark and Virginia Martin, his wife, were both cousins of Gov. William Clarke, who accompanied Merriwether Lewis in his exploring expedition to Oregon in 1804. They were also cousins of General George Rogers Clark, who established the Commonwealth of Kentucky. We cannot help pausing over this name. There is something so pathetic in the fact that, despite all his services, George Rogers Clark died poor, neglected, and prosecuted for debts contracted in the very service of his country whose flag he hung to the breeze over the present States of Indiana, Ohio, Illinois, Michigan, Wisconsin and Minnesota.

It was George Rogers Clark who founded the city of Louisville, Kentucky, and in Cave Hill cemetery rests his body, marked only by the simplest little stone bearing this inscription: "General George Rogers Clark; Born O. S. Nov. 9, 1752; died Feb. 13, 1818." This great figure in "The Winning of the West" lies almost forgotten.

Samuel Clark descends from John Clarke—the family sometimes spelled the name with an "e." "John Clarke was in York county, Virginia, before 1645. He was born in England in 1614. He had an elder brother, William, born in 1610, and a sister, Cecelia. They were children of Sir John Clarke and his wife, Elizabeth, a daughter of Sir William Steed, of England." The family coat of arms is described thus:

Clark Coat Of Arms

Quarterly, or, on a bend engrailed azure, a cinquefoil of the field: two argent on a chevron gules, between, columbines azure, as many crescents, or, three azure, a cross between five billets, soltaire, argent, in each quarter: four on a cross sable, five crescents argent. (See article by Frances Cowles, genealogist, in Nashville Banner for May 29, 1916).

We are constantly hearing evidence of Thackeray's assertion that in colonial days younger son of noblemen came to America.

Children of Virginia Martin and Her Husband, Samuel Clark

(1) Martin; a Methodist preacher. He married Charity Ann Battle, a sister of General Joel Allen Battle, who was Colonel of the Twentieth Tennessee Regiment during the War between the States. Charity Battle descended from Charity Horn . Martin Clark died in 1859. His wife died in 1880.

(2) Sally; married Gen. John Sumner Russwurm. John S. Russwurm was a cousin of General Thomas Summer, who gave him a large estate in land. His home was near Triune, Tenn. From here he moved with his family, making his home near Smyrna, near Murfreesboro. The writer has many of General Russwurm's letters, written to her grandfather, Captain John Hughes (1776-1860). We will copy one of these letters later. General Sumner also left his cousin a good sum of money; but freed his slaves. General Sumner is buried on Sumner's Knob, near Nolensville, Tenn. This was on his estate.

Sumner Coat Of Arms

Ermine two chevrons or. The crest is a lion's head erased, ducally gorged, or.

General John Sumner Russwurm was of New England descent. A letter written by General Russwurm to Captain John Hughes (1776-1860), which we copy elsewhere, shows that he was visiting his mother

in the North.   Her mother was of the Sumner line.   In regard to
the ancestry of this family, we will quote Frances Cowles, genealogist:
"In the little town of Bicester, Oxfordshire, there stands to this day the
picturesque church of St. Edburg, the most interesting spot in all England to the visiting Americans of the name of Sumner. · This church,
it is said, was erected in 1400 with the same material and upon the same
site of a much more ancient building.   Here lies buried the body of Roger
Sumner, and here, in 1605, was baptized his son, Wm. Sumner, the
father of the Americans of the name.   Roger, the father, was born in
the little town of Bicester.   He married Joan Franklin in 1601.   William was their only child. ₍ He married Mary West and had six children, the eldest two of whom were born in Bicester and the four youngest in Dorchester, Mass.   Here William, the father, held many important
offices.   His children were: William, born 1625, married Elizabeth
Clemen, of Dorchester, and later moved to Boston.   He had ten children.   Roger, the second son, was born in Bicester.   He married Mary
Josselyn, of Hingham, Mass., and had seven children, who established
a distinguished family.   The third son, George, married Mary Baker.
Samuel, the fourth son of William and Mary West Sumner, was born
in Dorchester and with his wife, Rebecca, went to South Carolina.   In-
crease, the fifth son, also went to South Carolina with his wife, Sarah
Stapler.   Joan, the only daughter, went South with her husband, Aaron
Way.   A Southern family, founded by William, settled in 1690 at
Nansemonde, Va.   His sons were James, John, Jethro, William and
Dempsey.   Jethro had a son, General Jethro, who was in the North
Carolina line during the Revolutionary war.   William, who moved to
Boston, had a son, William, born 1656.   His son, Hezekiah, born 1684,
married Abigal Bedwill; and their son, William, of Middleton, born 1705,
married Hannah Clark, and had seven children.

Gen. John Sumner Russwurm, a cousin of Thomas E. Sumner, whose
remarkable will is on record at the courthouse in Franklin, Tenn., was
one of the legatees of Thomas E. Sumner.   He gives him fifty shares
in the Tennessee State Bank; five hundred acres of land; two thousand
dollars in cash; silver and furniture; rifle and shot gun; large Bible and
all of his books except Blaie and Wesley's 'sermons' (these he leaves to
his wife); and his father's, Jethro Sumner's, sword, "in remembrance
of him who wore it with honor in defense of his country's freedom....
and may he never draw it but in defense of his country, nor sheathe it
without honor."   He also leaves a gold stock buckle to Gen. Russwurm.
Then he makes J. S. Russwurm one of the executors of his will.   In
this will he disposes of "my half of the eight hundred acres in Ohio,
granted to my father, Jethro Sumner."

Of course this would make Jethro Sumner's descendants eligible
to membership in the Sons and Daughters of the American Revolution.
He was general in the North Carolina line.   This will was probated in
the October session, 1819, in Franklin, Tenn.

In his will Sumner sets all his negroes free, providing for them in
their newly acquired freedom.   He leaves them in charge of a society

in Pennsylvania, denominated Pennsylvania Society for the Abolition of Slavery. In case of the society's refusal to take the negroes under its care, "I leave them in trust to the Bishops of the Methodist Church."

Children of Gen. John Sumner Russwurm and His Wife, Sally Martin Clark

Elmira; married Dr. James Ridley. They were parents of Judge Granville S. Ridley, of Murfreesboro, Tennessee, and Ally Ridley.

Virginia; married W. B. Gordon.

Roseline; never married.

Sally; married a Mr. Miles.

William; married a Miss Eason. Their son, Dr. William Russwurm, lives in Helena, Arkansas (1914).

Judge Granville S. Ridley was for years a leading member of the Murfreesboro bar. He, in 1886, was elected to preside over the Criminal Circuit, composed of Davidson and Rutherford, serving eight years.

Judge Ridley enlisted during the latter part of the Civil war in a cavalry regiment that was stationed at Greensboro, N. C., which was made up of many friends of his boyhood days, and, in order to reach his regiment, he rode horseback from the old home near Smyrna, Tenn., to Greensboro, N. C.

Children: Pauline, Mildred, Elizabeth, G. S. Ridley, Jr., Thomas, James, Howell and W. T. Ridley.

Three of his sons served with distinction during the World war. G. S. Ridley became captain, James Ridley was lieutenant in the Murfreesboro Gun Company, and Thomas Ridley was an aviator, seeing service in France in 1918.

Judge Ridley died at his home in Murfreesboro, June 29th, 1921. His death was very sudden. He complained of feeling badly, and asked his wife to bring him a glass of water; but before she reached his side he became unconscious and soon after died.

James A. Ridley was twice cited for bravery. He was awarded the Distinguished Service Cross for heroism at St. Quentin Canal, Bellecourt, France. Sept. 29, 1918. This can be seen in citation issued by headquarters of the Thirtieth Division. Ridley was 1st Lieut. of 113 Machine Gun Battalion.

Children of Rev. Martin Clark and His Wife, Charity Ann Horn Battle

1. Wm. Martin Clark; married Mary Elizabeth Blackman. He was a man of varied talents, was successful physician and served as Secretary of State Board of Health. He was at one time owner and editor of the Nashville Banner. He was author of a popular agricultural book "Grasses of Tennessee." His children are:

   a. Annette; married Joseph J. Green. They have one child, Elizabeth Blackman, married Marion Eugene Rozelle, and they had one child, Maynette, married James Albert Stephenson, of South Bend, Ind.

   b. James B. Clark; married Lucy Pecantel. He served for a long time on the Nashville Banner staff. In 1910 he became editor of the Chattanooga News. Children: Mrs. Elsie C. Jenkins, of Montgomery,

Ala.; Mrs. Mason Meullet, of St. Louis; Hays; Olive; Malon.

c. Battle Clark; married Mary B. Finch. He is member Nashville Banner staff. His son, Finch, served overseas in World war.

d. Wm. Clark; married Julia Detzel. Children: William, served overseas through entire World war; Hays, ran away and enlisted in naval service when 16; had citation for bravery when 18.

e. Annie Clark; married William Tippens. Children: Clark B.; Albert H.; Wm. Dalton; Mary Elizabeth; Margaret Martin (Clark) Owens; James Clark. Wm. Tippens and son, Albert, served overseas.

f. Olive Clark; married John Smith.

g. Mary Lee; married James Culbert. Children: Ann; Battle; Jane and Elizabeth are twins; Mary; Olive; Catherine.

h. Martin Clark; married Margaret Lilliard. Their son, Martin, served in World war.

i. Russwurm; married Sallie Wallace.

(2) Susan Clark, daughter of Reverend Martin Clark and his wife, Charity Ann Battle, married Dr. William Blackman, who was a brother of Dr. Wm. Clark's wife. Their two daughters were: Jessie Blackman, who married Colonel William Hodge, of the U. S. army (1860-65), and lives in New York; Martin Clark Blackman died of yellow fever 1878; and Lizzie Blackman, who married Dr. Reginald Stonestreet, an Englishman, who lived in Nashville, Tenn. Their son, Martin B. Stonestreet, became ensign U. S. navy in 1917, soon after America's declaration of war on Germany. On July 2, 1917, he was married to Esther Harrison Whiting, a Washington belle, the Bishop of Washington being the officient.

(3) Bettie Clark, daughter of Rev. Martin Clark and his wife, Charity Ann Battle; married Frank Armistead.

a. Sue Armistead; married John C. Cook. Their eldest daughter was Mildred Edwin Crutcher and twin daughters, Louise and Willie; sons: John C. Cook, who married Jonnie Rich; and Frank Cook, who married Annabel Hooper.

b. William Armistead; is a successful business man of Winston-Salem, North Carolina. He married Elnora Smith, a descendant of James Robertson, founder of Nashville. They have two children; girls.

c. Samuella Armistead; married Manlove. They have a son, Manlove, Jr., who served with the American army in France the three years of war.

(3) Samuel Clark, son of Virginia Martin and her husband, Samuel Clark; lived on his large plantation on Red river, and was a frequent visitor to New Orleans. Here he would go to lay in his plantation supplies and to enjoy social life.

Children: Walter, Martin and Lucy. Another son, William, married a Mrs. Scales, and lived in West Tennessee. His son, Joe, was killed in the Battle of Shiloh. He had other sons and grandsons, Bill, Joe, Clark, etc.

V. Brice Martin, son of Captain and Reverend William Martin and his wife, Rachel Dalton; died rather young, leaving two daughters.

The name "Brice" is found in almost every branch of the family. "Brice" was the name of the vessel on which the immigrant ancestor, Joseph Matrin, came to America. Martin settled in Virginia, and married Susanna Chiles.

VI. Susan; daughter of Capt and Rev. W. Martin and his wife, Rachel Dalton, married a brother of Governor Gabriel Moore, of Alabama. Her husband was a son of Matthew Moore and his wife, Letitia Dalton. They were cousins. Another of her husband's brothers married a sister of General Edmund Pendleton Gaines, who was also a cousin.

VII. Mary; daughter of Capt. and Rev. William Martin and his wife, Rachel Dalton, married a Mr. Moon, born in Albemarle county, Va. One can see her name mentioned in a letter written from North Carolina by John Banner, her nephew, to her brother, General William Martin (in sketch of General Martin).

VIII. ———— Martin, daughter of Capt. (and Rev.) Wm. Martin and his wife, Rachel Dalton, married Charles Banner. He was a member of the House of Commons in Stokes county, N. C., 1797-1802. They were parents of John Banner, some of whose old letters the writer possesses. John Banner was a member of the House of Commons from Stokes county in 1829 (see Wheeler's History of North Carolina, Stokes county).

Colonel Jack Martin of "Rock House"

John, or Jack (as he is spoken of in history), Martin was a son of Joseph Martin and his wife, Susanna Chiles. He was a brother of Captain (and Rev.) Wm. Martin, General Joseph Martin, etc. These three brothers moved from Albemarle county, Virginia, where they were born, to the border counties of Virginia and North Carolina. Colonel Jack Martin and his brother, William, both settled in Stokes county, N. C.

In June, 1784, John Martin married Nancy Shipp, of Surrey county, N. C., an adjoining county. In 1770 the building of his famous home, "Rock House," was begun. This house was completed soon after his marriage in 1784; but, being an immense structure, a part of it was habitable before that time, and here John Martin made his home. And here, too, war councils were held. Men met at "Rock House" to devise ways and means in two wars, the Revolutionary war and the war of 1812.

John Martin went out to the war of the American Revolution as Lieut. in Capt. Joseph Henry Smith's company. Later he served in the same capacity under Minor, Smith, Philips and Robert Hill, and under Colonels Joseph Williams, Cleveland, Shepherd and James Martin. He marched first from the old Surrey Court House. He was in the battles of Chestnut Ridge, Surrey County, Colsons, Old Fields, and Alamance, In a skirmish near Broad river he was wounded by the Tories. His wife, Nancy Shipp, comes from a family which has given many distinguished men and worthy women to our nation.

We are always interested in the social life of our ancestors. I will copy a sketch of "Rock House" written by Mrs. Kittie M. Lea, of Tampa, Florida. Mrs. Lea is a granddaughter of Colonel Joseph Martin, of Stokes county, N. C., and a great-granddaughter of Colonel John Martin of "Rock House."

"Rock House, September 12, 1912. I am sitting on the steps of 'Rock House' writing this sketch. 'Rock House' was built before the Revolutionary war by Col. John Martin, being begun in 1770 and finished in 1785. It was here the officers would meet to discuss plans of operation.

"Colonel Martin, known in North Carolina history as Colonel Jack Martin, was a man of great bravery, and his people were of note in many ways in the early settlement of Virginia and North Carolina. His wife, Nancy Shipp, came also of a family of note, many of whom are still prominent people in Virginia. Nancy (Shipp) Martin was a woman of great bravery and managing ability. Their children settled in Virginia and North Carolina. Among their children and grandchildren have been many gifted men and women.

"I look through the windows and go up the steps, where for more than a hundred years the ancestors of our family, Colonel John Martin, General Joseph Martin, Captain William Martin and many other prominent members of the family moved and enjoyed life. It was here that General Edmund Pendleton Gaines was a frequent guest. Joseph Martin, a son of Col. John Martin, of 'Rock House,' married Hetty Gaines, a sister of General Edmund Pendleton Gaines. (Note: they were grandparents of Mrs. Kittie M. Lea and Dr. R. S. Martin, of Stuart Virginia.)

"I go down in the basement, where my great-gandmother had her great dining room. Here the most noted China in her day was kept.

"From the windows can be seen thousands of acres of land which belonged to Colonel Martin, remaining in the family down to time of the War between the States (1860-65).

"This land stretches out in valleys and hills and upon sides of the mountains. The valleys are in cultivation, with small farm houses dotting the landscape. I look out on the rock, now in plain view, where my great-grandfather, Jack Martin, sat to rest, while his wife went farther to see what the slaves were doing. On returning to where she had left her husband, she found him dead. They were both over seventy years of age, nearing the resting place of life.

"At that time there was little of cleared land where now are great fields of tobacco and corn.

" I have just been to the graves of Colonel Martin and his son, William, who in his fiftieth year met a tragic fate. He was killed by his overseer. The grave of Mary (Shipp) Martin is here. The headstones are in place and flowers are blooming about the graves. It seems sacrilege to destroy any part of this old building, which was nearly twenty years in erection. The graves, which are in full view of the front porch, should be guarded. I feel that the spirits of these noble ancestors, who once occupied these rooms viewing the surroundings, which are so grand, are near me, and through them I look back into the past, and realize the truth of what my father, John L. Martin, and my uncle, Colonel William F. Martin, both soldiers in the War between the States, have told me of the glorious past. Both were grandsons of Colonel Jack Martin.

"Some years ago I visited these ruins in company with my aunt, Lizzie Moore, a daughter of Col. Martin. She was a woman of great intelligence and what she told me of 'Rock House' history verified many things my father had told me. I could write for days on the things of history connected with this grand castle, as it might rightfully be termed. The house is four stories in height, all stone, even the floor in the basment is stone.

"From here can be seen Quaker's Gap, the Tory's Cave, Pilot Mountain and Hanging Rock. The walls of this house are in good condition, covered with Virginia creeper, English ivy, and with ferns creeping out from the crevices in rocks. All doors and windows are arched. The roof and part of the partitions burned fifteen years ago (1897). A border of goldenrod has sprung up on the top of the ruin as if to glorify the structure. The walls are over one yard thick, being plastered inside and out, and will stand centuries longer.

"North Carolina history tells us that in Nov., 1775, Col. John Martin, with others, marched from the western part of the state against the Tories in the northwestern part of South Carolina, and with the troops of that state defeated the Tories, capturing 400 of them."

Generation

Children of Col. Jack Martin and his wife, Nancy Shipp:

Mary; born April 23, 1785.

Elizabeth; born Feb. 5, 1787; married a son of Tom Claud.

James; born March 20, 1789; married a Miss Carter.

Joseph; born Feb. 4, 1791; married Christine Harmon Lyon, a daughter of James Lyon and his wife, Hettie Gaines, who was a sister of General Edmund Pendleton Gaines, hero of Lake Erie.

Virginia; born Aug. 10, 1794; died June 26, 1797.

John; born May 5, 1797; married Nancy Perkins. They had one daughter, Carolina Virginia Martin, grandmother of Capt. Jas. G. Anthony.

Samuel; born Jan. 29, 1800; married a Miss Penn.

George; born Oct. 30, 1802.

Thomas; born Jan. 18, 1805; married Miss Smith.

William; born Aug. 26, 1809; died 1859.

We are sorry we cannot give full lines of descent from this family; but will give the names of the children of the fourth child, Col. Joseph Martin, of Stokes county, N. C., and his wife, Christine Harmon (Lyon) Martin. They were married in June, 1818. He was educated at Philadelphia.

Children of Col. Joseph Martin of Stokes County, North Carolina, and His Wife, Christine Harmon Lyon

John Lyon; born June 20, 1820; died Nov. 10, 1865.

Elizabeth; born Nov. 7, 1822; married ———— Moore, a brother of Governor Gabriel Moore, of Alabama. She has one daughter, Mrs. E. A. Couraid, of Louisville, "Pilot View Farm," N. C.

Edmund Pendleton; born March 29, 1824.

James Gaines; born Oct. 16, 1825; married Martha Josephine Pringle.

Augustine Henry; born March 25, 1827.

Sarah Ann; born March 8, 1828.

Mary Frances; born May 20, 1830.

William Francis; born May 10, 1832.

Martha Josephine; born Nov. 4, 1833.

Margaret Isabella; born Aug. 23, 1835.

Amanda Gillum; born March 27, 1837.

Myra Gaines; born Oct. 5, 1839; married Nun and had one daughter, Fannie N. Owen.

Joseph Martin; born Feb. 25, 1843.

John Lyon Martin; married Eliza Meadows, Aug. 28, 1853. Their first child was Christina Frances Martin, named for her grandmother, but who, early in life, received the nickname "Kittie" and is universally known as Mrs. Kittie Martin Lea. Her husband, Henry Clinton Lea, was educated at Chapel Hill. He read law under Judge Dargon, of Mobile. He became captain in the 8th Alabama regiment, of which his kinsman, Hiliary A. Herbert, was colonel. Col. Herbert later became Secretary of the Navy in Cleveland's cabinet. Mr. Lea was member Constitutional Convention of Alabama in 1875. They had two sons to die young, Henry C. and Martin A.

Eliza M. Martin; died August 13, 1880.

Children of John Lyon Martin and His Wife, Eliza Meadows

Kittie Martin; born June 22, 1855; married H. C. Lea, and lives in Tampa, Florida.

Joseph Martin; born June 25, 1856; died in 1921.

Iola G. Martin; born Feb. 20, 1859; married Asy Meadows; lives in Jacksonville, Texas.

Martha N. C. Martin; born Jan. 7, 1862; married S. Y. Algood. She lives in Tampa, Fla.

Myra Lyon Martin; born Jan. 30, 1865; married Nickolas Wise; lives at Bay City, Texas.

Children of Kittie Martin and Her Husband, H. C. Lea.

William Martin Lea; married Janie Reynolds. They have two children, Kittie R., and Jane.

Henry C.

Martin Algernon.

Children of Martha N. C. Martin and her Husband, S. Y. Algood:

Evelyn Gaines Algood; married I. G. Hedrick.

Robert M. Algood.

Kittie Lea Algood; married L. N. Weatherly; lives in Tampa, Fla.

Marion Algood; married Anna L. Graham; had son, Jewell L., who served in World war.

Blanche.

Jowell Lyon.

Colonel William Francis Martin

Col. William F. Martin, son of Col. Joseph Martin of Stokes county, N. C., was born in the famous "Rock House," May 10, 1832. He married Jennie Wellborne, of a highly respected family. They made their home in Mobile, Alabama.

During the War between the States, Col. W. F. Martin commanded a regiment of cavalry, and was noted for gallantry on the field of battle. He died in 1883, and his wife two years later. After the death of his brother, John Lyon Martin, William F. Martin educated his brother's children.

Children of Col. William F. Martin and his wife, Jennie Wellborne:

Jennie Martin; married Wellborne Keith. They live in Alexandria, La.

James Lyon Martin; lives at Ruston, Louisiana. He is a man of note.

Joseph Wellborne Martin; lives at Pine Bluff, Arkansas.

Samuel Martin.

George Martin.

John Martin.

James Gaines Martin, son of Col. Joseph Martin of Stokes county, North Carolina, and his wife, Christine Harmon Lyon, was born Oct. 25, 1825. He had only one son, Dr. R. S. Martin, who lives in Stuart, Patrick county, Va. Here he has a private sanitarium; and was at one time President of Board of Physicians and Board of Examiners. He stands at the head of his profession in Virginia. His mother was Martha Josephine Pringle. Some of this family live now (1917) at Campbell, Stokes county, North Carolina.

William Preston Bynum
(A descendant of Col. Jack Martin, of "Rock House")

William Preston Bynum was born in McDowell county, North Carolina, August 1, 1861, and was the son of Benjamin F. and Charity Henrietta (Morris) Bynum. He was educated in the public schools and at Trinity College, North Carolina, from which latter institution he was graduated in 1883 and obtained his degree of A. M. He studied law in the law school of Dick and Dillard in Greensboro, N. C., and was admitted to the bar in February, 1884. For a short time thereafter he was associated in the practice with his uncle, an ex-justice of the Supreme Court of North Carolina, at Charlotte, N. C.

In 1887 he moved to Greensboro, N. C., where he has practiced continuously since that time in all the courts of the state and in all of the United States courts. In 1890 he was Republican candidate for State Senator from Guilford county. In 1892 he was Presidential Elector on the Republican ticket. In 1894 he was elected Solicitor for the Fifth Judicial District of North Carolina on the Republican ticket, which position he held until the year 1898. He was Judge of the Superior Court of North Carolina in 1898-1899. In 1899 he was appointed Special United States Attorney to represent the Government in the prosecution of a number of bank cases pending in the Western district of North Carolina. In 1911 and 1912 he was a member of the committee appointed by the United States Circuit Court of Appeals for the Fourth Circuit to assist in the revision of the rules of practice for the Courts of Equity of the United States. He was one of the Electors at Large for North Carolina on the National Republican ticket in 1912. In 1915 and 1916 he served as a member of the commission appointed by the Governor of North Carolina for the purpose of revising the system of court procedure and to formulate a uniform system of inferior courts in that state. He is a member of the American Political Science Association and American Society of Criminology. For four years he was President of the General Council of the American Bar Association and also served as a member of the Executive Committee of that Association for a term of three years. In 1916 he was the candidate of the Republican party for Chief Justice of the Supreme Court of North Carolina. In 1919 he was elected president of the North Carolina Bar Association, serving for one year. The same year he was appointed a member of the Committee of the American Bar Association to report on the United States Military Practice and Procedure. He is a member of the National Conference of Commissioners on Uniform State Laws. He was married in the year 1892 to Miss Mary F. Walker, of Charlotte, N. C., and has no children.

Some descendants of George Martin, son of Col. Jack Martin and his wife, Nancy Shipp, live in Kentucky. Among them Pocahontas, a daughter of George, married Martin, of Monroe county, Ky. Other descendants of Col. Jack Martin live in California, etc.

There is an extensive connection of the Bynums with the Hampton family, of which Wade Hampton, of South Carolina, was a member. Mr. R. P. Reece, of Winston-Salem, N. C., comes of the Hampton branch. His grandfather, Dr. Jno. Hampton, was born in 1795; is buried at Flat Rock church, Hamptonville.

John Martin and Nancy Perkins were married August 17th, 1820.

John Martin, son of Col. Jack Martin and his wife, Nancy Shipp, was born May 5th, 1797; died May 27, 1845. Nancy Perkins; born April 22, 1804, died June 15, 1853. Children:

William; born November 8, 1821.

Faithy; born July 15, 1823.

Elizabeth S.; born Feb. 22, 1825.

Thomas P.; born Feb. 24, 1828.

Mary; born Feb. 16, 1830.

John; born Jan. 1, 1832.

Henry P.; born March 28, 1834.

Emaline S.; born Sept. 15, 1835.

Victoria; born Dec. 27, 1837.

Carolina Virginia; born April 1, 1839.

Peter P.; born Nov. 2, 1841.

Carolina Virginia Martin and John Coy were married September 20, 1855. Children:

Mary L.; born Dec. 9, 1856; died March 9, 1857.

Flora L.; born July 21, 1858.

Nannie J.; born Aug. 17, 1860; died ——————.

Clara H.; born March 30, 1864; died ——————.

Carolina Virginia; born Nov. 21, 1866; died ——————.

Maude (half sister); born Jan. 19, 1869.

Flora L. Coy and Cassius M. Anthony were married Sept. 12, 1877. Children:

Floyd; born in 1878; died, 1882.

James G.; born March 14, 1880; married Pauline Rissman, of Alameda, Calif., Oct. 24, 1907. No children.

Charles C.; born in May, 1885.

Pauline; born October 12, 1890; married Thomas Townsley, of Indiana, September 5, 1914; no children.

Charles C. Anthony married Anna Smith, of Illinois. Children:

Wanda; died in infancy.

Doroth Lorraine.

Charles Clifton, Jr.

James G. Anthony; born March 14, 1880; graduated from Lebanon Indiana High School in 1900; graduated from Purdue University, in electrical engineering, in 1904; commissioned Captain Signal Corps U. S. Army, Feb. 1, 1918; promoted to Majority July 1, 1919; accepted commission in regular army July 1, 1920.

Charles C. Anthony; born in 1885; entered Purdue University in 1902 and left in 1906 without graduating; took up civil engineering; in 1914 was sent to Europe by New York State Commission to make a study of the principal European Spas for the purpose of improving the spa at Saratoga Springs; now manager of the Arrowhead Mineral Springs Co., Los Angeles, California.

Pauline Anthony; born October 12, 1890; graduated from West Lafayette High School and entered Purdue University in 1908; graduated in 1912; married Thomas Townsley, Oct. 5, 1914, and went to Columbia, Mo; to live.

Senator Thomas Staples Martin

Thomas Staples Martin, United States Senator, who has made such a brilliant record in Congress, is from Albemarle county, Virginia. He comes of the Joseph Martin and his wife, Susanna Chiles, line. One of his ancestors, Thomas Martin, settled on Hardware river in 1764, where his descendants have resided ever since. This Thomas Martin died in 1792. His wife was Mary ——————. They had ten children (see Wood's History of Albemarle County).

Thomas Staples Martin was born and reared at Scottsville, on the James, Albemarle county, Virginia, just twenty miles from Charlottsville, so near Monticello. He was imbued with Jeffersonian principles, and it is said of him that he was a devotee at the shrine of antebellum citizenship.

After his graduation from the Virginia Military Institute, Martin entered the office of his uncle, Judge John Schuyler Moon, a noted Chancery lawyer. His friend, Wm. H. Bumpus, of Nashville, Tenn., speaks of him in the following terms: "For three years of Buckingham courthouse with my uncle, Judge John Hill, Thomas S. Bocock, and N. P. Bocock, all great lawyers, we were so constantly thrown together as friends and students. I never knew a better student, a finer gentleman, a more modest, unaffected man. His mind was analytical and logical... .He made his first speech at Buckingham courthouse." Martin ran for United States Senator against Fitzhugh Lee, who had been Governor and who was a nephew of Robert E. Lee, the idol of Virginia and of the South. "It was the most intense battle of intellects in the memory of men; but the logic f Martin prevailed." He became Senator March 11, 1895, and continued in office until his death in 1919, 24 years. He was the administration's strong friend in the troublous days of the World war; and his death was a great blow to President Wilson. His death was doubtless hastened by hard-working during the war as Chairman of the Senate Appropriations Committee. He had most exacting and important duties in this capacity, which allowed him neither rest nor relaxation. He died at his post, during the great wrangle in the Senate over the ratification of the Peace Treaty and the League of Nations. On the day of his funeral, Nov. 14, 1919, the Senate was in recess that members might attend. Besides the Senate and House committees, Vice-President Marshall, Republican Leader Lodge, Administration Leader Hitchcock, of the Senate, and nearly one hundred members of the Senate and House made the journey to Charlottsville. Others who accompanied them were Secretary of the Treasury Glass and Thomas Nelson Page, former Ambassador to Italy, and other friends.

Senator Swanson, of Virginia, who was associated in political life with Senator Martin for many years, gives the life story of this man, whom he classed as "my best, dearest, and most intimate friend."

Senator Martin was one of the last Confederate veterans to sit in the Senate. He enlisted in the Southern army as a boy of 16. Senator Nelson, Republican of Minnesota, himself a Union veteran, joined in voicing praise of the dead Virginian (see Nashville Banner of April 10, 1920).

One of Senator Martin's most noteworthy achievements was when he inserted in the Senate Record the achievements of the second session of the Sixty-fifth Congress in which twenty-five specific acts of importance to the prosecution of the war are enumerated. This included legislation affecting the second and third Liberty Loan Acts; also the Man Power Act, extending the draft ages, and other measures, which would undoubtedly be passed, he said, before the end of the session.

A record was sent to me in May, 1918, by my cousin, Bettie Hairston Ingles, of Virginia, who was at that time in Atlanta, Georgia, with her daughter. I like to acknowledge my authority for assertions made, but in this do not know just where to make quotation marks.

Gov. Josiah Martin, Gov. Alexander Martin, both of N. C., and Joseph Martin were kinsmen.

James Martin Record

James Martin, nephew of James Martin and his wife, Anne Drummond, who was a daughter of Governor Drummond, of New Jersey, made some record of the Martin family given to him by his uncle, James Martin. He says, too, the account he gives was handed down by Alexander Martin, who obtained it from his half uncle, James Martin, who lived and died on the south branch of the Raretan river, New Jersey, in 1761.

Hugh Martin married a sister of John and Alexander Hunter, who also came from Ireland. Alexander Hunter was the father of Colonel James Hunter, who died at Beaver Island, North Carolina, and to whose memory a monument was erected near Guilford courthouse, where he fought during the Revolutionary war with signal bravery. He was an ancestor of Dr. Robert Hunter Dalton (1804-1900), whose manuscripts are so often referred to in this book. Dr. R. H. Dalton was related to the writer of this family history, Lucy Henderson Horton, through the Daltons and Hendersons.

Mrs. Ingles says from early records handed down in a paper written by one James Martin, who was a son of the immigrant, is given the name of Hugh Martin, who came to America at the age of 21. He was born in the county of Tyrone, Ireland, near the town Tuskilling, about 1700 He was the eldest son by a second marriage of Alexander Martin to Martha Coghran, of Coughran, who came over about 1723, landing at Newcastle, on the Delaware. His family consisted of Hugh, who had arrived two years previous; Thomas, Robert, Henry, Agnes and Esther.

Agnes married a Quaker, Dawson, and lived near Cowles Ferry on the Delaware in Pennsylvania. Esther married Francis Mason, who lived in the forks of the Delaware. He raised three or four as large, athletic sons as could be found in the county.

Alexander Martin, the father, did not live long. After his death his widow, Martha Martin, lived with her daughter, ———— Mason, until her death at seventy years or more.

William Martin, half brother of these children, moved to South Carolina, to a place called Powpon, on the Edisto river, and died there leaving only daughters.

James Martin, brother of Alexander, came to America and married Anne Drummond, daughter of Governor Drummond, of New Jersey. They had two sons, James and William, and several daughters.

The children of Hugh Martin and his wife, ———— Hunter, were: Governor Alexander Martin, of North Carolina; Col. James Martin, of Stokes county, North Carolina, a man of distinguished ability, being a Colonel in the Revolution, and who was the father of Judge James Martin, of Salisbury, who died in Mobile, Alabama; Thomas Martin; Samuel Martin (see page 181, Wheeler's History of North Carolina).

Thomas Martin graduated at Princeton, and then moved to Orange county, Virginia, where he taught a Latin school near M. E. Madison's. He was recommended to the Bishop of London for Episcopal orders, and, being quite an orator, he had the honor of preaching before the King and Queen of England in London. He then returned to Virginia and took charge of a glebe in Orange county, Virginia.

Samuel Martin, son of Hugh Martin and his wife, ———— Hunter, married a Miss Caldwell. He was clerk of the court of Mecklenburg county, North Carolina.

Jane Martin married Thomas Henderson.

James Martin, the writer of his family's history, married his cousin, a Miss Rogers, daughter of Thomas and Frances (Martin) Rogers.

Dr. William Martin, an eminent surgeon of London, left a son, William, doubtless one of the emigrants to America.

Miss Josephine Robertson, of Statesville, North Carolina, says that there were in the garret at "Belmont," home of her great-grandfather, General Joseph Martin, in Henry county, Virginia, letters from Governor Alexander Martin, which proved they were related. Letters from Josiah Martin were also there, proving his relationship. These lettters were, however, lost in the fire. The family notes received from Mrs. Ingles prove that they were related.

Josiah Martin, Governor of North Carolina in 1771, had married his cousin, Elizabeth, daughter of Josiah Martin, of Long Island. He was the last of the royal governors of North Carolina. Under his administration Martin Howard was Chief Justice of the Supreme Court, and Maurice Moore and Richard Henderson were Associate Justices.

"Governor Josiah Martin was by profession a soldier. He bore the rank of Major in the British army, being an Englishman by birth. He was a brother of Samuel Martin, a member of the British Parliament, who was distinguished by a duel fought with the celebrated John Wilkes in 1763" (See page 1—62, Wheeler's History of North Carolina).

The Martins married into the great Fanshaw family of England, which is fully extended in the "Heraldica Miscelanica." Henry Martin, born 1733, Controller of English navy, was created Baronet on the 28th of July, 1791.

Turning to the establishment of the family in England, Sir Bernard Burke gives the following: "The family of Martin is descended from Samuel Martin of Green Castle. He was descended from Joseph Martin, County Doublin, who maried Lydia, daughter and co-heir of George Thomas, of Antiqua and had—1st, Samuel; 2nd, Josiah, of Long Island, in U. S. A., who married Mary Yeamans, of Antiqua, who had—1st, Samuel; 2nd, Charles Yeamans, who died without issue; 3rd, William. Elizabeth, the eldest daughter, married her kinsman, Josiah Martin, Governor of North Carolina; Alice; Rachel, who maried Mr. Bannister, of Long Island."

Thus we have the family brought in clear touch with the American colonies. Their descendants can be traced in New Jersey, Virginia, North and South Carolina, Tennessee and Alabama.

Governor Alexander Martin's Branch

There were intermarriages in the Dalton, Martin, Hughes, Henderson and Winston families in the border counties of North Carolina and Virginia. Dr. Robert Hunter Dalton, from whose records we often quote, was an offspring of these unions. He descends from Thomas Henderson, son of Samuel Henderson (1700-1784) of Granville county, N. C., and his wife, Jane Martin, sister of Governor Alexander Martin of North Carolina, and sister of Col. James Martin of Snow Creek, Stokes county, North Carolina, and of Robert Martin. Gov. Martin, in his will, makes Col. James Hunter, whom he designates as "my friend and relation," his executor. This Col. James Hunter was a kinsman of Dr. Robert Hunter Dalton.

Dr. Robert H. Dalton himself married Jane Martin Henderson of a later generation. The will of Gov. Alexander Martin shows something of the relationship between these families. For other evidences of the relationship, see the Robert Hunter Dalton records, which are filed in the archives of Missouri Historical Society.

Gov. Martin's father, Rev. Hugh Martin, was a native of Tyrone county, Ireland. He settled in New Jersey in 1721, and here Alexander Martin was born the same year.

Mr. Bradley Martin of Palmyra, Tenn., loaned the writer the original will of Gov. Alexander Martin. We shall say in passing that Mr. Martin is a member of the North Carolina Society of Cincinnati. At the present time (1912) there are only seven members of the Society of Cincinnati in Tennessee, so exclusive is the order. Gov. Alexander Martin was also a member of this order.

Bradley Martin descends from Captain Gee Bradley, of the Third Continental Army, through his daughter, who married James Martin, brother of Alexander. They had two sons, Thomas and Bradley Martin, father of the living Bradley.

Mr. Bradley Martin says that one of his kinsmen, Hon. A. R. Ghalson, has a tea pot that was given to his great-great-grandmother Rogers by Gov. Martin, having the coat of arms inscribed upon it. The will of Gov. Martin is very interesting and we will take extracts from it. The will is dated "State of North Carolina, Rockingham County, November Sessions, 1807." He orders that "all my just debts be paid out of what crops I have on hand and out of the crops for the succeeding year, for which purpose all my hands will be kept together under overseers for said year without division," etc. He speaks of his brothers, James and Robert Martin, and his sisters, Martha Rogers and Jane Henderson. He owned a great deal of land, having a tract of 300 acres in Montgomery county, 200 in Anson, 400 in Rowen, 640 acres in partnership with Col. Ad Osborne in Buncome county, and 400 acres in Wilkes. These lands were to be sold for division between the above named brothers and sisters.

He gave his Danbury plantation, where he lived, to his brother-in-law, Thomas Henderson, and wife, Anna Jane Henderson, "on the condition that they maintain and support my mother, Jane Martin, in as decent and proper a manner with regard to clothing and provision as she has been accustomed to during her residence with me."

Danbury plantation comprised more than seven hundred acres of land. Prince, who was a servant to Gov. Martin's mother, was to be set free after her death. He gave Prince, under the name of Prince Martin, one hundred and forty acres of land, one horse, one cow, one calf, sow and pigs.

He gave to Thomas Henderson and Jane Martin Henderson, his wife, negroes named Peg and Nancy, and he gave to another heir a negro named Suck and one named Lewis. (We will say, incidentally, that these names were borne by negroes belonging to my grandfather Samuel Henderson. This Thomas Henderson and my grandfather both descended from Samuel Henderson (1700-1784) of Granville county, N. C. They owned negroes of the same stock).

Gov. Martin disposes of his gristmill, of his still, of his black-smith jack, and of the blacksmith tools. Adjacent to the Danbury plantation were two hundred acres, and also near were ninety-six acres. He gives land and negroes to his brother's natural son, called Robert, and to his brother's natural daughter.

Gov. Martin also had two thousand acres on Duck river. He gave to his natural son, "Alexander Strong, son of Elizabeth Strong, otherwise known by the name of Alexander Strong Martin," eight hundred acres in one tract and forty in another, "also four hundred and fifty acres, part of my Harpeth land in the State of Tennessee." He also gives his natural son negroes. One can see in the books at the court house in Franklin, Tennessee, that Gov. Martin had a large grant of land from North Carolina in what is now Williamson county, in Tennessee. He gives one of his Roger nephews land in Stokes county, N. C. Besides this, he owned three hundred acres of land in Stokes county, and four hundred and twenty acres in Guilford county. "I give and bequeath to my nephews, James Rogers, Samuel Rogers and Nathaniel Henderson, son of Thomas Henderson, the residue of my Harpeth land in the State of Tennessee, which rsidue wil contain one thousand eight hundred and fourteen acres, to be equally divided among them, equal in quantity and quality, each to have his choice according to the order their names stand in this."

Samuel Henderson, grandfather of the writer, lies buried on this land in Williamson county, Tennessee. A small, old-fashioned stone marks his grave.

Governor Martin disposed of his Cataban plantation in Linden county, the upper part including the ferry. He speaks of his nephew, Samuel Henderson, and of giving him land on the Cataban river. He gives to Thomas Henderson "lot of land lying in Raleigh city, adjoining Mr. Secretary White's lot, where he lives." Also house and lot in town of Martinsville, Guilford county, and half of all lots adjacent to that which he holds in partnership with his father, Thomas Henderson. He gives away a good many negroes. He gives someone "table furniture, suitable for breakfast and dinner." He sets some of his negroes free. He speaks of Prince Martin "being a true, confidential and faithful servant;" and further: "As to my man Ben, his services entitle him to this favor, from his great fidelity to me in his private capacity, but when his public services are considered, they must be deemed highly meritorious by his country. It is well known, and I hereby certify that he served his country three years in the Continental service under my command faithfully and with reputation as a soldier, and poor fellow, being an humble friend, companion and servant, bravely risked his life to obtain that liberty from British domination for his master and country, which liberty he was incapable of enjoying the sweets and benefits of, and conscious of this inability, and that the said Ben and his family may not become burdensome to the public, I hereby give and devise to him, under the name of Benjamin Harris Martin, four hundred acres of land lying on the Guilford road, and forty in Rockingham county. I also give and bequeath to the said Benjamin Harris Martin two good work horses, two cows and calves, two plows and two sows and pigs." Governor Martin binds himself to the State of North Carolina for the good behavior of Ben and his family, and of Prince for five years. He gives to Prince one hundred and forty acres on Guilford road.

We will pause to say that the United Daughters of the Confederacy are endeavoring to preserve, in their historical work, records of kindly feeling between the masters and the slaves in the Old South. The writer, Lucy Henderson Horton, contributed to records gotten up by Mrs. Owen Walker, State Historian U. D. C., passages from the will of Governor Alexander Martin, which set forth something of the sympathy between master and slave.

Governor Martin in his will further says: "I give and devise to my brother, James Martin, Col. James Hunter, Thomas Henderson and Alexander Martin, Jr., my warrant and entry of five thousand acres of land lying near the Iron bank of the Mississippi river, on the northwestern corner of the State of Tennessee, to be equally divided among them in quality and quantity, to hold to them and to each of their heirs and assigns forever." He gives to Arthur Hayes five hundred acres of land. This man was a kinsman of the Mr. Hayes who married a daughter of President Jefferson Davis of honored Confederate memory. He gives to Alexander Frohack his small sword, which was presented to him when Governor by his friend, Thomas Frohack, father of Alexander. He gives his "silver coffee pot and stand of silver with my sugar dish to my sister, Jane Henderson, my tea pot and milk pot to my sister, Martha Rogers," other silver to be equally divided. He gives his law books to his nephews. He gives his encyclopedia to one of the nephews and speaks of his "other books, medical and scientific and of miscellaneous nature." He also speaks of his Duke's cabin tract of land: "I give and bequeath to Dr. Samuel Henderson, Jr., my negro boy, Lemisic, to hold to him and his heirs and assigns forever." He gives to his natural son horses, cattle and hogs; also negroes. "Lastly, I constitute, appoint, and ordain my friend and relation, Col. James Hunter, to be the executor of this last will and testament, from the great trust and confidence I place in his honesty and integrity of which I have been witness." This will is written by Thomas Lane and Robert Napier. There are several codicils, which we shall not go into in detail except to say that Martin speaks of giving his silver branch candlestick to his brother, James Martin, Sr., also his gold stock buckle, his portrait, and his gold-headed cane. He gives his horseman sword to his natural son, also his silver spurs and gold sleeve buttons. Martin gives his household furniture to his sister and brother to continue in the Danbury house. He speaks of beds and curtains, of window curtains, hand irons, pictures, China press, book case, etc.

Alexander Martin moved from New Jersey, where he was born, to Virginia, thence to North Carolina. In 1776 he was appointed colonel of a regiment in the Continental line and marched with General Nash to join Washington. He was elected governor of North Carolina in 1782 and again in 1789. He deposited in the office of the Secretary of State at Raleigh "Letters of the Hon. Alexander Spottswood, late Governor of Virginia, respecting affairs of North Carolina, addressed to the ministry of the late Queen Anne."

We are told that Gov. Martin lived at Danbury "In affluence and open handed hospitality." His brothers were Col. James Martin of Snow Creek, Stokes county, N. C., who was a colonel in the Revolutionary war and who was the father of the late Judge James Martin, of Salisbury, who died in Mobile, Alabama, and Robert Martin.

We have already spoken of Col. James Martin of Snow Creek, a brother of Gov. Martin, having married a daughter of Captain Gee Bradley, of the Third Continental army. They had two sons, Thomas Martin and Bradley Martin, father of the living Bradley Martin, of Palmyra, Tenn. (1912).

The children of Bradley Martin of Palmyra, Tennessee, are:

Bailey, of Spokane, Wash.

Adaline O'Neal, of Palmyra, Tenn.

Bradley, Jr.

Elizabeth M. Cummings, of Nashville, Tenn.

Richard, of Clarksville, Tenn.

Tennie Moore, of Palmyra, Tenn.

Etta Lee.

Dorothy.

Alexander.

Some living representatives of the Robert Martin branch, brother of Governor Alexander Martin, are Mr. Bradley Martin, of London, England, and his son, Bradley Martin, Jr., of New York. These men are multimillionaires. In both London and New York they entertain most lavishly in a social way. The St. Louis Republic for June 2, 1912, speaks of Mrs. Bradley Martin of London as "one of the foremost hostesses of the day."

Robert D. Douglas, attorney at law, Greensboro, N. C., is a grandson of Robert Martin, Rockingham county, N. C., being a son of his only child, Martha Denney Martin, who married Hon. Stephen A. Douglas. We will give Robert D. Douglas' line of descent as written by himself, Nov. 11, 1916:

I. "Rev. Hugh Martin, a Presbyterian preacher, came to this country from the north of Ireland and settled in New Jersey. He had four sons, Governor Alexander Martin, James, Samuel and Robert. Perhaps there were others. He had two daughters, one of whom married ———— Henderson.

II. "The Robert Martin mentioned above settled in Rockingham county, N. C., and left a son, Robert Martin, Jr.

III. "The Robert Martin, Jr., mentioned above lived in Rockingham county, N. C. He was generally known as 'Col. Bob Martin,' and acquired a considerable amount of property, several times represented his county in the State Legislature, and left one child, Martha Denney Martin.

IV. "Martha Denney Martin, mentioned above, married Stephen A. Douglas. She left two children, Robert Martin Douglas and Stephen A. Douglas, Jr.

V. "The writer is the oldest child of Robert Martin Douglas." He was Robert D. Douglas, of Greensboro, N. C.

Stephen A. Douglas, the "Little Giant," as he was called, was one of the leaders of his party, being nominated by the Democrats in 1860 for President of the United States.

"Col. Bob Martin," spoken of above, served in the Senate of North Carolina from 1829 to '34 (see Wheeler's History of North Carolina, page 355).

"While living in Chicago, under the influence of his wife, Stephen

A. Douglas gave a portion of land for a Baptist college in that city. Hundreds of ministers have been educated in this college and seminary, and have circled the globe with their messages of love." (See Article by H. A. Brown, D. D. in Christian Index, titled Reminiscenses of Elias Dodson). Mrs. Stephen A. Douglas, when a girl in the home of Gov. Alexander Martin, became a convert through the ministry of Elias Dodson.

Captain John Martin

The first man of the name of Martin in America was Captain John Martin, who came to Jamestown, Virginia, in 1607. On page 131, Daughters of the American Revolution Magazine for March, 1918, it is said: "As a colonist, the actual record of John Smith does not bear comparison with that of John Martin. Smith spent but two years in Virginia, while Martin established prosperous communities in the self-governing commonwealth. When Martin visited England in 1616 and again in 1623 he labored in behalf of the colony."

A son of this man drifted to Albemarle county, Virginia, and here Abram Martin, grandson of Captain John Martin, was born. Abram was living in Albemarle county, Va., (Miss Anna D. Elmore, of Montgomery, Alabama, a lineal descendant, says) in 1685, because some of her old records show that his son, John, was born in Albemarle county in 1685. Miss Elmore is an authority on Martin genealogy.

History tells us that what is known as the "Plains of Abraham," near Quebec, where Gen. James Wolfe defeated the French, Sept. 13, 1759, was so called in honor of this Abraham Martin.

John Martin, son of Abraham Martin, had the following children:

Thomas Martin; born 1714.

Abram Martin, Jr.; born Feb. 7, 1716.

John Martin.

———— Martin; married a White.

Eliza Martin; married a Douglas.

Mary Martin, married a Clark.

Abram Martin, Jr., married Ellizabeth Marshall, who was born in Westmoreland county, Va., March 1, 1727. She was an aunt of Chief Justice John Marshall, as proved by old letters found in the families of Abram Martin. After the war of 1776, Abram was killed by the Indians while looking for land in Georgia.

John Martin, son of Abram Martin (2nd) was the father of Judge William D. Martin. Judge William Dickson Martin was a member of Congress from South Carolina, and was Judge of the Supreme Court of South Carolina.

Abram Martin had moved from Virginia to Edgefield District, S. C. Judge William D. Martin, his grandson, lived in Charleston in the same state. A tombstone still marks his grave here in St. Micheal's churchyard.

Children of Abram Martin, Jr., and his wife, Elizabeth Marshall:
William.
Barcley.
James.
John.
Marshall.
Matthew.
George.
There was one daughter, whose name we do not know.

William, the eldest son of Abram Martin (2nd) was a captain of artillery. He was killed at Augusta, Georgia. He married Grace Warren. We will say in passing that a chapter of Children of the American Revolution organized in Franklin, Tenn., by Mrs. Martha Jones Gentry in 1898 was called the "Grace Warren Chapter" in honor of this woman. The writer's daughter, Sallie Horton, was a member of this chapter.

Barcley Martin was a member of congress. He married Rachel Clay, a cousin of Henry Clay. She was born in Charlotte county, Va.

Matthew, the youngest son of Abram Martin, Jr., lived at one time in Bourbon county, Ky. He later settled in Bedford county, Tenn. His name is on the D. A. R. monument to the soldiers of the Revolution who are buried in Tennessee soil. This monument is on the publlic square in Nashville, Tenn. He was ancestor of Gus Sowell and his sisters, Lizzie and Jennie Hines, of Birmingham, Alabama, and of Mrs. Bettie Martin Thomas, wife of the late Atha Thomas, of Franklin, Tenn.

All of these sons of Abram Martin (2nd) were officers in the American Revolution except the youngest son. We find prominent names among Abram Martin's descendants. Two of General Martin's daughters married gentlemen of prominence. One was the wife of Governor Fitzpatrick of Alabama, who was also U. S. Senator. Susan Martin, another daughter, married Dixon H. Lewis, Senator from Alabama. He is said to have been physically the biggest man in the U. S. Senate. It is said that the hackmen in Washington did not like to serve him, for at one time in taking a seat in a hack his immense weight broke it to pieces.

John A. Elmore, of Alabama, was a cousin of Matthew Martin. George N. Tillman, son of Abram Tillman and his wife, Rachel Martin, of Nashville, Tenn., who at one time ran for governor of Tennessee, descends from Abram Martin.

Col. William Neil Hughes and his sisters, Mrs. Sarah Gifford, Mrs. Alice Smith, of Columbia, Tenn., his brother, General Hughes of Topeka, Kansas; Colonel Archelaus Hughes and Edmund Hughes, on their maternal side, descend from Abram Martin and his wife, Elizabeth Marshall.

The line of Mrs. Atha Thomas, of Franklin, Tenn., runs:

Abram Martin (2nd); married Elizabeth Marshall. Their son, Matthew, married Sally Clay, of Bourbon county, Ky. Their daughter, Bettie Martin, married Edward A. Mosely. Their daughter, Letty L. Mosely, born in Bedford county, Tennessee, married, first, Washington Whitaker. Their daughter, Bettie Martin Whitaker, married first, Ambrose T. Sykes. Issue: Stella Sykes, married Dorsey A. Jamison, a prominent lawyer of St. Louis, Mo. They have one daughter, Elizabeth, who married C. D. Smiley, of St. Louis.

Jesse Sykes, married, first, Jennie James, of Rutherford county, Tenn. They had one son, Ambrose G. Sykes, surgeon. Jesse's second marriage was to Berda Cunningham. They have one daughter, Willie.

Bettie Martin Whitaker married the second time in 1878. Her second husband was the Hon. Atha Thomas, of Franklin, Tenn. Among offices of trust that he filled was that of State Treasurer of Tennessee for two terms. Issue:

Atha; who died in childhood.

Woodlif; attorney at law in Minneapolis, Minn.

Spencer Martin; attorney at law in St. Louis, Mo.

Mrs. Thomas enters the Daughters of the American Revolution through her Martin ancestor.

We will go back one generation. Lettie L. Mosely married the second time Henderson Whitaker, a cousin of her first husband. Their children were: Rebecca, Loula, who married Dr. Crump; Gertrude, Larkin and B. A. Whitaker.

Something of the Marshall and Martin lineage is made plain in Habersham Chapter Lineage book number nine. This shows the relationship to Chief Justice John Marshall. (See "Women of the Revolution" and Johnson's Traditions, "The Women of the Century" and "History of Edgefield."

Another proof of the Revolutionary service of Matthew Martin can be found on page 673 of the American Monthly Magazine for September, 1904: "Captain Matthew Martin was born in 1763 in Virginia. He became a volunteer at the age of 17. He served under Generals Pickney, Sumter, Green and Colonel Clark. He was in four battles, among them Guilford, N. C."

These two Martin families, the Joseph and John branches, were distantly related.

When Henry Clay died we find an entry in the Diary of Dr. Samuel Henderson showing that his father-in-law, Captain John Hughes (1776-1860), whose wife was Sally Martin of the Martin-Chiles-Page line, learned by telegram of the death of Clay on June 29, 1852. Friendship between the Clay and Martin connection seems to have been cherished.

Many members of all the Martin branches belonged to the Baptist church. We learn from the Habersham Chapter Book, Vol. I, that the Moseleys came to America during the reign of Charles the First, in 1649. They had grants of land on Broad creek in lower Norfolk county, Va. Here they built a home, which they called Ralston Hall. This was also the name of their home in England.

Authorities: Johnston's Traditions, The Women of the Century, Mrs. Elliott's Women of the Revolution. See genealogical column of the Atlanta Constitution for July 7, 1901.

Edmund Pendleton Gaines

Authorities: The Gaines family as found in "The Lookout" for Jan. 27, 1917, Dictionary of United States History by Jameson, and Old Family Records.

Edmund Pendleton Gaines, son of Captain James Gaines and his wife, Elizabeth Strother, was born March 20, 1777, and died June 6, 1849. He served during the war of 1812, being promoted Major-General for services in defense of Fort Erie in 1814. He was commissioner to the Seminole Indians in 1816, and took command against them in 1817.

For his victory over the British at Fort Erie, Canada, August 15, 1814, he was voted a sword by the Legislature of Tennessee in 1819. Colonel William Martin (afterwards General, of Militia), of Williamson county, Tenn., General E. P. Gaines' kinsman and personal friend, was at this time a member of the Tennessee Legislature. He was also voted a sword by the Legislatures of New York and Virginia, and was given a medal by the United States Congress.

Gen. Gaines was three times married. His first wife was Frances Toulman, a daughter of Henry Toulman, first Territorial Judge of the Alabama portion of the Mississippi territory. His second wife was Barbara Blount, a daughter of Governor William Blount of Tennessee. By this marriage he had one son, Edmund Pendleton Gaines, Jr., who died in Washington, D. C. His third wife was Mrs. Myra Whitney, nee Clark, a daughter of Daniel Clark, a native of Ireland, who came to New Orleans in 1776 as Consul. The wife of Daniel Clark, mother of the wife of Edmund Pendleton Gaines, was a Creole, Zumille Carrier des Granges.

Mrs. Myra Clark Gaines was born in 1805 and died in 1885. She was for many years plaintiff in an extraordinary law suit to recover the estate of her father, Daniel Clark. Her claim included much valuable property in New Orleans, estimated at $35,000,000. She recovered a good deal of her claim. (For further authority, see Blount Family).

There have been intermarriages between the Martin, the Dalton, the Gaines and the Hughes families of the South since the early settlement of America. In Wales the Gaines and Hughes families have a common ancestor in Roderick the Great. We will quote from the Genealogy of the Gaines family, as found in "The Lookout" for Jan. 27, 1917: "The Gaines family of Virginia and Tennessee is descended from the five sons of Richard Gaines, who died in Culpepper county, Va., in 1750. This Richard was a descendant of the emigrant, James Gaines, who came to America about 1620 and who was a grandson of Sir John Gaines, of Newton, in the County of Brecon, Wales. The sons of this Richard Gaines, of Culpepper county, Va., were Francis, James, William Henry, Thomas and John Gaines."

Because of the intimate relationship with the William Henry Gaines branch of the family and Samuel Dalton's, of Mayo, family and the Martins of Stokes county, N. C., we will write more at length on this family.

Among the descendants of William Henry Gaines and his wife, Isabella Pendleton, we find Moore, Dabney, Strother, Woodson and Rice intermarriages. Mrs. Susan Letitia Rice Clotworthy, of Hillman, Georgia, is a granddaughter of Letitia Dalton Moore Gaines. This Letitia Dalton Moore married her cousin, John Strother Gaines. She was the daughter of Letitia Dalton and her husband, Matthew Moore. Letitia Dalton was a daughter of Smuel Dalton (1699-1802), of Rockingham county, N. C. Two of Letitia Dalton's sisters, Mary Dalton Hughes, wife of Colonel Archelaus Hughes, of Patrick county, Va., and Rachel Dalton Martin, wife of Captain (and Rev.) William Martin, who was born in Albemarle county, Va., later lived in Pittsylvania county, and who died in. Stokes county, N. C., were great-grandmothers of the writer of this record, Lucy Henderson Horton.

Mrs. Kittie M. Lea, of Tampa, Florida, a descendant of Col. Jack Martin, of "Rock House," Stokes county, is also a descendant of William Henry Gaines and Isabella Pendleton, his wife, through their son, James Gaines (1742-1830), and his wife, Elizabeth Strother. Their daughter, Hetty Gaines, married Joseph Martin, son of Col. Jack Martin, of "Rock House."

Another intermarriage between this family and the Martin family was that of Susan Martin, a daughter of Captain (and Rev.) William Martin (1742-1807) and his wife, Rachel Dalton, a first cousin of Joseph Martin, of Stokes county, N. C., who married a sister of Edmund Pendleton Gaines. She was also a first cousin to Colonel Joseph Martin, of Henry county, Va. Susan Martin married a brother of Samuel Moore. Samuel Moore's wife was Elizabeth Gaines. Hence descendants of these marriages are related.

We like to weave in original manuscript when possible. The writer has in her possession a good deal of the correspondence of General William Martin, of Williamson county, Tenn. He was a brother of Susan Martin Moore; and he was a brother of the grandmother of Lucy Henderson Horton, Sally Martin Hughes. Among General William Martin's old letters are found letters written by his sister, Susan Martin Moore, which prove her to have been a cultured woman and an affectionate sister. This letter was written to General Martin just one year before he died. In his old age he suffered financial losses by going security for his friends. She says, "It is extremely mortifying to me to learn that you have again been taken in by your pretended friends. I had hoped that your misfortunes heretofore would forever deter you from becoming responsible for any one except such as you might know to be unquestionable." She speaks of her sisters and says, "Poor sister Sally (Hughes)! How it pains me to know that she is suffering so greatly. Will you please tender to her my most devoted and affectionate love, and if I never see her more in this llife, I hope to meet her in the climes of heavenly bliss." She speaks of her sisters, Polly and Virginia.

We have already stated that two sons of Richard Gaines, who died in Culpepper county, Va., in 1750, William Henry and James, married sisters, Isabella and Mary Pendleton. Francis, son of James and Mary Pendleton Gaines, married Elizabeth Lewis. Their son, Thomas Lewis, married Lucy Patterson Henderson. Their son, John Wesley Gaines, Sr., married Frances Maria Wair. Their son is John Wesley Gaines, of Nashville, Tenn. Mr. Gaines has served as a member of the U. S. Congress. To this same branch belong Mr. John Mosby, of Nashville, Tenn., and Mrs. Dabney Scales, of Memphis.

In "Burke's Landed Gentry" the Hughes and Gaines families have almost identical lineage from Roderick the Great, King of Wales. To the genealogical student this is not strange, since the origin of most Welsh families lies, not in the name of the sire, but like name by which the brothers of the same sire are designated. Thus in Lewis ap (son of) Gynn originated the Lewis family. In like manner the Gaines and many others are shown in the chart of the "Royal House of Britain."

The early Virginia family of Gaines intermarried with the Hughes family of Virginia, both of Welsh ancestry; and in search for the antecedents of these two families was developed the fact that they had the same origin in Wales in Roderick the Great.

Mrs. Harriet D. Pittman in her "Americans of Gentle Birth and Their Ancestors" says that the Hughes and Gaines families of Virginia are descendants of the house of David Gam, Prince of Wales, who antedated the christian era (see Vol. I, pages 255 and 336). Gwynned, Gwyn and Wynne; later the name was spelled Game; then Gaines.

We find this record: "Gwyndie Chapel Llannwst, erected 1633 by Sir Richard Wynne Owen Gwynned, Prince of Wales, founder of the house of Gwyder Mendith, son and heir to Evan, son to Robertson Meredith, son of Evan, heir to David, son of Onfin, son of Caridock, son and heir to Roderick, Lord of Anglesia, son of Owen Gwynned, Prince of Wales."

Two Old Letters

We said that we would insert one of the old letters of General John Sumner Russwurm. This letter was written to my grandfather, Captain John Hughes (1776-1860):

"Fredericksburg, Virginia, Nov. 29th, 1826. Captain Hughes, Sir: As I went on to Philadelphia I could not sell my horse at any price. I therefore left him at this place. On last night I got here and this morning I went to see my horse and found him fat; and today I sold him for $120 with the saddle and bridle. Tomorrow morning I take the stage route for Abbingdon—you see it will be impossible for me to come through your neighborhood. I am very anxious to return home. I have not heard from there but once or twice since I left.

"I have been to Portland and made a settlement with my uncle's executor, though not to my satisfaction by any means, although what money I got was of great benefit to me, inasmuch as it enabled me to settle my mother in a more comfortable situation than that I found her in.

"I am in hopes you had a very comfortable trip to Tennessee, and that you found your friends and mine in good health. I should be very glad to hear from you and wish very much to hear from you on receipt of this. I shall expect you and your family in Tennessee next fall. I am in hopes you, William and Brice made my house your home while you were there. Give my best respects to your good lady, Mrs. Moon, and Col. Martin. I must come to a close by saying I wish you peace, prosperity and happiness. Your friend, John S. Russwurm. N. B.—I see from newspapers that General Houston and General White have been fighting a duel. I am truly glad that Houston sustained no injury. Be sure to write me and give me all the news. I have a bad pen. Yours, J. S. R."

This letter was directed to "Captain John Hughes, Penn's postoffice, Patrick county, Virginia." Eighteen and one-fourth cent postage was paid on the letter.

We will copy a letter of later date written by W. B. Gordon, the husband of Virginia Russwurm, who was a daughter of General John Sumner Russwurm.

This letter is addressed to Gen. William Martin, Franklin, Tenn.:

"New Orleans, February 3rd, 1842. Dear Uncle Buck: I wrote you from Austin, Texas, between the 15th and 20th of December, giving you the information you requested of me—but as our letter-carrying has been all the time imperfect, I entertain some doubts about your receiving the letter.

"I delivered in person your message to President Houston. He replied that he would be pleased to see you in Texas or anywhere else, that you occupied a high place in his estimation, and that he would be more than pleased to confer upon you any appointment in his gift, but that he has been so repeatedly called upon by citizens of U. S., and many of them his old and particular friends, too, that they had obliged him to reject the claims of all foreigners and confine himself to citizens of the Republic. He stated further that a great many persons had been guessing that his Cabinet would contain citizens of the U. S. and that he resolved to disappoint their conjectures.

"I advised you in my letter to abandon the idea of going to Texas, and do sincerely hope you will, as you would, in all probability, lose all you would carry with you. The affairs of that Republic at this time threaten strongly its overthrow and a destruction to the dearest interest of her citizens. Mobocracy has sway over most of the country, and the Constitution is nicknamed. The criminal laws have ceased to be a terror. Murders are as common as natural deaths in Tennessee. You need not think this an exaggeration, for there have been more than sixty murders within my hearing since the first day of last October. If any man of your region desires to be unsafe, both in person and property, send him to Texas. But very few persons in the Republic are satisfied, and I believe all would leave if they could do so.

"I expect to make my home in this city for some years. I am now as poor as I can ever be made. By dent of industry and management, I, however, hope to better my situation. My love to all of the friends—write me. You have the best wishes of, Your true friend, W. B. Gordon."

It seems odd that one who lives in the states should be called in Texas a "foreigner."

HENDERSON

Authorities: Burke; John Henderson, W. S., of Edinburg, Scotland, in his history of the Caithness branch of the family, written in 1884; Eleanor Lexington, genealogist; Orkneying, a Saga, by Dr. Anderson, published in 1873; Colonial Records of North Carolina by Saunders, Vol. II, 1713-1728; Wheeler's History of North Carolina; William Wirt Henry in First Legislative Assembly in America, found in Annual Report of the American Historical Association for 1893; Manuscript written by Thomas Henderson of Mt. Penson, now in hands of Thomas McCorry, attorney at law, Jackson, Tenn.; Diary of Judge Richard Henderson, president of Transylvania Company, found in North Carolina Booklet for January, 1904; papers written by Archibald Henderson, D. C. L., of Chapel Hill, N. C.; Diary of Dr. Samuel Henderson (1804-1884); Colonial Families of United States of America, by George Norbury Mackenzie, Vol. IV, pages 177-180; Henderson Chronicles, by John N. McCue; Ancestry and Descendants of Lieutenant John Henderson 1650-1900, by Joseph Lyon Miller. Indebtedness is acknowledged to James A. Henderson and to John Wesley Gaines, M. C.

Coat of Arms

Gules, three piles issuing out of the sinister side argent, in a chief of the last, a crescent azure between ermine spots.

Crest—A cubit arm ppr., the hand holding a star or, ensigned with a crescent azure.

Motto: "Sola virtus nobilitat."

Origin of Hendersons

Burke says in 1834 that the surname Henderson is of considerable antiquity in Scotland, the Hendersons having settled in the County of Fife, near Inver Keithing, more than four centuries ago. They came here at the time of the disintegrating and scattering of the Clan Gunn in Caithness, when the Mackeys and other of the celtic clans endeavored to bring about their extinction. While the main portion of the Gunn clan settled in Sutherland, some settled in Ross and some in Fifeshire.

James, first knight of Fordell, who fell at the Battle of Flodden Field, September 6, 1513, descended from the "Crowner," George Gunn, through his seventh son, Henry. Following Scandinavian custom, Henry's sons became known as Henrickson Henryson, or Henderson.

"The Gunns unquestionably descended from the Norse Vikings, who subdued and settled portions of Great Britain at an early date. The Gunns were descendants of Rognvold, Earl of Moeria, who was alive in 870. . . Two or three of the sons of Rognvold of Moeria were among the Vikings who led forays into England and the Orkneys, among them Torf Einer, sixth son of the Earl, and from him Gunni, or Gunnius, was descended, he being the first Gunn. Gunnius married a granddaughter of Roland, Earl of the Orkneys and Caithness claiming through her the half of these holdings as estate. Being opposed in this claim in 1231, he killed Earl John, the contestant, for which he was required to appear and answer at the Court of Norway, and his Orkney estates in consequence were taken away from him. Whereupon he retired to his estates in Caithness and became known as the great Gunn of Ulbster."

Thomas Sinclair (England) says: "From this center the Gunns spread into the highland districts of Caithness, as well as along the eastern seashore. Clyth was their early stronghold. They had two castles in this district, that of Castle Gunn, at East Clyth, and Halbury Castle, at Mid Clyth, traces of both being still extant."

Upon the scattering of the Clan Gunn, which took place soon after the death of their greatest chief, George Gunn, at the hands of the Keiths, about the year 1453, many of them took on new family names. Some of the descendants of his son William are known as Williamson, others as Wilson, those of Robert as Robertson, and those of John, Johnson. His sons were James, Robert, John, Alexander, William, Torquil and Henry. As we have said before, through this youngest son, Henry, descended the Henderson of Caithness, Fifeshire, etc. To fortify this assertion England has tradition upon tradition. John Henderson, W. S., of Edinburg, who published a history of the Caithness branch of the family in 1884, asserts this idea.

We note the fact that some of the family have been beheaded for stoutly defending the rights of man, while some have missed being hung for cattle "lifting," a notable example of which was John Gunn, the original of Roderick Dhu in Scott's "Lady of the Lake."

Eleanor Lexington, genealogist, in the Times-Democrat, tells us that George Henderson, of Fordell, successor of James, who fell on Flodden Field, was granted lands in the shires of Fife and Edinburg by Queen Mary of Scotland, and his wife was one of her maids of honor.

Pedigree Earl of Moeria to Henry Gunn

Dr. Anderson in his introduction to "Orkneying a Saga," published in 1873, gives a genealogical table of the Norwegian Earls of Orkney

(1) Rognvold, Earl of Moeria, died 890.

(2) Torf Einer, Earl of Orkney, died 910; sixth son.

(3) Thorfinn (third son), Earl of Orkney: died circa 963; mother: Grelanga, daughter of Duncan, Earl of Duncansby.

(4) Holdver (fifth son), Earl of Orkney; died circa 980.

(5) Sigurd the Stout, slain at Clontarf 1014; mother's name unknown, daughter of Malcolm II, King of the Scots. (Note—In his time the Norse discovered America or Vineland.)

(6) Thornfinn (fifth son), Earl of Orkney; died 1064; mother: Ingibiorg, daughter of Earl Finn Arnason.

(7)   Erlend, Earl of Orkney, died 1098; mother: Thora, daughter of Sumavlidi.

(8)   Oepakson.

(9)   Gunhold; mother, Kol (Kalison).

(10)   Rognvold (Kali Kolson), Earl of Orkney; died 1158; canonized 1192.

(11)   Ingigerd; mother of Eirik Slagbrellir.

(12)   Ragnheld; mother of Liteef Skalli and Gunnie Andreson.

(13)   Snaekoll Gunnison; who lived in 1232, having fled then to Kelben Hougas Castle, on the Island of Vigr (Weir) after slaying Earl Johnson, of Harald Maddason, the last of the Norwegian earls of Orkney. From the same source William the Conqueror is descended, his ancestor being Horlf, conqueror of Normandy and son of Rognvold, Earl of Moeria, who died 890.

Pedigree of First Gunn to Henry Gunn

To Henry Gunn and his sons, according to Thomas Sinclair, the line runs thus:

(1)   Snae Koll Gunnison (the first Gunn).

(2)   Son of Snae Koll, name unknown.

(3)   James de Gunn; grandson of Snae Koll Gunnison.

(4)   Ingram de Gunn.

(5)   Sir Donald Gunn.

(6)   Sir James Gunn, of Ulbster.

(7)   George Gunn (the coroner), died 1453. The sons of George Gunn were: James, Robert, John, Alexander, William, Torquil and Henry. The children of Henry were known as Henryson, or Henrickson, gradually becoming Henderson. From him the Hendersons of Fordell descend.

We will quote from Eleanor Lexington, genealogist, in The Times-Democrat: "Henderson of Fordell is a term of distinction, and well known throughout the United Kingdom. One progenitor was Robert, a man of prominence in the reign of James the Third. James of Fordell (1450-1513) was a great figure in the times of James the Fourth, Lord Justice and King's Advocate, and he received a charter under the great seal. Accompanying James in the unfortunate expedition into England both he and his eldest son lost their lives with their royal leader at the Battle of Flodden."

Robert Henryson, referred to by Eleanor Lexington, went down to conclude negotiations for the marriage of James of Scotland to Margaret, daughter of Henry VI, of England. During the festivities of this occasion he was styled the "Rhymer of Scotland." (See Henryson, Encyclopedia Britanica).

Robert Henryson, the Scottish poet, is spoken of in the New American Enclyclopedia, Vol. IX, as "Henryson of Fordell, father of James Henryson, who perished in the Battle of Flodden Field. His principal work is his collection of fables, thirteen in number, which was edited by Dr. Irving in 1832. Among his other writings are the

"Tale of Orpheus Kyng, and How He Gied to Hewyn and Hel to Seek His Quene," (Edinburg 1508); "Testament of Cresseid," a poem which was suggested by Chaucer's Troilus and Cressede, being also a sequel to that work in connection with which it often appears; "Robin and Makyne," printed in Percy's "Reliques," and several smaller poems which have been printed in different works.

Dunbar, the darling of the Scottish muse, in his Lament, printed in 1508, speaks of "Gude Mr. Robert Henryson" as among the departed poets. This man of letters was a schoolmaster at Dunfermline, Fifeshire, Scotland. This town is 16 miles from Edinburg and was the birthplace of Charles the First, of England.

We cannot pass unnoticed the name of Alexander Henderson, who died in Edinburg, Scotland, in 1646, and whose death was publicly mourned by the nations. As a theologian, he stood second only to John Knox. He was author of the "Solemn League and Covenant." This was wider in its scope than the "National Covenant," which affected Scotland alone, while the former affected the three Kingdoms. Alexander Henderson was chaplain to Charles I and mediated between the king and parliament.

"George Henderson, sucessor to James of Fordell, was granted lands in the shires of Fife and Edinburg by Queen Mary of Scotland; and his wife was one of her maids of honor. He, too, gave his life for his country. His son, James, married Jean, daughter of William Murray, Baron of Tullibardine. James Henderson was a man of parts, and in great favor with James VI, who conferred a singular favor on him in terms of great honor both to himself and the family.

"James Henderson of Fordell is hereby excused from attending the wars all the days of his life, in consideration of the good, faithful services, not only by himself but also by his predecessors of worthy memory in all times past without defection at any time, from the royal obedience that become good and faithful subjects. Dated at our place at Holywoodhouse, February 27, in the 21st year of our reign." This was signed by the king. It was just one year after the death of his beautiful but unfortunate mother, Mary, Queen of Scots. On his mother's forced resignation of the crown, James had been proclaimed king of Scotland in 1567, when only an infant.

On the death of Elizabeth, queen of England, in 1603, James VI of Scotland, succeeded to the throne under the title of James I of England. Four years later, in 1607, colonists came to Virginia from Great Britain and settled at Jamestown on the James river in Virginia. These men were loyal to their king. They named their settlement in honor of King James, and the noble river was also named in his honor. Among these colonists in 1607 was Thomas Henderson (see manuscript written by Thomas Henderson, of Mt. Pinson, now in hands of Thomas McCorry, attorney-at-law, Jackson, Tenn.) He was born in Fifeshire, Scotland. That he was a younger son of Fordell, see "Colonial Families of the United States of America," by George Norbury Mackenzie, Vol. IV, pages 177—180, where his coat of arms is that of Fordell. We shall give additional proof of this fact later.

Those epic ships of 1607, the "Susan Constant," "The Discovery," and the "The Godspeed," bore in their bosoms English, Scotch, Irish and Welsh.

The Henderson manuscript, we referred to above, records the fact that Thomas Henderson moved from Jamestown to Blue Springs. One of his sons was Richard Henderson, who married Polly Washer. The writer, Lucy Henderson Horton, is a lineal descendant of this union through Samuel Henderson (1700-1783), of Granville county, N. C. Polly Washer was a daughter of Ensign Washer. They reared a family in Hanover county, Virginia, consisting of one daughter and four sons. Edward, Samuel, Nathaniel and Leonard. Their daughter married a man by the name of Travillian, who moved to South Carolina.

Ensign Washer

With the first colonists to Jamestown came Ensign Washer. He had held the office of Ensign in Great Britian. We find Washer a member of the House of Burgesses in the first legislative assembly ever held in America. This assembly was called by Sir George Yeardly, Governor-General, to meet at Jamestown, July 30, 1619. Two burgesses were to be elected from each plantation. William Wirt Henry tells us, in a paper read before the National Historical Society in 1893, that Captain Christopher Lawne's plantation, afterwards known as the Isle of Wight, was represented by Captain Lawne and Ensign Washer. (See report of the American Historical Association for the year 1893, page 308, in article by William Wirt Henry entitled "The First Legislative Assembly in America." See also page 179, Colonial Families of the United States of America, by George Norbury Mackenzie, Vol. IV.)

If one reads this article by William Wirt Henry he can see that England's nobility was represented in this first legislative assembly in America, in Virginia in 1619. In the days of Cromwell there were still many royalists, and their ranks were increased by the cavaliers who fled from his vengeance. Down to the days of the Revolution and afterward the Virginia planter and the English country gentleman were very much the same type

"Modern Democracy saw its beginning in England in the Virginia Court of the London Company; in America it had its earliest practical demonstration at Jamestown in the Virginia House of Burgesses, formally assembled in 1619. This first free parliament, responsible to the will of the people, antedated the first British ministry responsible to the people by 164 years.

"The charter secured for the Jamestown settlement in 1608 and 1612 was the forerunner of Marston Moor in England and the Declaration of Independence in America." A notable man who figured in this Legislative Assembly at Jamestown in 1619 was Captain John Martin.

Will T. Hale tells us in "Romance and Beginnings of Dixie" that "Captain Smith left Virginia in September, 1609, when Jamestown was an assemblage of fifty or sixty houses, made of wood, some of them two stories high. . . . Had one looked on that new settlement some day in the seventh year of the seventeenth century, he would have seen men going about their duties in Monmouth caps, Irish stockings, and coats-of-mail. . . . On their tables dishes were of wood, iron or pewter."

It is marvelous to think of the great things in embryo in the year 1607 at Jamestown, Virginia. Professor Moses Cort Tyler says "Since the earliest English upon these shores began to make a literature as soon as they arrived here, it follows that we can fix the exact date of the birth of American literature. It is that year 1607." Professor Tyler goes on to say that we claim the three writings of Captain John Smith while a colonist at Jamestown. The first of these was "The True Relation of Virginia," written soon after reaching Jamestown.

Captain Smith's second writing was to the London Company in which he tells of the utter unsuitableness of most of those with him to found a colony. He complained that many of the colonists were of those called gentlemen—such as do not know how to work. He added "When you send again I entreat you rather send me but thirty carpenters, husbandmen, gardeners, fishermen, blacksmiths, masons, and diggers up of tree roots well provided than a thousand such as we have." Smith's third writing was in reference to the Chesapeake Bay, printed in 1612. His first writing, the general history, has preface addressed to "The illustrious and Most Noble Princess, the Lady Frances, Dutchess of Richmond and Lennox" (see article written by S. A. Link in Nashville Banner, Nov. 17, 1906).

Thomas Henderson, who came from Fifeshire, Scotland, in 1607, to Jamestown, Virginia, the old manuscipt of the Henderson's tells us, "was the father of numerous children." While his son, Richard Henderson, who married Polly Washer, lived in Hanover county, Va., some of the family drifted west and lived Albemarle, Augusta and Orange counties of the same state. Samuel, son of Richard Henderson and Polly Washer, moved with his family to Granville county, N. C., and was the ancestor of the family of which we write at length.

John N. McCue in his Henderson Chronicles, published in 1915, gives us a roster of the descendants of Alexander Henderson of Fordell, County Fife, Scotland, three of whose sons immigrated to the American colonies prior to 1740, settling first near Alexandria, Va.; later some settled in Augusta county.

Dr. Joseph Lyon Miller, of Thomas, West Virginia, wrote "The Ancestry and Descendants of Lieutenant John Henderson (1650-1900), carrying out the Augusta county line. It is interesting to note the similarity of Henderson names of Fordell Manor, Fifeshire, Scotland, and the names of the descendants of Thomas Henderson, who came to Jamestown, Va., in 1607, and of the lines given by John N. McCue and Joseph Lyon Miller.

Thomas Henderson, who came to Jamestown in 1607, was a lineal descendant of Sir James Henderson, of Fordell, who fell on Flodden

Field. This James Henderson was Lord Chief Justice to James IV of Scotland.

We find a descendant of Thomas Henderson living in North Carolina in 1717, Thomas Pollock by name. By consulting Colonial Records by Saunders, Vol. II, 1713-1728, we find the record of a letter "sent of a kinsman of Captain Henderson, Thomas Pollock, to Sir Robert Pollock," dated April 3, 1717, in North Carolina, in which he speaks of owning property in Glascow. He also asks about relatives by the name of Hamilton, and in closing gives us some idea of the irregularity of letter carrying in those days. He says "Please direct your letter to me in North Carolina to the care of Mr. William Willistead, merchant in Boston in New England."

John, James and Samuel Henderson, who settled in Augusta county, Va., about 1740, were sons of William Henderson and Margaret Bruce, and grandsons of John Henderson, Gent. of Fifeshire, Scotland.

"John Henderson was an Ensign in the Augusta militia in the French and Indian war and in 1758 received fourteen shillings pay. His will was recorded in Augusta county in 1766.

"Samuel Henderson was also in the Augusta militia in 1758, and received a like amount of pay. His will is recorded in that county in 1782."

This man was great-grandfather of Mrs. Jane Henderson Duke (Mrs. Walter G.), of Richmond, Va. He had son John born in 1775. He had a son Joseph born in Orange county, Va., Sept. 16, 1832. Joseph's first wife was Mary Ellis; his second wife was Hannah Terrell, of Orange county, Va. They had seven children, two sons, Joseph and John, are living (1904) in Greenbrier county, West Virginia. Three of their daughters live in Richmond, Va.: Mrs. Wright, Mrs. Ware and Mrs. Duke. Mrs. Moncure lives in Louisa county.

Hon. John Wesley Gaines, who descends from the Hendersons of this section, has furnished us many official records, proving service in Colonial wars. These we will give later.

On page 15 of Henderson Chronicle, by McCue, it can be seen that Elizabeth Henderson married Benjamin Stuart, son of Archibald Stuart and Janet Brown. Benjamin Stuart was great uncle of Archibald Stuart, who was Secretary of the Interior in President Taylor's cabinet. He was also a great, great uncle of J. E. B. Stuart, of Civil war fame, and great, great, great uncle of Hon. Henry Carter Stuart, Governor of the Commonwealth of Virginia in 1915.

The writer of this record has an old letter written in 1829 by Archibald Stuart, father of General J. E. B. Stuart. This letter was written to the writer's grandfather, Captain John Hughes. She also has an old letter proving that the Henry Carter Stuart branch is related to our Hughes family through the Hanbys. (See copies of these letters under "Hughes"). We simply mention these facts to show that old Virginia families were related. Indeed, it is often asserted that all old Virginia families intermarried.

The John N. McCue book gives a galaxy of brilliant names found among the Virginia Henderson connection. On page 14 we find the name of the brilliant humorist, "Mark Twain." He was born in Missouri, where descendants of Samuel Henderson (1700-1783), of Granville county, N. C., settled. Among them the name of Senator John B. Henderson, author of the Thirteenth Amendment to the United States Constitution, that of freeing the negroes. Senator Henderson later made his home in Washington City. "Boundary Castle" is his home there. Samuel Henderson, grandfather of the writer, went to Missouri to live in 1808. It was then called Louisiana Territory. He settled on land which has been incorporated in the city of St. Louis.

On page 14 of McCue's book we see that Alexander Henderson (1777-1859) married Margaret Hart, of Kentucky. His second wife was Elizabeth Morrison. Of this last union comes Mrs. Amelia Beard, wife of Chief Justice W. D. Beard of the Supreme Court of Tennessee. In this same line is given the name of William Jennings Bryan.

Mrs. Amelia Henderson Beard, wife of Judge W. D. Beard, was a daughter of Robert M. Henderson, born Oct. 6, 1813; married Morrison. Robert Henderson was a son of Alexander Henderson, who moved from Virginia to Kentucky, and married, first, Margaret Hart; second, Elizabeth Morrison. He was the son of Alexander Henderson, born in Virginia in 1755. It is interesting to note that Mrs. Amelia Henderson Beard brought about in Tennessee the federation of woman's clubs.

The McCue book states the fact that three brothers settled near Georgetown, Virginia, about 1740, but later moved elsewhere. Dr. J. P. Henderson, of Chicago, Illinois, descends from one of these brothers. He is a grandson of John Grant Henderson, born May 4, 1793. The sisters and brothers of John Grant Henderson were Nancy, born Nov. 8, 1782; Alexander, born July 20, 1785; Samuel, born June 25, 1788; Elizabeth, born May 9, 1793.

Susanna Hart, of this same family, married Isaas Shelby. Nathaniel Thomas and David Hart were associated with the Transylvania Company, of which Judge Richard Henderson was president. Judge Henderson was a son of Samuel Henderson (1700-1783), of Granville county, N. C., and grandson of Richard Henderson and Polly Washer.

Hon Carter Harrison, once mayor of Chicago, was of the David Hart line, as was also Lieut. Governor Archibald Dixon, senator, and author of the Kansas-Nebraska bill.

Bennett Henderson, son of John Henderson and his wife, Frances Moore, was born Sept. 28, 1750; died Jan. 18, 1829. He married Elizabeth, daughter of Col. Charles Lewis, of Buck Island, and his wife, Mary Randolph, who was a daughter of Isham Randolph and sister of Mrs. Peter Jefferson, mother of Thomas Jefferson. Bennett Henderson was a member of Lieut. George Celmore's company, which marched to Williamsburg, May 2, 1775, to demand satisfaction of Lord Dunmore for the removal of Powder. He was Magistrate of Albermarle county in 1783. The town of Milton was built on his land.

General Bennett Henderson Young of Louisville, Ky., a veteran of the Civil war, was a grandson of this man. He was commander of the

Confederate veterans when the first reunion of the Blue and Grey was held. This reunion of the veterans, both of North and South, was held in Franklin, Tenn., in the fall of 1914. His patriotic utterances on this occasion no doubt went a long way toward unifying North and South and fitting them for the gigantic struggle upon which they were about to enter—the World war.

General Young, in his address at Arlington during the Confederate reunion in June of 1917, turned to President Wilson, who was on the platform, and told him that, if need be, call for a draft of men between 70 and 80 and that he would get "some really great soldiers," soldiers who had already demonstrated on the field of blood "that the Anglo-Saxon, in defense of his principles, is without fear." He added, "Please, Mr. President, tell the Kaiser that we will be there and that when peace is dictated with the sword at the gates of Berlin, the American men who love liberty and democracy more than they love life will be there under the Stars and Stripes, contending not for land, not for money, but for human liberty and for the destruction of the most baneful government the world has ever seen." General Young was twice Commander-in-Chief of the United Confederate veterans. He, with the help of S. A. Cunningham, acquired the ground for the magnificent monument to Jefferson Davis, leader of the Southern Confederacy. This monument is a tribute of the South to her beloved leader, and is built near Fairview, Kentucky, where Jefferson Davis was born June 3, 1808. This monument will tower above all others except the Washington monument. It is to be an Egyptian obelisk.

General Young is a many sided man. While eminently successful in his profession, that of law, he sometimes writes, for the blind, stories about birds and nature in a way that makes these things seem very real to them. Gen. Young reads them himself to the blind of Louisville.

When the first reunion of the Blue and Grey was held in Franklin, Tenn., brought about by the efforts of the U. D. C. Chapter No. 14 and the local bivouac, the badge worn by all these veterans was beautiful. On a large button was a figure of a veteran in grey and one in blue, clasping hands.

We will quote again from the McCue book: "Captain Wm. Henderson, with his brother, John, marched to Williamsburg July 11, 1775, under George Gilmer. Later he was commissioned captain in the 9th Va. "John Henderson, born before 1757 in Albemare county, Va.; died 1790 in Albemarle county. He married Frances Moore, daughter of John Moore and his wife, who was a daughter of Matthew Jowett. (Note: She was a French Huguenot.) John Moore was a brother of William Moore, some of whose business papers the writer has. They were sons of Bernard Moore. He was High Sheriff from 1757 to 1780, and Magistrate in 1783. Henderson was a private in 1775 under Charles Lewis." On pages 18 and 19 of the same book we see that the Missouri family, children of Daniel Henderson and his wife, Martha Steele, were prominently connected with U. S. Senators, Governors, a Minister to France, member of Congress, Secretary of the Interior, and members of the Supreme court of North Carolina, etc. The North Carolina Hendersons descended from Samuel Henderson (1700-1783), of Granville county, N. C., who was born in Hanover county, Va., and of the third generation in America. The Kentucky, Virginia and Missouri Hendersons were one and the same family. They, having been in America, at least the Thomas Henderson branch, since the English settlement at Jamestown, Va., in 1607, have been scattered over the South, principally in North Carolina, Virginia, Kentucky, Missouri and Tennessee. One branch of the family drifted to Alabama, Governor Charles Henderson, of that State, being a representative of this branch. He is a lineal descendant of Samuel Henderson (1700-1783), of Granvillle county N. C.

Judge Richard Henderson, president of the Transylvania Company, which made a treaty and purchase from the Indians of Kentucky and Tennessee as far south as the Cumberland River in 1775, with his two brothers, Samuel and Nathaniel, were the first of the Henderson name to go to Kentucky (see Dairy of Judge Richard Henderson as found in North Carolina Booklet for January, 1904). Later his kinsmen from Virginia and North Carolina followed him to Kentucky. The Hendersons intermarried with the Kavanaughs of Kentucky. On pages 24 and 25 it can be seen that James P. Henderson, son of Bennett Henderson and his wife, Elizabeth Lewis, who died in 1835, married Margaret C., daughter of Richard Pollard and his wife, Pauline Rives, and granddaughter of Robert Rives and Margaret Cabell, his wife. Margaret Cabell was a daughter of Col. Wm. Cabell and his wife, Margaret Jordan.

William C. Rives, brother of Pauline Rives, did service as U. S. Senator and as Minister to France: Mrs. N. E. Baskett, of Lexington, Missouri, is descended from a kindred branch.

We wish we could trace the lineage of Miss Augusta Brandford, of Knoxville, Tenn., whose grandfather, Judge Henderson, was a noted lawyer.

Judge M. H. Meeks

Judge M. H. Meeks, of Nashville, Tenn., is a son of John Henderson Meeks, whose Maternal grandfather was John Henderson, a captain in the Revolutionary war. The U. S. Government has placed a slab to mark his grave in McNairy county, Tenn., near Selmer. Judge Meeks' grandmother was Elizabeth, daughter of Capt. John Henderson.

Captain Henderson was a man of wealth and had great family pride. He was positive in his convictions and would uphold them even at the fear of personal strife. He was an intimate friend of Gen. Andrew Jackson, and sometimes entertained him at his home.
Descent of John Wesley Gaines, M. C., of Nashville, Tenn.:

John Wesley Gaines is son of Dr. John Wesley Gaines and his wife, Martha Frances Wair, who were married March 28, 1853, in Davidson county, Tenn., where his wife was born in 1834. He was a son of Thomas L. Gaines and his wife, Lucy Henderson.

Lucy Henderson was a daughter of John Henderson, Jr., of Albemarle, county, Va., and his wife, Frances Moore. This is proved by the will of her father and mother. Her mother's will is recorded in Warren county, Ky., in 1818. In this will "my daughter, Lucy, wife of Thomas L. Gaines," is spoken of. We have the verified copy of her father's will, made earlier.

John Henderson, Jr., of Albemarle county, Va., was a son of John Henderson, Sr., of Albemarle county, Va.

Mr. John W. Moseby, of Nashville. Tenn., is grandson of Thomas L. Gaines and his wife, Lucy Henderson, through their daughter, Sarah Elizabeth, wife of William T. Moseby. Mrs. Susan Powell Scales is a granddaughter through their daughter, Malvina H. Winchester.

John Henderson, Sr., of Albemarle county, Va., owned land in that county in 1745. (See Woods.)

Children of John Henderson, Sr., and his wife ———————:
John.
Bennett; married Elizabeth Lewis.
William; married Rebecca Hudson.
Elizabeth H.: married David Crawford.
Susan H.: married John Clark.
Mary H. Bullock.
Hannah H. Bullock.
Frances H.; married John Thomas.

In Wood's History of Albemarle county Va., we are told that this Bennett Henderson was "the second son of John Henderson, Sr., and died comparatively young. Within the next fifteen years his widow and all of her children had moved to Kentucky," to Warren county.

Children of John Henderson, Jr., of Albemarle county, Va., and his wife, Frances Moore, as shown in the will which was proved 1790:
Bennett.
Matthew.
William.
Mary; married Lewis.
Frances; married Hines.
Sarah; married Clark.
Elizabeth; married Martin.
Susanna.
Lucy; married Thomas L. Gaines.

The will of John Henderson is recorded in Albemarle county, Va. It bears the date of January 16,1790.

The will of Frances Henderson, wife of John Henderson, mentions her daughter, Lucy Gaines, wife of Thomas L. Gaines, (see Wood's History, 277-280). Witnesses to the will were Micajah Clark, Bennett M. Clark and Sarah C. Hines, who proved this will recorded in 1818 in Warren county, Ky., where they resided.

Children of Bennett Henderson and his wife, Elizabeth Lewis, daughter of Col. Charles Lewis, Jr.:

John; married Anna B. Hudson.

William.

Sarah H.; married John Kerr.

James.

Charles.

Isham.

Bennett; married Polly Crockett.   He was grandfather of General Bennett Henderson Young.

Hillboro.

Eliza H.; married John H. Hullock.

Frances H.; married Thomas Hornby.

Lucy H.; married John Wood.

Nancy H.; married Matthew Nelson.

(See Wood's History of Albemarle county, Va.)

The pension file (pension department) of Richard Gaines, of Albemarle county, shows that he served under Capt. Bennett Henderson in the Revolutionary war.

Some known descendants of John Henderson, Jr., through his son, Bennett Henderson, are General Bennett Henderson Young, Chief Justice Robertson; Governor and Justice Clarke, of Kentucky; Prof. A. B. Martin, of Lebanon, Tennessee; the two John Bullock Clarkes, members of Congress from Missouri; John Wesley Gaines, member of Congress from Tennessee; Mr. John W. Moseby, of Nashville, Tennessee; and Mrs. Susan (Powell) Scales, of Memphis, Tenn.

The Hendersons of Hanover county, Va., later of Granville county, N. C., and of Albemarle, Orange and Augusta counties, Va., members of which drifted to Tennessee, Kentucky and other Southern states, are all related.

Pleasant Henderson, born 1756 in Hanover county, Va. (brother of Judge Richard Henderson), enlisted in 1775 in the Revolutionary war; was later Major; Clerk of the Superior Court of Orange county in 1782; resident of Boonsboro, Ky., and moved to Tennessee in 1831; was then pensioned and died Dec. 10, 1842, in Carroll county, Tenn. Nathaniel Henderson, brother of the Colonial Judge Richard Henderson, was with him at the founding of Boonsboro, Ky. (see Dairy of Richard Henderson). He fought against the Indians at Boonsboro in the Revolutionary war. Some of his descendants drifted to Tennessee. Some of them are Judge John H. Henderson, Dr. Samuel Henderson and Mrs. Lucy Henderson Horton of Franklin, Tenn. William (brother of the Colonial Judge Richard Henderson) has among living descendants in Tennessee, Mrs. J. H. Kirkland, of Vanderbilt University at Nashville. Much can be seen of service in the Revolution of many Mosbys of Virginia, among them General Littleberry Mosby, who was a brother-in-law of Col. Robert Hughes, in McAlister's Virginia Militia.

Children of Thomas L. Gaines and His Wife, Lucy Henderson

Lucy Ann Gaines.
Pauline Frances Temple.
Mary Isabella.
Thomas Pendleton.
Sara G. Mosby.
Frank Asbury.
Martha Susan G. Petway.
Rebecca Hudson.
Malvina Henderson Winchester.
John W.

Thomas L. Gaines was living in Kentucky in 1818, but in 1836 moved to Nashville, Tenn., and died there in 1858. His wife died in 1854. He was enumerated in Todd county, Ky., census of 1830 and in the Nashville census of 1840.

Proof of the Revolutionary Service of John Henderson, of Albemarle County, Virginia, and of Others of the Family Connection

Under Captain Charles Lewis, John Henderson and sixteen others, an "Independent Company," marched to Williamsburg, Virginia, May 2, 1775, to demand satisfaction from Lord Dunmore for removing powder to his ship (See Lossing and Woods, supra). Other men of this family connection who served in the Independent Company were William Henderson, Robert Hudson Martin, Micajah Chiles, John Martin, Sergeant and Corporal Thomas Martin and John Bennett.

That John Henderson was a captain of Virginia is proved by records, viz: "1776-1779—John Bradshaw (his declaration, 1833) Augusta county, Va., volunteer, 1776, private to 1779 in Capt. John Henderson's company." (See Abstract of Augusta county Records, page 491.) 1780—"Captain John Henderson's company was in service at Cabin Point," etc. (see McAlister's, pages 14 and 15).

John Wesley Gaines

"John Wesley Gaines, son of Dr. John Wesley Gaines and his wife, Maria Wair, was born in Davidson county, Tenn., August 24, 1861; graduated at the University of Nashville; at Vanderbilt University he took the degree M. D. in 1882; but instead of practicing medicine he turned his attention to law, becoming a member of the Nashville bar in 1884; was presidential elector on the Cleveland ticket in 1892; in 1896 was elected to the fifty-fifth Congress of U. S. and was a member of Congress from 1897 to 1909. During his term in Congress he was active in Democratic leadership. He was the first to propose by resolution a new plan, or line, of procedure to secure reforms in the Reid-Cannon rules, by appealing direct to the voters, by a plank in the National Democratic platform, which was done at Denver in 1908, a Democratic House being the result of this plank and campaign. He was first to suggest and was active in the passage of the Federal law against the issuance of free passes (Amendment to Hepburn Act). He began the movement to secure legal proceedings against the tobacco trust, upon the refusal of the Attorney-General to proceed against the trust without evidence of guilt, he proceeded to collect evidence, and appointed an "Evidence Committee," which committee devised and organized the Dark Tobacco Grower's Association of Tennessee, Kentucky and Virginia. He made an active fight to maintain the circulation of "Clean Money," and was otherwise active while a member of Congress. (See Page 419, Who's Who in Tennessee, Paul and Douglass Co.)

Since his retirement from Congress, he has been engaged in the practice of law in Nashville. Here he takes an active interest in promoting the care of the Hermitage, home of Andrew Jackson.

On February 17, 1886, Mr. Gaines was married to Louise Lytle Cole, daughter of Col. Edward Cole, a prominent capitalist of Nashville, Tenn. Their son, an only child, John Wesley Gaines, Jr., served with credit in the World war.

Henderson of Fordell

We do not consider simple statement of the fact that Thomas Henderson, who came to Jamestown, Virginia, in 1607, and others of the line who come to America later, were of the Fordell line sufficient proof that this is true.

In an old book printed in London in 1707 and owned by Dr. Joseph Lyon Miller, of Thomas, W. Va., is written in quaint, faded characters the following family record:

"Wm. Henderson, Gent. and Margt. Bruce, mard. Feb. 7, 1705. John, son to Wm., born'd Febry. 9, 1706. James, son to Wm. born'd Janry. 17, 1708, dyed Sept. 1719. Sam'l, son to Wm., born'd November 28, 1713.

"Grandsons of John Henderson, Gent., of Fifeshire, Scotland: Wm. Henderson, dyed Augt. 1, 1736, aet. 61; born'd April 30, 1676. Margt. Henderson, dyed December 15, 1739; born'd March 1, 1680. Aet 59. Jean Henderson Stuart, dyed in child-bed, March 1739. Aet 19. John Henderson, dyed May I, 1776. Aet 60. Sam'l Henderson, dyed Janry. 19, 1782. This record set down from the memory of Jas. Henderson, now aet. 75."

And on the next page is this record:

"Jas. Henderson and Martha Hamilton mar'd June 23, 1738. Martha Henderson, dau. to Audley Harrison Hamilton, Gent., and Eleanor Adams, his wife. Jas. Henderson's living children: David, Wm., John, Jas., Sarah, Jos., Jean, Sam'l.; Archibald and Margt. passed away." On the fly-leaf is written "Jas. Henderson, His book, Virginia, 1740."

We are further indebted to Joseph Lyon Miller, M. D., of Thomas, W. Va., for tracing connection with Fordell. He says the record mentions "John Henderson, Gent., of Fifeshire, Scotland."

Judging from the birth of William Henderson, Gentleman, in 1676, his father, John Henderson, was probably born about 1650. He was a son of one of the four younger sons of Sir John Henderson, owner of Fordell during the reign of Charles I. According to Burke, Sir John had a distinguished command in the army of King Charles and was a lineal descendant of James Henderson, first Knight of Fordell.

Dr. Joseph Lyon Miller says, "An old family record, carrying the family back across the ocean to 1676, shows the connection with the Fifeshire, Scotland, Hendersons. A letter written from London in 1772 to my gt. gt. gt. grandfather, Lieut. James Henderson, of Augusta Co., Va., speaks quite freely of the Earl of Orkney, Lord Basil Hamilton, the Duke of Hamilton, and other relations of my gt. gt. gt. grandmother, Eleanor Hamilton Henderson, and so establishes our Hamilton kinship." He says that this letter was recently discovered among other family papers.

It is not surprising that children of younger sons of this family connection should have come to Virginia when we remember that in 1704 the Earl of Orkney was appointed Governor of Virginia. He was Governor for forty years, and drew two-thirds of the salary, 1,200 pounds, he received, while 800 pounds went to the Lieut. Governor. Yet he himself never visited the province. Alexander Spottswood was one of his Lieutenant Governors (see page 179, The Colonial Era, by George Park Fisher). Eleanor Lexington says "Famiy characteristics are hatred of effeminacy and scorn of cowardness and physical pain."

Another thread of connection of the Virginia Hendersons with the Fordell of Fifeshire, Scotland, line is found in the fact that Dr. Joseph Lyon Miller has an old family paper in which all money is reckoned in L. S. D., thus giving some idea of the date of the paper. On the back of this paper is a crudely drawn shield, bearing devices that have been irdentified as indentical with those of the Hendersons of Fordell. It also bears the Fordell motto: "Sola Virtus Nobilitat." Dr. Miller also has an old gold faced watch on the casing of which is the Fordell coat of arms. He also has old letters showing Hamilton connection in Scotland.

We will here give Joseph Lyon Miller's line of descent: Joseph Lyon Miller is the son of Henderson Miller, a son of Sarah Henderson Miller. She was a daughter of Colonel John Henderson of the 106th Virginia regiment War of 1812. He was a member of the Virginia Legislature, 1809-1820, with the exception of 1815 and 1816. He was a son of Lieut. John Henderson, of the Battle of Pt. Pleasant, 1774, and of Morgan's riflemen in the Revolution. Lieut. John Henderson was a brother-in-law of General Andrew Lewis, etc. He was a son of Lieut. James Henderson of the French and Indian war, who was a son of "William Henderson, Gent.," and Margaret Bruce, who were, according to the old record, married February 7, 1705.

"William Henderson, Gentleman," was son of John Henderson,

Gentleman, of Fifeshire, Scotland, Fordell Manor. He was one of the younger sons of Fordell."

Main Line of Fordell

As a similarity of given names between the main line, Fordell, and the Virginia and North Carolina Hendersons may be of interest, we will quote from Burke the generations from 1625 to 1850. It was in 1625 that Charles I succeeded James I (VI of Scotland) to the throne of England. "Sir John Henderson married Margaret Monteith, heiress of Randeford, by whom he had five sons and five daughters, and was succeeded by his eldest son, John Henderson, Esq., who was created a baronet of Nova Scotia July 15, 1664. Sir John married and had heirs." His wife was Margaret, daughter of Sir John Hamilton, of Obieston, Lord Chief Justice Clark, by whom he had two sons and two daughters.

The record says further: "Sir John Henderson died in 1683 and was succeeded by his second and only surviving son, Sir William Henderson, who married Miss Hamilton, a daughter of Sir John Hamilton of Mountain Hall, by whom he had four sons and a daughter. He died in 1709 and was succeeded by his eldest son, Sir John, who married Christian, daughter of Sir Robert Anstruther Bart, of Balkaskie, by whom he had three sons and five daughters. He was succeeded by his second and eldest surviving son, Sir Robert, died Oct., 1781. Married Oct. 3, 1748, Isabella, daughter of George McKenzie. Esq., of Fernie, by whom he had issue John, his successor, and Sir Robert Bruce (Henderson), present baronet (1834)."

Sir Bruce died childless and the estate descended to his first cousin, George Mercer, who assumed the name of Mercer Henderson. In 1858 he married Alice, a granddaughter of the fourth Earl of Roseberry. Georgena Wilhelmena, Countess of Buckenhamshire, is his sister's child. They are late representatives of the Hendersons of Fifeshire, Scotland. (See Burke's Landed Gentry.)

To prove connection between the Augusta county, Virginia, Hendersons and the Henderson branch which came to Tennessee, we will copy an old letter written Dec. 1, 1756, by John Andrew Henderson of Augusta county, Virginia. This man was the great, great grandfather of Mrs. C. A. Mee, wife of the mayor of Cleveland, Tenn., and was read at the meeting of the Ocoee Chapter, D. A. R., in January, at which Mrs. O. A. Knox was hostess:

"Augusta, county, Va., Dec. 1, 1756. Dear John: I have wanted to write you for some time to say that I am going to get married, but you know there is no good opportunity for sending letters your way. You know the lady (for we have talked about her charms before. I refer to Miss Mary Russell) to me the loveliest and most adorable of her sex. We expect to be married on Christmas day, and the neighborhood will be there. I think Miss Anne G. (Givens) will be there, and this will bring you, rain or shine, no difference what. We will stay at my or her father's until the weather opens in the spring; then we may take uplands on the Holston; but they say 'Injuns' are worse there than in the Greenbrier, and I don't want to take any chances on Mary's silky hair adorning any head but her own. Father will give us 100 acres if we stay here. This is what he gave to brother James. Tell Uncle James, Aunt Martha and the rest of the boys that they must all come to the wedding, too. We are going to have plenty to eat and drink, and we are going to dance until we wear our shoes out. There is no news here, but lots of sickness, for we all have colds. All the news is that I am going to get married, and don't you forget it, Jack. Give my best regards to my uncle and aunt and to the rest of the family. Your friend and cousin, J. Andrew Henderson."

We see that Andrew Henderson did come to Holston to live, as did his kinsman of the Samuel Henderson of Granville county, N. C., branch.

Jamestown

Three ships went to Virginia in 1607, the "Susan Constant," "The Goodspedd," and "The Discovery". Drayton, poet laureate, later wrote a poem to these men who went to Jamestown, Va., in 1607, beginning:

"You brave, heroic minds,
Worthy your country's name,
That honor still pursue,
Go and subdue,
Whilst loitering hinds
Lurk here at home with shame." etc.

Quaint stanzas, these of the poet laureate.

The fort first built at Jamestown was triangular-shaped with demilune at each angle, mounting a cannon. They called it Fort James, but soon the settlement was called Jamestown. For a church they nailed a board between two trees and stretched an awning over it. Reverend Robert Hunt read the Episcopal service and preached twice every Sunday (see Old Virginia and Her Neighbors, by Fiske).

We have proven elsewhere that Thomas Henderson came from Scotland to Virginia in 1607, settling first at Jamestown and later at Blue Springs. We have also proven that he was of the Fordell branch of Fifeshire, Scotland.

Dr. Joseph Lyon Miller, who descends from the Henderson of Augusta county, Va., of the same family, that of Fordell, has an old heirloom, an old gold-faced watch, bearing the Fordell crest. He has also old letters which prove unmistakably the relationship to Eleanor Hamilton Henderson. In this way he has proof of descent from the Earl of Orkney.

Some of the Hendersons, first of Jamestown, Va., later of Hanover county, Va., of the same state, drifted to Albemarle, Augusta and Orange counties, Va. Here they were joined by kinsmen, who came from Fifeshire, Scotland, "prior to 1740, and settled first near Alexandria, Virginia," but later moved to counties mentioned above. The relationship of these Jamestown Hendersons and those of Albemarle, Orange and

Augusta counties was testified to by Governor and U. S. Senator James P. Henderson of Texas. (See diary of Judge John Hughes Henderson now in possession of his son, Captain Thomas P. Henderson, of Franklin, Tenn).

The migrations of people in the early days largely followed water courses and valleys between mountains; they moved by ways of least resistance, People from Augusta county, Va., came to East Tennessee to live, among them Rev. Gideon Blackburn, who was born in Augusta county, Va., August 27, 1772. When a young boy he came with his parents to Washington county, Tenn., then to North Carolina, and we are told in "The History of the New Providence Church," by Will A. McTeir, that Blackburn studied theology under Dr. Henderson, near Dandridge. This may be seen on page 36. Dr. Henderson, referred to, was a kinsman both of the Augusta county Hendersons and of the Hanover, Va., later Granville, N. C., Henderson.

James P. Henderson

James P. Henderson was born in 1808 and died in 1858. He was the first Governor of Texas (1846-'47). He was U. S. Senator in 1857 (see Vol. II, The New People's Enclyclopedia of Universal Knowledge). On pages 24 and 25 of book compiled by John N. McCue entitled "A Roster of the Descendants of Alexander Henderson of Fordell County, Fife, Scotland, three of whose sons immigrated to the American colonies prior to 1740, and settled near Alexandria, Virginia," we can see that James P. Henderson was a son of Bennett Henderson and Elizabeth Lewis. Elizabeth Lewis Henderson died in 1835.

James P. Henderson married Margaret C., daughter of Richard Pollard and his wife, Pauline Rives, and granddaughter of Robert Rives and his wife, Margaret Cabell (daughter of Col. Wm. Cabell and Margaret Jordan). William C. Rives, brother of Pauline Rives, did service U S. Senator and Minister to France. The writer notices similarity of names in the Thomas Henderson of Jamestown branch, some of whom later settled in Hanover county, Va., and still later in Granville county, N. C., also in Kentucky, Tennessee, Missouri and Alabama with the Albemarle, Augusta and Orange county families. She also notices similarity of names, through wills, of negroes belonging to these several branches.

Both families intermarried with the Martins and Bullocks of Albemarle county, Va.

Henderson Genealogy

(Generation I in America)

Thomas Henderson came from Fifeshire, Scotland, in 1607, to Jamestown, Va. He later settled at Blue Springs. Some years later another branch of the same family, which had intermarried with the Hamilton, Bruce and Stuart families in Scotland, came to Virginia.

Members of these two families later drifted to Albemarle and Orange Counties, Virginia.

Generation II in America

Thomas Henderson was the father of numerous children, among them Richard Henderson, who married Polly Washer. They reared a family in Hanover county, Va., consisting of one daughter and four sons: Edward, Samuel, Nathaniel and Leonard. Their daughter married a Mr. Travillian, who moved to South Carolina.

Generation III in America

Samuel Henderson (1700-1783), son of Richard and Polly Washer Henderson, was born in Hanover county, Va., in 1700. There he was High Sheriff for some years. He married Elizabeth Williams, daughter of John Williams, of Hanover county, in 1732, she being then eighteen years of age. This Samuel Henderson moved with his family to what is now Granville county, N. C., in 1740, and settled on Nutt Bush creek His family intermarried with the Martins and Hunters of this section. Enfield was their seat of justice (see North Carolina Booklet for January, 1904; also Wheeler's History of North Carolina). Samuel Henderson (1700-1783) was High Sheriff of Granville county.

Elizabeth Williams' father was John Williams, who was born in Carnavon, Wales, in 1679. He immigrated to Hanover county, Va. His wife's name was Mary. Their children were:

Daniel.

John; married Frances Bustin.

William.

Charles.

———— Williams; married a Mr. Graves.

Children of John Williams and his wife, Frances Bustin:

Mary Ann.

Elizabeth; married Shadrack Flewellen.

There were other children, among them Sallie and twin sisters, Lucy and Rebecca.

Williams Coat of Arms

Williams (Penryn Co., carnar von, bart) Gu. a chevron, between three saracen heads affrontee, couped at the shoulders ppr.

Crest—A saracen's head as in arms. Motto: "Heb ddun heb ddym dduwadygan." (71 different families).

————

Thus we see that Samuel Henderson, son of Richard Henderson and his wife, Polly Washer, and grandson of Thomas Henderson, who came to Jamestown in 1607, was of generation III in America (see pages 177-180 of Colonial Families of the United States of America, Vol. IV, by

George Norbury Mackenzie. This carries the familly back to Fifeshire, Scotland, and shows that they bore the Fordell coat of arms.

Children of Samuel Henderson (1700-1783) and His Wife, Elizabeth Williams.

Mary.
Judge Richard Henderson; president of the Transylvania Company.
Nathaniel.
Elizabeth.
Ann.
Susan.
John.
William.
Samuel.
Thomas.
Pleasant.

Note: I draw upon a paper written by Thomas Henderson of Mt. Pinson, Tennessee in 1834. He descended from Thomas Henderson of this generation. This paper is now in the hands of Thomas McCorry, attorney-at-law, Jackson, Tenn., son of Judge Henry W. McCorry.

Generation IV in America

Mary, daughter of Samuel Henderson and his wife, Elizabeth Williams, was born in Hanover county, Va., Jan. 10, 1734. She married Jacob Mitchell. Her children were:
Jacob.
Samuel.
Richard.
Thomas.
Edward.
Willi: m.
Mrs. Ruth M. Halle.
Mrs. Elizabeth M. Bean.
Mrs. Jelico M. Nott.
Mrs. Susan M. Dyer.

Elizabeth, daughter of Samuel Henderson (1700-1783) and his wife, Elizabeth Williams, was born in Hanover county, Va., Feb. 19, 1738. She married John Beckham. They moved to Powlet, S. C. Children:
John.
Susan.
Elizabeth.
Henrietta (and several others, names unknown).

Ann, daughter of Samuel Henderson (1700-1783) and his wife, Elizabeth Williams, was born in Hanover county in 1739. She married her cousin, Daniel Williams, of Granville county, N. C., afterwards moving to South Carolina. Their children were: Samuel, Daniel, Joseph, Richard, William, Davis, Betsy, Nancy, Nuttie, Polly Washer.

Ann Henderson Williams died in 1831, ninety-three years and six months old.

Susan, daughter of Samuel Henderson (1700-1783) and his wife, Elizabeth Williams, was born in Granville county, N. C., April 23, 1743. She married R. Learcy. Children: Aso, Bennett, Thomas, Robert, William, Henrietta, Polly, married and lived in Kentucky; Betsy L. White.

John, son of Samuel Henderson (1700-1783) and his wife, Elizabeth Williams, was born in Granville county, N. C., Oct. 24, 1774. He married the widow of Solomon Alston, of Granville county. His children were: William, Joseph, Betsy H. Fernandes, Sally H. Haile.

John; died aged eighty-four. Joseph, his son, was the father of Mrs. Walter G. Duke—Jane Henderson Duke—of Richmond, Va., also of Mrs. Wright, and of Mrs. Ware.

Samuel, son of Samuel Henderson (1700-1783) and his wife, Elizabeth Williams, was born February 6, 1746, in Granville county. He was married in Boonsboro, Ky., in June, 1776, to Elizabeth Calloway, daughter of Col. Richard Calloway, just two weeks after she had been captured by the Indians. Their child, Fanny, born in June, 1777, was the first white child born in Kentucky. Samuel Henderson died at Winchester, Tenn., aged 80 years. His children were: Fanny H. Gillespie, Richard, Pleasant, Alfred, Susan H., Betsy H., Sally H., Dascia H. Estil.

Thomas, son of Samuel Henderson (1700-1783) and his wife, Elizabeth Williams, was born March 19, 1752, in Granville county, N. C. In 1778 he married Jane Martin, sister of Governor Alexander Martin of N. C., and of Col. James Martin of Snow Creek, N. C., Robert Martin, Thomas and Samuel Martin. Children: Alexander, Samuel, born March 25, 1787; Polly H. Lacey, Jane H. Kendrick, Nathaniel, Fanny H. Springs, Thomas, died November, 1831; aged seventy years.

Mrs. Louisa Brodnax, of New York, descends from Thomas Henderson. Miss Mary Louise Dalton, of St. Louis, Mo., who served a term as D. A. R. State Historian and in whose honor a U. D. C. chapter at Wintzville was named, also descends from Thomas Henderson through his son Alexander, who married Mary Wallace. Alexander Henderson and his wife, Mary Wallace, were parents of Jane Martin Henderson, who married Dr. Robert Hunter Dalton about 1832. R. H. Dalton was the grandfather of Mary Louise Dalton, who was the Librarian of the Missouri Historical Society. Mrs. Louisa Brodnax, of New York, and her son lost their money by unfortunate investments on Wall Street, and after this she became genealogist. She was sent by families in New York to England to make research in the archives there. She was a brilliant and most lovely woman. She died in London at St. Bartholomen's Hospital, Dec. 6, 1911.

We are indebted to Dr. Robert Hunter Dalton for valuable manuscripts, which are recorded in this book under the head of "Dalton."

The children of Alexander Henderson and his wife, Mary Wallace, were: Hamilton, David, George, Thomas and Wallace Gaston. Their daughters were: Mary Wade, married Dr. John I. Chalmers; Fanny, married Judge J. W. Chalmers; Sarah, married Mr. Calloway, of North

Carolina; Jane, married Dr. Robert Hunter Dalton; Elizabeth, married Cyrus King; Louisa, married Archibald Glenn, of New Orleans, and Kate, married Dr. J. C. Wimbish, of Texas.

In regard to Thomas Henderson, son of Thomas and Jane Martin Henderson, we will copy from paper written by Harry McCorry Henderson, who was born in 1848.

Thomas Henderson, who was born in Rockingham county, N. C., moved to Raleigh, where he published the first paper in North Carolina, "The Raleigh Star." He married Ann Fenner, the daughter of a celebrated doctor. Her brother, Dr. Erasmus Fenner, was a celebrated physician and surgeon of New Orleans, where he died about 1870. His only son, Judge Charles Fenner, is now practicing law there. He was commander of the famous Washington Artillery during the War between the States, and has been Chief Justice of the Louisiana Supreme Court ever since. Her other brother, Dr. Robert Fenner, was a celebrated physician of Jackson, Tenn. None of his children survive.

Thomas Henderson and his wife moved to West Tennessee and settled on the noted Indian Mound, Mt. Pinson, in what is now Henderson county, which was named for him. He was a prominent figure in the early days of West Tennessee. His children were: Richard, who was a graduate of West Point and was killed in Florida at the Dade massacre during the Seminole war; Calvin, who had no children surviving him. William Fenner was born in Raleigh, N. C., and reared at Mt. Pinson, Tenn. He moved to Texas in 1836; fought Indians in the early days; surveyed land and afterwards practiced law. He kept up his law practice until after the Civil war, after which he never practiced again, as he said he would never address negroes as "Gentlemen of the Jury." He died at Corsicana, Texas, in 1890 at 73 years of age.

William F. Henderson married Mary McCorry, of Jackson, Tenn., by whom he had two children, Harry McCorry, who was born in Corsicana, Texas, Sept. 13, 1848, and is said to have been the first white child born in that county; and Corinne Henderson, who lives in Jackson, Tenn. William F. Henderson, after the death of his first wife, Mary, married again. By his second wife, Louisa Edwards, of Lafayette, Christian county, Ky., he had a son, Calvin, and a daughter, Jennie, who live in Ft. Worth, Texas (1919).

The other children of Col. Thomas Henderson, of Mt. Pinson, were: Thomas, who was a wholesale merchant in New Orleans before the Civil war. When the war broke out he organized the Henderson Scouts, and was wounded at the Battle of Shiloh. His scouts made such a fine reputation as fighters that the company of which his brother, Samuel, was First Lieutenant, was divided. He was made Chief of Scouts for General Forrest, while Sam was Chief of Scouts for Joseph E. Johnston.

Captain Tom married three times, leaving one daughter, Susan, by his second marriage. She married William Butler, of Jackson, Tenn. By his last marriage Captain Tom left two sons, Thomas and William, both of whom live in Memphis, Tenn. After the Civil war, Thomas and Samuel Henderson formed the cotton commission and brokerage firm, which did a large business until 1873 when it failed during the great panic of that year. Samuel, whose history is related above, died in New Orleans, leaving a large family. One of his sons, Samuel, is a lawyer and in partnership with Judge Charles Fenner and his son, under the name of Fenner, Henderson & Fenner.

Alexander Henderson served in the army during the Mexican war, being wounded in that struggle. He was a lawyer and died at Seguine, Texas. He left two sons, Nathaniel, a lawyer and surveyor, at Wichita Falls, Texas; and Alexander, who lives on his farm near Austin, Texas. He also left three daughters, Corinne, Burch and Maria Nathaniel, who was a stockman in Texas and a sugar farmer in Louisiana, left children. I do not know how many survive him.

Corinne Henderson married Judge Henry McCorry of Jackson, Tenn. They had two sons, Thomas, who was killed during the Civil war; and Henry, who was a prominent lawyer of Jackson and died there, leaving a large family. She also left two daughters: Mary, who married Judge Freeman and is now a widow with two children; and Corinne, who never married.

Harry McCorry Henderson's children are: William Fenner, who lives somewhere in Washington State; Mary, Florence, Louisa, Edith, who lives at Port Laraca, Texas; Corinne, Frankie, deceased; Harry McCorry Henderson, who is at present (1920) in the marine corps, stationed at Ft. Lyon, Colo.; Thomas Richard Henderson, Harlingen, Texas; and Rosser, who is in the Second Division, San Antonio, Texas.

Harry McCorry Henderson died August 2, 1910.

The children of Calvin Henderson of Ft. Worth, Texas, are: Harry McCorry, who was a Major in the 36th Division during the late World war, and lived in Ft. Worth; Jessie, who married Robert Dow, of Calsbad, N. M.; and Kathleen, who lives in Ft. Worth; and one other daughter.

We will give a copy of Thomas Richard Henderson's Divisional Record, which shows where he was in the army during the World war: He was in the Third Division, Third Stationary Train; was stationed at Brohl, Germany, August 3, 1919; his number, 1,193,617; Sergeant; joined regiment Nov. 16, 1917; G. O., 76, H. S. D., landed in Europe April 28, 1918.

Service in Europe—Training Period: Chateam Villair, May 18, 1918, to May 30, 1918, served in Marne defensive from 15th July to July 18, 1918; served in Meuse Argonne offensive from Oct. 4 to Oct. 31, 1918; Aisne defensive June 1-5, 1918; was in Army of Occupation December 1, 1918 to Aug. 3, 1919; no citations; no wounds; was never in hospital; attended no special schools; grades held: Private, Corporal, Sergeant; Particular Duties in Organization, Personal Sergeant. Served in Meuse-Argonne and St Mihiel offenses.

Signed: Lieut. Colonel, Aeruedgley, Medical Corps, U. S. A. Comdg. Third Sanitary Train.

Pleasant Henderson, son of Samuel Henderson (1700-1783) and his wife, Elizabeth Williams, was born in Granville county, N. C., June

9, 1750; married Sarah Martin, daughter of Col. James Martin, of Snow Creek, North Carolina, in 1780. He was a member of the North Carolina Society of Cincinnati (see Volume III, American Historical Magazine). Children: James M., born 1787; William, born 1789; Maurice, born 1791; Tippo L., born 1798; Mark, born 1795; Pleasant, born 1802; Alexander, born 1807; Elizabeth Jane, born 1798.

William, son of Samuel Henderson (1700-1783) and his wife, Elizabeth Williams, was born in Granville county, N. C., March 5, 1748; married the widow Nelson of Nelson's Ferry, on Sante Lo. C.; died in 1787. William Henderson shared the restless spirit of the day, and in early life went to South Carolina to live, where he had relatives by the name of Travyllian. He served during the Revolutionary war from this state, being in several battles, among them that of Eutaw Springs. Later in life he removed with his family to Tennessee, settling near Dandridge. Children:

(1) Betsy H. Taylor, who moved to Attekapas. She was living in 1834.

(2) Ethelred Henderson, who moved to an adjoining county, Granger, in 1834.

(3) John Henderson, who lived near Dandridge, Tenn.

There were other children whose names we do not know.

Ethelred ' Henderson, son of William Henderson (born 1748), son of Smuel Henderson (1700-1783) and his wife, Elizabeth Williams, was born in Jefferson county, Tenn., but on reaching manhood moved to Granger, an adjoining county. Here his son, William Albert Henderson, was born in 1814. Here also his grandson, the Honorable William A. Henderson, was born in 1839.

Honorable William A. Henderson

William Henderson was born in Granger county, Tenn., in 1839, but after the death of his father, Wm. Albert Henderson, his mother carried her two children, Mary and William, to Knoxville to live. Granger county adjoins Jefferson, the birthplace of this man's kinsman, Senator John B. Henderson, of Missouri and Washington, D. C. Indeed descendants of Samuel Henderson (1700-1783) of Granville county, N. C., came westward and settled in Greene, Jefferson, Granger and Knox counties, Tenn.

Wm. Henderson attended and graduated from the Uniersity of Tennessee, and while assiduously pursuing his study of law, at the same time carried on the duties of teacher. He entered the firm of William Cocke, an uncle of Mrs. Overton Lea, member of the noted Virginia and Tennessee family of this name. The firm then became Cocke and Henderson. Henderson was a famous jury lawyer and became council for the East Tenn., Va. & Ga. railroad. On the organization of the Southern, Henderson went to Washington in 1895 as

General Council of that system. He tried to retire when he was 70 years old, but was impelled to take the position of General Solicitor of the Road, which position he filled until his death in 1921.

Henderson has written and lectured much on historical subjects, and has brought light to musty records from almost forgotten archives. Besides this, Ramsey, the historian, turned over his material to him.

He has filled many positions of honor. He was vice-president of Tennessee Historical Society; trustee of University of Tennessee; vice-president of Board of Centennial Exposition, etc.

After the fall of Fort Sumpter he joined the Confederate States army and served with distinction until the close of the war between the States.

To wide and accurate knowledge of law he added shrewd judgment of men, a general sunny disposition, an agreeable, rippling humor and keen wit, to which he added a fund of anecdotes always apt. In anecdote he even surpassed Tennessee's great master in that line, Hon. Eb James, of Chattanooga, in aptness and brevity. He sometimes electrified the bar of Tennessee at bar associations with a humorous address—something rich, rare and racy."

Hon. Wm. A. Henderson died in July, 1921, and is buried in Knoxville, Tenn.

His wife, Harriet Elizabeth Smiley, was born and reared in Springfield, Vermont. Of this union were born two children: Mrs. Mary Henderson Kirkland, wife of J. H. Kirkland, Chancellor of Vanderbilt University, at Nashville, Tenn.; and Mrs. Anne Henderson McDaniel, wife of Mr. Sanders McDaniel, of Atlanta, Ga. And they have one daughter each.

Mary Henderson Kirkland.

Mary Henderson, a daughter of Hon. Wm. Henderson and his wife, Elizabeth Smiley, was born at Knoxville, Tenn. She is the wife of Dr. James H. Kirkland, Chancellor of Vanderbilt University, Nashville, Tenn. She is a woman of culture and grace, and proved herself a most capable war worker during the great World war when, as president of the Tennessee Society of the Colonial Dames of America, by her example and under her direction, much valuable war work was done to aid the Allies. She was president of Colonial Dames of Tennessee more than five years, retiring in May, 1920. On her retirement from office the Nashville Tennessean speaks of the "extraordinary service which Mrs. Kirkland has given as war president." Indeed her services have been given special mention by the National Society Colonial Dames of America. On her retirement from office Mrs. Bruce Douglas proposed resolutions which received the hearty endorsement and approval of the members. This was in appreciation of the invaluable services of Mrs. Kirkland during the five years she was president.

This deserved special notice in the history of the Tennessee Colonial Dames: "Be it resolved that this organization owes to its retiring war president, Mrs. J. H. Kirkland, the heartiest thanks for her unselfish service during the stirring years just passed. It is due to her untiring energy in organization and to her zeal that the war records of the Colonial Dames are one which all may point to with pride. First in every patriotic undertaking she impressed the board and members of the organization with a deep sense of their responsibility by her personal supervision and the inspiration of her presence. She saw that each obligaton assumed was creditably discharged. Be it further resolved that this motion be spread upon the society's war records."

We will give extracts from the Report of Chairman of War Work of Colonial Dames resident in Tennessee, Mrs. C. B. Wallace:

"To relate our War activities throughout the state would require essentially a history of all the War relief societies in the State, for the Dames have been engaged in every enterprise organized by the Government in its conduct of the war.

"We are particularly proud of our Red Cross War Work, for in this field we are pioneers in Tennessee. To us belongs the honor of the first organized Red Cross Auxiliary in the State. In a commodious building loaned by the husband of one of our state officers this work was begun on the day following that fateful one which saw the President asking Congress for a declaration of war . . . .

"The special work of our National Society has been loyally recognized by a contribution of $1,200.00 to the Hospital Ship provided by the society.

"In each Liberty Loan drive our members took active part, buying and selling bonds in public and in private. In this way we have bought and sold Liberty Bonds to the amount of $900,000.00 and our purchases and sales in Thrift Stamps have amounted to $63,350.00. It must be remembered that this report represents only one third of our membership (many failed to report and quite a number of those reporting failed to state the amount of their purchases). In the Woman's Registration for War Service, and in the sales of Thrift Stamps and War Certificates, in house-to-house canvasses for War activities, in the drives for Red Cross, Y. M. C. A., Y. W. C. A. and Belgian, French and Armenian Relief, in campaigns for Books for Soldiers, Linen for Red Cross, War Salvage, and in Canteen and Motor Car Service our members have taken active and efficient part, both as individuals and officers.

"Our president has set us an inspiring example leading in every form of War work with notable zeal and self-sacrifice. She has served efficiently in the following organizations: Chairman for Nashville for War Savings and Thrift Stamps, Director of Nashville War Salvage Association, Assistant Chairman of Liberty Loan, Director of Women's Organizations in campaign for books for soldiers, Director of Emergency Hospital for Vanderbilt University, and member of Tennessee Budget Committee. In all of these organizations our membership has been actively employed."

After reporting the making of Hospital garments and of much knitting being done by the Colonial dames, the Chairman of War work adds: "We are proud and grateful to be able to record from our membership of 159, 45 sons of Colonial Dames have been in service. Six of these valient sons have made the supreme sacrifice," etc.

Mrs. Kirkland invested in Liberty Loan bonds and personally sold $75,000.00 worth. She worked on hospital garments. She canvassed for the fatherless children of France.

In the early years of Mrs. Overton's administration as President of Colonial Dames resident in Tennessee Mrs. Kirkland took an active part in establishing our mountain work at "Leamont," in Van Buren county. During Mrs. Kirkland's administration, tablets were placed to mark the site of the Colonial Fort Louden and Fort Assumption. She was elected honorary president for life of Colonial Dames resident in Tennessee in May, 1922.

James Henderson

John Henderson, son of William, son of Samuel (1700-1783), was the father of James Henderson, who was the father of Senator John B. Henderson, of Missouri, later of Washington, D. C.

James Henderson was born about 1800 at Dandridge, Jefferson county, Tenn. At about 21 years of age he went to North Carolina and Virginia to visit relatives. In Pittsylvania county, Virginia, he was married and here later his son, Senator John B. Henderson, was born.

Senator Henderson says: "My father had numerous brothers and sisters; among these brothers were John, Thomas J. and Samuel; and sisters, Anne and Fanny, and others. Some of the descendants of Fanny Henderson are now (1899) living in Marietta, Georgia, named Lewis."

Senator John B. Henderson

John B. Henderson was born in Pittsylvania county, Va., near Danville, in 1826.

"His father took him to Lincoln county, Missouri, when he was a very small boy, and he was but ten years old when both his parents died, leaving a small estate with which to educate their children. Such is the childhood history of John B. Henderson. He was a sturdy boy, vigorous, physically, and endowed with a strong and inquisitive understanding. He managed to secure an excellent education, for his was a mind that would not be denied. To him books were not mere printed pages—they were tools to be employed to fashion his mind and conscience for a useful and enviable position in society. Like so many other eminent American citizens, he taught school and studied law the while. At the age of twenty-two he was admitted to Pike county bar, and then his fortune was made."

I am copying from a sketch of John B. Henderson, by Savoyard, published in the Nashville Banner, April 28, 1905:

"A sketch of this man would be valueless without a glance at political conditions in the border states in 1861. He was Southern born, Southern reared, and Southern in thought and prejudice. But he loved the Union with all the devotion of a loyal heart, and his clear mind saw nothing but calamity for the American people in its destruction, and therefore he was a Southern Union man and opposed secession with all the energies of his nature, mental, moral and physical.

"No one not on the ground can understand the embarrassments and dangers that the Union men, and Southern men, too, endured in the states of Missouri and Kentucky.

"In time John B. Henderson became not only a successful lawyer and a skillful practitioner but a profound and eminent jurist. He pleaded before Chase and Waite and Fuller.

"Mr. Henderson was elected to the Legislature from Pike county in 1848, when he was a very young man, only twenty-two. In 1860, he was a delegate to the Charleston convention, where he supported Douglas. Upon his defeat for Congress in Aug. 1860, Mr. Henderson became a candidate for elector on the Douglas ticket, to be voted for in November, and his speeches in that behalf were execeptionally strong pleas as against the radicalism of the hour.

"And now a time came when Henderson and every one else were drawn in to the vortex of politics. Upon the election of Lincoln, South Carolina seceded. Secession meant war. He was chosen a member of the convention that was called to take action upon the question of secession, some time known as the 'Long Parliament' of Missouri. In that convention he was a leader and a conservative. He was a Southern man, a Democrat, and slave-holder. His father was a Tennessean, his mother, a Virginian, himself a Missourian, but his mind was ever eminently judicial, and he could see nothing but ruin for the weaker side in a war such as that which was impending. And so, like John G. Carlisle, a much younger man in the Kentucky legislature, he opposed secession with all the force of his character and all the logic of his mind. It was such men as Henderson and Carlisle who saved to the Union Missouri and Kentucky.

"When the war of minds gave place to the war of swords, Carlisle remained a war Democrat, but Henderson joined the Republican party and was appointed Brigadier General in the state militia. It was the great war Senate of which he was a member.

"He took his seat in the U. S. Senate, Jan. 29, 1862, when less than thirty-six years of age. His committee assignments show the esteem in which they held him: Finance, Foreign Relations, the very aristocracy of the Senate. Here he sat in council with Fessenden and

Sherman, devising ways and means, here he consorted with Sumner
and King to steer the craft of state clear of foreign shoals.

"Mr. Henderson was a slave-hollder, but like thousands and thousands of other Southern men, immense numbers of them in the Confederate army, he would have welcomed gradual emancipation as a solution
and as settlement of the slavery question.   With Lincoln he believed
that sudden emancipation would work injuriously to both races; but to
show how little masters of situations are even the strongest men in
times of revolution, Mr. Henderson was later author of the thirteenth
amendment to the Federal Constitution, which abolished slavery and
abolished it instantly.   The sword, however, had made the longer
continuance of the institution impracticable.

"As early as 1863 Mr. Lincoln foreseeing the inevitable end of the
war, set about the work of reconstruction. (Thadeus Stephens advo-
cated a bill confiscating the property of every disloyal man in the
seceded states and distributing the proceeds among the negro slaves.
Congress was with him as to the suspension of the constitution and
passed a bill embodying that idea in 1864 which Mr. Lincoln killed by
a "pocket veto"). The Lincoln plan is described by John B. Henderson:

"The duty of Congress is not to destroy the State or to declare
it a suicide and proceed to administer on its effects.   On the contrary,
the duty clearly is to preserve the State to restore it to its old republican forms.   Its duty is not to territorialize the State and proceed to
govern it as a conquered colony.   The duty is not one of demolition,
but one of restoration.   It is not to make constitution, but to guarantee
that the old constitution ore one equally republican in form and made by
the loyal citizens of the State, shall be upheld and sustained. If the majority of the people of a State conspire to subvert its republican forms,
the majority may be, and should be put down by the Federal power,
while the minority, however few, sustaining republican forms, may be
constitutionally installed as the political power of the State.'

"It is possible, barely possible, that, had Lincoln lived his plan
would have prevailed, and the country would have escaped its most
doleful and most infamous chapter—the carpet bag regime. Henderson,
Trumbull, Doolittle, Foster and other Republican senators were in
accord with Mr. Lincoln, but the assassination of the President devolved
the responsibility upon another, the radicals triumphed and the rest is
history.   Mr. Henderson was one of the famous seven Republican senators who voted 'not guilty' upon the impeachment charges of President
Johnson.   Associated with him were Fessenden, Trumbull, Grimes,
Ross, Fowler, Van Winkle.   Johnson's trial before the Senate in 1868
resulted in his accquittal, as the President's enemies mustered one less
than the neccessary two-thirds vote.

"In 1872 he accepted the Republican nomination for Governor, but
was defeated by Silas Woodson, his Democratic competitor."

We have been quoting from the "Savoyard's" sketch of this man.

But, since we are writing family history, we pause to say that Silas Woodson was related to the writer through her grandfather, Captain John Hughes (1776-1860.)

About 1890 Mr. Henderson moved with his family to the National Capitol. Here "he was an ornament to its best society and one of the most respected men of the nation. His home in Washington was on Corner Sixteenth Street and Florida Avenue. When his new home was being built the following description of it appeared in a Washington paper:

"Washington is to have a new architectural thrill in the 'palazzo' the splendid Venetian Gothic palace ex-Senator John B. Henderson is building here on the very highest point of Sixteenth St., from which one gets a view of the entire city. There will be nothing like it in America. The first story will be entirely of pure white Vermont marble, the upper part of white marble stucco, with many balconies and with polished marble columns supporting the arches of the windows. The rooms in this second story will open on a loggia—an attractive feature for Washington where strong sunshine and bright skies make a climate much like that of central Italy."

When McKinley was elected to his second term as President, a leading editorial in Harper's Weekly suggested to Mr. McKinley in the formation of his cabinet to "put in strong men like John B. Henderson," etc.

This man leaves a son, John B. Henderson of "Glenwald," Ballston, Va.

Miss Augusta Bradford, of Chattanooga, whose father served on the bench, is a great-granddaughter of Andrew Henderson, of Dandridge, Tenn., from 1800-26 a faithful elder here in the Presbyterian church.

Nathaniel Hendersoon

Nathaniel, son of Samuel Henderson (1700-1783) and his wife, Elizabeth Williams, was born in Hanover county, Va., Dec. 1, 1736. He was quite a small child when his father moved to Granville county, N. C. He married, first, the widow of Sugan Jones, of Warren, an adjoining county to Granville, by whom he had one son, Nathaniel. He was married a second time to a widow, ———— Morgan, by whom he had two children, Samuel and Elizabeth Young. Col. Richard Henderson, his brother, president of Transylvania Company, says in his famous journal kept while on his way to, and while at Boonsboro, Kentucky: "Sunday, 7th (May, 1775) Went into woods with my brothers, Nathaniel and Samuel and Captain Boone, after a horse left out on Saturday night," etc. In this same journal Richard Henderson writes: "Thursday, 27th (April, 1775) Employed in clearing fort lot, and Mr. Luttrell, Nathaniel Henderson and Samuel Henderson all assisted me." It is interesting to note that Kentucky made for her State Building at

the Jamestown Exposition a reproduction of this Boonsboro fort.
From Wheeler's history of North Carolina we learn that Nathaniel
Henderson, at the time of his death, was a member of the Tennessee
legislature. He had moved to Hawkins county, Tenn. He was appointed Justice of the Peace for Hawkins county, Feb. 28, 1794, by
Gov. William Blount. His son, Samuel, had a land warrant in Hawkins for Revolutionary war service. He is said to have been a man of
good mind and great benevolence of heart. In his address was disposed to be sarcastic, though not with view of giving offense.

Nathaniel Henderson was interested in the Cumberland settlement. His name is signed to "The Cumberland Compact" issued at
Nashboro, 13th May, 1780 (see page 187 Andrew Jackson and Early
Tennessee History by S. G. Heiskell). The author of this "Cumberland
Compact" was his brother, Judge Richard Henderson (see pages
178-9, Andrew Jackson and Early Tennessee History by S. G. Heiskell).

Alexander Martin, twice Governor of North Carolina, received a
military grant of several thousand acres of land in what is now Williamson county, Tenn. Martin died a bachelor and in his will gave
a small part of this land to Nathaniel Henderson. This can be seen
by referring to the old records at the Court House in Franklin. All
that is now owned of this land by the family is a little burying plot
where rest the bodies of his son, Samuel Henderson (1759-1828), and
his wife, Lucy Ryckman Henderson. These two graves are marked
by little, old-fashioned stones such as were so much used in the early
years of our republic. On one grave is the inscription —"Samuel Henderson. Born Nov. 29, 1759. Died Dec. 5, 1828." On the other stone is
the inscription—"Lucy Henderson. Born Nov. 15, 1765. Died July
14, 1843".

Children of Nathaniel Henderson

Nathaniel, (1756-1803).

Samuel, (1759-1828).

Elizabeth H. Young.

Nathaniel (son of Nathaniel Henderson, who was born in Hanover county, Va., Dec. 1, 1736, and died 1789); was born in Granville
county, N. C., in 1756. He was twice married, and both times he married widows. His first wife was the widow of Sugan Jones, of Warren
county. This county adjoins Granville county, N. C., the home of the
Hendersons. Nathaniel II was the only child of this first wife, who
lived to majority.

After reaching manhood, he felt the lure of South Carolina as had
relatives previously mentioned in this book. Two of his father's sisters, after marriage, had moved to South Carolina to live. His aunt,
Elizabeth, who had married John Beckham, lived at Powlet, S. C.,

and his father's sister Ann, born 1739, who married her cousin, Daniel Williams, had also moved to South Carolina to live. She died at the advanced age of ninety-three years. It is interesting to note the fact that one of her daughters was named "Polly Washer" Williams. Thus was handed down the name of a lineal ancestor, Polly Washer Henderson, who was a daughter of Ensign Washer, who served in the first legislative assembly ever held in America, that which met at Jamestown, Virginia, in 1619. Ensign Washer represented Captain Lawne's Plantation, afterward known as Isle of Wight Plantation.

Another daughter of Ann Henderson Williams was named "Nutty" in memory of the creek, "Nut Bush Creek," on which Samuel Henderson (1700-1783) had first settled in Granville county, N. C. (see original manuscript written by Thomas Henderson, of Mt. Penson, now in the hands of Thomas McCorry, attorney-at-law, Jackson, Tenn).

We see this strong local attachment manifested in the name of one of the children of Nathaniel's younger brother, Samuel Henderson (1759-1828). This Samuel named one of his daughters "Levisa," in honor of the noble river on which Boonsboro, Ky., was founded. Kentucky river was first called "Levisa" river (see McAffee MSS).

This last mentioned Nathaniel Henderson died in Edgefield, S. C., in 1803. He was great-great-grandfather of Governor Charles Henderson, of Alabama, and of Mrs. H. M. Weedon (Julia Henderson Weedon) of Troy, Ala., and of Mrs. Ella Henderson Brock. Dr. H. M. Weedon volunteered his services to his country during the great World war, and served thoughout the war as Major in a Medical corps.

Children of Nathaniel Henderson (1756-1803)

(His will was probated in Edgefield, S. C., in 1803. In this will he speaks of his sons and daughters).

Children: Richard, Thomas, William, Mary, Martha, Nathaniel. This last, Nathaniel Henderson, was born in Edgefield, S. C., but moved to Clark county, Ala., and died there in 1821.

Children of Nathaniel Henderson, who died in 1821

Children: James, Mary, Eli. Eli Henderson, born in Edgefield, S. C., 1803; moved to Pike county, Ala. He married Susan Darby. He died in 1857.

Children of Eli Henderson and His Wife, Susan Darby

Children: William Nathaniel, Augustin, born in Ala., 1831, died 1877; John, James Monroe, Lafayette, Martha, Susan Adelaide, Mary.

Augustin Henderson (1831-1877); married Mildred Elizabeth Hill. Their children are: Fox, married Sallie Wilkerson; Ella, married Wiliam L. Birch; J. C., married Nettie Talbot; W. J., married Julia Knox; J. E., married Mattie Hilliard; Governor Charles Henderson married Laura Montgomery; Julia, married Dr. Hamilton M. Weeden.

Nathaniel, son of Nathaniel Henderson (1756-1803) and his wife, Nellie, married a Miss Branson, whose father was a Tory and who returned to England during the Revolution but later came back to South Carolina. Both of these Nathaniel Hendersons, father and son, saw service in the Revolutionary war. Mrs. Hamilton M. Weedon of Troy, Ala., a descendant of theirs, secured their Revolutionary war record from Columbia, S. C. She also secured the will of her great-great-grandfather, which was probated in Edgefield, S. C., in 1803. One of the brothers of Mrs. Weedon married his wife in Warrenton, N. C. History was thus repeating itself. It was in Warren that Nathaniel Henderson (born 1736), his lineal ancestor, had "married the widow of Sugan Jones, of Warren."

Governor Charles Henderson

Charles, son of Augustin Henderson and his wife, Mildred Elizabeth Hill, was born in Pike county, Ala. His wife was Laura Montgomery. He has held many offices of trust in his State. In his announcement for Railroad Commissioner of Alabama he said among other things: "We have received only an insignificant portion of the wealth which has been held in hiding within a rich soil, beneficent climate. Infinitely more should be accomplished and in much more rapid strides. The future welfare of the people lies largely in the transportation problem..... We must strive for justice, for equal opportunities for local and State thrift so we may develop and rank with the most opulent."

Charles Henderson was Governor of Alabama from 1914 to 1918. He succeeded Emmet O'Neal. The exercises of inauguration, Jan. 18, 1915, took place on the balcony of the capitol in Montgomery, Ala., where Jefferson Davis was made President of the Confederate States of America. Here he took the oath of office, following the custom of Alabama executives. The same Bible with which Jefferson Davis was sworn in was used. This brought Governor Henderson into office to serve during the great World war, and through one year of reconstruction. And we find him making energetic endeavor to aid in winning the war.

Soon after Gov. Henderson's inauguration effort was made to enlarge the facilities of the department of archives and history. Thomas M. Owen, L. L. D., a kinsman of the governor, had already done work as historian and archivist.

The royal town of Troy owes much to this man's family and forbears. They were people of great wealth.

Mrs. Ella (Henderson) Brock

Ella Henderson; born in Pike county, Ala., Jan. 16, 1855; married in 1879, William Lowndes Brock, who was one of the leading merchants of Montgomery.

Mrs. Brock was a member of the "Cradle Chapter" United Laughters of the Confederacy. She was a devout member of St. John's

Episcopal church. She died Jan. 18, 1920. Her husband had passed away twenty years before. We will quote from a local newspaper: "Endowed with strong mentality and never-wavering in following her code of Right, always genial, loving her friends in her home and as she would meet them out in the world, ever receiving a warm welcome from all, her retiring nature sought no social display, but found its true contentment in the seclusion of her own beloved home."

Surviving her were her brothers, J. C. Henderson and former Governor Charles Henderson of Troy and J. E. Henderson of Enterprise, a sister, Mrs. H. M. Weedon of Troy and two daughters, Mrs. Lamar Fields and Mrs. Harvey R. Spangler, both of Montgomery, Ala.

Samuel Henderson (1759-1828)

Samuel Henderson was son of Nathaniel, who was born Dec. 1, 1736. Nathaniel was son of Samuel Henderson (1700-1783), of Granville county, N. C. Samuel Henderson (1700-1783) was son of Richard Henderson, of Hanover county, Va., and his wife, Polly Washer, daughter of Ensign Washer, who was a member of the House of Burgesses, which met at Jamestown, Va., in 1619. He represented Captians Lawnes' Plantation, later known as "Isle of Wight Plantation."

Richard Henderson, of Hanover county, Va., was son of the immigrant ancestor, Thomas Henderson, who came to Jamestown, Va., in 1607-8, where he first settled; later he located at Blue or Yellow Springs, near Jamestown.

Thomas, this immigrant ancestor, was born in Fifeshire, Scotland (see pages 177, 178, 179, 180, Colonial Families of the United States of America, Vol. IV, by George Norbury Mackenzie). We give, as an additional authority, manuscript written by Thomas Henderson, of Mt. Pinson, Tenn., in 1834.

We cannot trace Ensign Washer's lineage back in Great Britain, but on page 220, Virginia Magazine of History and Biography, 1907-8, it is said that a good per cent. of the Burgesses before 1700 are known to have been of gentle birth. And since Washer held the office of Ensign in Great Britain at a time when only men of gentle birth held military office, even that of Ensign, we infer that Ensign Washer was of gentle origin. One cannot help wondering if he did not sometimes attend religious services at the Old Brick Church, called St. Lukes, Isle of Wight. This building still stands and is the most remarkable seventeenth century building in the original English colonies.

The coat of arms of this American Henderson family is the Fordell coat of arms:

Arms—Gules, three piles issuing out of the sinister argent, in a chief of the last a crescent azure between ermine spots.

Crest—A cubit arm ppr., the hand holding a star or, ensigned with a crescent azure.

Motto—"Sola Virtus Nobilitat."

It may be interesting to note something in regard to the dominant

Henderson family of Scotland of late years. We see in Burke's Landed Gentry (1834) that the seat of Henderson of Fordell is Fordell, Inverkeithing, County, Fife.

"Lineage: The estate of Fordell which has been in the Henderson family nearly five hundred years was left by Sir John Henderson, the last bart. of Fordell (the son of Sir Robert Bruce Henderson) successively M. P. for County Fife, and for Sterling, to his only child and heir, Isabella Anne, who married 1818, the Admiral of the Fleet, Sir Philip, Charles Henderson Calderwood Durham G. C. B.   She died without issue and the estate of Fordell descended to Lady Durham's first cousin, George Mercer, who thereafter assumed the name of Henderson in addition to and after that of Mercer." In 1858 he married Alice, a granddaughter of the fourth ‾Earl of Rosebery. Georgiana Wilhelmina, Countess of Buckinghamshire, is his sister's child.

Samuel Henderson, son of Nathaniel, was born in 1759 in Granville county, N. C., but moved with his father to Hawkins county, Tenn., and married Lucy Ryckman, who was born and reared in Cumberland county, Va., a county adjoining Hanover county, the former home of the Hendersons. We learn this from the diary of his son, Dr. Samuel Henderson (1804-1884), written while his mother, Lucy Ryckman Henderson, still lived. This diary now (1919) is in the hands of Captain Thomas P. Henderson, of Franklin, Tenn. She was of Dutch descent.

Samuel Henderson's (1759-1828) grandfather, Sámuel Henderson (1700-1783), had moved from Hanover county, Va., about 1745 to what is now Granville county, N. C. Samuel, the subject of our sketch, was married in Green county, Tenn., March 14, 1785, while this was part of the short lived "State of Franklin." The State of Franklin was composed of Davidson, Green, Washington, Hawkins and Sullivan counties. In November, 1785, a convention met at Greenville to ratify the constitution of the State of Franklin, which constitution had been made at Jonesboro, Dec. 14, 1784. John Sevier, at this convention in Greenville, was chosen Governor of the State of Franklin; Langdon Carter was Speaker of the Senate; William Cage, Speaker of the House of Commons; and David Campbell, Joshua Gist and John Henderson, Judges of the Superior Court (see page 93, Wheeler's History of North Carolina). This John Henderson was a kinsman of the subject of our sketch. William Cocke was to represent the State before Congress. In September, 1787, the Legislature of the State of Franklin met for the last time in Greenville.

Some time after his marriage Samuel Henderson (1759-1828) moved to Knox county, Tenn., and settled on the Holston river, about four miles from Knoxville, on the opposite side of the river. Here their children were born. All their children were girls except the youngest, Samuel, who was born 1804.

The writer has, framed and hanging in her home, an old land warrant which belonged to Samuel Henderson (1759-1828), showing 100 acres in Hawkins county was conveyed to him in 1791, through

Isaac Taylor. This warrant is dated "Western Territory South of the Ohio, Sep. 19, 1791." This old land warrant reads:

"The Estate of Isaac Taylor, Desd. to Samuel Henderson Jr. one hundred acre Land Warrant; Hawkins County, W. T. So. of Ohio. This day came James Henderson before me, James White, a Justice of the Peace for Hawkins county, and made oath that He Heard Isaac Taylor assume on Armstrongs one Hundred Acre Warrant to Samuel Henderson, and further Saith not. Sworn to before me this 19th of Sept. 1791. James White, Jcp.

This day came Samuel Henderson as above and made oath that he never received any satisfaction for the above Warrant sworn to this 19th of Sept. 1791. James White, Jcp"

He was my grandfather. He belonged to Ninth Regiment North Carolina Continental Troops. This regiment was commanded by Colonel John P. Williams, Lieut. Col. John Luttrell, Major Wm. Polk (see North Carolina Register). He enlisted Nov. 26, 1776. His name is on the tablet on the court house in Franklin, Tenn., placed there in honor of Revolutionary soldiers buried in Williamson county, Tenn., by "Old Glory" Chapter D. A. R. Samuel Henderson's name is also on the monument to Revolutionary soldiers buried in Tennessee. This monument was projected by Mrs. James S. Pilcher, when State Regent D. A. R. The monument stands in front of the court house in Nashville, Tenn. I received permit from D. A. R. headquarters at Washington for bar on my Daughters of the American Revolution pin, bearing name Samuel Henderson as one of my Revolutionary ancestors. This permit I sent to the D. A. R. official jeweler and procured the bar on my pin.

Early in the American Revolution men would sometimes enlist for a short period. We do not think that Samuel Henderson served during the whole of the war. When sixteen years old, in 1775, he was with his father, Nathaniel Henderson, for a while at Fort Boonsboro on Kentucky River.

Judge Richard Henderson, President of the Transylvania Company, which had made a treaty with the Indians at Sycamore Shoals on Watauga River, March 17, 1775, and purchased from them all of what is now Kentucky and Tennessee as far south as the Cumberland River and a corner of southwestern Virginia, kept a diary while on his way to found Boonsboro, and after beginning work here. His Diary can be found in North Carolina Booklet for Jan. 1904. The original diary, yellow with age, is jealously preserved in the Wisconsin Historical Society Library.

Richard Henderson and the Transylvania Company engaged Boon and his party to cut out the Wilderness Trail, that historic pathway to the vast "hinterland" poetically phrased by a Cherokee chieftain as the "dark and bloody ground."

The D. A. R. have marked this "Trail". To this the writer contributed.

Judge Richard Henderson speaks, in his diary, of his brothers,

Nathaniel and Samuel, being with him here at Boonsboro, and one entry shows that he and these two brothers, on one morning, were the only ones at work on the Fort. I have always been interested in locating and marking historic spots since becoming a Daughter of the American Revolution. In February, 1900, thinking it a good way to record the location of historic spots I wrote for J. Franklin Jameson, Ph. D., who was compiling a large volume of his "Dictionary of United States History," twenty-five items. He retained the contribution as data, but did not deem it worthy of financial recompense. While I was Regent of "Old Glory" Chapter D. A. R. (1904-5), I brought before the chapter a good many historic spots I had located. On February 1, 1906, after I had been elected State Historian by the D. A. R. at our State Conference in Memphis, November, 1905, I wrote to Miss Desha in Washington, one of the founders of D. A. R., seeking her interest in marking some of these historic spots. Miss Desha was a woman much interested in patriotic work, and was on the National committee for marking historical spots. The places I then asked her to use her influence in having marked were Sycamore Shoals on Watauga River as the place where the Transylvania company, with Col. Richard Henderson at its head, had signed a treaty with the Cherokees, March 17, 1775. Here too the over-mountain men rendezvoused, October 7, 1780, before going to do battle at King's Mountain. We are happy to remember that D. A. R. chapters in Knoxville, Bristol and Johnson City, in 1910, appropriately marked Sycamore Shoals with a monument. The shaft bears this inscription on one side: "Here was Negotiated the Treaty Under Which Transylvania Was Acquired from the Cherokees, March 17, 1775."

The other historic spot about which I wrote Miss Desha was the site of Fort Prud home on, the third Chickasaw Bluff going down the Mississippi, built by La Salle in 1682. That La Salle built Fort Prud home at this time can be seen on page 115, "Opening of the Mississippi," by F. A. Ogg. The site of this fort is where the river makes a majestic turn, in Riverside Park at Memphis, Tenn. I also made an effort to get our D. A. R. State Conference to mark this spot in 1906.

Everyone knows the romantic story of Elizabeth and Fanny Calloway and Jemima Boone being captured by the Indians, and how at great peril they were recovered by their friends. Elizabeth Calloway, just two weeks after this time was married to Samuel Henderson, an uncle of the subject of our sketch. This romantic story afforded Fennimore Cooper an incident in his book "The Last of the Mohicans."

I will give references from Virginia Entries which show something of this man's possessions in lands: "Surveyed June 23, 1780. Samuel Henderson enters 1,000 acres on preemption lying on the trace from Boonsboro to the lower Salt Spring on Licken adjoining his settlement at the Sycamore forrest all round and to run down the Creek for Quantity" Book I, page 410, Virginia Entries. Also "assess of Abram Mitchell, 1.000 acres on the waters of Licken Creek on the Hunter's trace from Boonsboro to the lower Salt Spring adjoining all around his settlement." Book No. I, page 410, Virginia Entries "Surveyed May 23rd, 1780. Samuel Henderson enters 400 acres upon a Treasury Warrant on the waters of Brashers Creek adjoining James Allen's entry made on the north side of his own land and to run southwardly and eastwardly, beginning at Allen's South East Corner of his following entry of 500 Acres," Book No. I, page 288, Virginia Entries. In book No. I, page 25, Virginia Entries, we see that he entered 400 acres at one time and 400 acres at another time. Thus it seems that he possessed in Kentucky at least between three and four thousand acres of land in vicinity of Boonsboro.

The younger Samuel Henderson (1759-1828), who was married in 1785, ten years after the founding of Boonsboro, named one of his first children "Levisa" in honor of the old name given to Kentucky river upon which Boonsboro was founded. All of this man's children were girls except the youngest child, who was born in 1804 and was given the name of his father, Samuel Henderson. I will say in passing that this last Samuel was my father, and that he did not marry until he was in his fortieth year. I am one of his younger children, so in this way tradition is close.

The restless spirit of the times seems to have had possession of this man. In 1808 he moved with his family to Louisiana Territory, settling on a farm in the vicinity of St. Louis. Great river courses have always shaped the lives of men. In America it was through the rivers they generally found their homes. This land is now a part of St. Louis. They went all the way by water in a little boat, down the Holston to the Tennessee river, down this to the Ohio, along this to the Mississippi, then up to St. Louis.

It is interesting to note the state of St. Louis at this time. From the St. Louis Republic of July 12, 1908, we learn that St. Louis in 1808 had two hundred houses. Of these, fifty were built of stone. These were whitewashed. The houses stood in the midst of gardens and orchards. The settlement occupied three streets, now named Main, Second and Third. There was one school-master, Trudeau, who lived and taught in the same house. This was the only school around here. My father, Samuel Henderson (1804-1884), started to school here when very young.

Samuel Henderson (1759-1828) was in his new home near St. Louis in time to take part in the election of 1809 which "was held at Mr. Chouteau's house, lately occupied by Gen. Clark."

Samuel Henderson (1759-1828) and his wife had both for many years been members of the Presbyterian church, but here they found no Presbyterian church, so they joined the Methodist church. From the Diary of Samuel Henderson (1804-1884) we learn that his mother, in the Spring of 1787, joined the Presbyterian church in Knox county, and that her husband, Samuel Henderson (1759-1828), had already joined the church about a year earlier. The Methodist church had been established at St. Louis in 1806, and there was no Presbyterian church there until 1816. Rev. Gideon Blackburn, who aided in the establishment of the First Presbyterian church in Nashville, Tenn., also in Franklin, Tenn., visited St. Louis in 1816, and preached in a theatre then standing on Main street below Market street. Large and deeply interested crowds attended these services, and they prepared the way for the establishment of a church. The Methodist church was established in St. Louis in 1806. "The first preaching west of the Mississippi was clandestine, and was by John Clark, who, in 1798, crossed the Mississippi from Illinois at night and preached occasional sermons at Cold Water, near Florissant. The first regularly appointed was John Travis, who was sent to Missouri in 1806, when Protestant settlers were greatly increasing as the result of raising the American flag in St. Louuis in 1804. But Methodist foundation in St. Louis were actually laid by Jesse Walker, who held the first meeting in the month of December in a log cottage, 12x16 feet, which stood on the southwest corner of Third and Spence streets. Names were soon added to the membership of this church which were to become notable in the history of St. Louis, among them being the names of John Goodfellow, his wife and sister, Mrs. Caroline O'Fallon and Mrs. Kells, the mother-in-law 'of Samuel Cupples. When the congregation outgrew the cottage, a frame structure, 36x20 feet, with galleries on three sides, was erected on the northwest corner of Fourth and Myrtle streets." This was the church of which Samuel (1759-1828) and his wife were members. It is interesting to note the fact that the Samuel Cupples of today (1908) is true to traditions and is numbered among the noted philanthropists of our day. Among others of this church in St. Louis who are distinguished for the largeness of their gifts are Murry Charleton, John J. O'Fallon, S. M. Kinnard and Paul Brown.

During the agitation over the Missouri Compromise, through fear of losing his negroes, Samuel Henderson (1759-1828) came back to Tennessee about 1817, and settled in Williamson county, near Bethesda. Here he and his wife are both buried. Their graves are marked by little, old-fashioned tombstones.

My father, Samuel Henderson (1804-1884), always told us that Grandpa sold his farm for a mere song—for nothing much more than wagons and teams to bring them back to Tennessee. Now this land is incorporated in the city of St. Louis, and is of untold value.

Before leaving Missouri his daughters had married and settled in several states.

Lucy Ryckman, wife of Samuel Henderson (1759-1828), was born in Cumberland county, Va., a county adjoining Hanover, the home of the Hendersons. She came of an old Dutch family, some of whom settled in New York at an early date. Frances Cowles says in the Nashville Banner, July 6, 1916: "There isn't the slightest doubt that the old records would give some very interesting light on this fine old Dutch family. Harme Janse Ryckman was a resident of Albany between 1666 and 1667, and other members of the family were early settlers in New Amsterdam, now New York. A Captain Albert Janse

Ryckman, who was Mayor of Albany in 1702 and 1703, owned a brewery on the east side of lower Broadway, which included the south corner of Hudson street and Broadway. This property had formerly belonged to Peter Bronck, a member of the family for which borough of the Bronk, part of Greater New York, is now named. The family was also settled in Schenectady at an early date." Ary Ryckman owned a farm which included what is now Astor place. One branch of the family left New York for Virginia, settling in Cumberland county, Va. To this branch Lucy (Ryckman) Henderson belongs. While she still lived, her son, Dr. Samuel Henderson (1804-1884), writes in his diary that his mother, Lucy (Ryckman) Henderson, was born in Cumberland county, Va. Her father moved to Greene county, Tenn. We will fortify what we know of this family by a statement made to my brother, Judge John Hughes Henderson, in 1883 and recorded in his diary. This statement was made to him by Tapley Pyron, an old man then of nearly eighty years, a grandson of Samuel Henderson (1759-1828): "Lucy Ryckman Henderson's brothers, William and Abraham Ryckman, moved to Mississippi, and their descendants now (1883) are in that State and Arkansas. One of her sisters married Elisha Baker. He was a member of the Convention which framed the first constitution of Tennessee." Elisha Baker was one of the five men from Greene county in this constitutional convention which met at Knoxville, Jan. 11, 1796, in accordance with the proclamation of William Blount, Governor in and over the Territory of the United States of America, south of the Ohio river (see page 212 History of Tennessee—The Goodspeed Publishing Co.).

This was a notable convention, and the roll of members is illuminated by the names of Andrew Jackson, James Robertson, William Blount, William Cocke, Thomas Henderson, C. C. Claiborne, James Houston, D. Shelby, Edward Douglas, Leroy Taylor, John Tipton, Charles McClung, James White, Thomas Hardeman, John McNairy, David Craig, Elisha Baker.

"Another sister of Lucy Ryckman Henderson, Tobitha Ryckman, married John Strickland and settled in Kentucky. Tapley Bynum, father of Bradford and Ely Bynum, married another sister and settled in Kentucky. Elisha Baker's descendants are now (1883) in Missouri."

Lucy (Ryckman) Henderson was born November 15, 1765, and died July 14, 1843. After her daughters had all married, and had settled in different states, she made her home with her only son, Dr. Samuel Henderson (1804-1884). near Bethesda, Williamson county, Tenn. This son had such devotion for his mother that he would not suffer his heart to become so deeply involved that he should marry before she died. So he lived a bachelor. He married in his fortieth year. Lucy Henderson was active and full of energy even to her last days. Though she lived to be seventy-eight years old, it was no unusual thing to see her run from the house to the kitchen or negro cabins. She was five feet four inches in height, and of athletic build. Aside from more useful arts she taught her daughters to embroider and do fancy work. Some of this family did really beautiful fancy work.

The children of Samuel Henderson (1759-1828) and his wife, Lucy Ryckman, were all born in Knox county, Tenn., but all went with their father to Missouri in 1808 to live.

I. Ann; married Charles Pyron while living in Knox county, but she and her husband moved to Missouri in 1808. They were parents of Tapley, John and Sterling Pyron. Children of Tapley Pyron: Susan, born 1832, married W. B. Cullom, attorney at law, from Overton county, Tenn.; they lived in Missouri and California; Malissa married Johnson; Charles; Frances; Nancy, married Jordan; Addie, married Smith; Thomas.

II. Levisa; named for Levisa river, the old name given to Kentucky river on which Boonsboro had been built, married Bradford Bynum while her father lived near St. Louis, Mo. They went across the Mississippi river and made their home in Illinois.

III. Mary; married Oliver Brewer, and moved first to Missouri, but afterwards to Hampton county, Arkansas. Their descendants live now (1883) in Pike county, Arkansas, and elsewhere. They succeeded well in life.

IV. Mathilde; married Ely Bynum; lived in Kentucky.

V. Elizabeth; married John Strickland.

VI. Sally; married Henry Edwards. and lived in West Tennessee.

VII. Lucy; after being divorced from her first husband, by whom she had no children, married Thomas Gillespie. They moved to Texas, where they succeeded in life. They had one child, Thomas.

VIII. Samuel Henderson, son of Samuel Henderson (1759-1828) and his wife, Lucy Ryckman; was born October 8, 1804. He married Rachel Jane Hughes, March 14, 1844. He died December 9, 1884.

Samuel Henderson (1804-1884)

Samuel Henderson first saw the light in Knox county, near Knoxville, Tennessee. A kinsman of his father, John Henderson, of Greene county, had been chosen one of the Judges of the Superior Court of the short-lived "State of Franklin" in 1785. While visiting this kinsman Samuel Henderson (1759-1828) had met and loved Lucy Ryckman in Greene county and they were married March 14, 1786. Greenville was the capital of the State of Franklin.

The younger Samuel early had Methodist influences thrown around him. Because there was no Presbyterian church about St. Louis, whither they had moved in 1808, his father and mother had joined the Methodist church, which stood on the corner of Third and Spence streets, St. Louis. Living out from the village of St. Louis, Dr. Henderson says in his diary that his father's house was often a preaching place for the Methodist preachers, and a home for them. This boy started to school when quite young to Mr. Toureau, who lived and taught in the same house in St. Louis (see St. Louis Republic for July

12, 1908). Father has often told us that Tom, a faithful negro, went with him to school the first day through the woods and blazed the way with an ax so that he might find his way alone. His mother once dressed him like an Indian chief to please the Indians, and when the Indians came they wanted to take him to live with them. He remembered that in the long journey, in a little boat, from Tennessee to St. Louis, among their food was taken parched corn. This seems quite primitive. In those days they certainly lived the simple life. Parched corn when run through an old time coffee-mill could take the place of our breakfast cereals.

Emigration, in the olden time in America, followed the river courses. This family went down the Holston river, along the Ohio to the Mississippi river, then up the Mississippi to the vicinity of St. Louis. Families and friends often in their migrations would follow each other. The father of Senator John B. Henderson, of Missouri, in the early years of the nineteenth century went to Missouri from Tennessee to live.

We have stated before that Samuel Henderson (1759-1828) came back to Tennessee to live about 1817. He brought his family to Williamson county. Samuel Henderson (1804-1884) studied medicine under Dr. John L. Hadley, who had been a private student of Benjamin Rush, of Philadelphia, one of the signers of the Declaration of Independence. Dr. John Livingston Hadley was a grandson of Robert Livingston (1746-1818), who served on the committee of five which drafted the Declaration of Independence. He was also Secretary for Foreign Affairs 1781-1783. While U. S. Minister to France in 1801-1805 he and James Monroe negotiated with Napoleon Bonaparte the Louisiana Purchase (see page 375, Dictionary of United States History, by Jameson).

Dr. John L. Hadley, who married his first cousin, inherited what became known as "Hadley's Bend" in Cumberland river, from this grandfather. This vast landed estate, had been granted to Robert Livingston for diplomatic service. This estate reached out beyond the Bend and included what was afterwards known as "The Hermitage". The deed from John L. Hadley to Andrew Jackson can be seen in the State Archives at the capitol in Nashville. After I had been elected State Historian of the D. A. R., at Memphis in 1905, I visited the Archives, because we had been interested in the establishment of a department of Archives and History. On this visit Mr. Quarles, the Archivist, told me that he had rescued from the ash-barrel the deed to the "Hermitage" of the land sold by John L. Hadley to Andrew Jackson, President of United States.

The stay of this young man in the home of Dr. Hadley was to him a perfect delight. He writes back to his old friend, Rev. Henry C. Horton, in Williamson, of the "elegant and refining influences" about him. This large two-story brick house, the home of Dr. Hadley, still stands. When a girl I made several visits to Dr. and Mrs. Hadley in their home here. They were elegant old people, and their home was a large, old-fashioned, brick house with large cross halls in the center. The back part of this house was built while Tennessee was still a part of North Carolina. The rooms were papered when I was there in the old time landscape paper. In one room the story of Paul and Virginia was portrayed, in another room Venus and Adonis. "The Hermitage," near-by, still has this old-time landscape papering. On one of my visits to Dr. and Mrs. Hadley my father was with me. He and Dr. Hadley would talk of the days when Andrew Jackson lived at "The Hermitage," and of the hospitality of his home.

Dr. Hadley was in reminiscent mood. He told us of an incident in the home of Benjamin Rush in Philadelphia. He said that when he was studying medicine at Jefferson College, and was a private student of Benjamin Rush, he and several other boys were invited to take tea in the Rush home. While at the table, Mrs. Rush was explaining to the young men the mechanism of her new tea urn, when one of the boys remarked to Mrs. Rush that that reminded him of what Dr. Rush often told them: that they must look down as well as up for information. Dr. Hadley's face seemed to flush with shame when telling this incident. He said when it happened he felt as if he could sink through the floor, he was so ashamed of the boy.

On one of my visits to Dr. Hadley's in company with my father, Dr. Samuel Henderson (1804-1884), I made my first pilgrimage to the grave of Andrew Jackson, at the Hermitage, the Mecca of Americans. I saw and talked with Alfred, Jackson's body servant. When we were leaving, Alfred gave me a sprig of magnolia from Jackson's grave.

We will make quotation from the Tennessean and American of Jan. 20, 1918, in which is a sketch of "Vaucluse", the old home of Dr. John Livingston Hadley. The Government purchased Hadley's Bend for the great powder plant: " 'Vaucluse,' built by J. L. Hadley in early part of last century on land granted to Robert Livingston, his grandfather, as reward for diplomatic services, was among the most magnificent and splendid of Southern mansions in days before the Civil war and the scene of many interesting and romantic incidents."

This old home, like many other Southern homes, was a little commonwealth within itself, with the slaves' quarters and other accessories of an old-time plantation. On one side of the house at the front was a negro hospital, on the other a carriage house, while in the rear was an old fashioned garden with its wealth of flowers. Surrounding the whole was a red brick wall, five feet high, with false turrets every twelve feet. When, as a girl, I visited here, this wall fired my imagination and I fancied the turrets embattled as in the day "when Knighthood was in flower.' I have gone somewhat into detail about "Vaucluse," because it may be of interest to know something of the former life of a place which comes suddenly into national prominence as Hadley's Bend did when purchased by the Government after the United States entered the World war, on which was built a powder plant, the largest in the world.

Samuel Henderson (1804-1884), when young, clerked for nearly a year in a dry goods store in Nashville belonging to Dr. Hadley. He was here at the time "the stars fell," the time of that marvelous meteoric shower. 'Along in the twenties he went to Philadelphia to attend Jefferson Medical College. He traveled from Williamson county, Tenn., to Philadelphia, Pa., on horseback, a long horseback ride, it seems to us at this day. But men often preferred this to the stage coach. Father has often told us that Philadelphia at this time was not lighted on moonlight nights.

He practiced medicine after leaving Philadelphia for some years, but laid his practice aside long enough to take another course of medical lectures in Louisville, Ky., at the time the celebrated Dr. Samuel Gross was here. He had great admiration for Dr. Gross and friendship between the two men sprung up which lasted through life. Dr. Henderson, in his practice of medicine, would have Dr. Gross to come from Louisville to perform surgical operations. And when his son, Samuel Henderson (1852-1913), attended Jefferson Medical College in Philadelphia in 1872, Dr. Gross took a personal interest in the young man and would invite him sometimes to come and take breakfast with him in his home. After Samuel Henderson (1852-1913) had taken his degree in medicine Dr. Gross wrote the father in most appreciative terms of his son and insisted that he come to Philadelphia to practice medicine. This letter Dr. Henderson (1852-1913) preserved. Dr. Gross' fame extended to two continents. The University of Oxford, England, conferred upon him the degree D. C. L.

Samuel Henderson (1804-1884) was always fond of military affairs. When a young man he was colonel of a regiment of militia. This threw him with Gen. William Martin, of Williamson county, of whom he was very fond. March 14, 1844, he was married "at early candle lighting," as the record in the diary goes, to Rachel Jane Hughes, a niece of Gen. William Martin. They were married in her father's home, in the old house in which Gen. Martin had died more than a year before. Gen. Martin was a bachelor and made his home with his sister, Sally (Martin) Hughes. Dr. Henderson carried his bride to the home of a dear friend of his, Rev. Henry C. Horton. They were here for several months, when they came back to his wife's widowed father's to live. Rev. Henry C. Horton was the father of Mrs. Edward H. East, and grandfather of Mrs. Nathaniel Baxter, of Nashville. Their first child, Samuel, was born in 1845; died in infancy; and is buried in the old graveyard. His grave is beside that of the youngest child in this family, Levisa, who also died in infancy. After the birth of their second child, Sallie Martin Henderson, he carried his family to Franklin to live. An entry in the diary of Dr. Henderson is: "April 13, 1848. I removed to Franklin this day, having bought Dr. S. S. Mayfield's possessions." This home was on Maple avenue, where Mr. Alex Hughes Ewing now lives (1912). His lot in 1848 extended back and included what is now the Louisville and Nashville railroad depot, etc. A lot of residences have been built on part of this land. It is superfluous to say that town lots in 1848 were not

so valuable as now. This house was always the home of doctors.
Dr. Mayfield sold the place to Dr. Henderson. He sold the place to
Dr. Morton, and he sold the place to Dr. John Park, who lived here
for half a century, a most highly respected and beloved man, Dr. John
Park was grandfather of Mrs. A. H. Ewing.

This house, occupied by Dr. Samuel Henderson (1804-1884) and
his wife, was unchanged from the time of its erection until torn down
by Mr. A. H. Ewing, who had his present home built about 1910.
The original building was in colonial style with large hall in center
and double parlors on one side of hall with folding doors between.
On opposite side of hall were double rooms with folding doors. These
double doors folded back on their hinges in the old style. The front
door and solid mahogany, or cherry, stairway of the old residence are
preserved in the present edifice. Here they lived with delightful environment and their only child at that time, 1848, Sally Martin. It
seems that they should have been perfectly happy. But Father has
often told us of coming into Mother's room one day and finding her
bathed in tears. On asking the cause of this she replied, "Father
needs me in his home." He resolved then and there to go back to her
father's house to live, to "Rural Plains," as they called it. An entry
in Dr. Henderson's diary, June 20, 1844, shows that he bought from
Capt. John Hughes, his father-in-law, a tract of land on Big Harpeth
river on which was located the Harpeth Mills. This was in the day
before the merchant millers and was large for its time.

Samuel Henderson was a kind master. He always spoke of his
negroes as a part of his family. In his diary he says, "There have
been more than twenty cases of measles in my family this Summer."
Southern people never spoke of their negroes as slaves, they always
called them "servants." If a Northern man came South to live and
owned negroes he would call them his "slaves." The distinction made
a kind o' shiboleth.

I remember how the negroes all seemed to love "Master and Mis-
tess." They used to come sometimes at Christmas or on Father's
birthday, marching in procession, when two stout negro men at the
head of the procession would take Father on their shoulders and
carry him around the yard.

Dr. Henderson never sold negroes. He would buy negroes, but
would not sell them. He feared that they might fall into unkind hands.
He did sell for a small amount one negro, Lydia, to her husband, who
had been set free. Before Mr. Thomas Logan Douglas died he requested Dr. Henderson, his family physician and friend, to see that his
negroes, all of whom he freed by his will, were sent to Liberia in
Africa, if he should be living when Mrs. Douglas died. This was a
colony for emancipated slaves, founded by the American Colonization
Society, Dec. 31, 1816. Henry Clay was president of this Society.
Among old family papers we can see that in fitting out the negroes,
old-time wolsey-linsey was used. Lydia was the wife of one of these
Douglas negroes, and she went to Liberia with them. Father went

to Savannah, Georgia, and saw the Douglas negroes sail for Liberia.

Samuel Henderson (1804-1884) was a public spirited man. He was one of the projectors of the Nashville and Decatur Railroad, which was organized in July, 1851. He was a stockholder in this road and was one of the directors until it was merged into the Louisville and Nashville R. R. The building of the new Douglas church, along in the eighteen and fifties, was largely his work. This was built on a corner of Rev. Thomas Logan Douglas' place on the Lewisburg pike. Mr. Douglas intended to give the site to the Methodist church, but died without making a deed to the land, and when his widow died no deed had still been made. On winding up her estate, Dr. Henderson himself bought one acre of land on which the church stands, paying for this sixty dollars, and gave the lot to the Southern Methodist church. He bought this lot Nov. 25, 1852. We learn this from his diary. Henderson Academy was built principally at his expense. This was on the public highway just across the orchard from his home. It was a two-story brick building with two large recitation rooms down stairs, an entrance hall-way with two cloak closets and a stairway to the right, and a stairway to the left. On the second floor was one large auditorium and two small music rooms. When school first opened here Mr. Sterling Brewer and his wife taught, and Miss Laura Hardeman taught music. Later, when the writer started to school, Mr. Stokely Page, father of Williamson county's superintendent of public instruction (1916), Mr. Fred Page, had charge of this school. Mr. and Mrs. Brewer made their home at the "Red House" on my grandfather's place.

Samuel Henderson (1804-1884) believed in good roads. He aided in building the Lewisburg turnpike. He had that part of the pike upon which his home place bordered, built. He was Superintendent of the Nashville and Franklin turnpike. At opening of the War between the States he was made Captain of the Franklin Home Guards. His granddaughter, Mrs. Susie Miller, became a U. D. C. through him.

Dr. Samuel Henderson joined the Methodist church when he was about seventeen years old. He says in his diary that he "attached himself to the church at old Shiloh meeting house in the edge of Maury county." Rev. James Scott received his name. He lived the life of a true Christian. He was also an enthusiastic Mason. We will copy a record made many years ago of him as Mason, on paper with letter head "John Frizzell, Attorney-at-law, 164 Union St., Nashville, Tenn."

"In Hiram Lodge Oct. 25, 1836, Ch. 2, Ex. July 13, 1840. Council April 2, 1847, K. T. Feb. 4, 1848, H. P. Dec. 10; 1847. Grand King of this G. C. 1857."

An entry in Samuel Henderson's diary is: "Dec. 13, 1847. At a regular annual meeting of Franklin Royal Arch chapter I was elected High Priest of said chapter;" again: "Dec. 27, 1847. This day I was installed High Priest of Franklin chapter." "Jan. 8, 1848. I assisted in burying Nicholas Perkins in Masonic order." "Feb. 3, 1848. After having been elected previously to the degree of the Nashville Encampment, I this evening in Nashville received the degree of the Red Cross."

Feb. 4, 1848.   This evening I was made Knight Templar, and Knight of Maltā, with which I was well pleased." "Oct. 8, 1849. I am this day forty-five years of age. I attended the meeting of the Grand chapter of Royal Arch Masons at Nashville and was elected Scribe of said Grand chapter for the next year." "Nov. 30, 1849. On Friday met the companions at Hardeman's X Roads—Opened and organized a chapter of Royal Arch Masons to be called Triune Chapter, No. 30." Oct. 14, 1850.   Attended a meeting of the Grand Chapter at Nashville, and I was elected Grand King."

An entry in Samuel Henderson's diary is: "June 22, 1852.   Mrs. Frances Love (formerly Mrs. Thomas Logan)Douglas died   . . . burial services were conducted by Bishop Soul." "Nov. 24 and 25. At sale of Mrs. Love's estate I bought the (Douglas) church lot of one acre for which I pay ($60) sixty dollars." Dec. 5, 1853, he speaks of getting off the Douglas negroes to Liberia by way of Nashville, Tenn., and Savannah, Ga. (We note the fact that in the great World war Liberia casts her lot with the Allies struggling for Liberty, Aug. 4, 1917.)

Dr. Henderson was an old line Whig "of the strictest sect." When the war beween the states was brewing he took the same position that Robert E. Lee, John Bell and some other devoted Southerners took.   He did not want to see the Union dissolved.   This was the first stand taken by the Whigs.   Whigs were conservative.   But when Tennessee seceded, he said "My heart is with my people;" and he did all in his power to aid the South.   He helped Col. John McGavock equip a company of soldiers.   His own sons were little boys, so he aided some of his nephews who joined the army.   Samuel Henderson, however, was a firm believer in the constitutional right of a State to secede from the Union.   Indeed, this had never been doubted either by the North or the South.   It is interesting to recall the fact that the first Confederacy thought of was a Northern Confederacy 1803, which was to begin with the secession of Massachusetts. Col. Timothy Pickering, who had held many offices of trust, and at this time was a Representative of the State of Massachusetts in U. S. Senate, was one of the leading secessionists of his day.

As U. D. C., I wrote for Confederate Archives my Reminiscences of the War between the States.   In this paper is given some of my father's experiences during the war.   I remember well his great indignation at not being allowed to vote during the terrible reconstruction days.

In his diary during the war he tells of negroes running away to go to the Federal camps.   An entry is: "April 13, 1863.   The Federal soldiers have taken every horse, mare and mule that I have, leaving me but two little work mules and two mule colts.   They have broken into my smokehouse repeatedly and taken all my hams.   They have taken a good deal of my corn, and all of my hay, and nearly all my fodder. My health is very bad.   I will certainly go crazy."   After this he went with his children up to Mr. Frank Hardeman's to live. I remember that he carried what provisions he had, among which was a barrel of molasses that had escaped the Federal's eyes.   Here we remained four months. Two months of this time he was violently ill. In August, 1863, he sent his two oldest daughters, Sallie and Mary, North to school. The schools in the south were broken up, and he was anxious that his children be well educated. Dr. D. B. Cliffe, a Union man, who was carrying his own daughter North to school took these two girls under his care along with his daughter. To show how irregular schools were in the South when they attempted to open them at all: he started his two young sons, John and Samuel, to school in Franklin to Mr. Atha Thomas on Sept.21, 1863, and Oct. 22 was their last day at this school.

While at Mr. Hardeman's we devoted every forenoon to study. On Aug. 24, 1863, he carried his two little daughter's Lucy and Sue, to Col. McGavock's, to study under the family governess. Here we made our home for several months. Col. McGavock had sent most of his negroes to Louisiana to save them from the Federals. So while Sue and I were at Col. McGavock's, three of our negroes, Manda, Jane and Aaron worked there. In November of this same year his two work mules were stolen and he was left with only two mule colts.

We are glad to see a rift in the clouds in April, 1864. Dr. Henderson made a visit North to his daughters in school. Here, far from the madding turmoil of war, he could for awhile relax.

The day before the terrible battle of Franklin an entry in his diary: "Nov. 29, 1864. The Federal Calvary, when falling back to Nashville, formed a line near my house and looked for an attack. There were about four thousand men in line. They took my gray horse and work mule." This line of battle was just in front of our home, behind a rock fence . They theatened to shell our house.

The day after the fearful Battle of Franklin, Dr. Henderson's home was thrown open for wounded Confederate soldiers. Our house was full of wounded men. Father even took one wounded soldier in his own room. Being a physician and surgeon he did much for these soldiers. The writer recalls with pride the fact that sometimes soup was given her to feed these wounded men, and she would hand them water, etc. This was indeed a privilege.

July 3, 1865, Dr. Henderson had business in West Tennessee. He tells of leaving home June 26 in his buggy, with Dr. Leander Hughes, for Gibson county. He said that he passed over roads that had not been worked since the war began. There were no bridges. He says they "swam the horse across the Tennessee river and the buggy went over in a canoe." In 1861 his health was wretched and he was too old to take active service in the war, so he was made Captain of the Home Guards. The writer remembers with what a thrill she would watch this company of old men drill. They sometimes carried their walking canes as guns, but this did not dampen her ardor.

Samuel Henderson was a man of heroic mould. His beloved wife had died in 1858, leaving him with six little children, the oldest not yet ten years of age. Rev. Wm. M. Green said of him at the time of his death: "Here we enter the jeweled chamber of this man's character.

Turning away from the grave of his wife he gave himself, mind, heart and body to the care of his children.   Even the practice of medicine he abandoned.   He became a mother in all its meaning of watchfulness and earnest solicitude.   The moral, religious training and education of the children were his.   How beautifully they have repaid him.   How they have vied with each other in cheering his old heart and alleviating his pains.   They seemed to think that they could not do too much for him, and they could not.   Now that he is dead they have a precious legacy in the memory that they had such a father,. and we pronounce his life a success because of the character of his children."

Again, Dr. Wm. M. Green says, "If a chilvalric man is one who moves out boldly to the front with a matured conviction, Dr. Henderson was the soul of chivalry, with him there was no want of decision and no absence of resolution.   When a clear sense of right, evolved from the religion of Jesus, pointed out to him his duty, he moved toward it wth no falterng step.   The two-faced, characterless man he had an utterable contempt for.`   No thought ever crossed the mind of Dr. Henderson that by doing the right he would suffer materially in character or business.   That simpering and truckling policy which dwarfs and deforms so many business men was unknown to him.   In the muscle of this man there was energy, in his mind there was intellect, in his heart love, and in his life an accomplished mission.   When he passed the portal into the other life the angels whispered one to another, "There goes a man."

When Dr. Henderson died, Dec. 9, 1884, the physicians of Franklin and vicinity met in the office of Dr. John S. Park to take action and draft suitable resolutions in regard to his death.   Dr. W. M. Gentry was called to the chair and Dr. Wm. White was appointed secretary. The chair appointed Drs. D. B. Cliffe, J. S. Park and J. P. Hanner a committee to draft suitable resolutions.   The physicians of Franklin acted as honorary pall-bearers.   He was buried with Masonic honors, Hon. Burke Bond officiating. Masons acted as pall-bearers.   He died in a home he had built for his daughter, Sallie M. Smithson, in West End on Main street, Franklin.   This is a two-story brick house, and is now (1916) the home of Mr. Dorsey Crockett.

The writer never saw character so visibly written on any man's face.   Here truth and honor were apparent to the most casual observer.

Judge John Hughes Henderson (1849-1915)

John H. Henderson, son of Dr. Samuel Henderson (1804-1884) and his wife Rachel Jane Hughes (1818-1858), was born in the old ancestral home near Franklin, Tenn., Dec. 18, 1849.

The custom that prevailed in the South, of giving to each son, at his birth, a negro boy was here observed.   The grandfather, John Hughes (1776-1860), made a deed of gift to this child, of a negro boy, Manuel. Judge Henderson laughingly used to say that he was a slave owner in his own right.

Dr. Samuel Henderson (1804-1884) believed, in rearing his children, that it was best to give them as much freedom as possible. So he was strict with us only where principle was concerned. In minor matters we could have our own way. Perhaps this developed initiative, at any rate John Henderson was a manly boy. I remember how father often consulted his boys in regard to his business.

His school days begun at Henderson's Academy, but when still quite small the two brothers, John and Samuel, started to school in Franklin to Mr. Atha Thomas. Later they attended the Campbell school for boys in Franklin. This was conducted by Messrs. Patrick and Andrew Campbell. These brothers received their education in Edinburg, Scotland. Under them John Henderson made splendid progress in his studies. He took an extensive course in Latin and Greek, mathematics, etc. So when the Campbell brothers needed an assistant teacher, they proposed to John Henderson to teach several classes a day in Latin, and in this way pay for his tuition. This was in the days following the war. While this helped father financially, he believed that it would be fine training for his boy also. So in this way he paid for his own tuition. He had, however, attended school in Hayesville, Ohio, for more than a year. He left home for Ohio just a day or two before Abraham Lincoln was killed in 1865. I remember Father's great anxiety. He feared that some fanatic might try to wreak vengeance on Southern boys in the Northern schools. But this fear, we are happy to say, proved groundless.

He kept up his friendship with his college chums all of his life. During Reconstruction days he would write and tell his Northern friends of conditions in the South as seen though a boy's lenses. These boys, seeing things in an unprejudiced way, would write to him letters filled with indignation that such things should be done by the Federal authorities in their cruel effort to change social conditions in the South. They thought that the South was justified in resorting to any means to protect herself.

John Henderson chose the Law as his profession, as many of his name before him had done. He took a law course at the University of Virginia. Here he felt himself fortunate in being under the tutilage of Prof. Minor. In 1873 he came home from Virginia and begun the practice of his profession in Franklin, Tenn.

When, quite young, being a boy of strenuous habits, he became Agent for the Louisville & Nashville Railroad at Franklin. Here he succeeded Mr. Charles Marshall, who went to New Orleans to accept a responsible R. R. position. He commanded a fine salary. At the same time he was pursuing his study of the law. As a boy and a man he had many warm friends. He was one to inspire confidence. He gave up his agency for the Railroad in order to take his law course at University of Virginia. His education was obtained not altogether within school walls. He belonged to a debating society, where young men would meet and argue the issues of the day. In this he took delight. He was often called on at patriotic gatherings to address large audiences. The writer remembers that he was one of the chosen speakers at the court house in Franklin when the whole country was in gala attire on July 4, 1876, the one hundredth anniversary of the birth of our nation.

John Henderson joined the Methodist Episcopal Church, South, at old Douglas church, near Franklin, July 26, 1859. He often made public talks before the church assemblies when appointed. At Christmas services in 1883 he made an address which was warmly received on "He shall have dominion from sea to sea, and from the rivers to the ends of the earth." At one time he took the impetuous Peter as his subject. He often represented his church as lay member at the Tennessee Conference. On Children's Day, May 15, 1887, in the M. E. Church, South, in Franklin he made a tender talk about Christ taking a child in his arms and telling the people they must become as little children. His heart could warm up on this subject because of his great love for his own little children.

A year later he writes in his diary, June 27, 1888, of the birth of his son, the first John Hughes Henderson. Then he says, "As I believe I have done every time on similar occasions heretofore, I have gone down on my knees and have dedicated this little boy to God." He said he had rather his boys would be "honest, upright, Christian men than be President of the United States." To this baby, John Jr., Amanda, a negro woman who had nursed the father, became nurse.

Since I am trying to portray something of the real man, I will tell a little incident connected with Amanda. In her old age Amanda had softening of the brain. Sometime she would roam around at night without any definite aim. Once she was locked up as a vagrant. She said to the keeper: "If my Mars. Johnnie (she always called his name as she did when he was a child) knew I was here he would take me away." On finding out whom she meant by "Mars. Johnnie," they phoned Judge Henderson. It was a late hour at night and bitter cold. So he took in his arms a bundle of warm clothing for her to use that night, and the next day gave Amanda a room to stay in.

Many of his talks were made in this church at Franklin, of which he had been a member since early boyhood. Here he was a member of the Board of Stewards and of the Board of Trust. For many, many years he taught a class of young ladies in the Sunday-school.

July 1, 1886, he addressed the State Normal Institute. His subject was "Education in the South." In this address he "paid his respects" to George W. Cable, and discussed the bill pending in Congress known as the Blair Education Bill.

John H. Henderson was member of the Judicial Convention which nominated Democratic candidates for Supreme Judges. An entry in his diary reads: "I received today, from Gov. Peter Turney, a commission as one of his Aides on his Staff with the rank of Colonel—very much to my surprise." On the same date he says, "In present Supreme Court in Nashville I am interested in eight cases, of which I gain six and lose two."

He attended a meeting and banquet at the Maxwell House in Nashville of the Alumni of the University of Virginia, April 15, 1894. There were twenty present. He responded to toast.

John H. Henderson filled Judge McLemore's place on the Bench for some time.

In 1894 he was candidate for Attorney-General and Reporter for Tennessee. To this office he was not elected. His ability, we think, was universally acknowledged, but he was too straightforward for the modern politician.

He served as associate Justice on the Supreme Bench of Tennessee, 1907-8.

He loved the South with a perfect devotion, and was sometimes asked to make talks at the decorations of the graves of our Confederate soldiers. He was master of ceremonies when the Confederate monument was unveiled on the public square in Franklin, 1899. On that occasion Gen. George Gordon, of Memphis was with us, and the Governor of the State. There was the largest gathering of people ever known in Franklin. We will quote from Judge Henderson's introductory remarks:

"The occasion which bring you here is one to which we have all looked forward with interest. We are making history today. Future generations will point back with pride to this day: that their fathers and mothers, thirty-five years after the close of one of the bloodiest wars in history, when all passions had subsided, all animosities had been buried, and all sections of of our common country were at peace with each other as brothers, had paid this tribute of affection to the memory of their countrymen.

"A generation has passed, and this is, in part, the work of a new generation. To have done this sooner would have perhaps been too soon. There might have been in the tribute some malignity, some vindictiveness. But we are prompted by nothing of that sort. The corner stone of this monument is love, every rock in its foundation is cemented in love, every stroke of the chisel that worked out its beautiful symmetry was made in love: love pure and simple, welled up in grateful hearts, as a token of which we transmit this monument to posterity," etc. Judge Henderson goes on in his modest way to give the glory of its erection to others, but he was one of the first promoters of the movement to build this monument. It was unveiled by a niece of his, Sue Winstead, and Leah Cowan, whose father was an officer on Gen. Forrest's staff. These little girls drove in the procession in a beautifully decorated pony cart.

John H. Henderson was elected president of the Tennessee Bar Association in 1904. The Review-Appeal of July 7, 1904, says: "Mr. Henderson's established position in the front rank of the bar of Middle Tennessee, and his high personal character amply justified the partiality of his associates ." The session of the State Bar Association held at Chattanooga during his presidency was among the most brilliant ever held in the State. The Chattanooga News, on this occasion, pays tribute to his young lady daughter who accompanied him. It says: "Many charming ladies are with the lawyers, and the favorite with them all perhaps because of her rare beauty and charming manner is Miss Henderson, of Franklin. She is the daughter of Judge Henderson, president of the Bar Association."

His address to the Bar Association was much praised by the press of the State. To give some idea of his estimate of a lawyer, we will quote from an address made by him before the Tennessee Bar Association several years before this, in 1901. His subject was "The Twentieth Century Lawyer." After looking at various phases of his subject he said in conclusion: "We, among ourselves, are accustomed to say that the law is a great profession; that the lawyer, true to the ethics of his profession, is the highest type of a gentleman that we have, and the greatest benefactor of his race. If he is a lawyer in all that the word means, he is a conservator of the peace, a promoter of happiness in the domestic relations; he discourages lawsuits; his fee is largely an incident, instead of an incentive to his labor. He is an indispensible factor at the birth and upbuilding of governments," etc. The writer knows positively that Judge Henderson discouraged the bringing of lawsuits which tended to embitter family relations among his clients. She knows of some cases where he refused to bring suit for divorce from wife or husband when he knew that he might receive good fee.

In 1907, as we have said, Judge Henderson was called to the Supreme Bench of Tennessee. A notice in the Review-Appeal June 20, 1907, is: "Judge J. H. Henderson, of the Supreme Court, spent Sunday and Monday at home. Last Saturday he delivered the opinion of the Court in several important cases." While he served, decision was made in regard to title of the Gray property on Seventh avenue, purchased for the Governor's mansion. It was during this time that the Supreme Court declared the anti-race-track gambling law, passed by an act of the last Legislature, to be constitutional.

When he ran for re-election to the Supreme Bench he was indorsed by members of the Bar from the three sections of Tennessee, East Middle, and West Tennessee. He had a most hearty indorsement from his own Congressional district, the Seventh, and one hundred and sixty-eight members of the Memphis Bar gave him endorsement. In this Memphis endorsement is said when making selection for his successor "Judge Wilkes had the whole Bar of Middle Tennessee to draw from, and it was therefore a mark of eminent distinction when his choice fell upon Judge Henderson. Judge Henderson was in no sense an applicant for the position but accepted it chiefly for the purpose of showing his appreciation of the honor conferred upon him. "From that time until after the death of Judge Wilkes, Judge Henderson sat as Special Judge of the Supreme Court, making a splendid record, thoroughly satisfactory to the Bar and the public. A natural laudable ambition to secure an endorsement of that record prompts Judge Henderson now to stand for election at the hands of the people.

"For many years Judge Henderson has been one of the ablest and most popular lawyers of the State. He has long been one of the most active members of the Tennessee Bar Association; was at one time its president and is entitled to a large share of its credit for the good work it has done in promoting beneficial legislation.

"Judge Henderson has always been a stalwart Democrat, and has been in the forefront of all his party's battles. As a man, as a lawyer, as a Democrat, he is worthy in a high degree of the high position for which we urge him."

In 1910 there was a great revolt in Tennessee against a political machine which had been built up. A mass meeting of Democrats was called to meet in Nashville on May 18 to reorganize the Democratic party. Judge Henderson's views on this matter can be seen in Nashville Banner, May 10, 1910. Independent Democrats of the State of Tennessee assembled in convention at Ryman Auditorium in Nashville, Sep. 14, 1910, and adopted a Democratic platform. Of this Democratic platform committee J. H. Henderson was chairman. The opening sentence of this platform reads:

"We, the representatives of the Democratic party of Tennessee, acting by authority derived directly from the people, do declare our allegiance to the time-honored principles of the national Democracy," etc. This flatform can be found in full in Nashville Banner for Sept. 14, 1910.

At the time of the adoption of this platform hundreds of old Confederate soldiers, among them the writer's husband, Henry Claiborne Horton, marched to the convention, to the tune of Dixie, each man wearing an American flag. They were led by a man who was chief of artillery under the intrepid Forrest. This was a movement of the people seeking purer politics.

John H. Henderson had a large and lucrative practice, and he worked hard. He was sometimes found at his desk after the midnight hour.

He was married to Elizabeth Ewin Perkins in May, 1879. Theirs was a hospitable home. We can say, without fear of our assertion being called in question, that they entertained more largely than anybody in Williamson county. People in this county in ante-bellum days entertained quite as much. Notwithstanding changed conditions, they kept up the custom of the Old South, an open door.

Lizzie Perkins comes of an old and influential family. Her father, Samuel Perkins was of this well known family of Tennessee; and her mother, Theresa Ewin, was born and reared in Kentucky. Mrs. Perkins was a woman gifted in conversation and she was quite literary. The Perkins family were people of wealth and influence.

The three last years of Judge Henderson's life were full of suffering, which he bore with fortitude and without complaint. During this time a daughter, whom he idolized, passed away.

William H. Johnston sums up the character of this man in these words: "Judge John Hughes Henderson was a Christian citizen, devoted churchman, faithful advocate, man of peace, public almona, family arbiter; worthy, confident, wise adviser, loving husband, indulgent father, and exemplar par excellence."

His death-bed scene was the most beautiful thing the writer ever witnessed.

Children of John Hughes Henderson and his wife, Elizabeth Ewin
    Perkins:

Samuel; born July, 1880, died in infancy.

Thomas; Attorney-at-law: married Lucile Carter of Virginia.

Theresa Ewin; married Edward Hamilton, Attorney-at-law, Nashville, Tenn.

John; died early.

Sarah Martin; died 1912.

John Hughes.

Captain Thomas Perkins Henderson

Thomas P., son of Judge John Hughes Henderson and his wife, Elizabeth Ewin Perkins, was born in Franklin, Tenn., May 9, 1882. He is a lineal descendant of Captain John Hughes of the War of 1812, and of Colonel Archelaus Hughes, Captain William Martin and Samuel Henderson of the Revolutionary war. He is grandson of Dr. Samuel Henderson (1804-1884), who was a Captain of the Franklin Home Guards during the War between the States in 1861. On his maternal side he is grandson of Samuel Perkins, who served during the War between the States and who was son of Thomas F. Perkins and his wife, America Cannon, daughter of Colonel Newton Cannon, who served in War of 1812 and later was Governor of Tennessee.

Thomas P. Henderson was at first Captain, National Guard, Tennessee, commanding Company "I," 1st Tenn. Artillery. He was in training at Fort Oglethorpe, Ga., May 13, 1917, to May 30, 1917, and resigned to accept commission in 1st Tennessee Field Artillery, in process of organization.

As soon as America declared war on Germany he offered his services to the Government, and began at once to recruit a battery.

Franklin, Tennessee, occupies a unique place in the annals of the 114th Field Artillery. Half of the Regiment's captains are from this Williamson county town: Capt. T. P. Henderson, Capt. Enoch Brown and Capt. Reese Amis. But Henderson is the only commander in the regiment who recruited his own volunteer battery. His battery was the first company to leave Williamson county for war. He attended the first training camp at Fort Oglethorpe. After recruiting his battery he had official notification from Washington that it was the first battery in Tennessee to reach war strength. This regiment was originally First Tennessee Regiment. On later date when merged into the regular army they were known as 114th Field Artillery, 30th Division.

On the night before these men left for camp at Columbia, Tenn., July 20, 1917, the Army Comfort Circle gave a most enthusiastic entertainment at the Auditorium in Franklin. The boys were entertained in our homes. Tom, when thanking the people for what they had done for the boys, declared this the proudest day of his life. The camp at Columbia, Tenn., was named in honor of him, "Thomas P. Henderson Camp."

Sep. 5, 1917 the First Tenn. Field Artillery entrained for Camp Sevier, at Greenville, S. C. They sailed for France, May 26, 1918.

July 14, 1918, Tom wrote me from France: "Am in training camp, all of us aching to get to the front and do our turn." They attained their desire at St. Mehiel and in the stupendous Meuse-Argonne battle. Tom Henderson was first with the 30th Division, serving later with the 89th Division and with the 33rd Division. When starting home from overseas they were again placed in the 30th Division.

Gen. John J. Pershing told the American Luncheon Club in London, July 16, 1919, that the American offensive, known as the Meuse-Argonne battle, cut the German lines of communication and made further resistance impossible (see Nashville Banner for July 16, 1919).

"This long and bloody battle of the Meuse-Argonne pales the greatest of Civil war conflicts into insignifigance." In the Saturday Evening Post page 7, May 10, 1919, it is said that "the Meuse-Argonne was the greatest battle in American history." That long-drawn struggle began Sep. 26, and did not end until the finish, Nov. 11, at 11 o'clock. "Had not the Argonne position been forced, a Spring campaign might have been necessary."

We will copy passages from letters written by Captain Henderson to his wife, Aug. 28, 1918. He tells some things about the trip to the front. They traveled two days and nights. He speaks of his men being comfortably accommodated and of a magnificent, up-to-date palace car for the officers. "This was the nicest car I ever rode in. I think it was intended for some General and got on our train by mistake.... We have seen all the Fighting rivers." He says of Battery F.: "as far as enlisted personnel is concerned, 'is there.' They are not scared; they do not get excited, and in fact while firing under fire are calmer and cooler than when drilling in a test drill."

Captain Henderson writes his wife later in this terrible Meuse-Argonne campaign of how hot his guns were with incessant fire. Then he tells how grateful they are for an opportunity to bathe in the River Meuse. The battery fought through the whole of this Argonne campaign of 42 days of almost continuous fighting.

On March 31, 1919, the 114th Field Artillery, returned from overseas, paraded in Nashville. I never saw so immense a throng of people. Their welcome was glorious. The poor, dear Confederate veterans marched ahead of the regiment. The Ward-Belmont girls formed, near the triumphal arch, on steps as a living flag.

Battery F, 114th Field Artillery, returned to the States minus eleven of its brave boys who left Tennessee.

He was Captain, National Guard, Tennessee, commanding company I, 1st Tennessee Infantry, Second Officers' Training Camp, Ft.

Oglethorpe, Ga., May 13 to May 30, 1917, resigning to accept commission in First Tenn. Field Artillery, in process of organization.

He enlisted for military service June 1, 1917, at Franklin, Tenn., as a Provisional Captain in First Tennessee Field Artillery section of the National Guard; was mustered into Federal service July 30, 1917; assigned originally to raise and command Battery F, 1st Tennessee Field Artillery, the designation of the regiment being changed September 14, 1917, to 114th Field Artillery, and being part of the 55th Field Artillery Brigade of the 30th Division, U. S. Army.

Home Rendezvous, Columbia, Tenn., July 25 to Sept. 9, 1917. Here the camp was named in his honor—Camp Thomas P. Henderson. His was a company of volunteers, recruited by him in Tennessee from Williamson, Maury and Lawrence counties.

This company embarked from Hoboken, New Jersey, on Karoa, May 26, 1918. They were in Camp de Coetquoidan, France, June 16 to Aug. 21, 1918, when they went to Toul Front. He first went into action August 29, 1918, at 11 p. m. Bernecourt, Toul Sector. He participated in the following engagements: Defense Toul Sector, August 28 to September 11, 1918; St. Mihiel Offensive September 12 to 15; Defense Argonne Woods, September 22 to 25; Meuse-Argonne, September 26 to October 8; Defense Wouvre Sector, October 10 to November 10; Wouvre Offensive, November 10 to November 11, 1918.

He arrived at Newport News. Va., on U. S. S. Finland, March 23, 1919, from St. Nazarie, France. He was discharged from service at Ft. Oglethorpe, Ga., April 24, 1919, as Captain Field Artillery.

He is a lawyer. Was first of the firm, Henderson & Henderson, being associated with his father, Judge John H. Henderson.

Children of Captain Thomas P. Henderson and his wife, Lucile Carter:

Thomas Perkins Henderson.

Elizabeth Henderson.

Theresa Ewin, daughter of Judge John Henderson, and his wife, Lizzie Perkins, married Edward Hamilton, attorney-at-law, of Nashville, Tenn. Their children are Sarah Martin and Mary, and one son, who died in infancy.

Dr. Samuel Henderson, Jr. (1852-1913)

Samuel Henderson, son of Dr. Samuel Henderson (1804-1884) and his wife, Rachel Jane (Hughes) Henderson, was born at the old home in Williamson county, Tenn., June 27, 1852. He attended the Campbell School in Franklin under Messrs. Pat and Andrew Campbell. These men taught for many years and on their roll is found the names of many notable Southern men. His training in the larger school of life came during the war between the States, and in the even more trying reconstruction period. Sometimes we think the manhood following the war, developed under such adverse conditions, was as great a glory to the South as the chivalry of her sons who took up arms.

Dr. Samuel Henderson and his father, Dr. Samuel Henderson, Sr., both took the degree, M. D., at Jefferson College, Philadelphia, Pa.

Here the subject of our sketch came in contact with the celebrated Samuel Gross, M. D., D. C. L., etc. Dr. Gross took in him a personal interest, having known his father. On the graduation of Samuel Henderson, Jr., Dr. Gross urged the father, in flattering terms, to see that his son began the practice of medicine in Philadelphia. His whole life, however, was given to his native home.

He inspired confidence and impressed one as a man of reserve force. His kindliness of nature found expression through his practice. Much of this was done with no expectation of pecuniary reward. His professional services were often given to his father's old slaves. A beautiful tribute paid him by those who had shared his services was that "he was the friend of the widow and orphan." He was genial and social in his nature, and had many warm friends to whom he was devoted. He had a strong sense of justice. He was a member of the Odd Fellows order, in which he took great interest. This order in Franklin showed appreciation of this man by placing a framed picture of him in the lodge room. In preamble and resolutions passed by Odd Fellows lodge at time of his death is said: "He took an interest in civic affairs, was dependable to be on the moral side of all public questions, and was especially interested in the public improvement of the town, of which he was at the time of his death an alderman. Many years ago he became a member of Franklin Lodge I. O. O. F. and in his life he exemplified the tenets of the order in a marked degree. He had filled many offices of the order, and for many years, as if by common consent, as each Noble Grand was inducted into his position, it was announced that Brother Samuel Henderson was selected as Right Supporter to the Noble Grand. . . . . He was of a sunny disposition and bore life's burdens and cares with a smile, bringing good cheer with him wherever you found him."

Samuel Henderson joined the Methodist Church, South, when seventeen years of age. He served for years as member of the Board of Stewards in Franklin. The writer, who knew the man's life intimately, asserts with confidence that he was one of the purest of Christians all his life. The devotion of his only brother, Judge John H. Henderson, to him was something beautiful. The love of his sisters for him was scarcely less. His was of a nature that drew people to him.

Marrying when he had just reached his majority, he was the father of a large family of children when he himself was not much more than a boy. He was a public-spirited man. As a member of the municipal board of Franklin he effected much good for his town. The proposition to have cement pavements all over Franklin was his, and he suggested ways and means of doing this. A member of the municipal board said to the writer the day of Dr. Henderson's death: "The paved streets of Franklin will be a monument to Dr. Henderson's memory." It was he who first laid plans for the erection of the Auditorium, which is connected with our public school building, thus supplying a long-felt need for Franklin.

Articles read by him before the Williamson County Medical Society were sometimes printed in the "Nashville Journal of Medicine and Surgery," edited by Charles S. Briggs. One of these contributions can be found in the March, 1908, issue of this publication.

Dr. Henderson suffered with heart trouble. He spoke so seldom of his own suffering of any nature that many of his friends did not realize that death might come to him at any time. He was a man of bouyant nature, and always looked on the bright side of things. So when he died suddenly, September 15, 1913, the community was shocked. He had been home only two weeks from a most happy visit to his daughter, Mrs. John H. Harrison, in Los Angeles, California. His obsequies were attended by an unusually large number of people from all over the county.

Rev. W. B. Taylor wrote of him in the Christian Advocate, Oct. 2, 1913: "Dr. Henderson was among my first acquaintances when I came to Franklin three years ago. His approach to me was of such a manner as that a true friendship was begun which has grown stronger with the passing of years. He was one of a few busy professional men who was above the average in his attendance at church, and the mid-week prayer-meeting was his choice of all the services. As a physician he ranked among the ablest of his profession. A prominent physician once said to me: 'Sam Henderson is one of the best diagnosticians and general practitioners in the State. His only difficulty is his modesty.

"Dr. Henderson came of one of the best families of Williamson county, nor did the family name ever suffer at his hands. As a citizen he was public-spirited, aggressive, and always on the right side of all matters of public interest. He was a devoted father, and always at his best when at home with his family. His death was sudden and unexpected— a severe shock and deep grief to the entire community, where he is seriously and sadly missed in every sphere of our community life.

"The funeral services were conducted at the Methodist church by the writer, assisted by Revs. W. J. Collier and W. T. Haggard. While his mortal body sleeps in Mount Hope, his spirit is forever with the pure and good.—W. B. Taylor."

Samuel Henderson was married in November, 1873, to Florence Morton. Their children are: Samuel Morton, Mrs. Mazie Fleming, son, Sam Compton; Mrs. Louise Harrison, John P., Mrs. Susie Virginia Miller; child Catherine; Warren, who died in early manhood. By a second marriage to Bettie Hughes he had a son, Brown, who died in early manhood. John H. Harrison, who married Louise Henderson, held responsible position in U. S. Census Bureau. They have one child, Sam H. Harrison.

Sallie Martin (Henderson) Smithson (1857-1899)

Sallie Martin Henderson was born September 14, 1847, at the old home in Williamson county, Tenn. She was a daughter of Dr. Samuel Henderson (1804-1884) and his wife, Rachel Jane Hughes. She was one of the cheeriest, happiest of children, and was, indeed, a comfort to her father at the time of his supreme sorrow, the death of his wife. At this time Sallie was not quite eleven years of age. Now, too, the mother instinct, latent in the child's nature, manifested itself in her thought for her younger sisters and brothers. We have often said that she was a "little mother" to us. She married Feb. 9, 1871, Capt. Geo. W. Smithson. He was a Lieut. under Col. W. S. McLemore of the 4th Tennessee Confederate Cavalry during the war between the States. At the time of his marriage he was merchandising in Franklin, a member of the firm of House & Smithson. Theirs was an ideally happy home. They lived, and both died, in the two story brick house in West End, which was given to them by Mrs. Smithson's father, Dr. Samuel Henderson. This house is now (1916) the home of Mr. Dorsey Crockett. She was educated at the Tennessee Female College and in Ohio. Her last term in school was at the D. C. Elliott Academy, a finishing school for young ladies, in Nashville. She was fond of the piano and of her guitar, and would, as a girl, often sit on the doorsteps at evening and sing to her guitar accompaniment. The only patriotic club she ever joined was the U. D. C. We will quote from a newspaper article written at time of her death by Rev. Herschel B. Reams:

"Added to her charms of personal grace and beauty were the endowments of a strong intellect and a great heart.....In her home as wife, mother, hostess, she honored and magnified these good offices, and contributed abundantly to the happiness of all. Naturally bright and cheerful, she was easily a source of power and pleasure in every circle. "In sickness and in health she had that faith which inspires courage and is adequate to victory."

She died October 26, 1899. Her children are: Janey, married Rev. Walter J. Bruce; children, Walter, Jane, Mary, Frances; George Henderson, merchant; married Pattie Bolton; children, George,, Hattie; Sarah; Mary Sam, married Newton C. Perkins; banker; child, Sam; Sallie.

Mary Jane (Henderson) Warren (1849-1915)

Mary Jane; daughter of Dr. Samuel Henderson (1804-1884) and his wife, Rachel Jane Hughes, was born in the old home in Williamson county, Tenn., Jan. 17, 1849. She was educated at the Tennessee Female College, the Franklin Institute, and in Ohio. On Dec. 19, 1883, she married Rev. W. R. Warren, a wholesale and retail book merchant in Nashville, Tenn., He was for many years a member of the Tennessee Conference of the M. E. Church, South. A monument to his work here is found not only in the lives of people among whom he labored, but in the churches he was instrumental in building. Most of the Methodist churches built around Nashville during his active ministry received much aid from him. After his retirement from active work in the ministry, he built East End Methodist church. He was a man of most kindly heart. He took nieces and nephews, the orphan children of Dr. S. D. Baldwin, author of "Armageddon," and a sister of Mr. Warren's former wife, into his own home. When their health was failing, Mr. Warren took charge of a church in Colorado, so as to have them in a healthy climate. And on their account he later moved to New Mexico.

She was given to much charity. This was so quietly done that "the right hand knew not what the left hand did." She joined the M. E. Church, South, when very young and was always a consistent member. While her home was in Nashville she was a member of the Tulip street church. Their home was on Woodland street, near the old home of Bishop McTyeire and Dr. Thomas O. Summers, those bulwarks of Methodism. At time of her death she was making her home with a niece, Sue H. Winstead, in Franklin. She died May 29, 1915, leaving no children.

Susan Virginia Henderson Winstead (1855-1889)

Sue, daughter of Dr. Samuel Henderson (1804-1884) and his wife, Rachel Jane Hughes, was born in the old home in Williamson county, Tenn., June 9, 1855. She enjoyed robust health. She was a girl and woman of splendid domestic qualities. She had something of the artist nature and was always trying to beautify her home. She was above the average height and was of splendid presence, and always dressed in exquisite taste. During her father's illness of almost one year she was his constant attendant. With deft fingers and the tenderest care she ministered to his every need.

"After a long engagement, which thoroughly tested the love of both, she was married to Mr. M. P. G. Winstead, Oct. 18, 1888. This union of hearts was in every way congenial. Not quite fourteen months of wedded bliss had elapsed, when the wife and mother, apparently in the best of health, while sitting in her chair, died suddenly with heart failure. Her infant, two weeks old, was baptized by Rev. W. R. Warren on the occasion of the funeral and received the name of its mother. It was a striking coincidence that this mother and her child shared the same fate. Both became motherless in infancy. A faithfully kept family register shows that she was baptized Sep. 15, 1855, when three months old, and that she joined the M. E. Church, South, at Douglas, Aug. 18, 1869."

M. P. G. Winstead, when a beardless youth, responded to the call of our Southland. He enlisted in the Confederate army, and was severely wounded at the Battle of Perryville, losing one leg.

"Dr. Samuel Henderson, of precious memory, and father of the deceased, gave himself without stint or hindrance to the training of his children; he was a physical, moral, intellectual and religious father; he trained them up in the way God wanted them to go, and they have not departed from it, for a more robust family in principle and religion I have not known. No wonder that Mrs. Sue V. Winstead was just the woman she was, with such a training, true to her husband, family and friends, and true to her church and her God." This was written by Dr. William Green at time of her death.

A friend of hers, signed "T. P." wrote for the press, "As I sat last night with other friends to watch beside her bier, I recalled the scene of one short year ago when I saw her standing on the very spot where her bier rested, a happy bride beneath a yoke of fresh, bright flowers—fit emblems of a union of unshadowed happiness; alas that it vanished almost with their perfume.

"It is indeed a fruitless effort to attempt to portray the character of Susie Henderson. Tender and loving to infancy, kind and patient with children, genial and affectionate to the aged, cheerful, tender and untiring in the sick room, she was the embodiment of all that is beautiful in woman. She was social in the highest degree."

She left one child, Sue H. Winstead.

Lucy Henderson Horton

Lucy; daughter of Dr. Samuel Henderson (1804-1884) and his wife, Rachel Jane Hughes, was born Jan. 14, 1851, at the old ancestral home in Williamson county, Tenn. This was the old home from which General William Martin, her grandmother's brother, went out to the War of 1812. Martin was Major at Pensacola and was aide on General Andrew Jackson's staff, with title of Colonel at New Orleans, and distinguished himself. Mrs. Horton owns the old red sash worn by Colonel Martin on the battlefield of New Orleans.

Lucy Henderson attended school at "Henderson's Academy" until she was nine years of age. After this she was in school at the Tennessee Female College in Franklin, Tenn., which was under the presidency of C. W. Callender, and later of Bishop R. K. Hargrove. From 1865 to 1868 she attended the Institute in Franklin, Rev. A. N. Cunningham, principal. We will say in passing that while she was Regent of "Old Glory" chapter D. A. R. (1903-1905) she brought about a planting by the chapter, of memorial trees on the school campus to Revolutionary heroes, and again to these pioneer educators. She herself planted the Bishop Hargrove memorial tree, and again the Patrick Henry memorial tree.

Growing up as she did in the country she imbibed a passionate love of Nature. The trees, the birds, the flowers were like personal friends to her. It seemed to her that the sky bent more lovingly above her home, which sheltered a devoted family, than anywhere else.

Her father's confidence in his friends was such that he lost large sums of money about the time this girl finished school. Eager to be of some aid to her father, she sought a certificate of scholarship from Bishop R. K. Hargrove. Bishop Hargrove not only gave her the certificate but secured for her a position to teach in the Tennessee Female College.

She was married May 30, 1878, in the Methodist Episcopal Church, South, in Franklin, by Rev. William Burr, to Henry Claiborne Horton, of

Alabama. For eleven years after their marriage they made Alabama heir home. Since this time Franklin, Tenn., has been their home.

Lucy H. Horton is a club woman. She was one of the charter members of "Old Glory" chapter D. A. R., which was organized in 1897, she at that time, being made chapter Recording Secretary. Her national number in this order is 20,744. She filled the office of Secretary for six years, when she was elected Chapter Regent. When the State D. A. R. conference met in Memphis, Tenn., in Nov., 1905, she was elected State Historian N. S. D. A. R. This office she filled three years, and in April, 1910, at the D. A. R. congress in Washington she was elected Tennessee's Vice State Regent N. S. D. A. R.

She has served on six National Committees: Children of the Republic Committee, while Mrs. John A. Murphy, the founder, was National Chairman, and while Mrs. Gardner was National Chairman; Committee to Locate Historic Spots; Committee to Prevent Desecration of the Flag; Memorial Continental Hall Committee; Committee on Immigration; and Committees on Real Daughters.

She became a member of Colonial Dames of America resident in Tennessee in 1904. She served on Educational and Hospitality Committee, etc., and in 1921 was elected Second Vice-President of Colonial Dames of America resident in Tennessee, when Mrs. Frank W. Ring was President, and Mrs. H. C. Tolman was First Vice-President. The number engraved on her Colonial Dames Recognition Pin is 296. She entered the order through her ancestor, Samuel Henderson (1700-1784), of Granville county, N. C. That her first Henderson ancestor came to America in 1607 can be seen in Colonial Families of the United States of America, by George Norbury Mackenzie, Vol. IV, pages 177-180. Thomas Henderson, the emigrant ancestor, came to Jamestown, Virginia, in 1607.

Lucy H. Horton is member of Ladies' Historical Association of Tennessee; United Daughters of the Confederacy; Society for the Preservation of Virginia Antiquities; United States Daughters of 1812; and of the Hermitage Association. She was elected State Historian of the United States Daughters of 1812 in 1915, and being re-elected, served to 1922. She was then made State Vice-President.

As part of her work as Tennessee State Historian of the D. A. R., she filed in the State Archives at the Capitol in Nashville a record of work done by the D. A. R. of Tennessee, consisting of eighty-eight (88) type-written pages. She begins this record with the organization of D. A. R. work in Tennessee, by Mrs. J. Harvey Mathais, first State Regent, and carries it through the administration of Mrs. James S. Pilcher; Mrs. H. S. Chamberlain; Mrs. Charles B. Bryan and Miss Mary Boyce Temple. Lucy H. Horton served as State Historian D. A. R. during Miss Mary Boyce Temple's first administration.

The D. A. R. flag, which was presented to the Cruiser "Tennessee" in Hampton Roads just before the American Squadron started on its celebrated Pacific cruise in 1907, was Mrs. Horton's suggestion before the State D. A. R. conference at Memphis in 1905, and she was appointed by Mrs. Charles B. Bryan, State Regent, to get up the banner and procure money to pay for same from chapters over the State. This she did. The chapters responded promptly. This banner was presented at the hands of Miss Mary Boyce Temple, who was then State Regent. Mrs. Horton, who, on account of illness, could not be present, sent "Greetings" which was read by Mrs. Dabney Scales for her. This is a handsomely embroidered banner of white silk, bearing in the center the coat of arms of Tennessee, beneath this is the insignia of our order, and under this a scroll with the words "Presented by the Daughters of the American Revolution of Tennessee, 1907."

The Cruiser "Tennessee" was later known as the "Memphis" when the great dreadnaught which was to bear the name Tennessee was building. The "Memphis" was lost in San Domingo waters, but the Captain and his wife managed to save this banner, and when the dreadnaught "The Tennessee" was ready to go into commission in 1920 this banner was presented to this new battleship.

Lucy H. Horton, before serving on National Committee Children of the Republic, organized and conducted in Franklin the first Children of the Republic Club in Tennessee, Feb. 1, 1907, with an average attendance of forty-two. While on National Committee to Prevent Desecration of the Flag she placed the American flag in every school-room in Williamson county, and in many of these schools they gave salute to the flag daily. The students would rise to their feet and, looking toward the flag, all say in concert, "One country, one language, one flag;" then, as pupils filed out, each one would give the West Point salute to flag. When Mrs. J. M. Dickenson was National Chairman of Committee to Prevent Desecration of the Flag, she wrote Mrs. Horton that she highly approved of the simple words "One country, one language, one flag," which Mrs. Horton originated as salute to our flag, because so much was expressed in a few words.

Mrs. Horton was early interested in locating historic spots. In 1903 she read a paper before "Old Glory" chapter at an evening celebration in the home of Hon. Atha Thomas, when many guests, ladies and gentlemen were present. The title of this paper was "Bits of Tennessee History." She had made research in the State Archives at the capitol at Nashville for assertions made by her. In this paper of Mrs. Horton's seven important historic sites were located by her. These sites she, from time to time, urged the D. A. R. to mark.

It was in 1900 that she called the attention of "Old Glory" chapter D. A. R. to the fact that in the old Presbyterian church in Franklin, in 1830, a treaty with the Chickasaws was held by John H. Eaton and Gen. John Coffee, and this fact was incorporated in her report to the D. A . R. State conference in Nashville in 1903; the first State conference in Tennessee after its organization at Chattanooga in 1901.

On Feb. 1, 1906, Mrs. Horton wrote to Miss Mary Desha, at Washington, one of the three women who originated the D. A. R. order and who was interested in marking historic spots, asking her influence in having the site of Fort Prudhomme, built by La Salle in 1682 at the third Chickasaw bluff going down the Mississippi river, marked. This bluff is at Memphis, Tenn. In this letter of Feb. 1, 1906, she also sought Miss Desha's influence in having markers placed at Sycamore Shoals on Wautauga river to indicate the fact that here the over-mountain men rendezvoused before going to do battle at King's Mountain, Oct. 7, 1780. And here the Transylvania Company, with Col. Richard Henderson at its head, made a treaty with the Cherokees, March 17, 1775; and made the Transylvania purchase. To Mrs. Horton's appeal Miss Desha replied favorably.

Mrs. Horton's historical paper "Bits of Tennessee History" was published in The American Monthly Magazine for Nov., 1903, pages 347-352. Other historic spots located by Mrs. Horton in this paper in 1903 was the old Spanish fort, "St. Charles," at New Orleans. She called attention to the fact that from this third Chickasaw Bluff (now Memphis, Tenn.), DeSota first saw our majestic river, the Mississippi, April 25, 1541. Here also was located one of Spain's cordon of forts where she exacted toll of the flat boats from Kentucky. She called attention to the fact that Gen. Joseph Martin, with other adventurers, tried to make a settlement in Powell's Valley in 1769. This included Cumberland Gap. Another historic site noted by Mrs. Horton was the land office of Col. Richard Henderson at French Lick (now Nashville, Tenn.), established in 1779. These historic sites, as we have said, were located by Mrs. Horton in 1902 or before that time. Some of them have been appropriately marked by the D. A. R.

Mrs. Horton, as representative of "Old Glory" chapter D. A. R. to the second State conference, that which met in Nashville in Nov., 1903, in her report to this conference, states the fact that the Natchez Trace, and Boone's Trace, or the Wilderness road, were two of our early highways.

She was a delegate to the eleventh Continental Congress, N. S. D. A. R., which convened in Washington, D. C., in Feb., 1902. At this time Mrs. Charles H. Fairbanks was President-General. At one of the social functions in Washington Mrs. Horton was so glad to meet Clara Barton and Susan B. Anthony. She said to Miss Anthony, "You have broadened life for women." Miss Anthony's reply was, "I have taught you that life is worth living, haven't I?"

When tracing her Martin descent in 1897 preparatory to joining the D. A. R., she found in an article written by Stephen B. Weeks and published in Report of American Historical Association for the year 1893, entitled, "Gen. Joseph Martin and the War of the Revolution in the West," that Mr. Weeks was indebted to the Draper Manuscripts for some of his information regarding Gen. Joseph Martin. This led Mrs. Horton to be interested in the Draper Manuscripts, which were stored in the Archives of Wisconsin.

When Mrs. Horton was State Historian N. S. D. A. R., her report read before the D. A. R. State conference at Knoxville, Nov., 1907, shows her deep interest in the necessity of making effort to secure copies of the seven Draper Manuscripts, which relate entirely to early Tennessee history, for our State Archives. In this report she states the fact that she had corresponded with Mr. R. G. Thwaites, Secretary and Superintendent of the State Historical Society of Wisconsin, and asked for what sum of money we could have these seven manuscripts typewritten. His reply was that he thought it would cost between two and three hundred dollars, possibly less than two hundred dollars. But to Mrs. Wilkinson, of Memphis, Tenn., is due the glory of having secured type-written copies of some Draper manuscripts which relate to Tennesee. Mrs. Wilkerson succeeded Mrs. Horton as State Historian D. A. R. She secured the money and the Memphis D. A. R. chapters sent a man to Wisconsin to do the typewriting. Mrs. Wilkinson read her report before the D. A. R. State Conference at Murfreesboro, Tenn., in Nov. 1911, which proved her interest in the Draper Manuscripts. And in 1913 she had three typewritten copies made and placed, one copy in the Capitol at Nashville, one copy in the public library in Memphis, and one copy in Knoxville. The State is greatly indebted to Mrs. Wilkinson for her splendid work.

Mrs. Horton's State Historian's Report in 1907 further shows her interest in the State Archivist work. Mr. Quarles had shown her the original Constitution of Tennesee, which he had rescued form the ash barrel, after being placed in charge at the Capitol, and the original deed to the Hermitage made by John L. Hadley to Andrew Jackson, which was also saved from the fire. We remark in passing that Mrs. Charles B. Bryan, of Memphis, while State Regent (1903-5), did much toward creating in Tennessee a Department of Archives and History. Indeed she had the bill creating this Department presented to the Legislature.

Mrs. Horton's report showed that she had located many old papers, letters and documents, some of which were her own old family papers. She had also located old furniture and other relics, because all of these things bespeak history. Her endeavor was to make accessible to future historians material comparatively little known. She also reports the D. A. R. banner for the Cruiser "Tennessee" having been made and having been presented to this battleship by Miss Temple.

She was appointed by Mrs. Bryan to read a paper before the State Conference at Memphis, in 1905, on Immigration; and while Mrs. Horton was State Vice-Regent of Tennessee, 1910-1912, she took an interest in immigration and various other branches of D. A. R. work. She was State Chairman on Immigration.

She for three years served as chairman of the Social Service Committee of her Church Missionary Society, her work ending in 1916.

Soon after the great European war began the Woman's Peace Movement was launched. This must not be confused with the "Pacifist" movement. This appealed to Mrs. Horton. So in September, 1914, she moved that her Missionary Auxiliary in Franklin go on record in favor of universal peace among nations and the abolition of militarism. This they did, and thus they fell into line with the Woman's Peace Movement in America. This movement is the same that later,

July, 1915, was headed by Mr. William H. Taft. They had no hope of bringing about cessation of the present war. But when this war is over to help render impossible another such war. At this early date, stange to say, Henry Cabot Lodge and some other Republicans who afterwards fought so desperately in the United States Senate the ratification of the Peace Treaty of Versailles and the League of Nations Covenant, were in favor or a League of Nations which might prevent war.

On Oct. 1, 1914, Mrs. Horton at a meeting of "Old Glory" chapter D. A. R., moved that we memorialize the State D. A. R. Conference which was to convene at Knoxville, Nov. 9, 1914, to this same end. This motion carried, and she was authorized by the chapter to memorialize the State Conference, which she did as follows:

"Seeing the horror of the European war, and the demoralization which necessarily accompanies it, all of which is unworthy of twentieth century civilization, and believing that the whole world should be free from the thralldom of militarism and be thus enabled to advance to higher civilization, "Old Glory" Chapter Daughters of the American Revolution memorializes the State Conference Daughters of the American Revolution to the end that as a State Conference this organization fall in line with the Woman's Peace Movement in America and go on record as favoring universal peace among nations and the abolition of militarism. (signed) Lucy H. Horton; Pattie G. Rhodes, Regent; Com."

Later, on Jan. 1, 1920, when "Old Glory" chapter D. A. R. met in the home of Mrs. W. W. Campbell, Mrs. Horton made motion that, while public opinion is crystalizing on the subject, "Old Glory" Chapter Daughters of the American Revolution go on record as favoring a speedy ratification of the Peace Treaty and League of Nations Covenant by the United States Senate. This motion carried. Mrs. Horton, when reaching home, wrote a short report of "Old Glory" Chapter for the Daughters of the American Revolution Magazine, and this was published in the March, 1920, number of magazine. It can be found on page 169.

Mrs. Horton served as secretary of Franklin Chapter No. 14 Daughters of the Confederacy under Miss Annie Claybrooke's regency. She and Miss Claybrooke designed the medal to be presented in the schools in Franklin for best papers on Confederate history.

Mrs. Horton wrote for Confederate Archives, during Mrs. Owen Walker's term as State Historian U. D. C., a history of the "Shelby Greys," Company A, Fourth Regiment Tennessee Infantry. This was the company to which her husband belonged. She was indebted to Mr. James Beasley, of Memphis, for much data.

She also filed in Confederate Archives a sketch of Henry Claiborne Horton's life, and her own "Reminiscences of the War between the States." All of these papers passed through the hands of the U. D. C. Chapter No. 14 at Franklin, Tenn., and are included in "Historical Papers United Daughters of the Confederacy, Tennessee Division, 1910-12."

In United States Daughters of 1812, Mrs. Horton is one of the charter members of Thomas Hart Benton Chapter at Franklin, Tenn This order she entered through her grandfather, Captain John Hughes (1776-1860), who served both in civil and military life. He was a member of Virginia legislature in 1798, at time of passage of the famous Madison Resolutions, and later. John Hughes (1776-1860) was an enlisted soldier in War 1812. Mrs. Horton's work as State Historian of U. S. Daughters of 1812 takes the form of "Soldiers of World War Who Are Descendants of Heroes of Former Wars."

Her membership in patriotic orders is in unbroken chain from Colonial days to time of War between the States.

During the Spanish-American war she worked through the Army Comfort Circle which was organized by Mrs. Henry F. Beaumont, July 12, 1898.

World War Work

Lucy H. Horton became a member of the Red Cross Society in Franklin, Tenn., which organized for active work soon after America was declared to be in a state of war with Germany. She was a member of the executive board. When the Williamson county branch of the Council of National Defense was organized by Miss Susie Gentry in Franklin in Aug., 1917, she was elected honorary vice-chairman. She was a member of Army Comfort Circle, also organized by Miss Gentry in 1917. She knit seventy-two articles for soldiers and made forty-three articles for soldiers. She made public talks throughout the county during Red Cross drives and Liberty Loan drives, etc. She collected data of Williamson county war work; and, as State Historian U. S. Daughters of 1812, has written many names of soldiers of World war who are descendants of soldiers of former wars, and has given sketches of them. All of this will be filed in the State Archives and in Archives of U. S. Daughters of 1812 at Washington, D. C.

When "Old Glory" chapter met, May 6, 1920, Mrs. Lucy H. Horton was elected delegate from this chapter to the League of Women Voters which was to be launched at the Capitol in Nashville, Tenn., May 18, 1920.

Mrs Horton joined the M. E. Church, South, at Old Douglas, when twelve years old. While living in Montgomery, Alabama, she was a member of Court street Methodist church, during Mr. Andrew's pastorate. He was a son of Bishop Andrew. She has only one child, Sallie Horton, who married Edward E. Green, a banker of Franklin, Tenn.

Lucy Henderson Horton Is

Sixth in descent from Thomas Henderson, who came to Jamestown, Va., in 1607.

Sixth in descent from Ensign Washer, member of House of Burgesses in 1619.

Fifth in descent from Richard Henderson, who married Polly Washer,
daughter Ensign Washer.
Fourth in descent from Samuel Henderson (1700-1783), of Granville
county, N. C.
Third in descent from Nathaniel Henderson, Revolutionary soldier.
Second in descent from Samuel Henderson, Revolutionary soldier.
Third in descent from Colonel Archelaus Hughes, of the Revolution.
Fourth in descent from Leander Hughes, of Goochland county, Va.
Fifth in descent from Orlandar Hughes, of Goochland county, Va.
Fourth in descent from Samuel Dalton (1699-1802), of Rockingham
county, N. C.
Third in descent from Captain, later Rev. William Martin, a Revolu-
tionary soldier, brother of Gen. Joseph Martin and of Col. Jack
Martin, of "Rock House."
Fourth in descent from Joseph Martin and his wife, Susanna Chiles.
Fifth in descent from John Chiles.
Sixth in descent from Walter Chiles II, member of House of Burgesses.
Seventh in descent from Walter Chiles I, and his wife, Mary Page.
Eighth in descent from Col. John Page, member of the King's Council.

Sallie Horton Green

Sallie Horton, the only child of Henry Claiborne Horton and his
wife, Lucy Henderson, spent the first ten years of her life in southern
Alabama, in and near Montgomery, where her parents were then living.
At ten years of age she entered school in Nashville Tenn., at a small
private school, and the next year she was in school at Mrs. Clark's
suburban school. Later her parents bought a home in Franklin, Tenn.
Here she attended the Tennessee Female College, which was the
Alma Mater of her mother. She was married to Edward E. Green,
cashier and general manager of the National Bank of Franklin. They
have two daughters, Lucy Henderson Green and Marion Hyde Green.
These two girls were educated in a small private school in Franklin
and both attended and graduated at Battle Ground Academy under Dr.
R. G. Peoples. Later Lucy H. Green was for one year in school at
National Park Seminary, Washington, D. C. The following year she
was in school at Ward-Belmont, Nashville, Tenn., where she graduated.
In May of this year she was honored by being crowned May Queen.
She was made President of the Twentieth Century Club, a social club,
and was Assistant Editor of "Mile Stones," the School Annual. Marian
Green is also attending Ward-Belmont.

Henry Claiborne Horton (1835-1914)

Henry Claiborne Horton was born near Bethesda, in Williamson
county, Tenn., Dec. 23, 1835.
In the early years of the nineteenth century two brothers, Claiborne Horton (born 1780), the grandfather of the subject of our sketch,
and Henry Cato Horton (born about 1781), moved from Hanging Rock,
near Camden, S. C., to what was then Davidson county, Tenn., set-

tling near Bethesda. In 1850 Henry C. Horton (born 1781), father of Mrs. Edward H. East, Claiborne and William Horton, Mrs. Miranda Sharpe, Mrs. Sallie Lavender, etc., carried his family to Memphis, Tenn.; to live. In 1858 Henry Hollis Horton (1811-1881), son of Claiborne Horton, following his uncle, moved with his family to make his home in Memphis. He engaged in the mercantile business, and was a member of the Chamber of Commerce at time of opening of war between the States (see Art Supplement to the House Warming Edition of the Evening Scimitar, 1903, page 56, in article headed, "When Memphis Merchants Formed First Exchange").

In Memphis, Henry Claiborne Horton (1835-1914), son of Henry Hollis Horton, enlisted in the Confederate army in 1861, becoming a member of Shelby Greys, Company A., Fourth Regiment, Tennessee Infantry, Strahl's Brigade, Cheatham's Division, Army of Tennessee. The "Shelby Greys" were organized in Feb., 1861. They drilled in Irving Block. The officers were: Captain James Somerville; First Lieut. Luke W. Finley; Second Lieut. W. R. Hutchison; Third Lieut. Thomas H. Francis. They were mustered into the State service at Germantown, Tenn., May 15, 1861. Before this date the "Shelby Greys" were ordered down the river to quell a negro uprising. So this man saw service before Tennessee seceded. I will quote from the Commercial Appeal of May 15, 1909. This was when the Confederate Veterans held a reunion in Memphis. This quotation is from article entitled, "Forty-Eight Years Ago Today": "The Shelby Greys were Memphians. Their members were from the most distinguished families of this city. They gave a good account of themselves during the war. There were many transfers from their company and most of these were in the nature of promotion to other organizations. The organization was in eighteen pitched battles and was under fire almost every day during the advance of Sherman from Chattanooga to Atlanta. When Hood cut loose from Atlanta and came north, the company was part of his army and was in the fights at Franklin and Nashville."

Henry Horton's mess-mates were James E. Beasley, who after two years was promoted to Gen. Strahl's staff; Bevely Thurman was Horton's bed-fellow. He was a musician. He had a splendid voice and started out to the war with a guitar and violin, but soon lost these; W. H. Wheaton and two Torian brothers. Thurman's negro servant cooked for their mess. Two other of these men carried body servants. The battles in which he engaged were: Belmont, Mo.; Shiloh, Tenn.; Perryville, Ky.; Murfreesboro, Tenn.; Chickamauga, Tenn.; Missionary Ridge. Tenn.; Resacca, Ga.; Rocky Face Ridge, Ga.; New Hope Church, Ga.; Elsbury Mountain, Ga.; Atlanta (July 22), Ga.; Atlanta (July 28), Ga.; Jonesboro. Ga.; Franklin, Tenn.; Nashville, Tenn. (see record made by Mr. James E. Beasley, in Memphis Commercial Appeal, May 15, 1909, in article entitled, "Forty-Eight Years Ago Today").

The first man killed in the company at the battle of Shiloh was an orderly sergeant who stood just behind Mr. Horton. A cannon ball ricochetted and struck this man, killing him instantly.

Once, after the Battle of Murfreesboro, when no danger was suspected, Capt. Francis and several of his men, among them Henry Horton, were lying down under a tree when a cannon ball was hurled among them and wounded Capt. Francis in the foot. The wound was so serious his foot was amputated. On a following day Horton and an Irishman were under a tree and a cannon ball burst over their heads and part of it struck the Irishman, scattering his brains on Horton. In telling of this incident Mr. Horton laconically remarked, "I got away from that tree."

Perhaps the closest call he had was at the battle of Missionary Ridge. I will give an account of his experience here as dictated by himself and over his signature: About three hundred men, he among the number, were detailed to go into the valley and support a picket line. The pickets fell back to the main line on the ridge. While awaiting orders these men got into a deep rifle pit near the base of the ridge. From this pit they watched the Federal regiment, three lines deep, advance toward them. The fire from these men in the trench was most deadly. It looked as if half the regiment of Federals went down. This fire was kept up for about twenty minutes. Hardly a man in the trench was killed. But before the flanking enemy they had to retreat. Some of the men surrendered. This little band under hot fire had a steep ridge to climb. While doing this about half of the three hundred lost their lives. It sets one thinking of Tennyson's "Charge of the Light Brigade," so hazardous was the run. On the run up the ridge Henry Horton was struck by a bullet in rebound from a little tree.

Mr. Horton stood picket near Spring Hill the night before the Battle of Franklin. The next morning he captured a Federal and took his horse. He rode the horse beside his Colonel who was killed on Franklin's field that day. He asked of his Colonel permission to visit his grandmother, who lived near Franklin. This was granted. But later in the day seeing that a battle was imminent, he hitched this horse behind a rock fence just beyond where Mr. James Rodes now lives (1914), and entered with his regiment in battle. Here he fought at the locust thicket, where the battle was most fierce, and was among the Confederates who climbed the breastworks of the enemy. Next morning he found his horse where he had left him. He made a short visit to his grandmother. She had ready for him a splendid suit of Federal clothes from which she had cut the U. S. buttons and had put on others, and which she had dyed beautifully.

At Nashville he was sent out with others on the skirmish line, and during the fight, unknown to these men, the main body fell back. When this skirmish line was ready to retreat they found themselves alone, inclose proximity to the enemy. Some immediately surrendered, but Henry Horton endeavored to escape, and was shot in the back, his knapsack saving his life. Thus he was captured by the enemy.

In the lining of his clothes he had slipped gold coins which served him many a good turn while a prisoner at Camp Douglas, near Chicago. The night of his capture he and many other prisoners were made to stand in the rain in a muddy horse lot all night.

In April, 1865, he started on exchange. They learned after leaving Camp Douglas of Lee's surrender. These men were stopped at Point Lookout, Maryland, and held there until the middle of July.

His father, an intense Southern sympathizer, with many other Tennesseans, had refugeed in South Alabama, near Wetumpka. Here Henry Horton went. And since it was mid-Summer and too late to put in a crop, he rafted lumber on the Alabama river to Montgomery. With the first money he made he paid a debt contracted while in prison. In Alabama he married his first wife, Sallie Jackson, daughter of Absolem Jackson, of Elmore county, Ala., of a noted Southern family. She had five brothers in the Confederate army. He married his second wife, Lucy Henderson, daughter of Dr. Samuel Henderson (1804-1884), of Franklin, Tenn., in 1878.

Mr. Horton said that during the war he never really suffered for something to eat. Sometimes his " rations" were meager but he would eke out his little store. He said, too, that he never saw the time when he could not have one clean shirt.

Lieutenant Beverly Thurman was killed at Battle of Jonesboro.

Entered by Lucy Henderson Horton, his wife; Sallie Horton Green, daughter; March 14, 1914.

The above sketch of Henry Claiborne Horton is included in War Records of Tennesseans to be filed in Tennessee History Building by Tennessee Woman's Historical Association.

In addition to the war record of Henry Claiborne Horton, I would like for posterity to have a more intimate knowledge of the man's personal character. He was a man of medium height, and of athletic build. When seventy-five years old, he stepped along with the elasticity of a boy. He always looked much younger than he really was. Perhaps this was owing to the fact that he lived much in the open air. While in Alabama his plantation, which was on the Alabama river and Jackson's lake, several miles from his home, necessitated a ride almost every day. Then he owned cattle which ranged over a large territory, and he would ride many miles, sometimes on horseback, sometimes in his buggy, keeping an eye on his cattle. The four years of the War between the States when the sky was the only roof above his head, caused him to fall in love with outdoor life.

In his business dealings he was as honest as the day is long. I recall an instance where he once sold a grey horse. The prospective purchaser was much pleased with the animal and offered him a certain price. But Mr. Horton pointed out its defects and the sale ended in the purchaser paying less for the horse than he himself had at first proposed. Both men, however, seemed satisfied. He always paid cash for everything, and when he died he did not owe a debt to any man. He was a man of very positive and decided character. One always knew exactly where he stood. At the time of the Democratic revolt in Tennessee, in 1910, he was one of the old Confederate veteran who marched through the streets of Nashville to the convention hall when the Democratic party was reorganized. He was given a seat on the platform and was heartily in accord with the movement. This was a spontaneous call all over the State for purer government.

Negroes, without exception, loved to work for him, although he had the ante-bellum Southern way of ordering them around. They knew he was their friend. Besides, negroes like a decided and positive character, especially when it is tempered with justice.

Henry Claiborne Horton, we think, is a lineal descendant of Barnabas Horton, the Pilgrim father, who was born in 1600 in Mousley, Leicestershire, England, and who was son of Joseph Horton. Barnabas came to Massachusetts in 1635, in a vessel called the "Swallow." In 1640 he went with twelve other Puritans to Long Island, and they founded Southold. Eleanor Lexington tells us that "any Horton of today who can hark back to Barnabas is eligible to Colonial Societies. for Barnabas was a magistrate and member of the court." We will give his line of descent from Barnabas Horton as closely as we are able

Authorities: Horton Genealogy, published in 1876 together with supplements; "Spirit of '76" for April 1902, page 267; Frances Cowles, genealogist, in Nashville Banner for Feb. 27, 1915. page 10; Eleanor Lexington, genealogist.

From "Spirit of '76" for April, 1902, in article "Genealogical Guide to the Early Settlers of America," page 267, we find—"Horton: Barrabas Horton, Hampton 1640, went to Southold, L. I. 1662; favored Conn., and was next year made officer."

In this most reliable magazine, "Spirit of '76," one can see references in regard to Barnabas Horton and several contemporaries of name Horton as follows:

References: Baird's History of Rev. N. Y., 415-5; Bangor M. Hist. Mag. V, 197; Elv Gen., 25; Horton Fam. Gathering (1876), 13 p p.: Horton Gen. (1876), 259 p p., supplement (1870), 80 p p.; Williams Hist. Danbury, Vt. 167.

In Dictionary of United States History by Jameson on page 377 the statement is made that "the English settled the eastern portion of Long Island, N. Y., in 1640:"

1. Barnabas Horton; born in Mousley, Leicestershire, England, died at Southold, Long Island, New York, in 1680 (see page 9 of Horton Genealogy). The tombstone which marks his grave at his old home also proves this.

2. Joshua; son of Barnabas Horton, was born at Southold, L. I, in 1643; married, 1667, Mary Furthell. She died in 1729 (see page 11 Horton Genealogy).

3. Joshua Horton; Ensign, was son of Joshua Horton and his wife, Mary Furthell. He was born at Southold, L. I., in 1669. He married first, Elizabeth Grover, second, a widow, Mary Gillam. He died in 1744 (see page 170, Horton Genealogy).

4. Ephriam Horton, son of Ensign Joshua Horton; married Martha Vail.

5. Joseph Horton, son of Ephriam Horton and his wife, Martha Vail; was born at Southold, 1708.

6. Joshua Horton, son of Joseph Horton; was born 1730 (see page 170, Horton Genealogy).

(We think that this is Joshua Horton, the explorer, who came to what is now Tennessee in 1766 with Col. James Smith, of Pennsylvania, and Uriah Stone, for whom Stones river was named, and Wm. Baker and a negro servant. They named Cumberland mountains and Cumberland river in honor of the Duke of Cumberland.

Joshua Horton was the first patentee of land in what is now Tennessee (see page 125, History of Tennessee, Goodspeed Publishing Company).

The Hortons of whom we write claim descent from Joshua Horton, the explorer. So, if this man is the explorer, it makes connection to emigrant ancestor straight.

Smith gave such glowing account of this country that Isaac Linsey and four others from South Carolina visited the place (see J. G. Cisco in Nashville American, May 1, 1904). The Hortons of whom we write came to Tennessee from Hanging Rock, South Carolina.)

7. William Horton, son of Joshua Horton; was born in 1758. He has descendants of name Ephriam.

8. Claiborne Horton, son of William Horton, was born 1779; married Margaret Ingram, of South Carolina.

9. Henry Hollis Horton, son of Claiborne Horton; was born 18—; married his cousin, Rebecca Horton, daughter of Amos Horton.

10. Henry Claiborne, son of Henry Hollis Horton and his wife, Rebecca Horton; was born Dec. 23, 1835; married, first, Sallie Jackson, of Alabama; second, Lucy Henderson, of Franklin, Tenn. He died Aug. 19, 1914. His only child is Sallie Horton Green, wife of Edward E. Green

William Horton, son of Joshua Horton, was born in 1758. He married and two of his sons came from Hanging Rock, S. C., near Camden, to what is now Williamson county, Tenn., in the closing years of the eighteenth or early years of the nineteenth century and settled near Bethesda. This part of Tennessee was known at that time as Davidson county. These sons were Henry Cato Horton, grandfather of Mrs. Nathaniel Baxter, of Nashville, Tenn., and father of Mrs. Edward H. East. of Nashville, Tenn. The other son of William Horton who came to Williamson county, Tenn., was Claiborne Horton, grandfather of Henry Claiborne Horton (1835-1914).

Sally Horton, daughter of Rev. Henry Cato Horton (born 1781), was born at Bethesda, Williamson county, Tenn., in 1827. She married Fletcher Lavender. and they moved to Memphis. Tenn., where their only child. Laura Lavender. was born in July, 1849. She married Hon. Nathaniel Baxter. of Nashville. Tenn.

Children of Hon. Nathaniel Baxter and his wife, Laura Lavender:

Amanda Baxter; married Robert Jackson, of Nashville, Tenn.

Lollie Baxter; married Robert Mattox, Atlanta, Ga.

Both of these sisters had sons who distinguished themselves in the World war. Baxter Jackson, son of Robert Jackson and his wife, Amanda Baxter, was Captain in command of a company in 114th Field Artillery until the signing of the armistice. He was then detached from his command and sent to Bourges, Belgium, where he was assigned to duty in the Central Records Office of the American Expeditionary Forces, being in charge of the casualty department of that office. In 1919 he was promoted to rank of Major in the Field Artillery service. After returning to Nashville Major Jackson became assistant cashier of the Cumberland Valley National Bank. In 1920 he left Nashville for New York City to become Assistant Cashier of the Chemical National Bank of that city.

Robert Maddox, of Atlanta, Ga., son of Robert Maddox and his wife, Lollie Baxter, served in France. He continued with the American Expeditionary Forces after the armistice was signed. Later he entered the banking business in Atlanta, Ga. When bankers formed the Cotton Export Corporation in Oct., 1920, we find him taking an influential part.

This family has inherited the old English love of nature. This finds expression in their splendid country homes, that of Mr. Nathaniel Baxter near Nashville, and 'Woodhaven," the country home of Robert F. Maddox, near Atlanta, Ga.

The home of Mrs. Edward H. East, in Nashville, has been the scene of many brilliant entertainments. She was one of the first members of the W. C. T. U. in Nashville, and was a personal friend of Frances E. Willard. She promoted the establishment of the Y. W. C. A. building in Nashville.

Judge Edward H. East, husband of Ida Tennie Horton, was a lawyer of exceptional ability. He had signal success both in chancery and as a criminal attorney. Andrew Johnson, while President of United States, who knew well this man's ability, offered him a position in his cabinet; but Judge East declined the offer. This was in the hard reconstruction days and Judge East said his family needed the money he could make at the practice of law. This was more than his salary would be as a cabinet official.

Horton Coat of Arms

A lion rampant, argent, charged on the breast with a boar's head, couped, azure; a bordure engraved of the second.

Crest: A red rose seeded and barbed proper.

Motto: "Pro Rege et Lige" (For King and Law).

———

Gov. James D. Porter is a descendant of Barnabas Horton.

Edward Edmund Green

Edward Edmund Green, son of Joe John Green and his wife, Elizabeth Hyde (daughter of Edmund and Jane Hyde), was born Feb.

14, 1864. He was educated in the Campbell School in Franklin, Tenn.

In 1881 he entered the National Bank of Franklin, "The Old Bank." And after the retirement of Mr. J. L. Parkes he became cashier and general manager of this bank. He was Captain of "Perkins' Rifles," a Franklin military company; member of Methodist Episcopal Church, South, and was for twenty-five years Steward in same; for twenty-five years member of the Municipal Board in Franklin, Tenn.; a Mason; a Democrat.

By his first marriage, to Emma Lillie, he had one child, Bates Lillie Green. By his second marriage, to Sallie Horton, in Dec., 1900, he had two children, Lucy Henderson Green and Marian Hyde Green.

During the World war he was County Chairman of Williamson County Liberty Loan Committee for 1st, 2nd, 3rd, 4th Liberty Loan Bonds, and for the 5th, or Victory Loan Bonds; and Williamson county paid more than her quota in each loan. Upper rooms of the National Bank building were handed over to workers for the Red Cross from the time America entered the war until May, 1919. This was done at his suggestion, free of cost. He contributed in many ways to war relief. He also has done much for the destitute poor in his county. He is public spirited and has done much to build up his town.

Edward E. Green inherited from his father a Masonic certificate which had been given to his grandfather, Sherwood Green, at Warrenton (Bute or Warren county, N. C.) in the year of Masonry 5801. This certificate was framed and hung for years in home of E. E. Green. Warren county was cut off from Bute county, N. C. It is a border county to Virginia. And we see in Vol. 6, Virginia Magazine of History and Biography, page 525 and 26, that Col. John Green, Lieut. Robert Green and Gabriel Green were members of the Virginia Society of Cincinnati.

E. E. Green inherits from his father a Masonic apron which was originally given by Gov. James Turner to his ancestor, Sherwood Green. Sherwood Green and Thomas E. Sumner, son of Gen. Jethro Sumner, came to Williamson county, Tenn., from Warren county, N. C. Their wills are both recorded at the court house in Franklin, Tenn.

We will give Edward E. Green's line of descent:

Authorities: Wheeler's History of North Carolina; North Carolina Register, 1900-1901; Virginia Magazine of History and Biography, Vol. 6, etc.; Old family Bible record; Masonic certificate which was given to Sherwood Green at Warrenton, N. C., in year of Masonry 5801; "Who's Who in Tennessee;" "Culpepper County Virginia" by Raleigh T. Green, published in 1900.

Edward Edmunds Green, born Feb. 14, 1864 is son of

Joe John Green, born 1824, and his wife, Marion Elizabeth Hyde. He served during the War between the States (1861-65) in Clayburn's Brigade. His second wife was Nettie Clark, daughter of Dr. William Clark, of Tennessee. Dr. Clark was at one time owner and editor of Nashville Banner, and was State Health Officer. He was son of

Sherwood Green, born in Warren county, North Carolina, in 1791. He moved to Williamson county, Tenn. He was son of

Thomas Robert Green. He was son of

James Green and his wife, Elizabeth Jones. James Green was born in Culpepper county, Va., and here died. His son, Thomas Robert, moved to Warren county, N. C. James Green was son of

Robert Green, born 1695, and his wife, Eleanor Dunn, of Scotland. He came with his father to King George county, Va. He took up large tracts of land in 1735 in what was, in 1712, Essex, in 1721 Spottsylvania county, but in 1749 was Culpepper county. He was son of

William Green, the emigrant, an Englishman, who was an officer in the bodyguard of William Prince of Orange (see "Culpepper County Virginia," page 61, etc., by Green, published in 1900).

We are told, in the old Green manuscript, that Sherwood Green, who moved from Warren county, N. C., to Williamson county, Tenn., had a large family of children, and at his death left each child six hundred and forty acres of land. The books at the court house in Franklin, Tenn., show that he possessed much valuable land. This branch of family was related to men of Turner name of Warren county, N. C. Governor Turner was of this connection.

Hartwell Hyde, of this family connection, an officer in the Revolutionary war, came from Halifax county, N. C., to Williamson county, Tenn., in 1803. His daughter, Haley Jane Hyde, married Gabriel Fowlkes, near Triune, Tenn., March 27, 1806. Hartwell Hyde's father and mother died in Hale, Northhampton county. Hartwell Hyde enlisted in the American army either in Halifax or Northampton county. Mrs. R. Fowlkes Michail, of Parma, Missouri, says (1920) "We have an old military commission dated July 4, 1794, at Newburn, N. C., and signed by the Governor and Secretary of State of North Carolina, whereby Hartwell Hyde is made Captain of Militia of Halifax County." Her father was a cousin of Mr. H. P. Fowlkes, of Franklin, Tenn., and of E. E. Green, of Franklin, Tenn. H. P. Fowlkes was a member of Sons of the American Revolution through his ancestor, Hartwell Hyde.

Joe J. Green, father of E. E. Green, was a cousin of Isham Green Harris. Isham Green Harris was Governor of Tennessee three times. In 1848 he was made a Congressman. He served for years as United States Senator, retiring in 1901.

Judge Richard Henderson (1735-1785)

Richard Henderson, son of Samuel Henderson (1700-1783) and his wife, Elizabeth Williams, was born in Hanover county, Va., April 20, 1735. In Wheeler's History of North Carolina, page 102, we are told that "his ancestors by his father's side were from Scotland, and his mother's side (Williams) from Wales..... His early education was as good as the state of the country afforded. He studied law with his cousin, the late Judge Williams, for twelve months When he applied for license to the Chief Justice of the colony, whose duty it was to examine applicants, and on his certificate a license to practice was issued by the Governor, he was asked how long he had read, and what books? When the limited time was stated, and the number of books he had read, the Judge remarked that it was useless to go into any examination, as no living man could have read and digested the works he had named in so short a time. With great promptness and firmness, young Henderson replied that it was his privilege to apply for a license, and the Judge's duty to examine him; and, if he was not qualified, to reject him; if qualified, to grant the certificate. The Judge, struck with his sensible and spirited reply, proceeded to a most searching examination. So well did the young man sustain himself that the certificate was granted, withencomiums upon his industry, acpuirements and talents. He soon rose to the highest ranks of his profession: and honor and wealth followed."

Richard Henderson was appointed by the Crown one of the Supreme Judges of North Carolina, Martin Howard being Chief Justice, and Richard Henderson and Maurice Moore, Associate Justices, They held their office until 1773 when, because of troubled times in political matters, the courts were closed.

This man, with mind ever on the alert, the following year, 1774, organized the Transylvania Company, consisting of Richard Henderson and John Williams of Granville county, N. C.; William Johnston and James Hogg; Thomas Hart, John Luttrell and Nathaniel Hart of Orange; while Leonidas Henly Bullock, of Granville, and David Hart, of Orange, held half-shares, making eight shares in all. The company signed a treaty with the Cherokees, March 17, 1775, at Sycamore Shoals on Wautauga river. Gen. Joseph Martin was attorney for the company and entry taker for the Powell's vallev division of the purchase. Transylvania consisted of Kentucky and Tennessee as far south as the Cumberland river, and a corner of southwestern Virginia.

On the occasion of the purchase Oconostota, a Cherokee orator, called Chief Warrior and head prince of the Cherokee nation, made an eloquent and pathetic appeal to his people to hold their lands. But, in spite of this the treaty was signed. Oconostota's elegant Indian treaty pitcher, called "the pitcher of the Chiefs," used at this time, can be seen now in the rooms of the Tennessee Historical Society at Watkins building, Nashville, Tenn. It is of beautiful blue ware. This pitcher was presented to the Historical Society by Mrs. James K. Polk. The writer is very proud that, as early as 1906, she wrote to Miss Dasha at Washington, a prominent D. A. R., seeking her aid in having Sycamore Shoals on Wautauga river marked as the spot on which the Transylvania treaty was made by Judge Richard Henderson and others with the Cherokees. Also as the site on which the over-mountain men rendezvoused before doing battle at King's Mountain. Proof that Mrs. Horton had located this historic site and six other important sites can be seen in American Monthly Magazine for Nov., 1903, pages 347-352. One of the proud achievements of Bonnie Kate, Sycamore Shoals and John Sevier Chapters D. A. R., was to erect a monument at Sycamore Shoals on Wautauga river bearing inscription to mark these events. On occasion of the unveiling of this monument, in June, 1910, our U. S. Senator Robert L. Taylor, who was born almost on this identical spot, was orator of the day.

The government of Transylvania was patterned after that of the Carolinas—it was a proprietary government, and Richard Henderson was the first of the Proprietors. In Carolina this would have constituted him Palatine, just as the Duke of Albemarle was Palatine in 1669, or John, Lord Berkley, later, etc. However, Transylvania was short-lived, and things were not consummated. Edward Hyde, Earl of Clarendon, who had been Lord Chancellor of England, was one of the proprietors of Carolina. In proprietary governments the proprietor performed those acts of government which in royal governments were performed by the crown.

The diary kept by Richard Henderson while on his way to, and while in Transylvania, together with the address made by him at the opening of the first legislative assembly in what is now Kentucky, is found in its original form in the Draper Manuscripts in the State Library at Madison, Wisconsin. Here is founud, too, Richard Henderson's plan of old Boonsboro Fort. Much of this can also be found in North Carolina Booklet for January, 1904. In his diary he speaks of stopping several days at Martin's Station in Powell's Valley with Gen. Joseph Martin, because they could not go further with their wagons until Boone and a company of men had cleared a wagon road.

He speaks several times of his brothers, Nathaniel and Samuel, being with him at Boonsboro, of their helping to build the fort, etc "Little or no iron was used in the construction of Boonsboro Fort. At each corner was a two-story loop-hole blockhouse to act as a bastion. The stout log cabins, thirty in number, were arranged in straight lines so that their outer sides formed part of the wall, the spaces between being filled with a high stockade." The fort was in the form of a parallelogram, about two hundred and fifty or sixty feet long, and half as wide. The houses had high, sloping roofs, made of huge clapboards and they were held in place by long poles fastened with withes. The open space within the stockade served as a playground, muster field, etc. Here was kept a small school, where the wife of Kentucky's first Governor, Mrs. Isaac Shelby, was educated. She was a woman of fine mind and was well educated as is proved by a deposition in her own handwriting in the Madison Circuit Clerk's office at Richmond, Ky., in the case of Clay vs. Little. This could not be excelled for its beautiful penmanship, pure English and exquisite refinement. The daughter of the first Chief Justice and the wife of one of Kentucky's earliest Attorney-Generals were trained and reared in the fort.

Around the walls of the old fortress were fought the battles that gave to Kentucky the name of "Dark and Bloody Ground." The fort had just been completed, in 1775, when the savage emissaries of Great Britain killed three of its inhabitants. This was followed, in 1776 and 1777, by repeated assaults from the Indian allies of King George III and his commandant at Detroit on the Lakes. Proclamations from the Chief of the British forces in Canada offering protection to all who would abandon the principles of our Revolutionary forefathers were freely scattered around the fort. The officers were promised the same rank in the regular army of Great Britain which they had in Virginia or Carolina, but all was without avail to induce the men of Boonsboro to quit their allegiance to these States, or the cause of the young republic. During the years from 1777 to 1782 they were furnished with arms and munitions by Virginia and participated in many skirmishes with the Indians led by trained Canadian officers. They constituted a small but an important part of the soldiery of Virginia in the remote West. Tours of military duty ranging from three to nine months at a time were performed by many of them, for which some of them obtained pensions at a later period as Revolutionary soldiers of the United States. They served under George Rogers Clark, James Barnett, John Montgomery, Richard May, Nathaniel Hart and others. Other compatriots left the old pioneer fort on the Kentucky river for short periods of service and fought with Gen. Gates at Saratoga, or suffered with Washington at the battles of Still-water, Germantown, Brandywine and Yorktown, or followed Isaac Shelby to victory at King's Mountain, North Carolina."

Boonsboro chapter, D. A. R., of Kentucky, is composed almost entirely of descendants of the early settlers at Boonsboro.

Two weeks after the rescue of Betsy Calloway from the Indians she was married to Samuel Henderson, brother of Judge Richard Henderson, and their daughter, Fanny, born one year later, was the first white child born on Kentucky soil. Fanny Henderson married Gillespie.

Fort Boonsboro was begun one day after the battle of Lexington was fought. They however, did not receive news of the battle until June following. Later on in this same year Lexington, Ky., some miles north of this place, was founded and named in honor of the battle. We are glad to see that the name of Transylvania still lives in the name of the old University at Lexington.

In 1792, when Kentucky was admitted to the Union, Boonsboro was one of the largest towns in the State, but in 1810 it had almost ceased to exist, and now for long years has been a cornfield. "Ilium fuit." But the "divine elm," as Richard Henderson called it, under which the convention was held in 1775, still stands in lonely grandeur, well guarded. This tree is twenty-two feet in circumference.

When the ter-centennial of Jamestown was celebrated in 1907 the Kentucky building was replica of old Fort Boonsboro. As we strolled down the broad board walk on the water front at the Norfolk exposition and found that this fort was built in a dense grove of trees, just as the real fort of long ago stood, the delusion seemed perfect. So much so, that we involuntarily looked about for the majestic elm, under which the first legislative assembly of what is now Kentucky met and made laws and elected a member to the Continental Congress. (Authorities for what is written regarding Boonsboro: Walter Clark, Chief Justice N. C.; Mrs. Sallie Gibson Chenault; American Monthly Magazine for March, 1906; Stories of Great Americans for Little Americans, by Edward Eggleston; Diary of Judge Richard Henderson.)

We always like to know something of the social atmosphere in which people live. We are told in North Carolina Booklet for January, 1915, page 122, that "In the middle years of the eighteenth century, attracted by the lure of rich and cheap lands, many families of Virginia gentry, principally from Hanover county, settled in the region ranging from Williamsboro on the east to Hillsboro on the west. Hither came the Hendersons, the Bullocks, the Williamses, the Harts, the Lewises; the Taylors, the Bentons, the Penns, the Burtons, the Hares and the Sneeds. There soon arose in this section of the colony a society marked by intellectual distinction, social graces, and the leisured dignity of the landlord and the large planter..... the quaint old diarist, Hugh McAdew, says of the people of this social group that 'they were a people with abundance of wealth and leisure for enjoyment.' From this society came such eminent democratic figures as the father-in-law and preceptor of Henry Clay, Thomas Hart: his grandson, the 'Old Bullion' and 'Great Pacificator' of a later era, Thomas Hart Benton; Richard Henderson, known to his contemporaries as the 'Patrick Henry of North Carolina;' John Penn, signer of the Declaration of Independence, etc."

An English contemporary and acquaintance, in speaking of Richard Henderson's practice and advocacy as a lawyer in the North Carolina Superior Court, pays him this elevated tribute: "Even there, where oratory and eloquence are as brilliant and powerful as in Westminster Hall, he soon became distinguished and eminent, and his superior genius shone forth with great splendor and universal applause." Richard Henderson married the daughter of an Irish nobleman, Lord George Kelynge, or Keeling. His law partner married the widow of Lord Keeling (see page 8, N. C. Booklet for July, 1917).

James Hogg, who was elected delegate to the Continental Congress when this Transylvania assembly met under "the divine elm tree." organized and enacted laws, was, the historian Battle tells us, "one of

the most influential men of his day." He was a Scotchman of the same
family as Ettrick Shepherd, and whose wife, McDowal Aives, was second cousin to Sir Walter Scott (see page 350, The Occupation of Kentucky, by Archibald Henderson).

To prove something more of the social atmosphere in which Richard Henderson lived, he was intimately associated with Judge Maurice
Moore. The Supreme Bench of North Carolina in these colonial days
was composed of Martin Howard, Richard Henderson and Maurice
Moore. Maurice Moore was descended from an ancient Irish family
of which the Marquis Drogheda was the head in 1834. His grandfather, Sir Nathaniel Moore, was Governor of the two Carolinas in
1705. Maurice Moore also descended from the second child of James
Moore and his wife, ——— Yeamans, daughter of Sir John Yeamans,
who established the city of Charleston and was Governor of the two
Carolinas in 1670. Moore was Governor of the Carolinas in 1700 and
1719 (see page 47, Wheeler's History of N. C., Brunswick Co.).

Transylvania was short-lived. Gov. Martin, of N. C., declared the
purchase illegal because made by individuals instead of the crown. The
State of Virginia declared the same. But North Carolina granted the
company 200,000 acres of this, and the State of Virginia granted the
company 200,000 acres of land and the State of Tennessee made a
similar grant in Powell's Valley. In 1779 Judge Henderson opened a
land office at the French Lick, now Nashville, Tenn., for the sale of
the company's lands. "The following summer he returned home,
where in the bosom of his friends and family he enjoyed the evening
of life in peace and plenty." He died in Granville county, N. C., Jan.
30, 1785.

Cumberland Compact

On page 175 of Andrew Jackson and Early Tennessee History, by
S. G. Heiskell, we find: "We are disposed to believe eventually Richard Henderson may be shown to deserve to stand in the same class with
Cecil Rhodes and others..... as developers and builders of new countries."

Dr. Archibald Henderson, a lineal descent of Judge Richard Henderson, in a speech made before a joint meeting of the Mississippi Valley Historical Association and the Tennessee Historical Society in Nashville,
Tenn.. April 27, 1916, took as his subject, "Richard Henderson: the Authorship of the Cumbeland Compact and the founding of
Nashville." In this address Dr. Henderson contented that his ancestor,
Richard Henderson, has the right to stand as a founder of Nashville by
the side of James Robertson and John Donaldson. He was one of the
founders of Boonsboro and of Nashville.

Any one can readily see that the Transylvania purchase, made by
Col. Richard and his associates, and their efforts of settlement at Boonsboro, Ky., opened up the way for, and made the Cumberland settlement
easier.

The Transylvania purchase from the Cherokee Indians was made at Sycamore Shoals on Watauga river, March 17, 1775. "The Cumberland Compact" was signed at Nashboroug, May 13, 1780. It was in the winter of '79 and '80 that Robertson and Donaldson came to Cumberland. We have already seen that Richard Henderson had a land office in this new settlement on the Cumberland river.

John Donaldson, in his famous journal, makes references to Richard Henderson. On March 31 he says, "Set out this day, and after running some distance met with Col. Richard Henderson, who was running the line between Virginia and North Carolina. At this meeting we were much rejoiced. He gave us every information we wished, and further informed us that he had purchased a quantity or corn in Kentucky to be shipped to the falls of the Ohio for the use of the Cumberland Settlement We are now without bread and are compelled to hunt the buffalo to preserve life." There is glory enough in the founding of Nashville for Robertson, Donaldson and Henderson, all.

The Historian Putnam, in 1846, discovered the original document: "The Cumberland Compact." This is now preserved in the Archives of the Tennessee Historical Society. Putnam says, "As Richard Henderson and the other members of the Transylvania Land Company were here at this juncture, April 1780, he, Henderson, was foremost in urging some form of government."

Dr. Archibald Henderson says, "the Cumberland Compact is a mutal contract between the co-partners of the Transylvania Company and the settlers upon the land claimed by the company. The significant feature of the document is that it is an elaborate legal paper which could have been drafted only by one intimately versed in the intricacies of the law and its terminology. The indisputable fact that Richard Henderson, eminent as lawyer and jurist, was the only lawyer on the Cumberland in May 1780, and that his name heads the list of 230-odd signatures to the document known as the Cumberland Compact, has led one of the Justices of our Supreme Court, a deep student of the early history of Tennessee, the Hon. Samuel C. Williams, to state in print that 'without serious doubt Judge Henderson was the draftsman of the compact of government."

Mr. John H. DeWitt, President of Tennessee Historical Society, and W. A. Provine made affidavit on April 28, 1916, that the handwriting of this original "Cumberland Compact" is identical with that of Judge Richard Henderson's hand-writing on Salisbury court house records and in the original diary of Richard Henderson written in 1775. This demonstrates the fact that Judge Richard Henderson was the author of the Cumberland Compact. One of the signatures to the Cumberland Compact is that of Nathaniel Henderson, brother of Judge Richard Henderson. P. Henderson's name is also signed.

Children of Richard Henderson and his wife, Elizabeth Keeling:

Fanny H.; born 1764; married Judge McCay, of Salisbury

Richard; born July, 1766.

Archibald; born Aug., 1768.

Elizabeth H.; born 1770; married Alexander.

Leonard: born 1772.

John Lauson; born 1778.

All four sons studied the profession of their father. Leonard Henderson became Chief Justice of North Carolina. Archibald attained distinction, became member of Congress, etc.

Leonard Henderson

Leonard Henderson, Chief Justice of the Supreme Court of the State of North Carolina, was, as we have said, a son of Judge Richard Henderson, who served under the crown as associate Judge of the Supreme Court of North Carolina. Henderson, Ky., Henderson, N. C., and the county of Henderson are named in his honor.

Fanny Henderson, daughter of Judge Leonard Henderson, married Dr. William V. Taylor, who was born on James river in Va. One of their children, Lucy White Taylor, born in N. C., married Joel Addison Hayes, of Nashville, Tenn., son of Oliver Bliss Hayes. Their son, Joel Addison Hayes, married Margaret Howell Davis, a daughter of Jefferson Davis, President of the Confederacy. Their son, Jefferson Davis Hayes, was born in 1884. Their daughters are Varina Howell Hayes and Lucy White Hayes.

When President Davis died in New Orleans in 1889 he left no son to perpetuate his name. While the dead chief of the Confederacy lay in state, this boy asked to be given his grandfather's name. The bishop of the State, deeply touched by the circumstance, amid an awed silence laid his hand on the child's head and another on the cold forehead of the President and said, "I christen thee Jefferson Davis." The change of name was later made entirely legal by legislative enactment of three States, Louisiana, Mississippi and Virginia.

Young Jefferson Davis graduated from Princeton in 1907, and from Columbia as a mining engineer in 1911. He followed this profession in the West for several years, and then settled at Colorado Springs as Assistant Cashier of the First National Bank of which his father was President, and an eminently successful man.

His first military experience was with the National Guard on the Mexican border as a gunman in a battery of field artillery, and before his company was mustered out he was promoted to the rank of first lieutenant. On the following August the battery entered the Federal service, and after a period of training was ordered overseas. The vessel on which it crossed the Atlantic was the Tuscania, when that ill-fated ship met disaster, but it reached an Irish port in safety, and Lieutenant Davis and his comrades crossed over to France in due course. A recent letter from the front describes his work as observation officer for his battery. As such it was his duty to go aloft in an anchored balloon, watch the fire of his guns and signal orders to the gunners.

His friends say that Lieutenant Davis has inherited the indomitable spirit and staying power of his famous grandfather, and predict that he will win distinction as a soldier" (see Outlook).

The spontaneity of the South's homage to memory of her late President, Jefferson Davis, was seen by the writer in 1907 at time of Confederate reunion in Richmond, Va. Immense throngs were crowding the building of Confederate Museum, when in the North Carolina room it became known that these two men, J. Addison Hayes and his son, Jefferson Davis, were present. Streams of people grasped the hands of these two men. The remark was heard, "This boy has a double attraction—he springs from the Hendersons of North Carolina, and from our great President."

Jefferson Davis married Dore DeWitt, daughter of Dr. and Mrs. Theodore DeWitt, of Broadmoor, a suburb of Colorado Springs, Dec. 23, 1910. Their son, Jefferson Davis, Jr., was born Oct. 21; 1911.

Varina Howell Hayes, daughter of Joel Addison Hayes and his wife, Margaret Howell Davis, married Dr. Gerald B. Webb, of Colorado Springs. They have three children, two girls and one boy. Dr. Webb is a descendant of an English ducal family, we are told in Confederate Veteran for August, 1909. Margaret Varina, Gerald, Bertram and Robina are their children. "Dr. Webb is a specialist and has more than national reputation."

Jefferson Davis, President Confederate States of America, is so well known, history is full of his achievements, but we cannot refrain from mentioning something of his home life. It is said that with his family and friends around him "he was seen at his best, and that best was the highest point of grace and refinement that the Southern character has reached."

Jefferson Davis took his university course in Lexington, Kentucky, at old Transylvania University, where so many Southern boys were educated.

It s gratifying to note the fact that June 3, 1916, the 108th birthday anniversary of this man, was celebrated in U. S. Congress. Sectional feeling at that time had in large measure died out. Our entrance into the World war soon after unified the Nation.

We will quote from the Confederate Veteran of August, 1909, written after the death of Margaret Hayes, wife of J. Addison Hayes, who had died July 18, 1909: "Margaret Davis was educated at a convent in Paris, where Margaret of Italy and Princess Margaret of Bavaria were her closest friends. To distinguish her in this trio of "namesakes" she was called Pearl, the meaning of her name, and that jewel entered largely into her life pleasures. The friendship of the three Margarets never was lost nor laid aside.

Joel Addison Hayes survived his wife ten years. President Jefferson Davis and his family lie buried in beautiful Hollywood Cemetery at Richmond, Virginia, and beside them lies Joel Addison Hayes.

Archibald Henderson (1768-1822)

Authorities: North Carolina Booklet for July, 1917, and for Oct., 1917; Moore's History of North Carolina; Wheeler's History of North Carolina, etc.

Archibald Henderson, son of the Colonial Judge Richard Henderson and his wife, Elizabeth Keeling, was born in Granville county, N. C., Aug. 7, 1768. From his father "he inherited the legal acumen and forensic brilliance which elevated Richard Henderson at the age of thirty-three to the highest court in the colony, and won for him the title of the 'Patrick Henry of North Carolina.' From his mother, the daughter of an Irish nobleman, Lord George Kelynge, Archibald derived that refreshing simplicity of manner and ·dignity of demeanor which were signal traits of his personality."

He was educated at Springer College in Warren county. There were thirty pupils. Among them was Archibald Henderson's colleague in Congress, Robert Goodloe Harper. He studied law under his close relative, Judge John Williams. In early life he went to Salisbury, at the behest of his sister, Fanny, who was the wife of Judge Spence Mc-Cay, of this place. He seems to have had devotion for his sister's family. When he entered Congress from this district, in 1799, he carried with him to Philadelphia his little niece, Betsy McCay, and placed her in school here. He writes her father, "I have frequently taken Betsy to the theatre and it would astonish you to see how she is pleased with the performances." He also says he had placed her in a dancing school. She afterward became the wife of Hon. William C. Love, of Salisbury.

"During the Summer of 1801 there appeared a notice in the North Carolina Mercury and Salisbury Advertiser (Aug. 6) announcing the 'recent wedding of Archibald Henderson, Esq., Member of Congress, to the amiable Miss Sally Alexander, both of the town.' The union of the Henderson and Alexander families was doubly sealed by the marriage of William Lee Alexander, a native of Mecklenburg county, brother of Archibald Henderson's wife, with Elizabeth Henderson, Archibald Henderson's sister. In describing his acquaintances in Salisbury during the last decade of the century, Dr. Charles Caldwell says, 'Henderson had two sisters, by far the most accomplished women of the place.'"

I am quoting from "A Federalist of the Old School," by Archibald Henderson (born 1877).

Sarah and William Lee Alexander, whose brother was Dr. Nathaniel Alexander, of Mechlenburg, a graduate of Princeton, afterwards Member of Congress and Governor of N. C., were the children of Col. Moses Alexander and his wife, Sarah, daughter of Wm. and Jane Taylor Alexander. This Jane Taylor Alexander was descended from John Alexander, the youngest son of the first Earl of Sterling, who married Miss Graham, of Gartmore, Scotland and emigrated to America in 1659, settling in Stafford county, Va., in 1660.

"Children of Archibald Henderson and his wife, Sarah Alexander, were: Roger, who died in infancy; Archibald and Jane Caroline. Archibald: born Jan. 8, 1811, was educated at Yale and at University of Virginia. Dec. 14, 1840, he married Mary Steele Ferrand. Jane Caroline married in 1845, Hon. Nathaniel Boynton, a native of Massachusetts, afterwards a member of Congress from North Carolina, and Associate Justice of the North Carolina Supreme Court."

Archibald Henderson had a large and lucrative practice of law, and Moore, the historian of North Carolina, pays tribute to this man. He says, "He was one of the ablest lawyers ever seen in the State, and possessed virtues to match his intelligence" (see History of N. C., Vol. I, page 428, footnote). Archibald DeBow Murphy said of him that he was "the most perfect model of a lawyer that our bar has produced." The esteem in which he was held by the bar of North Carolina is shown in the magnificent monument at Salisbury erected to Archibald Henderson by the North Carolina bar. The inscription on this monument is eloquent in his praise.

When a young man he carefully cultivated the classics in literature. He was an excellent Shakespeare scholar. He and a friend of similar literary taste, Dr. Charles Caldwell, met on stated evenings to study polite literature.

Mr. Henderson is described as a "large man, physically, with a noble forehead, aquiline nose, compressed lips, firm-set jaw, somewhat elongated chin, and an open countenance, kindly and benignant in expression." The writer will remark that this is a good pen picture of a Henderson of later date, Judge John Hughes Henderson, of Franklin, Tenn. This serves to prove the fact that family resemblance and family characteristiccs are hereditary.

Archibald Henderson was an ardent Federalist. Perhaps this arose in large measure from his great admiration of George Washington. He had seen Washington at Salisbury in 1791, when he himself was in his early twenties, and the "impression seemed so deep as to tinge the whole fabric of his life and thinking."

He was strongly opposed to slavery. Both he and his brother, Leonard,. were vice-presidents of the Raleigh branch of the American Colonization Society in 1819, the fundamental of which was to encourage emancipation of slaves, and to send them to Africa for colonization. This work was promoted in North Carolina in 1819 by Rev. William Meade, afterward Bishop. In 1820, at Chapel Hill, Major Pleasant Henderson was vice-president of this branch of the American Colonization Society.

I cannot help pausing to say that the negroes in the South would in time have been freed, had there been no war between the States, because gradual emancipation was taking place.

We can read something of Archibald Henderson's character by his life motto "Let justice be done, though the heavens fall." He always carried a cane with ivory head, upon which was a silver plate bearing this inscription in Latin: "Fiat Justitia Ruat Coelum."

"Archiballd Henderson had an immense legal practice before the Federal Circuit Court presided over by John Marshall. before the Supreme Court of the State. and in the Superior Courts."

This man died in 1822.

His son, John Steele Henderson, was a leading lawyer of North

Carolina, and for ten years was head of the State delegation in Congress. In him the family traditions of culture and of political sagacity have been admirably sustained. Both he and his wife descend from the famous English mathematician, Wallis, and some of their descendants have mathematical bent. Their son, Archibald Henderson, D. C. L., of Chapel Hill, N. C., has become authority on this subject. "It is significant that his works of literary criticism have been paralleled in almost every case by an article of note on some mathematical subject. In 1911, for instance, the year that saw the production of 'Interpreters of Life,' Cambridge University published Mr. Henderson's researches on the 'Lines of the Cubic Surface.'"

Archibald Henderson, M. A., Ph. D., D. C. L.

Archibald Henderson, son of John Steele Henderson, M. C., grandson of Archibald Henderson (1768-1822), and great-grandson of Colonial Judge Richard Henderson, was born in Salisbury, N. C., June 17, 1877. His earliest lessons were conned at the knee of his grandmother, who developed in him ability and avidity in reading French and English literature of noble type. This taste has found expression in his life work. He has done much literary work; his first published article appeared in 1905-06. These articles show his special qualities as critic. "All these essays showed his pronounced tendencies toward social thought, his understanding of questions and of the movements which would become paramount during the Twentieth Century."

His "Modern Drama and Opera" was issued from the press in 1911. Later there was a second publication under the same title, a book of 255 pages. This last covers very thoroughly the dramatists and composers of present-day fame. "Dr. Archibald Henderson, one of the foremost critics of dramatic literature," wrote the introductory chapter and an essential part of the book. This is a valuable reference book. The title index at the end of the volume refers to more than six hundred plays and operas.

His "European Dramatists" came from the press in 1913. Edwin Markham says in reference to this book, "Archibald Henderson stands today as the chief literary critic of the South, and in the forefront of the critics of the Nation." The Pall Mall Gazette, of London, says, "Dr. Henderson is one of the most vivacious of the younger writers of the day on matters of the theatre, and here he is at his liveliest."

Maurice Maeterlinck said of his "Interpreters of Life," "You have written one of the most sagacious, most acute and most penetrating essays in the whole modern literary movement." Many of his writings have appeared in great magazines and representative journals throughout the world, having been translated for this purpose into five different languages. He is a member of the "Drama League of America," and of the "Authors' Club of London."

He has done much valuable historical work. He is a member of the American Historical Association; Ohio Valley Historical Association; Mississippi Valley Historical Association; President of N. C. Literary and

Historical Association; member Drama League of America; Poetry Society of America; American-Scandinavian Society; Sons of the American Revolution; Phi Beta Kappa Society.

Among his historical works are: "Creative Forces in Western Expansion—Daniel Boone and Richard Henderson;" "The Invasion of Kentucky (1775)—Daniel Boone and the Transylvania Company;" The Mecklenburg Declaration of Independence;" "The Founding of Nashville, and the Authorship of the Cumberland Compact;" "The Star of Empire." This is the story of the westward expansionist movement in the eighteenth century as exemplified in the careers of Isaac Shelby and Richard Henderson.

Dr. Archibald Henderson has made invaluable historical sketches. When the Mississippi Valley Historical Association held its annual meeting in Nashville, Tenn., in April, 1916, an address before this body, "he brought evidence and proof of various nature to prove the fact that Judge Richard Henderson was undoubtedly the arthor of the Cumberland Compact.   He said that he had given the subject careful and diligent investigation, comparing various documents and writings of the time, and had arrived at this conclusion."

On June 23, 1903, Dr. Archibald Henderson was married to Miss Minna Curtis Bynum, of Lincolnton, N. C., "a lady of rare accomplishments having been awarded the degrees B. A. and M. A. from the University of N. C., in June, 1902.   She is the daughter of the late Rev. Wm. Shipp Bynum, a noted Episcopal preacher of his day."   Mrs. Henderson comes of a distinguished family.   Edwin Markham, a friend of Archibald Henderson, who has enjoyed the hospitality of their home at Chapel Hill, speaks of it as an ideal home, filled with joyousness and light by four beautiful children who are educated under governesses of three different nationalities.   This has been indeed a most congenial and happy marriage.

Edwin Markham wrote a noteworthy appreciation of this man for the Brooklyn Institute of Arts and Science bulletin.   He says: "In the ranks of the younger generation of authors I see against the American background of present day no more striking figure of international culture and literary attainment than Archibald Henderson, educator, orator, literateur and historian."   Mr. Markham further says of him, "In his 'Interpreters of Life' and 'The Modern Spirit' Henderson gathers up a half dozen characters conspicuous on the literary horizon of the century and shows the mood and meaning of their contibution to humanity: Ibsen, Maeterlink, Mereditah and Wilde. . . . This volume was hailed in France, England and America as a piece of creative criticism. . . . . . this gives the author international standing as critic."   . . .

A comprehensive article setting forth the work of this man appeared in the Charlotte Daily Observer of June 22, 1913.   Here it is said, "To understand and to interpret the trend of modern movements and the result of the breaking down of modern conventions has been the purpose of all his readings and all his journeyings.   On his varied trips